The Guardian University Guide 2009

The Guardian University Guide 2009

● what to study ● where to go ● how to get there

Edited by

Alice Wignall

theguardian

Published by Guardian Books 2008

2 4 6 8 10 9 7 5 3 1

Copyright © Guardian News and Media Ltd 2008

Alice Wignall has asserted her right under the Copyright, Designs and Patents Act 1988 to be identified as the editor of this work.

First published in Great Britain in 2008 by
Guardian Books
119 Farringdon Road
London EC1R 3ER

www.guardianbooks.co.uk

Guardian Books is an imprint of Guardian News and Media Ltd

A CIP catalogue for this book is available from the British Library

ISBN: 978-0-85265-097-4

Text design by Bryony Newhouse
Cover design by Two Associates
Maps by Tony Mills
Map of London boroughs by Ghost

Distributed by A&C Black Publishers Ltd

Printed in the UK by CPI William Clowes Beccles NR34 7TL

Contents

Subjects

University profiles

Preface

"Do you want to go to university?" asked my dad.

"Don't mind," I said.

"I think you should," he replied. "I think it'll suit you."

"OK," I said.

And that was how I decided I would go to university.

"What subject do you want to do?" asked my mum.

"English?" I asked.

"It is the only thing you're any good at," she said kindly.

And that was how I decided what I would study at university.

"And where do you want to go?" asked my sister. "It says here you can put down five choices."

We stared at each other blankly. We didn't know five places. We didn't know anything. We flicked through the giant book every sixth former had staggered home with that day, which listed all the institutions and their courses to be found in the British Isles, and ended up more confused than ever. In the end, we chose Exeter because we used to go to Cornwall for our summer holidays, Manchester because my grandma lived nearby, Bristol because Dad's friend Phil grew up there and we all liked him, Nottingham because it offered English and linguistics and, having never heard of the latter before, I was suddenly seized a passion to discover what it was all about, and Cambridge because my dad said it was the prettiest place he had ever visited. It wasn't the most rigorous research session ever undertaken before embarking on a potentially life-changing decision, but that (followed by the conditional offers and subsequent winnowing-by-eventual-A-level-results, of course) is how we decided which university I should go to. (And where I would learn that it is in fact all right to end a sentence with a preposition as long as you are aware that that is what you're doing and have taken a considered decision to do so in order to avoid an uglier sentence. But that is by the by.)

So if you are feeling adrift, panicked, uncertain or any particularly unholy combination of the three, please relax. It should be clear by now that my 17-year-old self was ten types of idiot. By virtue of simply picking up this guide, you have already shown more common sense, practicality, maturity, and general competence than I mustered during the whole application procedure and I not only managed to get to university but enjoy it too. Like most of my friends (not all of whom can be living secret adult lives of quiet desperation that paint the past an inaccurately roseate hue), I look back on my time at university as some of the best years of my life.

I did make what might be generously termed a faltering start. I was overwhelmed by the noise and the speed of everything. I was surrounded by posh people who had had, it seemed, a separate teacher at school for every book ("Oh yeah, Buffers took us for Dombey and Son, old Moleskin-Weskit took us for Middlemarch and Wiggers did The Very Hungry Caterpillar.") They were discussing literary critics while I was still wandering around the faculty library trying to get my head round the fact that people had written books about books. This seemed to me to be information it would have been useful to have had beforehand. On top of that, I was so homesick that I cried myself to sleep for six weeks straight. They wanted to send me home and told me to try again next year. But I'd already had a gap year and didn't want to be the only menopausal graduate of '97, so I stuck it out and things improved no end by the beginning of the second term. I found the normal people, learned with relief and a reawakened sense of karmic justice that most of the boarding school poshos balanced their academic advancement with social retardation, and realised that I now had three years to read all those books about books while they worked out how to talk to the opposite sex. In fact I enjoyed myself so much I ended up staying for four years instead of three, which didn't please my local education authority, but they stumped up the cash in the end.

So what did it have, in the end, to recommend it? Egads, boys and girls, it's almost impossible to put into words without sounding like the kind of old fart who will be attempting to lecture you soon in a draughty hall while you indulge alternately in a little hangover-banishing nap or vivid mental re-enactments of the sexual gymnastics you and this week's love of your life enjoyed a few short hours before. (I'm taking it as read that you know there will be plenty of drink, drugs, and sex around in a place where hundreds of young ladies and gentlemen live cheek-by-jowl and wholly unsupervised and that this is a) a very splendid state of affairs and that b) I need add no more than a minimal caveat to ensure your psychosexual health over the three coming years, namely – DO! Use a condom! And DON'T! Drink until your liver forces its way out of your body and skitters off down the sewers begging for succour.) But here goes.

You will make your best friends, who will probably last you a lifetime. People will catch you if you fall. You will be free to indulge your passions – be they academic, social, political (I never was one of the "We can change the world" types, but I doff my cap to anyone who manages to preserve an idealistic spirit until the age of eight, never mind 18) or anything in between – be an idiot, be a poet, be a nerd, be anything you want in as quick succession as you like without fear of retribution. You may not learn everything there is to know about your subject (I'm still not sure what linguistics is. Or are.) But you will have learned how to learn about anything, and more importantly you will have learned that you are as good as anybody. These two lessons, I assure you, will save your ass more times than you can count in the years to come, whatever you decide to do and wherever you decide to go. Good luck, and I hope you enjoy it. I hope you enjoy it all.

Lucy Mangan
Lucy Mangan is a writer, author, and Guardian columnist.

Introduction

Choosing university

Once upon a time, and not even all that long ago, making decisions about university was very much more simple than it is now. There weren't many and not many people went to them. That, obviously, wasn't a good thing: certain types of people, mostly from certain types of school, were expected – or at least encouraged – to go, while for the rest (the vast majority) higher education was something that happened to other people.

These days, fortunately, things have changed. And how. Recent figures show that more than a third of school-leavers choose to study for a degree and that number looks set to carry on rising. While once there were a small handful of universities, now there are well over a hundred. And don't even try to count the courses: you can study anything from aadvarks to zygotes and most things in between.

It is, frankly, an exciting time to be a potential undergraduate. You can decide to attend your local university, or travel to the other end of the country. You can opt to bury yourself in classical literature or theoretical science, or sign up for a vocational degree that will prepare you for a job in a cutting-edge industry. Perhaps you fancy an established, esteemed institution. Or maybe you're leaning towards something younger, leaner, perhaps more flexible. Part-time or full-time, years abroad or in industry, exams or coursework, town or country, campus or not, music, sport, fun, and games: it's all there for the taking.

And that's before we even get on to the great benefits a university education can give you. There is the obvious stuff, of course: the unparalleled opportunity to immerse yourself in study, the skills a degree will cultivate and the talents it will unearth. Your career prospects will improve, your social life will receive a kick up the backside, you'll get a taste of freedom and independence you probably haven't had yet and simply stepping out of your room in the morning will expose you to experiences and opportunities you haven't come across before.

There is a downside, of course. The many thousands of pounds of debt you're likely to tot up just being there, for one thing. If you're currently living on a few quid of parental allowance a week, contemplating owing £30,000 to a combination of banks and loans companies in three or four years' time is enough to make you feel a bit queasy.

But for better or worse it looks like tuition fees are here to stay. And, surprisingly perhaps, most students seem to have taken them in their stride. While numbers of applications to university did drop for courses starting in 2006 – the year fees were introduced – they were back up again for 2007, and again for 2008. Perhaps people are figuring their education and future is worth making a financial investment in. Maybe they think three years of fun is too good a chance to pass up, and they'll worry about the money later. Or perhaps they simply feel that university is something that shouldn't be missed, or left to those who don't have to worry about money. They're right! And it is worth mentioning – though we'll deal with finance more thoroughly elsewhere in the book – that whatever you think about the basic principle of having to pay for your education, the loans and fees system is at least worked out to make it straightforward to pay back what you owe, beginning with the fact that you only start to repay when (the government thinks) you can afford it.

Overall, it seems that the prevailing attitude among Britain's students is one of keep calm and carry on. Yes, the money stuff's a pain, but there's too much that's really great about being a student to let it worry you too much. There are lectures to go to, essays to write (in the middle of the night, more often than not), plays to be in, student newspapers to edit, student elections to campaign in, chemistry prizes to win, books to read, coffee to be drunk, bars to prop up, friends to be made, and a world to be explored.

Feel like joining them? Read on ...

Why go?

Why not? Really, what else have you got planned for the next three years? Something better than opportunity, freedom, experimentation, and education? If so, please, please write in and let us know what it is so we can do it too.

Because there's a reason so many people want to go to university – and why so many people who did look back on it as the best days of their lives (and why many who didn't regret it bitterly, or go, in the end, as mature students) – because it is, in short, brilliant. It's fun. It's a laugh. It's eye-opening and mind-expanding. If you have even the merest hint of a chance to go you should grab it with both hands and anything else you've got that grabs and thank your lucky stars every minute of the day for the glorious opportunity that's just come your way.

First, let's turn to the first purpose of university: education. It can get lost a bit amongst all the angst over student loans and excitement over freshers' week, but what you're there for is to learn. You'll never have another chance like it, and your brain and your life will never be the same. You can spend years simply soaking up knowledge about something you care about, something that fascinates you, perhaps something that will stand you in good stead in your future career. You will learn from experts and scholars. You will be challenged and pushed and you will love it.

And, of course, a university education is about more than just fastening in your mind chemical equations or dates of important historical events (in actual fact, you're likely to forget 80 per cent of all that information the moment your last exam finishes). What it will also give you is a new way of thinking, an ability to analyse and discuss on a deeper level, a critical approach to information and the skills to deliver your arguments and conclusion in a persuasive and coherent way. Sounds like things that, say, an employer might be interested in? You're right!

Which is why there is even a phrase to describe the material benefits a degree will offer you. It is the "graduate premium", and it means, basically, that if you have a degree you're going to earn more money than someone who doesn't. Now, obviously, it's not a rule without exceptions and we could sit here naming Wayne Rooneys and Victoria Beckhams all day. Nor is there any accounting for the graduate with a double first who elects to live out their life on a remote Scottish island, living off thin air and goodwill. But, yes, on the whole, getting a degree equals more money for you. It's also worth remembering that for some jobs a degree is an absolutely non-negotiable entry requirement and for many more it's pretty much expected that you will have one.

OK, enough of being serious. Let's talk about the fun! Chances are, going to university will see you leaving home for the first time and, my goodness, what place better to go to upon leaving the family nest. You are as free as a bird. You can party all night, eat cake for breakfast, wash less than once a week, cook roast dinner every night for a month, play Mozart at 7 am, and wear what the hell you like out on a Friday night. (You might want to remember that some of these things will really annoy your flatmates. On the other hand, what are they going to do? Ground you?) But at the same time as luxuriating in all this limitless freedom you're safely wrapped up in the cosy security of university life. Whether on campus or in a student flat, you're plugged into a community who are all doing exactly the same thing as you.

And then there are the people who you'll be sharing it all with. You might not believe it when you lay eyes on them for the first time, looking all nervous and sick on the first day, but the people you are at university with are going to be hugely important in your life; in some cases, for the rest of it. You'll never have such a pool of potential mates to chat to, hang out with and share your experiences with again. Among the gawky freshers at your first lecture will be people who will become friends for life. Front row, third seat in? That's the best man at your wedding. The girl chewing her nails by the wall? You'll go travelling for a year with her when you graduate. The guy who's just tripped over a chair and dropped his folder? The funniest person you will ever meet. (Oh, yeah, and he's going to turn out to be a famous comedian, so you really want to keep in touch with him.) And the one sitting in front of you, blocking your view of the stage. Well, remember that wedding we mentioned … ?

And you'll make these friendships while doing all the stuff that university allows you to do when you're not in the lecture hall or the library (which would be quite a lot of the time, then). Some of that is just sitting about, having a coffee break that lasts for three hours or fashioning a meal for six from three rashers of bacon and a packet of noodles in the communal kitchen. Some of it's even more fun than that. Universities attract things that students like to do – bars, venues, shops, and concerts. And universities themselves, or active student members of them, know that there's more to student life than work, work, work. Hence the proliferation of student media, student politics, student sport, student theatre, student music, student jam-making and student stamp-collecting. At any university you will find people who share your most bizarre and whimsical interests; in fact, you'll probably find a society dedicated to them.

Going back to where we started, university is about learning. But not only the things on your reading list. Without wanting to sound too corny, it will give you a chance to learn about yourself – from learning whether you're the type of person who is ever going to get out of bed at 6 am for an early-morning jog with your keen neighbour, to learning what you are really like, and what you really want. When you get your degree, you'll get a scroll with something fancy written on it. The rest of what you get at university isn't the kind of stuff you can write down anywhere.

Making a choice

Stick a pin in a map? It sometimes feels as though that's the most logical response to the array of courses and institutions on offer. Or maybe you have known since you were perched on your grandfather's knee that you'd always end up doing Italian at Warwick or physics at Newcastle. In which case, well done you. The other 99.9 per cent of readers might want to consider the following:

There is plenty of information out there for wannabe students. Picking up this book was a smart start, but it is only a start. Like over-eager participants at a speed-dating event, universities are just gagging to talk to you and will virtually trip over themselves in their eagerness to tell you all about what they have to offer. Even the briefest visit to any of their websites will enable you to find out more about their selling points and order a prospectus. Take a trip to your school or college careers service and you'll find a wealth of resources to help you narrow your search.

Don't forget the value of personal experience either. Other people's (do you have friends or family members who could impart some wisdom? Or even just tell you why they chose their university?) and your own. If you can manage it, attend as many open days as you can. There is no substitute for really getting a feel for a university's location and spirit than going for a wander round the campus, meeting some lecturers in your subject and chatting to some of the current students. There's more on open days in the Applying section, starting on page 28.

Equally, remember that this is your life, your education, and a lot of your own (future) earnings. Friends, teachers, and parents might all have strong opinions on the subject and, of course, you should listen to what they have to say. But if everyone wants you to do a nice humanities subject in the south-east, and yet you're drawn to study biology in Scotland, who's to say that you're wrong?

Think big. You might as well. Don't let your choices be narrowed by wanting to follow your current friends to where they're going (you'll make more, and keep the old ones too) or by wanting to choose a sensible option (who can even say what that is?) or stick to something you know you can handle (you never know until you try, and you might amaze yourself). Be realistic too. Have a think about what you like and what you are like. How do you study? What kind of environment do you like to live in? It's time for challenging yourself, but in a way that's going to enable you to flourish and only you know in what kind of atmosphere you're most likely to do that. There's more about the different factors to bear in mind in the Choosing a university section on page 18.

Money might play a part in your choice too. Remember that tuition fees are "variable". Yes, in practice most places charge the same – that is to say, the full amount – but a few plucky institutions are lighter on your pocket. Maybe you'd like to investigate them more thoroughly. Or perhaps you don't want your decision to be influenced by a few hundred pounds a year either way. What does really vary – and quite massively – is the financial support that different universities can offer. All are required to offer some kind of means-tested bursary for students paying fees but that can vary from the bare minimum to really quite lavish awards, depending on a whole host of criteria. At some places, a wealth of scholarships and prizes are on offer; others aim to boost their performance in one particular area by offering financial incentives to people who excel at that subject. If money is an issue for you, it's all worth some really thorough investigation. For more thoughts on money go to our Finance section on page 34.

The last thing to remember? Don't panic! If it seems as though there are a lot of options, well, that's because there are. And whichever one you finally settle on leaves another one – or several other ones – that could get you thinking: "I wonder if I really made the right decision?" It's best not to dwell on that too much or you'll never get round to deciding on anything. And forget, too, any notion that there even is a "right" decision. Furnish yourself with as much information as you possibly can but remember that at the end of the day you will still be taking a leap – albeit a well-informed one – into the dark. It's part of the fun. The nature of university is that you'll almost certainly end up having the best time of your life wherever you go, and swearing blind that University X was the only place you could ever have gone – and you'd have said exactly the same thing if you'd gone to University Y instead. You know, perhaps that map/pin thing isn't such a bad idea after all ...

Using this guide

Thorough research – and maybe a bit of guesswork and intuition – will form the basis of how you decide where to apply, and what you decide to study. We hope that this book will make a good starting point and a helpful reference.

The institution guides are intended to give a flavour of the universities and higher education institutions they cover. They will give you an idea of what a place is like, what its strengths (and, sometimes, weaknesses) are, anything especially noteworthy about it, and, of course, how expensive it's liable to be. You may already have a shortlist in your head, but browse through them anyway – you could come across some things that surprise you (we did when we were compiling them!). Of course, we can really only scratch the surface here, but the contacts will point you in the right direction to enable you to have a closer look.

Much of this book is given over to the Guardian's unique tables. These are an attempt to help you gauge how good a university is in a particular subject area. Don't make the easy mistake of assuming that a "good" university will teach everything well; every place has its weak spots. And an institution that you perceive to be lacklustre in other ways might turn out to have an internationally renowned department in just the subject you want to study. No matter how good a university's reputation in general, there's no point applying there if the subject you want to study isn't taught well there.

The overall Guardian score is a combination of a number of factors. These are: student:staff ratio; job prospects; the amount of money spent per student; the A-level score (or tariff) of the students who enter the university and a value-added score assess how well those scores are translated into degrees (how many grade Ds at A-level convert into 2:1s at degree level, for example); teaching quality, as rated by graduates of the course in the National Student Survey (NSS); and feedback, which is also taken from the NSS. These tables aren't perfect by any means, as the universities themselves are very quick to tell us, and each year we tweak the methodology, looking to achieve statistical nirvana, but we firmly believe that they are the most rounded league tables there are for prospective undergraduates.

When you examine the tables (divided into subject areas, rather than courses, so also investigate which subject your course comes under) it may be that you rate particular criteria as especially important to you, so examine the data carefully. If you think job prospects are the most important thing, look for universities and colleges that do well in that area; if you think you will benefit most from a lot of personal attention from your tutor, you'll want to consider the figures relating to staff/student ratios.

The overall league table (page 53) is really for interest only. The fact that one university comes top overall is neither here nor there if it doesn't do the course you want to do, or doesn't do it well.

We've also included a short introduction to each subject area, aiming to give an overview of what a course might involve and where it might take you. Space and the virtual impossibility of covering the almost infinite variety of courses on offer mean that these can really be nothing more than a starting point, but hopefully they'll get you thinking and give you some directions for further investigation.

While we've tried to ensure the web addresses in this book are correct, these things can change quickly. There's always Google if we have failed you. We have also tried to recommend useful and reputable sites but editorial policy can change and quality can lapse so we bear no responsibility if you find material there that is useless, wrong or offensive. We will feel quite bad about it, though.

Take your time, consider the choices ahead and make the decision that feels right. Arming yourself with the facts is a good first step. After that it's up to you ...

Choosing a university

All right, you've decided you're going to apply to university. Well done! Really the only little thing you've got to think about now is … where? Yes, things get a little bit more tricky from this point on. Narrowing the field from the literally hundreds of options can be a daunting task. But you should relax (at least a little bit): no one expects you to you to be a walking, talking encyclopaedia of facts and figures relating to every university in the land. Even we're not that and we've just spent months putting this guide together.

The best thing you can do is research, research, research. Have a quick look at a large group of institutions, narrow that down to a few strong contenders, really put in the effort to find out about those and that should leave you with some obvious choices.

But before you do that, you might want to consider some of the following criteria that could play a part in making your choice …

Stay or go?

The popular image of someone starting university is that of a nervous student loading up the family car with their worldly belongings and being driven hundreds of miles before being dumped at the door of a chilly hall of residence by an emotional mum, stoical dad, and, possibly, gleeful younger siblings.

What is less common is the idea that someone might leave home on the first day of their degree … and be back again in time for dinner and an early night in their own bed. And yet studying for a degree while living at home is an increasingly popular option. It cuts costs, of course (if you can persuade your parents or whoever you live with that they really do want to support your education by not charging you rent, or at least not at market value), and it's almost certain that your living environment will be more pleasant, quieter, cleaner, and provide better food than if you chose to fend for yourself on campus.

The expansion of the higher education sector means that many more people now have good universities nearby. And many universities are focusing, through recruitment drives or financial incentives, on attracting local students to register with them. In big cities, where you've got the attraction of excellent universities and the problem of high rents, it's always been pretty usual to find students who are happily still living at home.

You also might feel that you just quite like your family, thank you, and enjoy the idea of having a group of people to come home to who are compelled by long-standing affection or genetics to be supportive and interested in what you're doing.

But, then again, a large part of the point of university for many new undergraduates is that it gets them out of the house. For several months at a time. There's no doubt that – unless you happen to inhabit a mansion with extremely liberal (and deaf) family members – staying put in the house you grew up in is going to cramp your style. You might think you can cope with that now … but are you sure you're still going to be as sanguine when you're leaving the students' union bar early for the third night in a row so you can get the last bus home while everyone else is free to carry on partying because they all live on campus?

And let's not gloss over the fact that leaving home for the first time – no matter when or how you do it or how much you think you're gagging to get out of there – can be a bit of a wrench. Most first-year students admit (through probably not until the second year) to a bit of homesickness. But the nice thing about university is that it lets you experiment with the idea of living alone – yet all the while surrounded by friends, facilities and excellent support networks. And with lovely long holidays that let you go back to the family home for weeks on end and remember exactly why you wanted to move out in the first place.

Location, location, location

Remember all those times you've gazed out of the window and idly thought, "I wish I lived by the sea/by the mountains/in a big city/in the middle of the country/near a Test cricket ground"? Well, here's the thing: now you can! Nothing beats choosing a university for having a really good think about where you'd like to live and making it a reality. Always lived in the north and fancy seeing if they're really soft down south? Grown up amongst concrete canyons but secretly nurturing a desire to don a pair of walking boots and tramp up and down real grass-covered hills every weekend? Dying to live somewhere that other people pay to go on holiday to? It's all within your grasp!

First, you might want to think about how much you want to super-size your university experience. The lure of big cities is age-old: all those bright lights, the opportunity to lose yourself in infinite choice and variety, the chance to share it all with a diverse group of people and students drawn from all over the world. Cities also have a way of making you feel anonymous, almost invisible, as millions of people busily carry on with their lives all around you and pay you no attention whatsoever. In some ways that can be a liberating – almost exhilarating – experience. You can do anything and be anyone! In others, it can be terribly lonely. Only you know whether you're likely to sink or swim (though bear in mind that the insta-community of a university is likely to make the landing in a big city a little more soft than it might otherwise be).

Other downsides of city life: travelling around it takes a long time, even if the transport links are good; it's expensive, even if part- time work is easy to come by; you might even feel that cities offer a few too many distractions to happily sit with studying for a degree ...

Small towns – or even pretty medium-sized towns in which the university plays a big part – can be lovely places to live for a few years. Everywhere's quick and easy to get to; as you whizz around town on your bike you'll soon get to know it like the back of your hand, you'll see familiar faces wherever you go, and – especially if students make up a significant part of the local economy – there will be plenty of events and facilities laid on just for you. Sure, it gets parochial and claustrophobic from time to time; the fact that the whole place boasts only two cinema screens is a bit annoying; and the last time the local football team got anywhere near the FA Cup is when they took a coach trip to watch the final. Perhaps, if you're going to go small, it would be as well to check that there is a night bus to somewhere that doesn't shut down at 10 pm for when your feet get a bit itchy ...

Another thing to think about is just how far you want to go. It's easy, when that Ucas form needs filling in and your head is swimming with the contents of 14 different prospectuses, to think that that's not exactly a top priority. And you're probably right. But come reading week, when everyone else in your hall of residence is hopping on a train for the quick trip home to get some laundry done and a nice dinner cooked for them and you realise you're stuck in Norwich when your family is in Belfast, or Dundee when your best hope of roast chicken is in Penzance ... well, you might feel it's something you should have paid a bit more attention to. Obviously, it isn't a factor you should let limit you. But at least having an idea of how much it will cost, and how long it will take to get home should you suddenly want or need to, might not be a foolish idea.

One site fits all?

So, you think you've got it all sorted: you've picked the town or city you want to live in and are busily imaging yourself sauntering along its streets and paths, strolling home at midnight by the gleaming river or going for an early-morning jog through its parks. And then you find that you'll actually be based on a campus eight miles away and the only reason you'd be walking home by the river at midnight is because you missed the last bus.

Don't scrimp on working out *exactly* where you're going to be. A distance of a few miles, or being on the wrong side of the city from your faculty, or just not right in the centre of things, if that's where you want to be, can make a real difference.

Equally, do you want to live on a campus or not? Campuses are remarkable places: self-contained little towns full of just students! Plenty of them have everything you could possibly need right there: shops, banks, bars, cafes, launderettes, doctors, a sports centre, even a cinema or a pool. It can feel as though you're a privileged citizen in some weird student kingdom, and in many ways you are. Some campuses, too, are lovely to look at: rolling parkland and landscaped gardens. All right, you won't spend your *whole* time lolling around on the lawn on sunny afternoons. But you will spend *some* of your time doing that, and what could be nicer?

On the other hand, some campuses are just downright ugly and depressing. If you attend a campus university, you'll end up living off-site for some of the time, but you'll still have to go back most days. A town-based university might be a more appealing choice. These are places where the university buildings are scattered across a town or city, or part thereof. In some – usually the older ones – you're bedded right into the heart of the place where you live, which can really make you feel like part of something. Or sometimes just make you feel as though you're part of a tortuous experiment as you realise you've got five minutes to get from lecture to lab and it's a 20-minute journey across the city centre!

In the end, it just comes down to personal preference. We've said it before, and we'll say it again before the book's over: go for a visit. There really is no substitute for first-hand experience to get a real feel for a place and how much you're going to like it.

Party time

Oh, yeah, we all know about university, don't we? Three-for-one on alcopops and all the kebabs you can eat, all the while wearing nothing but a vest with ambition and a smile. And the best part is, your parents will never know! Unless they are on Facebook.

And we're not here to tell you that it isn't true – because, frankly, it is, and thank God you can do all that stuff at university because you could certainly never hold down a job and carry on in that fashion.

Nor are we seriously going to suggest that you pick a course on the basis of where has the best social life. You'd be an idiot. A happy idiot, at lots of parties, sure, but an idiot nonetheless. But even we will concede that there's more to university than work, work, work and your studies and your general sense of wellbeing will improve immeasurably if you can let your hair down in the manner that you most enjoy.

So if you're just assuming that a big part of your university social life will revolve around clubbing like a maniac, you might want to just make sure it will be easy for you to make that happen. Those cute little colleges tucked down country lanes? Not so many big-name DJs, as it happens. Similarly, if you're crazy about opera, ballet, classical music, theatre, art or live music, here's an opportunity for you to set up home somewhere where you've got easy access to all of them.

All universities have student bars and the like. But they are not all created equal. Nor do they all boast the same range of student societies and clubs. It stands to reason, most of the time, that the bigger the place the more diverse the offering, the higher the quality and the more opportunities there are to get involved. If you're especially ambitious in one area, you might want to think about the fact that some student organisations are held in national – even international – regard. No aspirant comedian's career was ever hurt by being a member of Cambridge's Footlights comedy troupe, for example, and some of the big student newspapers are recognised by professional journalists as being excellent training grounds for wannabe hacks. Some university sports teams compete internationally too. Picking the right place for you to have fun might be a ticket to more than just a degree.

Money matters

We've already talked about how tuition fees can vary from place to place (and country to country. Read the Finance section (page 34) carefully!) But there's more to the cost of university than that. Even as a student you don't get special dispensation from the economic forces that govern everyone else ... So, broadly speaking, London (and most of the rest of the south) and big cities are more expensive in terms of rent, transport and – oh, just everything, basically – while your quiet northern town is likely to be as cheap as the chips they serve (that will taste better than anything you find south of the Watford Gap).

London students do get extra allowances in their loans/grant package. Will it be enough to tide you over? Only you can decide. And you should remember that it's not all one-way. If you are planning on working part-time you might find that London and other expensive places are also the ones with the most ready supply of money-making opportunities, and, possibly, the highest wages.

Other things need factoring in. OK, you might be living in an "expensive" city – but you're on campus so everything's within walking distance, the bar's amazing and subsidised and because everyone's skint you've learned to be inventive with your money. Whereas your friend in a "cheap" town might not pay as much rent but a big night out means a trip to the nearest city: club prices on drinks and a taxi ride home. And she buys posh sarnies from M&S for her lunch every day because the campus caff is so dire.

It is, frankly, enough to make your head ache. But then so is looking at your overdraft after one year of student life. If you're worried about money it would be worth your while doing a little digging into exactly how pricey various places are likely to be.

Are you a snob?

It's not an especially palatable truth, but it does exist, so we might as well get it out in the open. In the minds of many – most, probably – people there's a snob's pyramid of UK universities. Right at the top sit Oxford and Cambridge, with the next most venerable institutions arrayed beneath them, the red-bricks beneath them and so on, until you get, at the bottom, to the "new" universities, the higher education institutions and the degree-awarding colleges.

Is it right? Is it fair? Well, and at the risk of causing Guardian-reader outrage, in some cases: yes. It stands to reason that institutions that have been around forever and a day have had the time to accrue the power, the position, the privileges, the experience, and facilities to earn a formidable academic reputation. That reputation attracts the best teachers and students, which in turn boosts their standing, and so it goes on. It's not just a perception; hard statistics (such as our own tables) often demonstrate (though the emphasis is on "often" – not "always") that the places you think are going to be the best are the ones that are.

Should you aim for the top? Again, a resounding yes! Of course you should aim as high as you possibly can. Do not let fears about certain places being "not for the likes of us" put you off. The institutions that are (rightfully) worried about their access figures really do have active programmes in place to encourage applications from everyone who fancies their chances. And while it is sadly true that some places – and, even more sadly, often the best places – are still overpopulated with people from one small section of society, that will only change by more different types of people going. And why not you?

And yet on the other hand ... you might, after sensible deliberation, decide that actually you'd rather be somewhere a bit more free and easy than a place that requires you wear a gown to dinner and listen to someone mumbling in Latin before you get to eat. And you don't need to scrimp on academic quality if you do. Equally, some people literally can't get into certain universities. If you're in a wheelchair, for example, ancient quads and narrow steps might be more of a pain than you can be bothered to cope with. (Not, of course, that it would be an insurmountable problem: Stephen Hawking manages Cambridge just fine and they don't come much more ancient-quadded than Cambridge.)

We've talked in the introduction about how we believe that you should look at the quality of your course, not just the institution. It's the basis of our subject league tables, after all. So if you fall in love with a brilliant course, a passionate tutor (in the platonic sense only, may we just add), a terrific campus or a great city that pulls you to a university "less good" than another one, what is to stop you going there? Nothing, we say.

Though of course we do still live in the real world. While we, and you, might know that course A is lacklustre and limp at University X, and vibrant and thorough at University Y, most lay people – and we mean employers here – only know that, in vague and general terms, X is "better" than Y and so their graduates get an easier ride. We can't pretend that doesn't happen. On the other hand, you might be surprised by how quickly it does filter through to the wider world which courses are better at which places. This is especially true on a course with a vocational bent: you can bet your bottom dollar that employers will have a keen grasp of where the best graduates are going to come from, and it won't just be because of centuries-old reputation.

Similarly, while those little specialist colleges may not have made much impact on the collective consciousness, if they are absolutely the best in the business when it comes to the handful of courses they teach, does it matter that Mr Bloggs in Bolton has never heard of them? In a word: no.

And don't disparage those HE institutions either. They provide significant proportions of graduates in creative arts, teaching, healthcare and land-based subjects, and they could teach some of the "better" places a thing or two about widening participation. If you're interested in non-traditional routes into higher education, or more flexible ways of learning, you could do much, much worse than looking at one of these institutions.

Oxbridge

But while we're on the subject of snobbery, let's take a look at that most thorny of subjects: Oxbridge. Oh, we could fill a book on this one topic alone. The history! The tradition! The ludicrous public school boys!

There are plenty of reasons for wanting to give Oxbridge a whirl. Both universities are ravishing to look at, for a start. You cannot kid yourself that they are not at the very top of any list of the country's – or the world's – universities. The education you get there will be first-rate, with brilliant – bordering on genius – teachers, excellent facilities and terrific resources. And, sick to the stomach though it might make you feel, the phrase, "Well, I was at Oxford/Cambridge" still carries a lot of currency out in the real world.

But then again, like Monty Python's Camelot, they are ever such silly places. All those traditions and quirks, the Latin and gowns, the language of its own each place has (battells, pidge, bops ... what does any of it mean?), the black tie and balls. It can all border somewhat on the surreal. Of course, all of that may have you salivating to get stuck in – and, if you're up for it, it certainly can be tremendous fun. On the other hand, you may think the whole thing is deranged ...

Applying to either is a bit more of a faff than to other places and you are virtually guaranteed an excruciating interview in which you pit your mock A-level wits against the person who wrote the defining work in your subject. And though of course we are not saying that other degrees aren't challenging or intense, the eight-week terms of Oxbridge, the sheer weight of expectation that seems to leech out of the walls and the one-on-one tutorial style of teaching does seem to lend studying there an extra dose of pressure that can either push you to strive for ever-greater things ... or push you right over the edge.

In the end, you may decide that it's not for you – and that's fine. But whatever you do, don't be put off by the idea that you are not for them. No matter what you think, the streets of these places are not filled with gals in gowns suddenly grabbing you to check that you know which fork you use with fish and whether it's better to say "sofa" or "settee". No one – least of all Oxford or Cambridge – is going to try to tell you that their student body isn't skewed more in one (socially privileged) direction than any other but, even so, they are diverse enough that everyone can find their own comfortable niche. In the end, all students are pretty much the same and reports from Oxbridge students consistently say that the "What school did you go to?" questions ceases to be of interest to anyone after the first five seconds of freshers' week chat.

And Oxford and Cambridge really, really are – no matter what anyone else might tell you – trying to get more people to apply. It's only sensible – the brightest and the best from all areas of the country and all different back-grounds coming to interview gives them the widest choice and the best chance of maintaining their reputations. It's obviously the case that people who've had money flung at their education are going to feel a bit more comfortable with the concept of Oxbridge than someone who'd never heard of it until they saw a rerun of Inspector Morse. But the people who run Oxbridge are – quite famously, actually – not stupid. They understand that people from expensive schools have been primed for it and that other people haven't. They have no vested interest in people from one section of society or another. You think your average bookish tutor, with her head full of advanced physics, cares what her student's mum and dad do for a living? Not at all. They are interested in rooting out potential and the ability to thrive in the system these universities operate. If you think you've got it and you fancy spending some time among the dreaming spires, for heaven's sake go and show them.

Open season

Turning from one atypical university experience to another ... if, for whatever reason, you decide you don't have the time or the money to commit to a full-time degree right now, don't want to move, don't want to give up your job or don't want to have to rearrange your life around a university timetable there is always the option of studying for a degree with the Open University.

The appeal is obvious: all you need is a computer and a TV, the fees are less, you can fit your study round whatever else you choose, and its academic reputation certainly stands up to scrutiny.

However, the Open is not by any means an easy ride. It still requires a big time commitment and because it's part-time each course lasts six years. Your staying power will certainly be tested – and you won't be immersed in the student experience as you would be on campus.

In any case, although we've included the Open in our institution guides, you won't find it in the league tables. That's not because it's not worthy of being rated, but because its unique set-up means that it can't be fairly compared with other universities.

Minority rule

Perhaps you think that your race, religion, sexuality or physical ability should play as much of a role in deciding where you're going to continue your education as you think it should in deciding what you're going to have for dinner tonight. If that's you, more power to you. And, indeed, you're probably right if you sense that universities, in general, are far more tolerant to different experiences and points of view among their populations than society in general. University governing bodies will certainly come down hard and fast on discrimination: it goes without saying that if you encounter any you should alert the relevant authorities straight away.

Ethnic minority students may find themselves among only a very few on their course – and the situation gets worse as you approach the top of the pile of UK universities. However, you may not be remotely bothered by that: you'll just take it as a chance to meet plenty of other people from different backgrounds. And it's unlikely that you'll be totally on your own, in any case.

But if being with significant numbers of people from the same race or religion as you is important, head to the big cities. At some of the new London universities, white students are the "minority" section of the student body.

Disabled students may sometimes feel that their way to university is barred – in very literal terms. Old buildings (even "new" universities can occupy ancient structures) with poor facilities for disabled students, coupled with ignorance about what needs to be done, might make for a frustrating mix. But persevere! There are laws in place to ensure that people with disabilities have equal access to education. Most universities will have a dedicated unit to help students with disabilities and ensure the institution meets its responsibilities and will (or should be) keen to make changes that need to be made. It may just require that you point out what needs to be done.

Finally, if you already know you are lesbian, gay or bisexual – or aren't sure but think that university might be a good time to find out – there is probably very little to fear about starting university. Although it would be naive to suggest that homophobia has been totally eradicated, campuses do tend to be fairly tolerant places and most universities will have a community of LGB students and, very likely, an active LGB society too.

If you're nervous about being out at university, however, or want to make sure that you've got ready access to a good LGB scene, you might want to give some thought to where you want to go. Sure, you may relish the thought of being the only out and proud student on some tiny rural campus – and good for you if you do – but if you're more inclined to just want to be one of many, then the larger cities are probably a commonsense option, along with places with an established gay scene.

Applying

You think you know what you'd like to study, and you've got a fair idea of where you might like to study it. Now all you have to do is make those vague inklings a reality by getting the application process under way. Although it can seem daunting to begin, with it's actually pretty straightforward — as long as you're prepared for what's coming up and when, you will be fine.

Open days

Not, strictly speaking, a mandatory part of the application process, but we do think that if you can possibly manage it, you should make attendance at a few open days a key stage in your application process.

Of course, it's probably not possible for reasons of time, money or basic inclination to visit every university you have even the vaguest interest in. But if you can, visiting at least the top handful of places on your wish list is a good idea. Scour prospectuses and websites all you like, but they are designed to give a good impression and that nice picture of a handsome building basking in the afternoon sun is handily cropped to leave out the damp 1960s monstrosity that spoils the view for anyone who actually sees it in person. Turning up and having a walk around might be the only way to get a real sense of a place and how you'll fit into it. It's also a great opportunity to meet students and tutors and talk to them about what you might be letting yourself in for. If you don't think you can fund open days independently, check with your school or college to see if they're organising any group trips (or if you could persuade them to).

Open days can be sprinkled throughout the year, though, unfortunately, the traditional season for them has always been mid-May — when many Year 12s are now in the midst of AS-level exams. Universities are (slowly, as is their way) catching on to this development and being more flexible, making them earlier or later in the year. They will be listed on university websites, and the Ucas website also carries details through its institution guide.

You may have to book a place on an official open day, or you may just be able to register your interest and turn up — university websites will have details. Official open days will probably offer you a chance to meet students and lecturers, have a look round facilities, accommodation, and the all-important bar, and give you a taster of academic life.

Have a think beforehand about what you really want to know and use the "Any questions?" slot at the end of the head of department's presentation to find out. Talk to students – and not just the ones officially designated to show you around – they'll probably be able to give you the best impression of the place you're considering spending the next three years.

If you can't make an official open day, you could always call the university and see if you can arrange your own. Ask if you can spend five minutes chatting to a tutor and looking at the facilities. Or you could create a totally ad hoc visit – just dropping by a campus and having a look around. You could probably corner a student or two doing that, but you're unlikely to get much of an idea of the academic side of things in the department you're planning to apply to.

If you *really* can't make any open days then at least cast your net a little further during your research. Student-union-produced alternative prospectuses and student web forums are a good place to start for the uncensored take on what a university is really like – just to balance out the utopian idyll presented in the pages of the official prospectus.

Applying

Application season begins on September 1 when Ucas starts accepting applications. Time was, a Ucas form was made of paper and was filled out by anxious students with a Biro clutched in one hand, a bottle of Tippex by their side and frowns of concentration on their faces.

These days you'll almost certainly fill out and submit your form online (and Ucas has a list of centres across the country that will allow you to access their website and fill in the form if you don't have the internet at home, school or college). Unless you are called for interview or asked to submit other examples of your work, this will be the only thing prospective universities have to go on, so it's more than worth making sure you don't make silly mistakes. Take some time to familiarise yourself with the form and think about your responses before you fill it in and click "submit".

Your personal statement is particularly important, and a chance to convince the weary admissions tutor who is on their 30th Ucas form of the day that you really are passionate about your subject and would be a joy to teach. This isn't an excuse to be economical with the truth – these people have made a living out of being clever, remember – but to really talk about why you're interested in the courses you've chosen and the subject; skills and experience you have gained through work, volunteering or placements, especially if it's relevant; and your ambitions and wider interests. Whoever looks at your form will have read the phrase "In my spare time I enjoy socialising with my friends" a hundred thousand times before, so try to be a little bit original.

You can choose up to five courses to apply for (though keep an eye out for entrance criteria; there's no point in applying to do something you don't have the right A-levels for), apart from people who want to study medicine, dentistry or veterinary courses: for those, you can choose up to four courses in one of those subjects, and use your fifth choice for another subject.

The closing date for most applications is January 15 (though see below for some exceptions). After it has received your application, Ucas will forward it on to the places you have applied to. And then all you have to do is sit back and wait for the responses to start coming in. They will be either a rejection, an unconditional offer, or a conditional offer (normally based on your exam results). Once you've heard from all of the places you applied to, you can decide which (if any) to firmly accept, accept as your insurance place (if your first choice makes a conditional offer your insurance place should be an unconditional offer, or a conditional offer based on lower grades or fewer tariff points) and decline.

If you miss the January 16 deadline for applications, from January 16 to June 30 you can make late applications, which universities may consider if they have places to fill – though obviously the most popular places will probably have filled their courses. You can also apply through Ucas Extra from late February if none of your first round of applications has led to the offer of a place, or none that you want to accept. Using Extra you can apply to courses with spaces left to fill, one course at a time. The details of these courses will be on the Ucas website.

Finally, if you miss the June 30 deadline for Ucas Extra, suddenly decide you want to go to university when you thought you didn't, or haven't yet managed to find a place on a course, you can apply through Clearing from mid-August. More information about that below.

Oxbridge

Wouldn't you know it but Oxbridge has a different Ucas applications closing date to the rest of the UK's universities – October 15, a good three months earlier than everywhere else. Which means that if you're giving Oxbridge a go you have to have your Ucas form shipshape and ready to go ages before your friends have even started to think about theirs.

It also means that while they're still dawdling over their personal statements you'll probably be packing your bags and heading to one or other of the universities for interview. These normally take place in December.

Also be aware that you can't apply to both Oxford and Cambridge in the same year. For application to Oxford, you will also have to complete an Oxford application form and return it to the university by October 15. This used to be the case at Cambridge too, but for entry in 2009 it looks as though you will only have to fill out the Ucas form.

Other courses

People applying to do courses in medicine, dentistry, veterinary science or veterinary medicine. The closing date for all these courses is also October 15.

Art and design

If you are planning to apply for art and design courses, things can become a little tricky. Essentially, there are two ways to apply for art and design courses. Applications for courses via Route A follow the same procedures as for non-art and design courses. Route B courses follow a different timetable and a different application process.

Some courses are listed as both Route A and Route B – the course is the same, whichever route you apply through. However, the university or college may prefer that you apply through one particular route, so check carefully. Route B course codes always begin or end with an "E".

Route A follows the same timetable as applications for courses at most other universities, but Ucas recommends that you apply by mid-November to allow the universities and colleges more time to ask to see your portfolio. (If you want to apply to the fine art course at Oxford, you must apply by October 15, in common with all other Oxford courses. There is no fine art course at Cambridge.)

Route B runs to a later timetable to allow time for applicants doing a foundation course in art and design to identify their specialisation and prepare their portfolio – although anyone can apply for a Route B course.

For Route B courses, you can list up to three choices in preference order. The deadline is March 24, but it is recommended that you apply by March 6 to avoid the last-minute rush. You will be asked to indicate your first choice, second choice, and third choice.

Your application will go to your first choice, which will decide whether to invite you for an interview and then whether to make you an offer. If you decide to accept the offer, your other choices will be cancelled. If you turn down the offer, or you do not receive an offer, your application will go to your second choice, and so on. Obviously, a highly prestigious institution is likely to have filled its places with people who put it as first choice – and so applicants who put it as their third are unlikely to get much of a look in.

You can also do Route A and Route B applications on the same form. You can apply for a mixture with up to a total of five choices. You cannot choose more than three Route B courses. The following examples show the combinations of choices that are allowed.

- 3 Route B + up to 2 Route A
- 2 Route B + up to 3 Route A
- 1 Route B + up to 4 Route A

If you decide to apply for a mixture of Route A and Route B courses, you can apply for Route A between September 1 and January 15 and then add your Route B choices later (but before March 24) via the Ucas website.

Clearing

Clearing is often synonymous with a mad scramble for a university place as the summer draws to a close – ending up with slightly baffled students wondering how come they're studying psychology in Scotland when they wanted to be doing chemistry on the south coast. But it needn't be a disordered scuffle: it can actually be a very sensible option, and given a little patience, a little flexibility, and by making sure you don't lose your head, you can end up on a course that is right for you. More than 30,000 people find a university place through Clearing every year: they can't all spend their first year wondering how they ended up where they did.

Clearing opens in mid-August, after exam results, and is a way of matching up students without a place with universities with places to spare. You are eligible for Clearing if any of these apply:

- you have not withdrawn your application
- you hold no offers
- your offers have not been confirmed because you didn't get the required grades
- you have declined your offers or not responded by the due date
- your offers have not been confirmed, and you have declined any alternative offers from the same university
- you sent your Ucas form in after June 30 (June 12 for Route B art and design courses). Ucas won't have processed it after this date, so you'll have to use Clearing

When Clearing opens, universities with spaces to fill will list their under-subscribed courses on the Ucas website and in newspapers, including the Guardian. You can then match up your interests and exam results with what's on offer and secure yourself a place on a course starting in a few weeks' time.

It goes without saying that you need an open mind and a degree of flexibility. You may not find the Italian course you are after – but how about film studies with Italian? You may also have to consider universities that weren't on your list before. That's when a cool head – and access to a guide such as this one – will come in handy.

On the other hand, don't get caught up in the momentum of Clearing unless you're sure it's the right thing for you to do. If you aren't sure that you will find something that's going to suit you, it may be better to take an unscheduled gap year and go through the whole application process again rather than make a rash decision and end up somewhere that's wrong for you or doing something you hate.

Applications at a glance

2008	
August	AS-level results
September 1	Ucas starts accepting applications
October 15	Deadline for applications to Oxford and Cambridge, and applications for dentistry, medicine, veterinary medicine, and veterinary science
December	Interviews for Oxford and Cambridge and some courses at other universities
2009	
January	Interviews
January 15	Deadline for Ucas applications to most courses
January 16	Late applications accepted by Ucas. Universities and colleges will consider them if they want to make more offers
Late February	If you have not received any offers or declined all offers you can apply for other courses, one at a time, through Ucas Extra
March 24	Deadline for "Route B" art and design courses. (Ucas recommends applications reach them by March 6)
June	A-level and AS-level exams
June 30	Deadline for late applications. Applications after this date are entered in Clearing
August	A-level and AS-level results. Firm offers are accepted. Clearing starts on A-level or Scottish Highers results day. Course vacancies are listed in the Guardian
September/October	University term starts

Finance

Few things in life are certain but, these days, finishing your university studies owing the government a pound or two has got to be one of them. When you first start contemplating higher education you'll very soon realise that it's not going to be a cheap ride – and we're not just talking about overindulgence in the union bar. Over the past few years, debt has become as much a part of the university experience as Pot Noodles and questionable student housing.

The government's decision to allow higher education institutions (HEIs) in England, Wales and Northern Ireland to charge variable fees of around £3,000 a year for their degree courses from 2006 added to already existing concerns that the cost of studying was becoming a barrier to students entering higher education. The National Union of Students estimates that a student beginning their degree in 2006, when the new higher-fee regime was introduced, would graduate with debts of around £27,000.

However, when you look at the detail, things might not appear as gloomy as you first thought. For a start, you don't have to pay your course fees until after you have graduated and are working, rather than finding the money before your first lecture; the government has reintroduced maintenance grants for students from low-income families and universities are offering bursaries and scholarships to tempt you into the fold. There is also extra financial help for part-time students, students with disabilities or those with children. And the threshold for student loans has been raised.

So yes, unless you're wealthy or meticulous in your budgeting you are likely to graduate in some debt, but it may be worth remembering that the investment you make in your education now should benefit you over the course of your working life. The government estimates that graduates earn on average 50 per cent more over their lifetime than someone who stopped studying after their A-levels.

We think it would be a shame for anyone to miss out on the opportunities that a degree offers because of worries about money – especially when there are lots of schemes in place to make the debt manageable. In this chapter we'll guide you through the maze of student finance and hopefully take some of the worry out of higher education's "F" (that's "fees", folks) factor.

Tuition fees

Let's start with the cost of your course. HEIs in England, Wales and Northern Ireland can charge students around £3,000 a year for full-time degree courses (Scotland has a different arrangement, which is outlined later in the chapter). This goes up a little every year, in line with inflation. So, for entry in 2008, HEIs are allowed to charge up to £3,145 a year. The government has yet to finalise the cost for 2009-10 courses, but if you consider charges for 2007-8 were £3,070 you can get an idea of how much you could pay.

Of course, while universities are allowed to charge this yearly amount it's actually up to the HEI how much it asks students to pay and not all of them are charging the full amount. Prices can vary between universities and courses, so it could pay you to shop around.

The important thing to note is that tuition fees do not have to be paid before you start your course, as they used to be before 2006. You can still pay upfront if you wish, and some universities may even offer a discount if you chose to do so, but most students are expected to pay after graduation.

To defer payment until after your studies, you need to take out a non-means-tested student loan for tuition fees from the Student Loans Company (SLC). The SLC will pay your fees direct to the HEI and you will not have to repay the loan until after you have graduated and are earning at least £15,000 a year. More on repaying your loans later in the chapter.

When the government introduced variable fees in 2006 it said it would review the price of courses in 2009 to assess whether the £3,000 limit needed to be raised. However, whatever the outcome of the review, this should not affect students thinking of applying to study in 2009-10.

Financial support

Aware that raising the cost of tuition fees would be as popular a concept as an empty beer keg at the students' union bar, the government has beefed up the financial support available to undergraduates so as not to put you off studying. Ministers also told HEIs that if they wanted to charge the full price for fees, they would have to do their bit to help ease the financial burden on students.

This has resulted in the reintroduction of non-repayable maintenance grants, university bursaries and higher borrowing levels to help towards the cost of living. The government estimates that around half of all students applying to university will be eligible for some form of non-repayable financial help.

Details of what is available are outlined below. All figures relate to UK students studying at English universities. The financial support for students studying in Scotland, Wales and Northern Ireland is outlined later in the chapter.

Student loans for maintenance

In the same way that you can take out a loan to cover the cost of your tuition fees, you can borrow money from the SLC to help cover your living costs while at university – such as accommodation, travel, food, clothes, nights out.

Anyone under the age of 60 can apply for a maintenance loan, although the amount you can borrow is pegged to where you are studying and where you will be living while taking your degree.

There are three borrowing limits.

Students living away from their parents' home and studying in London can borrow the most – for 2008 entry, this will be up to £6,475 in the first year of study.

Those living away from home and studying elsewhere in England can borrow up to £4,625 in their first year, while students who decide to live at their parents' home during their degrees, regardless of where in the country this may be, can borrow up to £3,580.

These amounts are likely to increase for 2009 entry.

If your course includes a placement overseas, the amount you can borrow could change. If you study abroad for a term or more you may be eligible for an overseas rate of loan. In 2008, the maximum loan you can take out while studying overseas is £5,510.

You will be automatically entitled to borrow 75 per cent of the maximum loan amount for which you are eligible, but whether you can take out the remaining 25 per cent will depend on family income and whether you are receiving any other student grants.

Maintenance loans from the SLC will usually be paid directly into your bank account in three instalments during the academic year.

Maintenance grants

Full-time students from low-income families (earning less than £60,005) studying in England can apply for a non-repayable maintenance grant to help with their living costs.

In 2008, students whose annual household income is £25,000 or less will receive a full grant of £2,835 a year. A partial grant will be paid on a sliding scale to students with household incomes of between £25,001 and £60,005.

Expect these figures to rise slightly if you begin university in 2009.

The money will be paid directly into your bank account three times a year.

If you receive a maintenance grant you will also be entitled to take out student loans, but the amount you can borrow will be slightly less – the government reasons you won't need to borrow quite so much if you receive a grant. For example, if you receive a grant of £1,260 or more, your student loan entitlement will be reduced by £1,260. The smaller the grant you receive the more you will be able to borrow.

Example: figures based on a student beginning their course in 2008-09, living away from home and studying outside London.

Household income	Maintenance grant	Student loan for maintenance	Total for 2008-09
£25,000	£2,835	£3,365	£6,200
£30,000	£2,002	£3,365	£5,367
£40,000	£998	£3,627	£4,625
£50,000	£524	£4,101	£4,625
£60,005	£50	£4,575	£4,625

Source: Directgov.gov.uk

Special support grant

This grant is similar to a regular maintenance grant – it's assessed using household income and is worth the same amount – but it is aimed at helping students pay for those extra costs that come with university, such as books, equipment, travel, and childcare. Eligibility rests on, among other things, whether you're a single parent, have a disability, or have taken time out of a course because of illness or because you've been caring for someone.

The difference between this award and the maintenance grant is that it will not affect the amount you can borrow as a maintenance loan.

University and college bursaries

As a condition of charging higher fees, HEIs have had to come up with their own bursary schemes to help students manage their finances – and they have come up trumps with the amount of money.

Anyone receiving a full maintenance grant will automatically be entitled to at least £300 a year from their place of study, if it is charging the full price (£3,145) for tuition, in effect allowing eligible students to cover their fee costs each year (maintenance grant + bursary = fee charge). Students receiving a £2,835 maintenance grant in 2008 will get at least £310 from their HEI. Universities and colleges are also offering bursaries to students who are eligible for partial grants.

However, many HEIs are offering far more than required. It is estimated that last year, students entitled to a full maintenance grant and studying at a university charging the full cost for fees, received, on average, bursaries worth around £1,000.

But it's not just students in receipt of maintenance grants who may be eligible for financial assistance. Some HEIs are offering money to students who live close to the institution or who apply from a partner school or college.

Some HEIs are also offering scholarships (and of significant sums too) to students studying particular subjects, or if they make the institution their first choice on the Ucas form. There are also sometimes awards available for academic excellence (usually based on your A-level grades). It doesn't take a genius to work out that universities use these tactics to increase the numbers of people applying in certain subject areas, or to attract people with academic prowess. But you could really benefit if you look out for an awards package that matches your course interests and abilities.

To fully benefit from the money that is on offer, you need to check what's available at the university you wish to attend. Most will have this information on their websites. It's important to do so as soon as you've decided on a course, as eligibility for some scholarships could be based on written exams, portfolios or interviews. More on applying for financial support later in the chapter.

Subject-specific bursaries and grants

While universities can offer specific bursaries and scholarships for certain subjects, it's also worth checking with umbrella bodies and societies to see what they are offering, particularly if you want to study a subject with a lower uptake, such as the sciences, technology, engineering, and maths (or STEM) subjects.

There is also extra money available from the NHS for specific nursing, midwifery, and other medical courses, and for social work degrees.

STEM subjects

Keen to encourage more students on to these very worthy, but perhaps not quite so sexy degree courses, some umbrella organisations are offering financial incentives, so you need to do your research.

The Institute of Physics (www.iop.org), for example, has its own university bursary scheme, aimed at increasing the number of students studying the subject at undergraduate level. The institute is offering 300 bursaries worth £3,000 over the course of a three-year degree course, or £4,000 for a combined master's course, to students studying at selected universities.

The Royal Academy of Engineering (www.raeng.org.uk), meanwhile, offers financial awards to exceptional engineering students, worth up to £5,000 over three years.

Aspiring scientists can also find financial help from the Nuffield Foundation, which is offering science bursaries to undergraduates to carry out research during their course.

And the Royal Society of Chemistry lists the institutions that offer scholarships for those studying the subject in the UK, as well as offering funding to attend its conferences (www.rsc.org).

Healthcare

If you want to study a medical or healthcare course you may also be eligible for financial assistance from the NHS.

Students taking nursing or midwifery degrees and diplomas (which lead to registration with the Nursing and Midwifery Council) could receive an NHS bursary (www.nhspa.gov.uk/sgu), which could cover the cost of your course fees and help towards living expenses.

Students taking a nursing degree can apply for means-tested maintenance grants, while those taking diplomas should be eligible for non-means-tested support.

Bursaries may also be available for students studying other medical courses, such as chiropody, podiatry, occupational therapy, physiotherapy, and speech and language therapy.

Be aware that receipt of an NHS bursary will reduce your entitlement to a maintenance loan, but at least that could reduce debts after your studies.

If you are offered a place on a relevant medical course, the HEI should notify the NHS that you are eligible for an award. The NHS should then send you bursary application details.

Things are slightly different for medical and dentistry students studying courses lasting five or six years, as you will only be able to apply for an NHS bursary in your final years of training. You are, of course, still able to take out student maintenance loans for the full duration of your course – although this amount will be slightly reduced after your fourth year of study. And you can still apply for a maintenance grant, subject to your family income, which means you could be entitled to receive that precious extra bursary from your place of study for at least the first four years of study.

Social work

If you are planning to do a degree in social work you may be eligible for a bursary to help cover living costs from the NHS Business Services Authority on behalf of the Department of Health. These bursaries are non-means-tested, but you have to study on an approved course and meet a few other requirements (such as being a UK resident and not receiving support for your studies from an employer), so check with your favoured place of study before you apply.

If you meet the criteria you will be eligible for a basic grant to help with living expenses and the cost of travel during placements. The bursary does not cover tuition fees, but you will be able to take out a loan to cover the cost of those in the same way as other students studying different courses. You will receive a higher grant if you are studying at a HEI in London.

Part-time students will also be eligible for these bursaries.

Teacher training

Although there have been discussions about tuition fees being waived for undergraduate teacher-training degrees and extra bursaries being made available, particularly to those taking their teacher training in subjects with a shortage of teachers, the extra benefits seem to have gone to students doing postgraduate courses rather than first degrees. So, if you take a regular bachelor of education degree you will be subject to the same financial package as other undergraduate students. If you decide instead to do a three-year degree in another subject and then apply for a postgraduate certificate of education (PGCE) you could get your hands on some extra cash and could qualify for a "golden hello" bursary when you start work, depending on the subject you teach.

Other financial help

Access to Learning Fund

As well as their own bursaries, HEIs also offer extra financial support to students through their Access to Learning Funds. These are set up specifically for those moments of financial crisis – an unexpected expense, struggling to keep on top of your bills, or if you think you may be forced to drop out of university for financial reasons.

You can apply for money from this extra pot of cash directly through your HEI, and it is up to it to decide whether you fit the criteria for help and, if so, how much money you will receive. Money from this access fund is usually treated as a non-repayable grant, but sometimes it takes the form of a short-term loan (which is probably still preferable to making extra payments on a credit card).

Priority for money from this fund is given to students from low-income families, those with children, students leaving local authority care, and those in their final year struggling to make ends meet as they approach the end of their course.

Students with disabilities

If you have a disability – mental or physical – you may be entitled to extra financial help while you study.

Disabled Students' Allowances help to meet any extra costs incurred because of your disability. For example, the money could pay for someone to help you get around campus a little more easily, or to pay for any specialist equipment to help with your studies.

Full-time students can get specialist equipment allowances of up to £5,030, and up to £20,000 a year for non-medical support from a helper. You may also be entitled to extra cash to help meet your travel costs.

Proof of your disability will be needed.

Students with dyslexia may also be able to get extra money, usually to help pay for a computer to aid study. Again, you will need to supply evidence of the condition, usually in the form of an assessment from a psychologist or teacher.

Students with children and dependents

If you have children and are taking a full-time degree you may be entitled to money to help meet the cost of childcare. It's also worth checking to see if you are eligible for Child Tax Credit.

Those with adult dependents can also apply for an adult dependents grant.

Both these grants are based on household income.

The Parents' Learning Allowance could be another source of welcome cash to help pay for course-related costs, such as books, placements, and extra equipment. Again the amount you get will be based on income, and the allowance does not have to be paid back.

Distance study

If you decide you would prefer to study by distance learning – perhaps your dream course is at a university in the north of England, but you can't bear to leave your home in the south-east – you may be able to get some funding. This largely depends on which course you are taking and income levels, so contact your local education authority or Student Loans Company for advice.

Funding for part-time students

For those who want to take a little more time with their studies, perhaps to fit it around work, you will be pleased to know that you can get financial assistance during your course.

Keep in mind that HEIs can set their own tuition fees for part-time courses, so it will be wise to check with the individual institution what it plans to charge for the entire degree before you sign up.

Your household income and the course you wish to study will determine your eligibility for a grant to help cover fees and pay for books, extra materials, and travel. It will usually be assumed your living costs will be met through work or savings if you are studying part-time. However, if your household income is low, you may be able to get some form of help with accommodation. It's always worth inquiring.

When to apply for money

It's important that you begin researching what you're entitled to as soon as possible. Don't wait until you have an offer of a place at university before applying for financial help, otherwise you could find yourself out of pocket come the first week of term.

You need only fill in one application form to get all the money you might want – although it is a whopper of a form!

The student finance application form covers tuition fees, maintenance loans, and grants, disability and childcare grants and can be downloaded from the government advice website, www.direct.gov.uk. You can also use this website to apply online for funding.

Alternatively, contact your local education authority or the Student Loans Company for a paper application form.

How to apply

To apply for loans and grants you will need to quote the course for which you have applied and name the university you wish to attend, even if you're not 100 per cent certain what you want to study or where you want to go. These details can be updated later. The important thing is to get your application in as soon as you can. If your details do change, make sure you tell your local authority straight away to avoid any future problems with your application.

If applying for a maintenance grant or loan, your application will need to be supported by evidence of household income, so warn parents, or partners, that they may be asked to show their payslips.

Once your form has been sent off, your local education authority will assess your eligibility and work out how much money you are entitled to receive.

Around six to eight weeks after applying for financial help you should get a letter from Student Finance Direct (SFD), which deals with applications, confirming the amount you will receive and when it will go into your bank account. If you open a new bank account before you start your studies, remember to tell SFD.

When you register for your course, your university will let SFD know you've arrived and signed up and you should start receiving your first student maintenance grant and loan payments. The university will receive the money to cover your fees directly, so you won't have to worry about that.

Getting your hands on a bursary from a university may involve a slightly different process. Some universities administer these bursaries themselves, others leave it to SFD to sort out. Check what the procedure is with your place of study. You may just need to tick the boxes on your student finance application form that allows SFD to pass your details on to the university on your behalf.

Repaying your tuition and maintenance loans

You will not have to start repaying your tuition fee or maintenance loans until after you graduate and are earning at least £15,000 a year.

The tax office will be notified of your earnings once you start your job and your repayments will be deducted automatically from your pay beginning the April after you graduate. If you decide to work for yourself straight after university, repayments will be collected through the tax self-assessment system.

The good news is you will not pay commercial rates of interest on your student loans. Instead, rates are linked to inflation, so, in real terms, you will be paying back what you borrowed, which means you shouldn't get any nasty surprises about how much you owe.

The rate you pay back will be around 9 per cent of your earnings above £15,000 gross a year. (This salary works out to be around £1,250 a month or £288 a week).

So, if you are earning £18,000 a year, you will pay back around £22 a month. Here's how:

An annual salary of £18,000 means you will be paid £1,500 a month gross, which means you are paid £250 over the monthly threshold amount of £1,250. The amount you pay back a month will be 9 per cent of £250, which works out to be around £22, which means a weekly payment of just over £5.

What you'll pay back

Income each year before tax	Monthly repayment	Repayment as % of income
up to £15,000	0	0%
£16,000	£7	0.6%
£17,000	£15	1.1%
£18,000	£22	1.5%
£19,000	£30	1.9%
£20,000	£37	2.3%
£21,000	£45	2.6%
£22,000	£52	2.9%
£23,000	£60	3.1%
£24,000	£67	3.4%
£25,000	£75	3.6%

Source: Student Finance Direct

You can, of course, choose to pay more each month. If you haven't paid off your loans after 25 years the government will write them off, so you may find it's not worth rushing.

And remember, the figures are recalculated as your income goes up (and down) so if your income drops to below £15,000 for any reason, your repayments will stop.

You may also be entitled to a five-year "repayment holiday", which allows you to take a break from paying back your student loans, perhaps because you want to save money for a house or start a family. Repayment holidays are for students graduating in or after 2011.

Studying in different parts of the UK

Where you live could affect how much you pay in tuition fees and how much you receive in grants and loans. Outlined below are the details you need for studying in Scotland, Wales, and Northern Ireland. Remember to contact individual institutions to find out about the bursaries and scholarships they may be offering.

Scotland

Students from Scotland studying in Scotland Scotland did not sign up to the university finance system established in England, Wales, and Northern Ireland, opting instead to introduce a graduate endowment, rather than yearly fees. This endowment was paid by students upon completion of their degrees. However, the Scottish executive recently voted to axe this requirement, which means Scottish students staying in the country to study will pay nothing for their tuition. Means-tested maintenance loans are available and those from low-income households can apply for non-repayable bursaries. You will not have to pay back your loans until the April after graduation when earnings hit £15,000 or more a year. Financial help may be available to cover travel expenses.

Students from Scotland studying in England, Wales or Northern Ireland Students will be subject to variable tuition fees, for which you can take out a non-means-tested fees loan, payable the April after you graduate if you are earning at least £15,000 a year. You will be entitled to apply for means-tested student loans, although borrowing limits may be slightly lower. You can also apply for a Students Outside Scotland bursary, which is dependent on family income and will reduce your loan entitlement. You may also be eligible to take out an Additional Loan, which is again dependent on household income. Financial help may be available to cover travel expenses.

Students from England, Wales, and Northern Ireland studying in Scotland You will be subject to yearly tuition fees of at least £1,700 (£2,700 for medical students) – bear in mind degrees from Scottish HEIs tend to last four years. You can apply for a non-means-tested loan to cover tuition and for means-tested maintenance loans and grants.

Those in receipt of a full maintenance grant will be eligible for a bursary of around £300 a year.

Wales

Students from Wales studying in Wales You will be subject to variable tuition fees, repayable the April after graduation when you are earning at least £15,000. However, all Welsh students staying in the country to study should be entitled to a yearly non-repayable, non-means-tested tuition fees grant, which should cover more than half the cost of your course. The money will be paid directly to your institution. Means-tested, non-repayable bursaries are also available from HEIs. You can also apply for means-tested maintenance loans. Assembly Learning Grants are also available to help those from low-income families to cover living expenses. Undergraduates training to be secondary school teachers may be eligible for extra funding during their school-based placements.

Students from Wales studying in England or Northern Ireland You will be subject to variable tuition fees, repayable the April after graduation if you are earning at least £15,000 a year. You can apply for a non-means-tested loan to cover tuition and for a means-tested maintenance loan. You can also apply for an Assembly Learning Grant to help cover living costs, dependent on household income. You may also be eligible for a bursary from your place of study.

Students from Wales studying in Scotland You will be subject to yearly tuition fees of at least £1,700 (£2,700 for medical students). You can apply for a non-means-tested loan to cover tuition, a means-tested maintenance loan and for an Assembly Learning Grant to cover living costs. Those in receipt of a full maintenance grant will be eligible for a bursary of around £300 a year from their place of study.

Students from England, Scotland, and Northern Ireland studying in Wales You will be subject to variable tuition fees, repayable the April after graduation if you are earning at least £15,000 a year. You can apply for a non-means-tested loan to cover tuition and for means-tested maintenance loans and grants. You may also be eligible for a bursary from your place of study. Scottish students can apply for a Students Outside Scotland bursary, which is dependent on family income, to help with maintenance.

Northern Ireland

Students from Northern Ireland studying in Northern Ireland You will be subject to variable tuition fees, for which you can take out a non-means-tested fees loan, repayable the April after graduation if you are earning at least £15,000 a year. You will be able to apply for a non-repayable, means-tested maintenance grant (the amount available is slightly higher than the amount offered elsewhere), and could be eligible for a bursary from your chosen place of study. You will be entitled to apply for means-tested student maintenance loans.

Students from Northern Ireland studying in England and Wales You will be subject to variable tuition fees, for which you can take out a non-means- tested fees loan, repayable the April after graduation if your salary is at least £15,000 a year. You will be able to apply for a non-repayable, means-tested maintenance grant, and could be eligible for a bursary from your chosen place of study. You will be entitled to apply for means-tested student maintenance loans.

Students from Northern Ireland studying in Scotland You will be subject to yearly tuition fees of at least £1,700 (£2,700 for medical students). You can apply for a non-means-tested loan to cover tuition and for means-tested maintenance loans and non-repayable grants. Those in receipt of a full maintenance grant will be eligible for a bursary of around £300 a year from their place of study.

Students from England, Wales, and Scotland studying in Northern Ireland You will be subject to variable tuition fees, for which you can take out a non-means-tested fees loan, repayable the April after you graduate if you are earning at least £15,000 a year. You will be able to apply for a non-repayable, means-tested maintenance grant (the Students Outside Scotland bursary for Scottish students) and could be eligible for a bursary from your chosen place of study. You will be entitled to apply for means-tested student maintenance loans.

》 Further information

Student Awards Agency for Scotland	↗ www.saas.gov.uk
Student Finance Wales	↗ www.studentfinancewales.co.uk
Student Finance Northern Ireland	↗ www.studentfinanceni.co.uk

Subjects

Reading the league tables

Hello, and welcome to the all-singing, all-dancing Guardian league tables. Well, not quite – though if you care to pop by the office, I'm sure we could give you a song – but we are pretty proud of our tables, and hope that they'll be useful in your quest to find the right university.

As with anything that involves statistics, however, university performance is open to quite a lot of interpretation and so here are some notes on how we put ours together.

The tables are compiled, in association with EducationGuardian.co.uk, by Campus Pi, an applied research department at Brunel University. The rankings are compiled from the most recent figures available – official 2006-07 returns from universities and higher education colleges to the Higher Education Statistics Agency (Hesa). They also incorporate data from the National Student Survey (NSS) 2007, published by the Higher Education Funding Council for England.

We have used seven statistical measures to contribute to the ranking of a university or college in each subject, weighted as follows:

- Teaching quality – as rated by final-year students on the course (10%)
- Feedback (assessment) – as rated by final-year students on the course (5%)
- Spending per student (17%)
- Student:staff ratio (17%)
- Job prospects (17%)
- Value added – comparing students' degree results with their entry qualifications (17%)
- Entry tariff (17%)

We don't publish the actual figures for spending, or for the Guardian's value-added calculation. These scores are marked out of 10 in bands, to allow for comparisons – spending on medical students is bound to be higher than on business students, for instance.

For each subject that it teaches, an institution is given a Guardian score, based on these seven measures. The Guardian score for each institution in each subject is derived from a weighted average of the standardised scores for each measure, converted into a scale in which the highest ranked institution gets 100 points and all institutions receive a positive score.

When it comes to the overall score for a university, the subject scores are weighted according to the number of students enrolled on the course taking first degrees – a department with 200 students counts more than one with 50.

The institutional table is determined using average standardised scores in each subject, as opposed to the average teaching score that is displayed for each subject. We believe this is a more robust methodology.

The number of institutions offering a subject now affects the influence of that subject in the institutional table. So, the institution finishing first in a small subject such as agriculture and forestry will not benefit in the overall table as much as the institution that finishes first in a subject such as business and management studies, in which 111 institutions are active.

We do not include research ratings or research funding – these are tables aimed at students taking first degrees and so concentrate on teaching and teaching resources.

Thresholds

To be included in a subject table an institution must be teaching at least 35 students.

We have also imposed a threshold on the overall universities table: an institution must feature in at least four subject tables. This excludes a number of specialist colleges – in music, for instance – which may be at the top of their subject rankings.

On the university ranking table, the following institutions do not have scores because they appear in fewer than four subject tables:

Arts Institute at Bournemouth

Bishop Grosseteste University College Lincoln

University of Buckingham

Central School of Speech and Drama

Conservatoire for Dance and Drama

Courtauld Institute of Art

University College for the Creative Arts

Dartington College of Arts

Edinburgh College of Art

University College Falmouth

Glasgow School of Art

Harper Adams University College

Heythrop College

Leeds College of Music

The Liverpool Institute for Performing Arts

Norwich School of Art and Design

Ravensbourne College of Design and Communication

Rose Bruford College

Royal Academy of Music

Royal Agricultural College

Royal College of Music

Royal Northern College of Music

Royal Scottish Academy of Music and Drama

Royal Veterinary College University of London

St George's, University of London

St Mary's University College, Belfast

School of Pharmacy

Stranmillis

Trinity College Carmarthen

Trinity Laban

University College Birmingham

Writtle College

The measures

Teaching quality
We have used results from the NSS, carried out for the third time in 2007, which questions final-year undergraduates about what they think of the quality of the course.

The full NSS survey results are available at www.tqi.ac.uk

We used the responses to four questions in the NSS under the heading of the "teaching on my course". These looked at whether staff are good at explaining things, make the subject interesting and are enthusiastic about what they teach, and if the course is intellectually stimulating. This column shows the percentage who "definitely agree" or "mostly agree" with these statements.

Feedback (assessment)
This column also taken from the NSS, derives from answers to five questions on feedback relating to whether marking criteria were made clear in advance, assessment arrangements were fair, feedback was prompt, whether they received detailed comments on their work and whether feedback "helped me clarify things I did not understand". We show the percentage who "definitely agree" or "mostly agree".

Spending per student
The amount of money that an institution spends providing a subject (not including the costs of academic staff, as these are already counted in the staff-student ratio) is compared with the volume of students learning the subject to derive a spend-per-student measure. This figure also includes the money the institution spends on central academic services, and per student.

Student:staff ratio (SSR)
SSRs compare the number of staff teaching a subject with the number of students studying it, to get a ratio where a low SSR is treated positively in the league tables. At least 25 students and two staff (both full-time) must be present in an SSR calculation. Year-on-year inconsistency and extreme values at either end of the spectrum cause several SSRs to be suppressed.

This is far from being as straightforward as it sounds and a lot of effort by the Guardian, Campus Pi and the universities has gone into trying to match them up. One size does not fit all, as we have learned (the hard way).

Job prospects
Based on the 2005-06 Destinations of Leavers from HE Return, we assess the proportion of graduates who find graduate-level employment, or study full-time, within six months of graduation. Graduates who report that they are unable to work are excluded from the study population, which must have at least 24 respondents in order to generate results.

Value added

Our attempt is to measure how well universities teach a wide range of students, not just the superstars. Scores employ a sophisticated methodology that tracks individual students from enrolment to graduation, comparing qualifications upon entry with the award that a student receives at the end of their studies.

Each student is given a probability of achieving a first or 2:1, based on the qualifications that they enter with. If they manage to earn a good degree then they score points that reflect how difficult it was to do so (in fact, they score the reciprocal of the probability of getting a first or 2:1). Thus an institution that is adept at taking in students with low entry qualifications and converting them into graduates with the best degrees will score highly in the value-added measure, as the number of students getting a first or 2:1 will have exceeded statistical expectations. At least 28 students must be in a subject.

Entry tariff

We take the average Ucas tariff points of first-year first-degree entrants to a subject, subtracting the tariffs for key skills and core skills. There must be at least eight students in this measure.

Scottish institutions are treated separately, with average tariff scores for Highers/A-levels only. These Highers/A-level tariffs are compared with the UK average for A-level tariffs. However, the total tariff scores of non-Scottish institutions are compared with the average total tariff score of non-Scottish higher education institutions only.

Caveats

Four universities – Liverpool Hope, London Metropolitan, Keele and West of Scotland – declined to provide data for these tables.

There are three joint medical schools: Brighton/Sussex, Hull/York, and the Peninsula medical school established by Exeter and Plymouth. These schools do not have individual institution profiles, but are linked from the tables through to the parent institution.

With regard to data provided by Hesa, it should be noted that Hesa does not accept responsibility for any inferences or conclusions derived from the data by third parties.

University rankings

This is the overall table, made up of the average Guardian score across the board.

Ranking	Institution	Subject appearances	Average Guardian score	Ranking	Institution	Subject appearances	Average Guardian score
1	Oxford	25	100.0	40	East Anglia	22	61.3
2	Cambridge	23	92.9	41	Nottingham Trent	25	60.9
3	London School of Economics	11	84.4	42	Goldsmiths	12	60.7
4	Warwick	22	81.6	43	Newcastle	31	60.4
5	St Andrews	18	78.4	44	Liverpool	31	60.1
6	Imperial College	14	78.1	45	University of the Arts London	4	60.0
7	UCL	29	76.6	46	Queen's, Belfast	34	59.8
8	Soas	7	74.3	47	Queen Mary	18	59.7
9	Edinburgh	34	73.4	48	Plymouth	30	59.3
10	Loughborough	24	72.9	49	Napier	13	59.1
11	York	23	72.5	50	Robert Gordon	15	58.6
12	Lancaster	23	71.8	51	Newman University College	6	58.5
13	Bath	20	71.1	52	Heriot-Watt	15	56.6
14	Exeter	24	70.9	53	Hull	26	56.4
14	Leicester	20	70.9	54	Brunel	23	56.2
16	Durham	25	69.2	55	Glasgow Caledonian	11	55.8
17	Dundee	20	67.8	56	Birmingham City	19	55.6
18	Aston	11	67.3	57	Oxford Brookes	26	55.4
19	Nottingham	32	67.2	58	Glamorgan	20	55.1
20	Glasgow	31	67.0	59	Gloucestershire	17	55.0
21	King's College London	23	66.5	59	Ulster	27	55.0
22	Surrey	21	66.4	61	Bangor	16	54.6
23	Aberdeen	20	66.1	62	Central Lancashire	21	54.2
24	Manchester	38	66.0	63	Bradford	19	54.0
25	Southampton	29	65.8	63	Brighton	22	54.0
26	City	14	65.4	65	Bath Spa	13	53.7
27	Leeds	37	65.1	66	UWE Bristol	24	52.8
28	Kent	26	64.8	67	Staffordshire	18	52.5
29	Strathclyde	22	64.2	68	Queen Margaret	6	52.4
30	Birmingham	37	64.1	69	Aberystwyth	19	51.1
31	Bristol	31	63.7	70	St Mary's UC, Twickenham	12	50.6
32	Cardiff	31	62.7	71	Anglia Ruskin	20	50.3
33	Sussex	24	62.4	72	Sunderland	15	49.9
34	Royal Holloway	18	62.2	73	Portsmouth	23	49.6
35	Essex	20	62.1	74	Worcester	13	49.4
36	Sheffield	31	62.0	75	Coventry	20	49.0
37	Bournemouth	12	61.8	76	Northumbria	25	48.5
39	Reading	23	61.4	77	UWIC	7	48.1

Ranking	Institution	Subject appearances	Average Guardian score	Ranking	Institution	Subject appearances	Average Guardian score
78	Sheffield Hallam	24	47.2	98	Derby	18	43.0
79	Northampton	15	47.1	99	Swansea Met	5	42.9
80	Chester	15	47.0	100	Hertfordshire	24	42.8
81	Teesside	18	46.7	101	Lincoln	18	41.4
82	De Montfort	21	46.2	102	Westminster	16	41.2
83	Swansea	20	45.9	103	North East Wales Institute	7	40.9
84	Newport	10	45.8	104	Edge Hill	14	40.8
85	Thames Valley	8	45.5	105	Abertay Dundee	6	40.7
86	Salford	21	44.9	106	Roehampton	19	39.4
87	Chichester	9	44.8	107	York St John	13	38.9
88	Kingston	26	44.4	108	Middlesex	17	37.9
89	Canterbury Christ Church	18	44.3	109	Liverpool John Moores	28	37.8
89	Huddersfield	19	44.3	109	Southampton Solent	14	37.8
91	Bedfordshire	16	44.2	111	East London	16	34.9
92	Manchester Met	29	43.8	112	Greenwich	27	34.2
93	Leeds Trinity & All Saints	8	43.7	113	Wolverhampton	24	33.9
94	Marjon (St Mark and St John)	6	43.6	114	Bucks New University	11	33.2
95	Cumbria	16	43.4	115	Lampeter	5	32.8
95	Winchester	12	43.4	116	London South Bank	17	32.1
97	Leeds Met	21	43.1	117	Bolton	9	28.3

Specialist institutions

Rankings for colleges that offer one, two, or three subjects, but do not compete with universities across a broad range of subjects.

Ranking	Institution	Subject appearances	Average Guardian score
1	Courtauld Institute	1	100
2	Royal Scottish Academy of Music and Drama	1	92.5
3	Royal Academy of Music	1	82.9
4	Conservatoire for Dance and Drama	1	77.2
5	Royal College of Music	1	70.4
6	Trinity Laban	2	69.0
7	The Liverpool Institute for Performing Arts	2	67.4
8	Rose Bruford College	2	67.1
9	Central School of Speech and Drama	1	62.7
10	Dartington College of Arts	3	59.0
11	Glasgow School of Art	2	58.8
12	St Mary's UC, Belfast	2	56.9
13	Buckingham	1	56.5
14	Royal Northern College of Music	1	50.9
15	Harper Adams UC	1	46.5
16	School of Pharmacy	1	46.4
17	UC Falmouth	3	45.1
18	Stranmillis UC	1	43.6
19	Arts Institute at Bournemouth	2	41.5
19	St George's Medical School	2	41.5
21	Heythrop College	2	38.4
22	Leeds College of Music	1	36.6
23	Royal Veterinary College	1	36.4
24	Bishop Grosseteste UC	1	35.6
25	Royal Agricultural College	2	33.6
26	Edinburgh College of Art	1	30.8
27	Norwich School of Art	1	25.2
28	Ravensbourne College	1	23.9
29	Trinity College, Carmarthen	3	23.1
29	Writtle College	1	23.1
31	University College Birmingham	2	22.7
32	University College for the Creative Arts	3	20.3

Art and design

Architecture

> Architecture is at the same time a deeply basic feature of social human needs and activity, and a field constantly requiring new ideas and innovation. Big and exciting challenges need to be faced by architects: meeting our dwelling needs in a sustainable way, keeping space meaningful in a society, improving the quality of our public spaces and so on. There is a big difference between producing buildings and spaces that somehow 'work' and making successful and innovative architecture that can become a meaningful and inspiring place for those who use it.
>
> It involves a holistic approach to space, place, and dwelling, which requires students to tackle multi-disciplinary projects and problems. Studying architecture means being exposed to all aspects and facets of what makes a place. Students are expected to look at a problem from the creative and artistic side, as well as from a cultural and historical and a technological and scientific perspective. But above all they face the challenge of integrating all of these into a designed final product — a building or a space. So, studying architecture means learning to be speculative, creative, and research-oriented whilst at the same time translating these skills into the ability to be concrete, practical, and focused on solving very real problems and making better places for people to use and enjoy.
>
> It is both a highly vocational subject leading to a very definite professional profile for which there is no job shortage, as well as something providing a variety of highly transferable skills, given its multi- and interdisciplinary character. Thanks to skills ranging from creative design, graphic, and spatial awareness to analytical and scientific reasoning, architecture graduates are amongst the most flexible and versatile around.
>
> **Dr Alex Aurigi**, *Director of Architecture, School of Architecture, Planning and Landscape, Newcastle University*

In the immortal words of the greatest architect of the 20th century, Le Corbusier, architecture is "the masterly, correct and magnificent play of masses brought together in light".

Sounds wonderful, but if you want to be one, you have to remember it's a very long course of study, comprising a three-year BA or BSc degree at university, a year of practical training in an architect's office, a two-year Dip Arch or BArch at university, and a further year of practical training before the final Professional Practice Examination.

Once you start your course, you will study across a wide range of subjects, from history and theory to IT, technology and management. If a five-year course is a daunting financial prospect, several schools of architecture offer a part-time alternative — taking five years for the BA or BSc degree and three years for the Dip Arch or BArch, during which you'll be able to work while you study.

The breadth of the subject will equip you with plenty of transferable skills, and for those who decide after taking their undergraduate degree not to pursue a career as an architect there will always be employment opportunities in IT and the media.

It is a myth that A-level maths and physics are a prerequisite for entry to architecture courses, but it certainly will be an advantage if you have a natural feel for geometry and three-dimensional form and some skill in drawing. Most universities will expect to see evidence of your abilities in a portfolio of work at the time of your application.

You will need a minimum of two A-levels if you enrol on leaving school, but the government's widening access policy encourages candidates from non-traditional academic backgrounds to enrol as mature students if they can demonstrate an aptitude for the subject.

In order to practise as an architect in the UK, it is also necessary to be on the register of architects, which is held by the UK statutory regulator, the Architects Registration Board. ARB is the sole body charged with prescribing the qualifications, so if you want to practise as an architect, it is important you check out whether or not the qualification you are thinking of is prescribed by the ARB. And if you want to be a member of the Royal Institute of British Architects the course needs to be recognised by it too – so check first.

Try to go and see a range of departments in action before making a choice. Course content can vary considerably according to research interests and institutional histories. Some courses are more technical and academic than others, and you will want to ask about their links with architects' practices and investigate what the work placements are like.

Another possibility is architectural technology, which is a relatively new profession and deals with the technical aspects of the specification, design, and construction of a building, often acting as the project manager, connecting client and architect. These courses are shorter than the full requirements for architecture "proper" – three years, or four with a sandwich course, usually followed up with a work placement.

---

66 You've got to be very self disciplined when studying for a degree in architecture. It's the quantity and quality of work expected and amount of time that you need to be in university that challenges me the most, but this also means you make great friends and help each other through. I love the diversity of the course – from history of architecture to design and environmental building science.

Eleri Akehurst, *third-year architecture student, University of Plymouth*

》 Further information

Architects Registration Board
8 Weymouth Street
London W1W 5BU

t 020 7580 5861
e info@arb.org.uk
↗ www.arb.org.uk

The Royal Institute of British Architects
66 Portland Place
London W1B 1AD

t 020 7580 5533
e info@inst.riba.org
↗ www.riba.org

Royal Incorporation of Architects in Scotland

15 Rutland Square
Edinburgh EG1 2BE

t 0131 229 7545
e info@rias.org.uk
↗ www.rias.org.uk

Royal Society of Architects in Wales

Bute Building
King Edward VII Avenue
Cathays Park, Cardiff CF10 3NB

t 029 2087 4753
e info@inst.riba.org
↗ www.architecture-wales.com

Royal Society of Ulster Architects

2 Mount Charles
Belfast BT7 1NZ

t 0289 032 3760
e info@rsua.org.uk
↗ www.rsua.org.uk

CABE (Commission for Architecture and the Built Environment)

1 Kemble Street
London WC2B 4AN

t 020 7960 2400
f 020 7960 2444
e enquiries@cabe.org.uk
↗ www.cabe.org.uk

↗ Online reading

Architecture www.architecture.com
Chartered Institute of Architectural Technologists www.ciat.org.uk
Design Council www.designcouncil.org.uk
The Architecture Foundation www.architecturefoundation.org.uk
Art and Architecture www.artandarchitecture.org.uk

Architecture

		Guardian score	Satisfied with teaching %	Satisfied with assessment %	Spend per student score /10	Student:staff ratio	Job prospects %	Value added score /10	Average entry tariff
1	Cambridge	100.0			10	13		6	533
2	UCL	99.4	98	74	10	12	93	7	463
3	Cardiff	84.6			8	15	98	6	485
4	Bath	84.4	93	65	8	20	92	8	479
5	Newcastle	74.6	87	68	6	19	91	8	446
6	Nottingham	74.2	84	51	8	18	92	7	431
7	Edinburgh	74.1	86	51	8	20	85	9	439
8	Liverpool	72.3	81	42	8	17	94	6	420
9	Manchester School of Architecture	70.3	78	45	6	14	95	5	410
10	Sheffield	69.0	91	43	5	15	93	3	448
11	Oxford Brookes	68.7	87	75	4	18	87	8	368
12	Glasgow School of Art	67.0			4	24	95		419
13	Northumbria	65.4	85	54	4	23	94	9	298
14	Dundee	63.7	80	65	6	17	87	4	395
15	Sheffield Hallam	60.7	92	66	4	28	94	6	296
15	Strathclyde	60.7	75	47	5	22	93	7	349
17	Glamorgan	60.0	76	57	8	18			194
18	Ulster	59.2	83	63	3		100	8	308

	Guardian score	Satisfied with teaching %	Satisfied with assessment %	Spend per student score /10	Student:staff ratio	Job prospects %	Value added score /10	Average entry tariff
19 Brighton	55.7	77	45	5	21	91	6	300
20 Queen's, Belfast	54.3	77	54	3	21	83	9	358
21 De Montfort	53.4	79	51	6	18		3	269
22 Lincoln	48.9	81	78	3	23	72	9	270
23 Birmingham City	47.8			3	23		9	253
24 Westminster	47.7	83	62	4	18	76	4	303
25 Southampton Solent	47.5	70	49	5	24			202
26 Plymouth	45.8	67	38	3	21	88	5	331
27 Robert Gordon	45.3			4	20		2	336
28 Portsmouth	44.7	86	70	3	28	80	4	312
29 UWE Bristol	44.0	82	53	4	23		2	282
30 Greenwich	42.2	68	55	8	23	83	2	233
31 Kingston	40.8	84	62	3	28		3	293
32 East London	40.6	76	56	6	27	93	1	232
33 Anglia Ruskin	40.5	70	48	8	27			243
34 Leeds Met	34.6	74	52	2	26	70	8	278
35 London South Bank	33.4	80	51	4	34		6	180
36 Liverpool John Moores	29.8	73	55	2	32	75	5	305
37 Huddersfield	29.2			4	35	85	2	271
38 Wolverhampton	28.4			3	27		2	178

Art and design

❝ 'The world is but a canvas to the imagination,' said the philosopher Henry David Thoreau — and how right he was. An art and design degree offers the opportunity to be creative, innovative, and original, as well as helping to develop skills for life after graduation, whatever direction you choose to go in.

Art and design covers a range of disciplines, from the more traditional fine art courses right through to fashion, product design, and graphics. They are hands-on courses, allowing students to focus on creating and developing, and are often taught by current artists who can help you to develop your ideas and creations. New technology has encouraged the evolution of courses into the 21st century, allowing students to use digital animation and video and moving image, alongside traditional paint and canvas.

Many courses require a foundation year, which provides the opportunity for you to improve your skills and will provide a better indication of which degree subject within art and design is the right one for you.

Studying a creative subject allows you to develop and see your artistic potential through teaching and learning — not just from tutors, but also from other students. We think that's the beauty of studying an art and design course, as it offers a collaborative environment within a vibrant community where people can freely exchange their ideas and experiences.

The creative industries are competitive and so an increasing number of business-facing universities are offering alternative module choices, such as marketing, giving you a wider range of skills for your portfolio.

Art and design is an inspiring and exciting field of study — one that will allow you to truly develop your interests, passions, and ideas.

Chris McIntyre, *Dean of the Faculty for the Creative and Cultural Industries, University of Hertfordshire*

Choosing a course in art and design could be the first step in achieving a career in fine art, graphics or textiles; or might just help you to a lifetime of art appreciation and personal pleasure. And either is fine. There is no need to feel that your degree is wasted if you don't turn out to be a designer or artist.

Whatever your eventual direction, you'll be entering a very broad church, with subjects ranging from design disciplines (anything from craft-based courses such as furniture design to multimedia work), to fine art (more traditional disciplines such as sculpture or installation art), to the history and theory of art and design, even museum studies.

For your course, you'll probably choose between one of three broad areas: fine art (including disciplines like painting, sculpture, photography, and tapestry), visual communications and design (think things like graphics, animation, illustration) and the applied arts (perhaps fashion, furniture or jewellery design). Once on a course you should have the chance to dabble in other areas, cross-fertilising ideas, and developing your imagination alongside your technical skills.

To do an art degree in art you will most likely need to have a foundation or diploma qualification, which in turn usually means having to do a one-year course after school or college. This foundation year will help you decide whether art and design is really for you before you commit to a further three years.

No one can guarantee that when you complete your studies you'll be able to make a living as a professional artist, but you will learn a wide variety of skills that can be utilised in, for example, design and media companies. You might also decide to go into arts management, work in a museum or gallery, or become an art therapist.

Most art and design courses are in the new universities, but there are some in various "old" universities, higher education colleges, and a few specialist institutions. Check the entry-level qualifications for the course, especially if you haven't done any work to foundation level – some will let you in on A-levels alone.

When making your choice, look closely at the facilities of the department. And investigate also the city's galleries, museums, and cultural life, as these will be invaluable research resources.

Study carefully the elements of the course you are taking and never just take the course name and assume the content is the same for every institution. See also who is teaching you – it could be that you will be studying under a designer or artist of international renown. And while the course content is important, do some research on the reputation of the institution you have in mind. Some are highly prestigious with well-established places on the art scene – it could mean a vital leg-up in your career as a practising artist.

For the more vocational courses – curatorship, for example – it is less important who teaches you than whether the course contains vocational elements that will help you achieve appropriate professional qualifications.

> 66 Studying art and design at university I have been encouraged to explore my artistic potential and think independently. The essence of what I have learned and practised has been more realistic in comparison to A-levels, with lecturers who work in the design field and have close connections to industry. This has enabled me to understand the possibilities of my designs. My studies have allowed me to believe in the potential of my ideas, not only during my studies but after graduation.
>
> **Jess Reed**, *final-year furniture student, Loughborough University*

» Further information

National Society for Education of Art and Design
The Gatehouse, Corsham Court
Corsham, Wiltshire SN13 0BZ

t 01249 714825
↗ www.nsead.org

The Arts Councils:
England – www.artscouncil.org.uk
Scotland – www.scottisharts.org.uk
Wales – www.artswales.org.uk
Northern Ireland – www.artscouncil-ni.org

The Association of Illustrators
2nd Floor, Back Building
150 Curtain Road, London EC2A 3AR

↗ www.theaoi.com

EQ (diversity in the creative industries)
Suite E229, Dean Clough
Halifax HX3 5AX

t 01422 381618
↗ www.thinkeq.org.uk

The Chartered Society of Designers
1 Cedar Court, Royal Oak Yard   t   020 7357 8088
Bermondsey Street   e   info@csd.org.uk
London SE1 3GA   ↗ www.csd.org.uk

The Institute of Engineering Designers
Courtleigh, Westbury Leigh   t   01373 822801
Westbury, Wiltshire BA13 3TA   e   ied@ied.org.uk
    ↗ www.ied.org.uk

The Textile Institute
1st Floor, St James's Buildings   t   0161 237 1188
Oxford Street   e   tiihq@textileinst.org.uk
Manchester M1 6FQ   ↗ www.textileinstitute.org

The Association of Photographers
81 Leonard Street   t   020 7739 6669
London EC2A 4QS   e   general@aophoto.co.uk
    ↗ www.the-aop.org

The Crafts Council
44a Pentonville Road   t   020 7278 7700
London N1 9BY   ↗ www.craftscouncil.org.uk

Design Council
34 Bow Street   t   020 7420 5200
London WC2E 7DL   e   info@designcouncil.org.uk
    ↗ www.designcouncil.org.uk

The Centre for Sustainable Design
University College for the Creative Arts   t   01252 892772
Falkner Road, Farnham   f   01252 892747
Surrey GU9 7DS   e   cfsd@ucreative.ac.uk
    ↗ www.cfsd.org.uk

↗ Online reading

Guardian.co.uk Arts and Entertainment   arts.guardian.co.uk
Arts Advice   www.netgain.org.uk
Graphic Arts Monthly   www.gammag.com
Adam (art, design, architecture and media)   www.adam.ac.uk
Design Week   www.designweek.co.uk
Design Museum   www.designmuseum.org

Art and design

		Guardian score	Satisfied with teaching %	Satisfied with assessment %	Spend per student score /10	Student:staff ratio	Job prospects %	Value added score /10	Average entry tariff
1	UCL	100.0			10	12		10	371
2	Brunel	90.0	89	70	9	15	70	8	353
3	Dartington College	85.5	88	75	5	9		9	307
4	York	82.3	82	51	7	17		8	475
5	Edinburgh	81.5	93	61	7	18			437
6	Loughborough	78.0	87	75	7	16	52	9	355
7	Newcastle	77.0			7	15	67	8	359
8	Plymouth	76.8	73	62	10	19	46	9	262
9	Lancaster	73.5	86	56	5	11			351
10	Goldsmiths	71.1	89	59	5	15	67	5	313
11	Southampton	70.5	71	45	9	20	50	10	352
12	Glasgow School of Art	70.1			7	14	54	5	350
13	Kent	70.0	81	65	6	18	64	8	272
14	Glamorgan	69.9	79	66	8	10	61	7	234
15	Brighton	68.6	82	64	8	18	57	6	295
16	Greenwich	68.4	77	69	7	23	75		234
17	Glasgow	67.3	87	54	3	17			398
18	Napier	66.0			7	19	59	8	276
19	Birmingham City	65.9	70	62	8	13	45	8	294
20	Dundee	64.8	74	65	8	13	45	5	320
21	Reading	64.5	78	46	5	16	53	8	303
22	Ulster	63.4	76	65	4	14	57	8	256
23	Nottingham Trent	63.3	78	61	6	20	72	4	298
23	Trinity College, Carmarthen	63.3	77	59	4	10			277
25	UC Falmouth	62.7	80	71	5	26	65	8	270
26	Leeds	62.2	69	53	5	21	59	5	384
27	Northumbria	61.6	75	57	6	18	63	6	274
28	University of the Arts London	60.5	72	56	10	22	49	4	313
29	Arts Institute at Bournemouth	60.1	89	80	3	21	51	4	296
30	Heriot-Watt	59.6	68	57	6	22	73	3	312
31	Gloucestershire	59.3	79	61	7	13	34	8	260
31	UWE Bristol	59.3	84	76	5	20	44	8	245
33	Middlesex	58.9	75	62	10	24	51	5	232
34	Essex	58.2	82	63	8	20		4	218
35	Huddersfield	57.9	84	73	4	19	48	7	247
36	Staffordshire	57.7	79	63	9	18	44	4	238
37	Kingston	57.5	82	63	4	18	58	3	289
38	Robert Gordon	57.1			4	16	47	3	330
39	UWIC	56.7	76	64	5	20	52	7	253
40	Coventry	56.6	77	59	6	32	54	9	282
41	Anglia Ruskin	55.7	72	55	5	19	46	9	253
42	Teesside	55.4	83	77	10	17	46	1	227
43	Roehampton	54.8	87	71	3	23	56	7	227
44	Central Lancashire	54.0	73	67	5	21	56	5	244
45	Bath Spa	52.6	70	57	5	18	45	7	255

	Guardian score	Satisfied with teaching %	Satisfied with assessment %	Spend per student score /10	Student:staff ratio	Job prospects %	Value added score /10	Average entry tariff
46 Sunderland	52.4	73	58	4	13	47	4	253
47 Chichester	51.5	86	65	3	16	35	3	305
48 Bedfordshire	51.3	71	62	5	23	49	8	207
48 De Montfort	51.3	72	62	5	18	48	4	252
50 Portsmouth	51.1	83	72	4	21	46	5	241
51 Manchester Met	50.9	70	62	4	18	51	4	265
52 Northampton	50.7	70	65	4	20	53	5	247
53 Chester	50.2	95	62	3	24	31	7	275
54 Westminster	50.0	87	66	5	19	30	3	296
55 Hertfordshire	49.5	79	60	6	17	49	2	239
55 Newport	49.5	70	66	4	23	51	8	224
57 Edinburgh College of Art	49.2			4	19	45	4	
58 Bucks New University	49.0	72	65	4	17	44	4	240
59 Cumbria	47.5	72	58	2	22	48	8	250
60 Southampton Solent	47.0	78	60	4	20	55	3	227
61 Derby	46.9	73	63	7	18	34	3	271
62 Liverpool John Moores	46.0	68	57	3	18	49	5	216
63 Norwich School of Art	45.4	80	68	3	29	48	6	
64 Oxford Brookes	45.0	74	59	3	27	32	8	296
65 Canterbury Christ Church	44.9	67	50	3	16	33	7	257
66 Swansea Met	44.8	74	53	3	20	46	7	213
67 Ravensbourne College	44.5	78	67	2	37	82	6	195
68 Hull	44.2	80	53	6	22	30	5	257
69 Aberystwyth	43.8	82	59	4	27	32	4	300
69 Bournemouth	43.8	74	49	2		61	3	270
71 Lincoln	43.5	83	71	4	26	41	2	265
72 Bolton	42.8	73	62	3	23	37	9	199
73 Salford	41.6	79	61	3	28	53	3	220
74 Leeds Met	41.0	72	63	5	23	49	2	234
74 East London	41.0	66	56	4	21	48	5	207
76 University College for the Creative Arts	40.7	69	57	3	22	50	3	227
77 Sheffield Hallam	40.2	75	58	4	19	36	1	264
78 Thames Valley	39.7	65	60	5		60	2	226
79 London South Bank	37.1	82	67	3	38			232
80 York St John	36.8	60	55	5	24	47	2	259
81 Wolverhampton	35.3	68	60	5	23	39	3	198
82 North East Wales Institute	27.9	61	41	4	18	31	2	204

Building and
town and country planning

66 Planners understand cities — it's what they're trained to do. They develop strategies — for developing London eastward along the Thames; for protecting Europe's historic townscapes; for renewing east European neighbourhoods suffering from decades of underinvestment and social neglect; for upgrading impoverished squatter settlements in Africa; for accommodating projected housing demand in environmentally sensitive regions. They are environmental managers, city shapers, community mobilisers, social entrepreneurs, regulators, inventors, and visionaries.

History and archaeology tell us there have always been planned cities, laid out according to grand designs. Ancient Babylon and Alexandria; the Chinese imperial cities; 18th-century Paris; Britain's 20th-century new towns. Some of these worked according to plan for a while — where their builders and rulers commanded sufficient power and resources. Most cities, even planned cities, however, take on a life of their own. They grow under the influence of millions of individual decisions about where to live, work, invest, play.

Shaping these processes has to be one of the most challenging and important jobs around. This has never been more so than now — the commencement of the urban century. Cities in the rich nations are reinventing themselves in a lively and creative urban renaissance — a dramatic turnaround from the decaying industrial cities of the 20th century. Cities are becoming bigger and more sophisticated.

There are now 30 cities in the world with over 7 million inhabitants, 24 of them larger than London. And as cities grow and city systems evolve, problems emerge — urban water shortages, regional growth disparities, destruction of valuable cultural and environmental assets, rural deprivation, urban poverty, overheated housing markets, congested transportation. Finding mechanisms to address these problems without compromising economic health and vitality is the planner's key skill. Planning is one of the oldest professions — evidence of its abiding importance.

Train as a planner and you're unlikely ever to be out of work. Few other jobs also give you the same kind of chance to shape the future.

Professor Chris Webster, *School of City and Regional Planning, Cardiff University*

We don't like to whinge, but creating tables for university subjects can, at times, be a little like tying knots in jelly. The problems come when you find that the figures tend to leave you grouping two (or more) only slightly related subjects. It happens elsewhere and it's not perfect, but here we've grouped together building and town and country planning. They're subjects that can be linked, but these are tables where you should take the rankings with just a small pinch of salt and do more research into the universities which interest you.

To start with building, university courses on building studies (or the built environment) focus on all aspects of buildings — except the design element that belongs to architects. It's a rather practical course, covering construction management, construction techniques, structural and civil engineering, and the planning of infrastructure for major building developments, including airports and railways.

The idea of a building course is to turn out one of the highly skilled professionals who gets to plan and build increasingly complex projects anywhere in the world. Building studies courses have largely developed from university schools of engineering, though many courses also have a grounding in urban policy and history – the best engineers and contractors understand the political ins and outs of projects, and one way of understanding the political sensitivities of particular projects is to understand their history.

The more closely focused courses – those containing engineering or architecture modules, for instance – often require specific A-level subjects, such as maths or physics. These types of degree will also draw more on your numerical skills, whereas more general or management-based building degrees will require a greater emphasis on communication and organisation. But because the learning-through-doing component is so essential in this field, courses are inevitably more "hands-on" than many arts subjects.

An increasing number of women apply to construction engineering and built environment courses; traditionally this has been a male-dominated preserve, but the times they are a-changing.

Most building-related courses are three- or four-year BScs. The range of degrees is so varied that few institutions offer exactly the same degree course so make sure you understand what you're getting into. Certain courses also offer the opportunity to attain chartered engineer status – this requires studying for the Engineering Council examinations – which may help you gain employment further down the line.

Four-year courses nearly always include a sandwich year in industry, which can be a great way to get to know the industry and find your niche in the job market. Ask about the provision an institution has for work placements.

Next up: town and country planning. The subject covers a wide range of activities – advising on the design of new transport systems, tourist sites, conservation areas and, of course, developments in our towns and cities. Issues such as regeneration and environmentally friendly and sustainable development are playing an increasingly important role in the subject.

Town and country planning degrees increasingly reflect the specialisms developing in the planning industry, with courses concentrating variously on things such as urban design, environmental impact, and transport issues. Most courses, though, offer at least one year of training in the general skills of town and country planning. From then on they diverge more – into town and regional planning, city and regional planning or civic design, for example – but they mostly cover a similar curriculum, just with different emphases. There's also the option of joint honours, in planning and geography, for example.

The distinguishing feature for many town and country planning students is the professional accreditation of programmes. The Royal Town Planning Institute (RTPI) accredits courses, meaning that students leaving an accredited course have privileged status and are more likely to get a job if they stay in the field. And as ever, look at the research specialisations of the teaching staff. Try to make sure that those who will be teaching you cover the specific areas you want to study.

With a recruitment crisis in many planning authorities, the employment prospects of graduates are very good, even for those coming from non-accredited courses. As well as being at the local town hall you could also end up in consultancy, environmental management, and rural community councils. After two years in practice, many graduates will sit further exams for professional qualifications, such as membership of the RTPI, the Chartered Institute of Housing or the Chartered Institute of Transport.

> Town planning is not taught at school yet it combines many subjects in the school curriculum, such as geography, art, and economics. The degree is varied and interesting. One day you can be looking at buildings, the next you can be discussing Donald Trump's planning application for a golf resort. As well as lectures and practicals, there are field trips that give you a taste of how the subject fits into the wider world.

Sarah Johnston, *third-year town and regional planning student, University of Dundee*

» Further information

The Chartered Institute of Building
Englemere, Kings Ride
Ascot, Berkshire SL5 7TB
t   01344 630700
e   reception@ciob.org.uk
↗   www.ciob.org.uk

The Association of Building Engineers
Lutyens House, Billing Brook Road
Weston Favell, Northampton
Northamptonshire NN3 8NW
t   0845 126 1058
e   building.engineers@abe.org.uk
↗   www.abe.org.uk

CITB-ConstructionSkills
Bircham Newton, Kings Lynn
Norfolk PE31 6RH
t   01485 577577
e   information.centre@citb.co.uk
↗   www.citb.org.uk

Town and Country Planning Association
17 Carlton House Terrace
London SW1 5AS
t   020 7930 8903
↗   www.tcpa.org.uk

The Royal Town Planning Institute
41 Botolph Lane
London EC3R 8DL
t   020 7929 9494
↗   www.rtpi.org.uk

The Chartered Institute of Housing
9 White Lion Street
London N1 9XJ
t   020 7837 4280
e   London@cih.org
↗   www.cih.org

BRE (Building Research Establishment)
Bucknalls Lane, Garston
Watford WD25 9XX
t   01923 664000
e   enquiries@bre.co.uk
↗   www.bre.co.uk

Centre for Education in the Built Environment
Bute Building, King Edward VII Avenue
Cardiff CF10 3NB
t   029 2087 4600
↗   www.cebe.heacademy.ac.uk

↗ Online reading

Cyburbia www.cyburbia.org
Construction Education www.constructioneducation.com
Construction Plus www.constructionplus.co.uk
The Chartered Institute of Logistics and Transport www.ciltuk.org.uk
The Landscape Institute www.landscapeinstitute.org
The British Association of Landscape Industries www.bali.co.uk
Internet Town and Country Planner www.vts.rdn.ac.uk/tutorial/town
Sapling (a portal site for architecture, planning, and environment) www.sapling.info

Building and town and country planning

		Guardian score	Satisfied with teaching %	Satisfied with assessment %	Spend per student score /10	Student:staff ratio	Job prospects %	Value added score /10	Average entry tariff
1	UCL	100.0	80	53	10	12		8	346
2	Loughborough	98.0	84	64	10	10	89	7	330
3	Salford	90.4			10	15	96	8	292
4	Cardiff	83.7	83	66	8	15		7	317
5	Gloucestershire	83.0	90	73	10	17		8	266
6	Glasgow Caledonian	80.5	81	54	7	18	88	9	336
7	Liverpool	78.8	82	42	7	17			329
8	Reading	75.4	80	36	5	21	100	9	334
9	Nottingham	73.5	84	51	7	18			350
10	Dundee	73.1	84	69	5	17			361
11	Glamorgan	67.6	76	57	7	18		8	215
12	Plymouth	66.7	83	44	7	16		5	285
13	Sheffield	64.5	81	49	5	15	85	1	371
14	Newcastle	63.5	75	37	5	19	91	6	314
15	Sheffield Hallam	63.3	82	59	4	28	83	10	258
16	Oxford Brookes	61.3	77	53	4	18	79	7	286
17	Nottingham Trent	58.8			7	20	93	5	250
18	Central Lancashire	58.6	58	51	8	24		8	269
19	Manchester Met	57.4	77	43	4	18			282
20	Northumbria	55.5	82	65	4	23	92	3	274
21	Heriot-Watt	53.6	69	53	5	15	82	2	282
22	Anglia Ruskin	52.5	75	53	7	27		2	288
23	Greenwich	52.1			8	23	76	7	199
24	Napier	51.2			3	24	94	5	238
25	Queen's, Belfast	51.1	72	53	3	21	72	5	328
26	Kingston	50.8	79	57	3	28	91	5	219
27	UWE Bristol	45.8	79	66	4	23	84	2	252
28	Portsmouth	43.6	84	61	3	28		7	226
29	Ulster	42.5	66	38	3		87	6	277
30	Birmingham City	40.7			3	23		6	203
31	Westminster	38.3	75	56	4	18	50	4	253
32	Liverpool John Moores	37.3	67	51	2	32	89	4	253
33	Wolverhampton	36.4			3	27		5	175
34	Leeds Met	32.4	68	53	2	26	65	5	226
35	Southampton Solent	31.8	70	49	4	24		1	
36	Bolton	31.5	83	58	2	38		6	172
37	London South Bank	29.5	80	51	4	34	72	4	176

Drama studies

> Drama explores and aids understanding and communication. Performance and social practices shape us as individuals and mould the ways in which we encounter and interact with people, objects, and situations in our everyday lives. Studying performance teaches us about cultures and histories, powers and ideologies, pasts and presents: it offers access to a wider comprehension of human identities and behaviour.
>
> Universities offer students the opportunity to work with leading academics in areas of both theory and practice, in live performance and on screen, across film, theatre, television, and new media. Our degree programme, for example, is not designed to teach vocational skills, but enables students to develop practical capabilities alongside critical and theoretical awareness. Key concepts are explored through a variety of teaching and assessment modes — including performance practice, writing, presentation, filmmaking, and archival research. The breadth of the curriculum and an emphasis on research-led teaching mean that students can study across a range of dramatic forms, or explore one form in greater depth.
>
> As the significance of the creative and cultural industries to Britain's economy increases, studying drama develops and enhances a set of critical, creative, and practical transferable skills. Whilst many graduates do go on to work in areas, such as acting and directing, scenic design, lighting and stage management, as well as producing, editing and sound design for the screen, these skills lend themselves to a variety of careers.
>
> **Dr Catherine Hindson**, *Lecturer in Performance Studies, University of Bristol*

Drama — kind of cool, and very popular. It's a fearsomely difficult course to get on to, but don't go thinking it will be all floodlights and applause.

For while theatre and cinema are extraordinary cultural phenomena, drama at university isn't all about performance, unless you're heading for one of the drama or dance schools to learn acting or dancing and nothing more. If you make that choice, bear in mind that not all the courses at drama schools have degree status, so they don't all appear in the tables in this book.

Many higher education institutions do, however, carry acting modules as part of a broad degree programme — mixing theoretical and practical, studying areas such as film, theatre, and radio, performance techniques, basic technical knowledge, and an academic understanding of historical and critical theory. You'll work with a wide cultural perspective and with a large dollop of critical theory. At the end of it all, you may want to delve into theatre design, production, writing or management. Employment prospects are decent, but there's a lot of competition as you bid for work in the theatre, TV, radio, or in arts management.

If performance is what you want, some drama schools have given their courses degree status, or you can do a joint honours degree, mixing acting with a more academic course. The big advantage is that with a degree qualification you will only have to pay standard university fees. Drama schools can in effect charge privately and it can cost upwards of £10,000 a year, and you may not have the benefit of a student bank account as you won't be technically eligible. However, many drama schools have awards and scholarships you can compete for, which may help you financially.

Courses are rigorous and often very practical – although there has to be an element of written work for courses to qualify for degree status. To begin with, you need to consider your skills, both academically and in terms of performing arts, to make that choice between a performance-based degree and wider theatre or cinematic studies. If you mainly want to act, the other elements of a degree-based drama course may only frustrate you.

It's generally best to think of drama in terms of a vocational degree and investigate accordingly. Does the institution have the expertise and equipment to help you in your specific area of interest? If it's TV, is the technical equipment there? If it's theatre design, does the place put on a number of plays to give you the practice? Are there links with full-time drama courses to provide the cannon fodder (actors) for your experiments?

You might want to specialise in directing, the history of theatre, textual analysis or arts management, so check the structure and choices available on the course.

And what are the contacts like with the real world? Does the institution offer work placements with professional companies to help you gain that vital experience and contacts book that's going to help you find a job on graduation? Some places, on the other hand, bar students from working outside for the duration of the course, reasoning that they're working hard enough already. Financially, this could be an issue, but it could also save you from running yourself into the ground.

And don't forget that in the job hunt later, reputation counts for a lot – much more than for most degrees. It can be a remarkably small world out there and people will know whether somewhere excels in particular areas, so bear that in mind when making your choice.

❝ Studying drama has been the most challenging, yet rewarding, three years of my life. The structure of the course is based upon the symbiotic relationship of theory and practice, which nurtures and develops each student's ability to move between action and thought fluidly. My knowledge of theatre has broadened immeasurably, and the course has encouraged me to question what I and other people believe, in order to form my own opinions.

Charlotte Dubrey, *third-year drama student, University of Exeter*

》 Further information

National Drama   ↗ www.nationaldrama.co.uk

The National Council for Drama Training
1-7 Woburn Walk   t 020 7387 3650
London WC1H 0JJ   e info@ncdt.co.uk
                                   ↗ www.ncdt.co.uk

The Conference of Drama Schools
PO Box 34252   e info@cds.drama.ac.uk
London NW5 1XJ   ↗ www.drama.ac.uk

Council for Dance Education and Training
Old Brewer's Yard   t 020 7240 5703
17-19 Neal Street   e info@cdet.org.uk
London WC2H 9UY   ↗ www.cdet.org.uk   》

National Operatic and Dramatic Association
58-60 Lincoln Road
Peterborough PE1 2RZ
t 0870 770 2480
e everyone@noda.org.uk
↗ www.noda.org.uk

Dance and Drama Awards
e dada@lsc.gov.uk
↗ www.direct.gov.uk/danceanddrama

Equity
Guild House, Upper St Martins Lane
London WC2H 8JG
t 020 7379 6000
↗ www.equity.org.uk

British Association of Drama Therapists
e info@badth.org.uk

↗ Online reading

The Stage www.thestage.co.uk
Arts Marketing Association www.a-m-a.co.uk
AisleSay www.aislesay.com

Drama and dance

		Guardian score	Satisfied with teaching %	Satisfied with assessment %	Spend per student score /10	Student-staff ratio	Job prospects %	Value added score /10	Average entry tariff
1	The Liverpool Institute for Performing Arts	100.0			2	13	80	10	401
2	Conservatoire for Dance and Drama	93.8	86	59		11	64	9	305
3	Warwick	93.3	97	63	8	11	43	7	422
4	Trinity Laban	91.0	85	57		8		8	260
5	Bristol	90.0	95	52	9	22	61	7	422
5	Birmingham City	90.0	88	55	8	13	69	9	280
7	Rose Bruford College	88.5	92	67	6	21	83	8	302
8	UEA	87.9	90	64	10	20	47	4	381
9	Loughborough	87.6	89	64	7	18	59	8	385
10	Royal Holloway	87.3	89	62	5	14	54	8	407
11	Lancaster	84.4	86	55	5	11		5	390
11	Queen Mary	84.4	94	69	5	11		6	369
13	Exeter	84.0	95	64	6	18	49	7	388
14	Central School of Speech and Drama	82.5	83	64	5	18	80	6	327
15	Goldsmiths	81.6	87	50	5	15	54	9	343
16	Birmingham	81.5	91	52	7	17	56	4	413
17	Manchester	81.1	87	48		17	48	5	416
18	Surrey	81.0	87	48	5	16			362
19	Plymouth	79.7	82	63	10	19	41	6	226
20	Glamorgan	77.8	77	58	8	10	50	7	277
21	Dartington College	77.7	89	71	5	9	46	7	263
22	Middlesex	77.4	82	51	10	24	63	5	303
23	Kent	77.3	88	80	6	18	56	4	333

	Guardian score	Satisfied with teaching %	Satisfied with assessment %	Spend per student score /10	Student:staff ratio	Job prospects %	Value added score /10	Average entry tariff
24 Bath Spa	75.5	91	71	6	18	44	9	269
25 Sussex	74.0	83	53	5	14			388
25 University of the Arts London	74.0	79	57	10	22	51	7	304
27 Glasgow	73.3	90	61	4	17		4	391
28 Essex	72.6	89	62	8	20	52	5	307
29 Gloucestershire	71.8	77	61	7	13		8	279
30 Hull	70.5	74	45	6	22	58	8	341
31 UWE Bristol	68.4	93	75	6	20	36	9	264
32 Westminster	68.2	81	61	6	19	47	7	299
33 Reading	68.0	87	68	6	16	32	4	328
34 Brunel	67.4	80	62	4	8	36	5	297
35 Liverpool John Moores	67.2	81	56	4	18	53	8	280
35 UWIC	67.2	89	70	6	20			265
37 Queen Margaret	67.1			4	20	67		271
38 Sunderland	65.7	80	61	5	13	36	8	263
39 Brighton	65.6	78	61	8	18	39	6	278
40 Manchester Met	64.9	92	66	4	18	58	3	267
41 St Mary's UC, Twickenham	64.7	88	69	2	21	50	9	249
42 Greenwich	64.5	77	69	10	31			223
43 Leeds	64.4	74	41	6	21	54	6	340
44 De Montfort	63.5	75	57	5	18	57	4	257
45 Salford	63.2	75	42	4	28	56	10	296
46 Huddersfield	61.5	87	65	5	19	42	4	271
47 Coventry	61.4	89	65	5	24	42	8	238
48 Arts Institute at Bournemouth	61.3	83	73	4	21	54	2	322
49 Chichester	60.5	85	54	3	16	54	2	310
50 Nottingham Trent	60.4	76	42	6	20	55	4	273
51 Trinity College, Carmarthen	60.1	83	59	4	10	35	2	265
52 Hertfordshire	58.0	85	73	3	19	55	3	246
53 Portsmouth	57.6	82	70	4	21	48	4	265
54 Northumbria	57.0	60	44	6	18	56	7	250
55 Staffordshire	56.9	79	63	9	18			222
56 Winchester	56.8	82	59	3	14	31	6	266
57 Ulster	56.6	88	61	4	14		2	234
58 Aberystwyth	55.8	84	63	4	27	46	5	287
59 Oxford Brookes	54.9	87	62	3	27			291
60 Newport	54.5	83	77	4	23		4	227
61 Kingston	53.4	77	51	4	18	39	6	243
62 University College for the Creative Arts	52.7	69	55	4	22	51	4	
63 Derby	51.7	75	62	7	18	17	5	263
64 Bolton	51.5	84	60	3	23			245
65 Queen's, Belfast	51.2	73	40	4	31		8	340
66 Leeds Met	50.9	59	57	5	23	44	7	260
67 Northampton	50.7	86	73	5	20	32	3	212
68 Anglia Ruskin	50.5	74	54	6	19		7	207

	Guardian score	Satisfied with teaching %	Satisfied with assessment %	Spend per student score /10	Student:staff ratio	Job prospects %	Value added score /10	Average entry tariff
69 Central Lancashire	49.9	66	48	6	21	48	3	268
70 Cumbria	49.1	70	52	2	22	48	5	291
71 Roehampton	49.0	82	52	3	23	39	5	256
72 Chester	48.6	82	60	4	24	42	3	274
73 Southampton Solent	47.7	79	62	4	20	35	3	240
74 Canterbury Christ Church	47.4	84	70	3	16	40	1	286
75 Wolverhampton	47.1	80	61	5	23	45	3	188
76 Lincoln	46.7	74	37	4	26	52	3	276
77 London South Bank	46.6	80	69	4	38		9	215
78 Bedfordshire	46.0	74	54	5	23	35	5	210
79 York St John	45.6	78	40	6	24	41	2	280
80 East London	42.8			4	21		2	210
81 Edge Hill	39.4	72	40	3	19	36	2	253
82 Bucks New University	39.3	79	66	5	17	25	2	179
83 Worcester	32.6	93	68	2		24	1	230

Music

❝ Why do people come to university to study music? Music is something you *do*, after all; most students have developed their love of it by playing or singing. Perhaps this has been in some kind of social situation — a choir, an orchestra — and perhaps those social aspects are as important as the music itself. It may seem strange, therefore, that so often reading music at university means studying 'history of' or 'analysis of' a particular repertoire. It almost seems as if that initial impetus has got lost somewhere along the line.

On the other hand, music is too interesting just to play. It has had a massive effect on society over the ages and in different places; more importantly, society has had a massive effect on music. Unless we think about that too, the fascinating web of associations that arise from engaging with different pieces and repertories just gets lost. That, we think, is the point of coming to university — to think, as well as to do. In studying music, we passionately believe in considering musical sources at first hand. As often as possible, we make the study of music begin from direct engagement with the music under consideration. Often this means experiencing music in performance — one's own, and that of others. Scores and writings about music also play their part; developing one's critical responses to music, whether in the form of essays, analyses, performances, or compositions, and finding a space within the material that you can really make your own.

Dr Nicky Losseff, *Senior Lecturer in Music, University of York*

There used to be a split between music colleges (or conservatoires), which offered diplomas, and the universities offering degrees. Much of that distinction has now gone and all the institutions offer degrees but, in general, the conservatoires still place more emphasis on the practical aspects of the music rather than the theory and history of the subject, whereas you could do a university degree in music that involves no performance at all.

However, the basics remain the same. After three years (or four at a conservatoire), you should come out with a BMus (although it could be a BA in some places and if you do a music technology degree, you could end up with a BSc). Courses vary hugely – you could choose to study anything from classical performance to how to run a recording studio – but they should all give you a breadth of musical knowledge and appreciation. On many courses you'll find similar core modules, likely to include composition, theory, history of music, performance, and analysis.

Aside from the core subjects, the choice for music degrees is vast, so decide whether the course of modules is of interest to you – whether it's performance, jazz, composition or conducting. In recent times, music degrees have tended to open out to wider influences, and popular music degrees are also experiencing a boom. And if you're heading for the technological end of the spectrum, make sure the facilities are all you would hope for.

Look at the specialisations of those who teach and what links they have. There may be a composer you admire working in the department, or there may be an orchestra or studio to which they have strong links that will help you gain experience via a work placement scheme. Investigate the extra-curricular scene too. As you might expect, music students are often involved in music performance and production beyond the requirements of their degree, sometimes to exceptionally high standards.

When applying, you'll almost certainly need two or three A-levels, including music or a BTec in music technology or studio techniques if that's the direction you're interested in. If you want to be a performer, you'll need to be grade eight in whatever it is you play, as a high degree of technical proficiency is essential. Some (the more old-fashioned) also require a minimum grade on the piano – usually about grade five or six – regardless of your instrument, as they make students do keyboard harmony.

The employment prospects are good, although making it as a performer is notoriously difficult. It's a competitive arena and not well paid, and a large percentage of musicians are self-employed and must teach or find other work to supplement their income. Other music graduates teach full-time or go into arts administration, while music technologists can find a home in the industry as sound engineers or technicians, or work in broadcasting.

Depending on the course you choose, music can in effect be a vocational degree, so it pays to think hard about what you plan to get out of it. And make sure that the way your work is assessed is the best way for you. Assessment methods vary tremendously (from practical tests to written exams and coursework) so don't be caught out.

> 66 The most refreshing difference between music A-level and music as a degree is the approach to learning. At university I have developed as a musician for my own benefit, not because I need to pass an exam. In my second year, I have chosen to focus on performance and musicology. Being able to tailor my degree towards a specialism has given me the opportunity to devote more time to developing the skills needed to attain my career aspirations.
>
> **Rosie Williamson**, *second-year music student, University of Sheffield*

» Further information

Associated Board of the Royal Schools of Music
24 Portland Place
London W1B 1LU

t 020 7636 5400
↗ www.abrsm.ac.uk

Association of British Orchestras
20 Rupert Street
London W1D 6DF

t 020 7287 0333
e info@abo.org.uk
↗ www.abo.org.uk

Musicians' Union

t 020 7852 5566
e info@musiciansunion.org.uk
↗ www.musiciansunion.org.uk

Incorporated Society of Musicians
10 Stratford Place
London W1C 1AA

t 020 7629 4413
e membership@ism.org
↗ www.ism.org

British Society for Music Therapy
61 Church Hill Road, East Barnet
Hertfordshire EN4 8SY

t 020 8441 6226
e info@bsmt.org

National Association of Youth Orchestras
Central Hall, West Tollcross
Edinburgh EH3 9BP

t 0131 221 1927
↗ www.nayo.org.uk

Access to Music www.accesstomusic.co.uk
Music Everything www.musiceverything.com
Awards for Young Musicians www.a-y-m.org.uk
Soundgenerator.com www.soundgenerator.com
Music for Youth www.mfy.org.uk
Youth Music www.youthmusic.org.uk

Music

		Guardian score	Satisfied with teaching %	Satisfied with assessment %	Spend per student score /10	Student:staff ratio	Job prospects %	Value added score /10	Average entry tariff
1	Royal Scottish Academy of Music and Drama	100.0			9	6	89	9	
2	Oxford	95.4	93	79	10	17	81	6	447
3	Royal Academy of Music	92.4	90	67	8	8	94	9	318
4	King's College London	85.1	95	64	6	16	87	7	446
5	Royal College of Music	82.6	84	60	8	11	96	7	310
6	Plymouth	81.5	89	64	10	19			214
7	Trinity Laban	79.1	95	60		8	74	5	301
8	Nottingham	78.0	91	51	6	13	74	7	442
9	Cambridge	75.6	80	62	10	20	70	3	469
10	Manchester	73.1	83	54		17	71	5	432
11	UEA	71.7	83	61	10	20			278
12	Ulster	70.1	88	61	4	14		9	278
13	The Liverpool Institute for Performing Arts	69.4			2	13	59	10	388
14	Southampton	69.0	92	63	8	20	61	8	338
15	Newcastle	68.2	89	54	6	15	67	8	345
16	York	68.1	89	63	7	17	73	3	389
17	Edinburgh	67.9	92	65	6	18	57	7	416
18	Royal Northern College of Music	67.3			3	10	90	6	
19	Glamorgan	67.2	79	60	7	10	73	4	305
20	Bristol	67.1	94	53	8	22	75	4	386
21	Birmingham City	66.9	80	68	7	13	81	4	295
22	City	66.8			9	10	63	3	295
23	Durham	66.3	74	37	6	14	70	6	441
23	Napier	66.3			6	19	74	7	330
25	Birmingham	65.9	85	62	6	17	66	3	430
26	Sussex	65.8	83	53	4	14			374
27	Sheffield	64.6	92	59	5	14	70	4	344
28	Goldsmiths	63.0	87	48	4	15	59	8	320
29	Lancaster	61.3	81	63	4	11	66	6	322
30	Bath Spa	60.5	93	63	5	18	66	8	259
31	Rose Bruford College	60.3	90	66	5	21		8	238
32	Bangor	60.0	95	87	4	14	59	2	286
33	Brighton	59.6	78	61	7	18		5	305

	Guardian score	Satisfied with teaching %	Satisfied with assessment %	Spend per student score /10	Student:staff ratio	Job prospects %	Value added score /10	Average entry tariff
34 Middlesex	59.2			10	24	58	9	210
35 Cardiff	58.8	88	64	5	16	70	2	334
36 Dartington College	58.7	83	62	4	9			257
37 Coventry	57.9	89	66	4	24		7	268
38 Essex	57.1	82	52	7	20		9	203
39 Liverpool	56.6	80	55	3	18	65	7	356
40 Leeds College of Music	56.1	74	40	4	12	69	7	299
41 Thames Valley	55.1	85	57	4		68	9	243
42 Brunel	54.4	73	52	4	8	70		303
43 Leeds	52.3	75	52	5	21	62	5	367
44 Surrey	51.9	89	50	4	16	67	1	335
45 Royal Holloway	50.9	77	53	4	14	55	3	356
46 Queen's, Belfast	50.7	92	72	3	31	56	7	367
47 York St John	50.2	89	44	5	24		7	247
48 Hertfordshire	49.5	79	61	5	17	52	6	242
49 Huddersfield	48.6	83	68	4	19	58	4	281
50 Westminster	48.5	80	60	5	19	56	5	262
51 Glasgow	48.2	82	33	3	17		2	357
52 Central Lancashire	47.5	82	55	5	21		6	295
53 Roehampton	45.7	85	51	3	23			252
54 Southampton Solent	44.7	79	61	4	20			224
55 Salford	44.4	83	50	3	28	58	9	260
56 Chester	43.9	82	60	3	24			270
56 Oxford Brookes	43.9	92	67	2	27		5	264
58 Hull	43.5	78	51	5	22	50	5	276
59 Derby	42.0	78	52	6	18			264
59 Cumbria	42.0	66	47	4	20			295
61 Wolverhampton	39.3	80	62	4	23	48	6	188
62 Anglia Ruskin	38.9	70	47	5	19		3	244
63 De Montfort	38.1	83	49	3	20		3	240
64 Canterbury Christ Church	37.7	89	64	3	16	65	1	230
65 Kingston	36.8	68	49	3	18	57	3	229
66 Chichester	35.3	84	61	3	16	38	2	243
67 Bucks New University	29.6	79	52	4	17	33	2	218

Engineering

❝ There is a skills shortage in the UK for qualified engineers who can undertake a broad range of jobs in areas like management, design, development, planning, marketing, and sales. Engineering courses covering a wide range of skills topics could set students above the rest when applying for jobs in industry. Courses cover a range of exciting and innovative topics, including mechanical, electrical, and electronic engineering. In large part they are highly vocational courses suited to individual interests and work needs.

A paid 12-month work placement in a local company is required in some full-time engineering courses, giving students valuable and essential experience in industry and improving their future career prospects. Some courses offer flexibility, with distance learning and work-based learning for people already employed in the industry who are looking to upgrade their skills. Engineering is fast-moving, exciting, and leads to excellent career prospects.

Professor Phil Picton, *Head of Division, Applied Sciences, Engineering, University of Northampton*

Asked to name five famous engineers, you might dredge up Isambard Kingdom Brunel, George Stephenson, and maybe James Watt from your memory. Don't know about you, but after that we'd be struggling.

Yet the profession includes an extraordinarily wide spectrum of practitioners, from the designers of great hydroelectric projects to the bloke who fixes your washing machine. The Royal Academy of Engineering has estimated that up to two million people in the UK could be classified as engineers in some way or another, and there are now courses available in anything from film production technology or motor sports engineering, to space technology or medical engineering.

And yet a large number of universities have seen a drop in applicants over recent years, while two-fifths of engineering students say they have no intention of actually becoming engineers when they graduate. That's a real shame because there are huge opportunities right now in UK engineering. Just about every discipline has a shortage of good engineers, and this is particularly acute in the civil and chemical engineering fields. This in turn means employment prospects are good, and salaries, which truthfully have never been spectacular, are now improving as companies chase fewer and fewer graduates.

All courses accredited by the Engineering Council UK are either three-year BEng (four years in Scotland), or four-year MEng qualifications and usually require students to have decent A-levels before applying. In some sectors, especially civil engineering and structural engineering, becoming chartered is a prerequisite to practice, but for all sectors you'll find the financial rewards are higher with it than without.

Once you've graduated, the possibilities are much wider than you might think. You don't have to restrict yourself to engineering – only about a quarter of registered chartered engineers work in manufacturing. You could find your way into financial companies, management consultancies, telecommunications, power and water supply, environmental projects, the armed forces, or the sophisticated IT operations of major banks.

But will you go for a BEng or MEng? Many universities run only the MEng. Look too at the system for gaining chartered engineer status which you can acquire two years after your MEng. Alternatively you could go for incorporated engineer status after taking a BSc, although remember the chartered engineer status is likely to be better rewarded in your pay packet.

It is important to find out how the course is structured, as general engineering degrees can vary hugely. So investigate what modules and options are available to you in the later years of the degree as you begin to specialise. Also, check to see what work placement opportunities there are and what the chances are for study abroad.

We've said this before too – check the research specialisations of the teaching staff and see if they tally with the areas you want to work in. There's no substitute for learning from the leaders in your field.

---

66 A degree course has given me the freedom to study at my own pace, but with much more individual help and many more resources compared to A-levels. I have found the most challenging part of the course is timekeeping – sticking to deadlines and keeping the delicate balance between work and leisure. I have really enjoyed the opportunity to take a placement year at Aardman Animations; it has given me an insight into the industry and will help me focus for my final-year studies.

Morgan Roe, *placement-year robotics and automated systems (engineering) student, University of Plymouth*

General engineering

The general engineering course is, naturally, the best general introduction to the subject and a way of getting into engineering without specialising too early. At the start of the course, you can study across the range and then usually specialise as you go on, graduating in one of the more specific disciplines.

Most MEng courses start with an introduction to engineering for the first two years before moving on to two years of specialisation. It will be based around a core of science, maths, and computing skills, the ability to interpret data, written, and oral communication, presentation skills, teamworking skills and creative approaches, as well as the skills of imagination married to practicality, which are essential to the problem-solving that is at the heart of engineering. It's from such a base that you go on to specialise.

» Further information

The Royal Academy of Engineering
29 Great Peter Street
Westminster, London SW1P 3LW

t   020 7227 0500
↗ www.raengbest.org.uk

Engineering Council UK
10 Maltravers Street
London WC2R 3ER

t   020 7240 7891
e   staff@engc.org.uk
↗ www.engc.org.uk

The Institution of Engineering Design
Courtleigh, Westbury Leigh
Westbury, Wiltshire BA13 3TA

t   01373 822801
e   ied@ied.org.uk
↗ www.ied.org.uk

The Institution of Engineering and Technology
Savoy Place
London WC2R 0BL

t   020 7240 1871
e   postmaster@theiet.org
↗ www.theiet.org

↗ Online reading

The Engineering Careers Information Service www.enginuity.org.uk
Engineer Girl www.engineergirl.org
Progressive Engineer www.progressiveengineer.com
The Engineer online www.e4engineering.com

Civil engineering

Civil engineering is arguably the most practical of the disciplines and has had the most recruitment problems after the Engineering Council UK's bid to improve academic standards. Strangely, civil engineers seem to be held in rather low regard in the UK, despite the fact that they are essential to our daily life. But at least you'll be pretty much guaranteed a job, possibly with consulting or contracting engineering companies or local authorities, central government or in banking, law, or in the City. You'll be a numerate problem-solver, and those are valuable assets in an employee.

As a civil engineer, you'd be responsible for the design, building, and maintenance of bridges, roads, railway lines, water supply, or sewage systems – facing up to the challenges that make up the creation and use of the infrastructure of a modern country. As well as the practical, it also offers opportunities in design, management, the environment, and buildings and bridges of all shapes and sizes.

You will be involved in studying structural mechanics, geology, surveying, fluid mechanics, and plenty of maths (maths and physics A-levels are essential and a humanities subject is also useful).

» Further information

The Institution of Civil Engineers
1 Great George Street
Westminster, London SW1P 3AA

t 020 7222 7722
↗ www.ice.org.uk

The Institution of Structural Engineers
11 Upper Belgrave Street
London SW1X 8BH

t 020 7235 4535
↗ www.istructe.org.uk

CITB-Construction Skills
Bircham Newton, Kings Lynn
Norfolk PE31 6RH

t 01485 577577
e information.centre@citb.co.uk
↗ www.citb.org.uk

The Chartered Institution of Building Services Engineers
222 Balham High Road
Balham, London SW12 9BS

t 020 8675 5211
↗ www.cibse.org

European Council of Civil Engineers
C/o ICE, 1 Great George Street
Westminster, London SW1P 3AA

↗ www.eccenet.org

↗ Online reading

The Institution of Highway Incorporated Engineers www.ihie.org.uk
Society of Operations Engineers www.soe.org.uk
New Civil Engineer Plus www.nceplus.co.uk

General engineering

		Guardian score	Satisfied with teaching %	Satisfied with assessment %	Spend per student score /10	Student:staff ratio	Job prospects %	Value added score /10	Average entry tariff
1	Cambridge	100.0	88	71	8	14	93	6	548
1	Imperial College	100.0			9	9		5	467
3	Oxford	99.1	83	66		10	87	4	526
4	Leicester	87.1	82	69	9	10	71	5	330
5	Bournemouth	84.9			7	11		10	264
6	Brunel	79.6	89	70	4	15	70	7	353
7	Warwick	77.7	67	49	9	14	83	4	395
8	Hull	74.9	82	67	8	15		3	251
9	Exeter	72.2	88	65	3	13	66	7	319
10	Durham	71.9	76	54	3	15	89	4	469
11	Central Lancashire	69.3	76	59	5	14		9	
12	De Montfort	66.5	77	58	4	11		6	211
13	Aberdeen	65.2	72	46	4	17	89		365
14	Birmingham City	57.8	71	64	4	12		4	211
15	Brighton	55.5	70	58	6	18	68	3	
16	Sheffield Hallam	52.2	77	56	3	18	50	8	246
17	Napier	50.0			2	19	63	6	
18	Greenwich	48.5	73	60	3	22		8	199
19	Glasgow Caledonian	35.8	76	58	3	21	56	1	333

Civil engineering

		Guardian score	Satisfied with teaching %	Satisfied with assessment %	Spend per student score /10	Student:staff ratio	Job prospects %	Value added score /10	Average entry tariff
1	Imperial College	100.0	74	51	10	12		4	462
2	Manchester	91.2	74	50	10	14	86	7	395
3	Dundee	89.5	85	53	5	14		7	380
4	Sheffield	87.2	76	52	5	12	93	7	428
5	Nottingham	86.9	80	57	9	13	91	3	390
6	Edinburgh	85.6	79	47	9	16		6	427
7	Bristol	82.3	87	62	5	15	91	4	440
8	Loughborough	79.8	87	74	4	26	96	7	354
9	Queen's, Belfast	78.8	77	53	4	18	97	7	370
10	Southampton	78.7	88	54	5	23		7	425
11	Birmingham	78.2	69	46	9	16		8	375
12	UCL	77.6	73	60	9	9		1	391
13	Surrey	76.4	74	48	7	15	93	3	340
14	Bradford	72.6	74	62	5	9		2	257
15	Newcastle	71.9	70	51	5	14	90	5	355
16	Strathclyde	70.3	58	28	4	16	94	9	
17	Liverpool	68.9			7	25		8	318
17	Portsmouth	68.9	79	72	3	21		8	256

		Guardian score	Satisfied with teaching %	Satisfied with assessment %	Spend per student score /10	Student:staff ratio	Job prospects %	Value added score /10	Average entry tariff
19	Bath	67.5	84	58	3	24	89	5	442
20	Cardiff	66.8	85	59	5	21	85	4	403
20	Glamorgan	66.8	65	50	3	18		9	
22	Heriot-Watt	66.1	82	48	4	13	84	5	380
23	Kingston	66.0	85	66	4	21		9	194
24	Coventry	65.6	78	65	3	21		9	255
25	Ulster	64.5	75	43	4	17		5	275
26	Nottingham Trent	63.1	73	61	4	21		7	210
27	Teesside	59.6	80	66	4	20			204
28	East London	58.2	86	64		26		9	216
29	Brighton	54.3	70	58	3	14			255
29	Leeds	54.3	72	46	7	23	85	3	347
31	Plymouth	51.6	76	53	4	16	83	4	263
32	City	51.0	65	51	6	21		2	281
33	Leeds Met	50.0			6	28		6	210
34	Glasgow	49.5	74	41	4	21		2	378
35	Salford	48.6	73	48	4	24			223
36	Greenwich	41.4	68	59	4	22		1	
37	Wolverhampton	34.1	45	48	3	18			159

Chemical engineering

		Guardian score	Satisfied with teaching %	Satisfied with assessment %	Spend per student score /10	Student:staff ratio	Job prospects %	Value added score /10	Average entry tariff
1	Cambridge	100.0			7	11		6	547
2	Newcastle	86.3	69	54	10	10			351
3	Manchester	80.4	76	54	9	15	86	3	421
4	Imperial College	78.6	85	62	8	15	77	7	469
5	Edinburgh	71.5	73	43	6	9			449
6	Birmingham	66.3	69	46	8	14		6	393
7	Nottingham	58.1	75	48	6	15	81	6	364
8	Leeds	54.2	68	43	7	15	84	6	288
9	Loughborough	52.6	87	67	4	16	74	6	364
10	Sheffield	52.1	73	47	4	14		3	351
11	Surrey	50.4	75	54	4	15			281
12	Aston	43.7	74	56	4	8			293
13	UCL	40.0	75	60	4	13		2	377
14	Strathclyde	39.6	83	62	4	20	79	6	316
15	Heriot-Watt	39.4	81	51	3	16			394
16	Bath	35.1	82	48	3	17	79	2	374
17	London South Bank	29.2	57	62	1	18		10	

Chemical engineering

Almost without exception, university engineering departments report that this discipline comes with great career potential, with some of the best salaries. Chemists and biochemists often need to stay on for a PhD if they're going to get the best jobs, but chemical engineers are straight in there earning the cash.

The jobs – of which there are plenty – could involve working in the chemical, process, food or pharmaceutical industry or in those areas of the City that deal with the large chemical engineering industry.

The subject is – to try to put it simply – about the practical application of chemistry on a large scale, involving the creation and efficient operation of facilities relating to the manufacture of almost anything, from plastic gizmos to cleaning products, from drugs to toothpaste. It's about building a process, one that's economically viable and environmentally responsible. Some students do shy away from working in an industry with a rather poor environmental image, but a big part of the subject is learning how to manage risks properly, and the emphasis on that is getting greater all the time.

» Further information

Institution of Chemical Engineers
Davis Building, 165-89 Railway Terrace   t   01788 578214
Rugby CV21 3HQ   ↗ www.icheme.org

↗ Online reading

ChemWeb www.chemweb.com
The Chemical Engineers Resource page www.cheresources.com
ChemSoc www.chemsoc.org
The Chemical Engineer Today www.tcetoday.com
The Association of Institutions concerned with Medical Engineering
  www.aime.org.uk

Electrical and electronic engineering

Electrical and particularly electronic engineering are among the few disciplines with a clear public perception of what might be involved. There is a very close link with computers, after all, and most people are familiar with this technology. But electrical and electronic engineering can cover a wide range of areas and skills. You could be involved in electricity generation, supply and distribution, software engineering, signal processing, control engineering, computer architecture, communications technology, networking, databases or e-commerce engineering. You'll also end up with a grasp of both the theory and the practical mechanics of electrical and electronic systems, microelectronics, silicon devices and nanotechnology.

Once you graduate, you'll find work in electronics companies, telecommunications of every kind, small systems houses, satellite businesses, and companies in finance – and the City will be keen on your expertise too. In fact, there are very few areas of the economy where your skills will not be useful.

>> Further information

Institution of Electrical Engineers
IEE, Savoy Place
London WC2R 0BL

t 020 7240 1871
⌐ www.iee.org

Engineering and Technology Board
10 Maltravers Street
London WC2R 3ER

t 020 7240 7333
⌐ www.etechb.co.uk

The British Computer Society
First Floor, Block D
North Star House, North Star Avenue
Swindon SN2 1FA

t 01793 417417
e bcshq@hq.bcs.org.uk
⌐ www.bcs.org

⌐ Online reading

Circuit archive www.ee.washington.edu/circuit_archive
Engology www.engology.com
Helpengine www.helpengine.org

Electrical and electronic engineering

		Guardian score	Satisfied with teaching %	Satisfied with assessment %	Spend per student score /10	Student:staff ratio	Job prospects %	Value added score /10	Average entry tariff
1	Imperial College	100.0	85	58	10	14	82	4	463
2	Edinburgh	99.6	81	50		11	92	7	419
3	Glasgow	99.4	82	51	10	11	61	9	380
4	Leeds	95.4	85	52	10	14		6	377
5	Queen's, Belfast	93.7	84	66	8	10	83	6	351
6	Manchester	92.2			10	10	75	3	351

		Guardian score	Satisfied with teaching %	Satisfied with assessment %	Spend per student score /10	Student:staff ratio	Job prospects %	Value added score /10	Average entry tariff
7	Birmingham	91.2	83	61	9	14	70	7	408
8	Essex	91.1	82	70	5	8		7	
9	UCL	90.5	71	59	8	9		4	391
10	Sheffield	89.3	83	56	5	10	83	6	357
11	Lancaster	88.4	86	56	8	8	62	6	340
12	Surrey	88.3	81	58	8	14	81	6	340
13	Bath	87.7	75	64	6	10	85	6	324
13	Loughborough	87.7	91	66	6	15	86	5	346
15	Strathclyde	87.0	86	65	8	10	73	4	351
16	Southampton	85.6	81	55	6	15	86	5	406
17	Bristol	85.1	89	49	6	14	85	4	415
18	Cardiff	84.6	74	59	7	13	81	7	353
18	Plymouth	84.6	85	75	8	10	54	8	247
20	Nottingham	83.8	80	59	8	12	83	5	331
21	UWE Bristol	81.7	90	51	3	19	80	10	273
22	Aston	80.4	74	56	3	8		7	293
23	York	80.0	80	49	7	10	75	3	384
24	Queen Mary	78.7	74	65	10	15	70	6	248
25	King's College London	77.8			5	16		8	297
26	Liverpool	77.2			6	13	72	4	350
27	Robert Gordon	75.6			6	20	82	7	337
28	Newcastle	74.4	80	59	7	14		2	342
29	Brunel	68.6	78	61	5	14	56	6	305
30	Reading	68.2			4	19	75	8	311
31	Coventry	68.0	78	65	3	8		8	227
32	Kent	67.6	75	68	6	14		7	223
33	Staffordshire	66.4	73	51	5	19		9	
34	Bradford	65.6	77	67	4	19	71	6	277
35	Ulster	64.3	78	56	4	11			225
36	Birmingham City	61.8			5	12	48	6	226
37	Oxford Brookes	61.1			3	19		9	224
38	Teesside	59.0	81	66	6	19	48	7	237
39	De Montfort	58.0	77	57	4	11	60	3	180
40	Portsmouth	55.0	74	55	3	19	69	6	228
41	Sheffield Hallam	53.4	78	58	4	19	56	7	186
42	Westminster	53.3	89	81	2	17		3	207
43	Heriot-Watt	53.0	76	49	3	17	76	1	335
44	Manchester Met	51.4	72	66	3	19	46	8	199
45	Derby	48.6	71	50	3	23	51	9	258
46	Glamorgan	42.0	65	50	4		25	8	208
47	Liverpool John Moores	41.5	66	55	3	18	56	3	196
48	Glasgow Caledonian	40.8	75	58	3	22	44	3	310
49	Huddersfield	40.6	76	64	3	25	46	2	267
50	Hertfordshire	40.3	70	59	3	20	58	3	192
51	Northumbria	38.3			3	20		1	256
52	Greenwich	35.5	61	49	3	22	55	5	198
53	Bolton	35.0	74	73	3	22		1	196
54	City	34.9	62	47	3	19	58	2	214

Materials engineering

Materials engineering is increasing in popularity largely due to its non-traditional status and good industrial links. However, there are comparatively few universities offering the course as it remains a specialist interest area and is an expensive course to run. It's really at the junction of chemistry, physics, and engineering and parts of the course can often be hidden away in other degrees as it takes in such a wide, multi-disciplinary approach. It's all about what everything is made of – the properties of materials, how to make them lighter, stronger, more heat-resistant, and cheaper than before – spanning a huge range from metallurgy to textiles and working from the atomic level upwards. It's currently big on recycling.

» Further information

Institute of Materials
1 Carlton House Terrace
London SW1Y 5DB

t   020 7451 7300
e   admin@materials.org.uk
↗ www.instmat.co.uk

Materials Engineering (UK)
Stephenson House
Railway Technical Centre
London Road, Derby DE24 8UP

t   01332 264452
e   reception@meg.co.uk
↗ www.meg.co.uk

Institute of Materials, Minerals and Mining
1 Carlton House Terrace
London SW1Y 5DB

t   020 7451 7300
↗ www.iom3.org

↗ Online reading

Engineering Talk www.engineeringtalk.com
Internet for materials engineering www.vts.rdn.ac.uk/tutorial/materials
The British Institute of Non-Destructive Testing www.bindt.org

Material and mineral engineering

		Guardian score	Satisfied with teaching %	Satisfied with assessment %	Spend per student score /10	Student:staff ratio	Job prospects %	Value added score /10	Average entry tariff
1	Oxford	100.0	88	69	10	9			522
2	Manchester	74.8	84	59	8	12	58	8	377
3	Bath	74.6	82	55	4	9			462
4	Imperial College	70.3	80	51	7	12		2	425
5	Leeds	67.3	68	48	8	11	72	7	328
6	Exeter	66.8	87	63	3	17			315
7	Birmingham	66.7	81	56	6	13		7	373
8	Sheffield	62.2	79	52	5	10			341
9	Loughborough	60.6	91	62	4	12	77	2	279
10	Queen Mary	50.1	67	50	6	18		5	301
11	Manchester Met	37.4	61	49	2	24	68	8	260
12	De Montfort	30.7	68	46	2	20	34		238

Mechanical engineering

There's a range of courses for mechanical engineering, including pure mechanical as well as aeronautical, automotive, and manufacturing engineering. Whatever you choose, you'll be looking at many of the same basics, including solid mechanics, fluid dynamics, thermodynamics, design, materials, propulsion, electrical drives, control systems, computer modelling, and applied engineering, before specialising in a chosen area.

After graduating, you can work in areas such as the car, boat, construction, oil and gas, renewable energy resources, and biomedical industries, or you could move to areas where your expertise and transferable skills will come in handy – IT or the City, perhaps. Either way, the chances are that you won't be on the dole.

» Further information

Institute of Mechanical Engineers
1 Birdcage Walk
London SW1H 9JJ

t 020 7222 7899
e membership@imeche.org.uk
↗ www.imeche.org

The Royal Aeronautical Society
4 Hamilton Place
London W1J 7BQ

t 020 7670 4300
e raes@raes.org.uk
↗ www.raes.org.uk

↗ Online reading

The Society for Experimental Mechanics www.sem.org
Icrank www.icrank.com
The Royal Institution of Naval Architects www.rina.org.uk

Mechanical engineering

		Guardian score	Satisfied with teaching %	Satisfied with assessment %	Spend per student score /10	Student:staff ratio	Job prospects %	Value added score /10	Average entry tariff
1	Teesside	100.0	74	77	7	17		10	
2	Imperial College	97.9	78	50	10	15	84	3	497
3	Southampton	92.5	87	55	6	12	81	6	425
4	Loughborough	89.8	88	68	8	12	80	3	378
5	Edinburgh	88.9	77	41	9	17	79	7	421
6	Nottingham	85.9	79	44	9	15	84	4	367
7	Bristol	85.2	87	51	4	16	84	4	461
8	Newcastle	84.7	78	54	8	17	84	5	367
9	Queen's, Belfast	84.6	80	52	5	14	90	6	360
10	Robert Gordon	83.6			8	18	91		318
11	Sheffield	83.1	80	49	6	17	76	7	383
12	Cardiff	81.5	75	61	6	17	75	7	370
13	Birmingham City	81.4			6	12		10	231
14	Bath	81.3	86	50	4	21	84	4	457
15	Glasgow	80.1	72	51	7	14	75	4	389

		Guardian score	Satisfied with teaching %	Satisfied with assessment %	Spend per student score /10	Student:staff ratio	Job prospects %	Value added score /10	Average entry tariff
16	Manchester	79.6	71	38	10	19	73	3	411
17	Leeds	78.5	71	40	10	17	67	5	350
18	Birmingham	78.1	74	49	8	17	68	5	386
19	Brunel	77.9	77	71	5	15	69	7	326
20	Strathclyde	77.7	71	54	6	16	76	7	332
21	Staffordshire	77.2	73	51	5	17		8	226
22	Surrey	75.7	75	46	7	15		5	302
23	Aston	75.3	67	47	5	15	77	7	297
24	Bradford	73.5	74	62	5	13		7	262
24	Sussex	73.5	66	51	5	16	67	7	351
24	UCL	73.5	68	44	9	12	65	1	375
27	UWE Bristol	72.5	87	41	3	15	71	6	247
28	Kingston	71.1	74	53	9	18	57	6	209
29	Heriot-Watt	69.8	64	46	6	17	75	3	367
30	Liverpool	69.6			8	20	76	2	363
31	Salford	69.5	68	38	4	14	76	8	217
32	Queen Mary	65.9	67	56	7	16	51	4	305
33	Ulster	65.0	76	57	4	21	86	3	229
34	Oxford Brookes	64.9			5	20	66	5	257
35	Sheffield Hallam	64.8	78	51	4	24	73	9	189
36	Northumbria	64.2			2	23	84	7	239
37	Coventry	63.0	78	67	3	32	73	9	239
38	Manchester Met	62.8	85	73	2	24		8	237
39	Hertfordshire	62.3	74	50	3	22	64	8	245
40	Portsmouth	61.7	71	54	5	22	69	5	219
41	Greenwich	61.4	69	64	3	22		5	208
42	King's College London	61.3			5	19		2	334
43	Wolverhampton	61.1	65	61	2	12	56	7	196
44	City	60.8	71	51	5	24	59	6	243
45	Plymouth	60.6	81	64	4	16	38	5	234
46	Huddersfield	58.7	73	61	2	25	60	8	224
47	Southampton Solent	57.5	82	65	4	29		7	256
48	Liverpool John Moores	57.4	74	63	2	14	63	2	225
49	Glamorgan	56.0	62	50	4	20		5	
50	Derby	55.8	69	59	3	16		4	
51	Swansea Met	52.8	79	60	4	16	34	4	192
52	Bolton	50.3	90	70	2	20		1	101
53	London South Bank	36.0	57	62		34	49	6	

Humanities

American studies

" American studies is the ideal interdisciplinary arts degree that allows students to continue their studies in history and English literature while adding courses in politics and film studies. The focus on America (normally the USA alone, but sometimes also Canada, and in one or two places Latin America and the Caribbean as well) gives an intellectual coherence to the degree. America has been, and remains, the dominant cultural, economic, and military influence in the world, and an American studies degree allows students to learn how this hegemony arose and why it has persisted so long. Many American studies degree programmes in the UK have study abroad opportunities that give students the chance to live in the USA for a year and really immerse themselves in the culture. An American studies degree is one of the few that leaves all career paths open, from the normal 'milk-round' jobs, to those which make specific use of the expertise in American culture that graduates should have.

Dr Tim Lockley, *Associate Professor, Department of History and School of Comparative American Studies, University of Warwick*

If you want to understand the nature of the modern world then there is no better way of doing it than to understand the diversity of the country that put a man on the moon, went to war with Britain, Spain, Japan, and Vietnam at various points in its history and still managed to invent jazz, fast food, and bourbon. If you are fascinated by America it makes sense to study it seriously at undergraduate level. While bits of Americana will be included on other courses – you can hardly avoid it if you're studying modern literature, politics or history, for example – you can also get stuck into America's contribution to all those areas and much else besides on an American studies course. What's included under that title varies a good deal, so take a look at the prospectus and find out as much as you can before committing yourself.

American studies is the very definition of a multidisciplinary course, giving you the chance to study literature, history, and politics, film and cultural studies with, possibly, some travel thrown in. It is also interdisciplinary in the way that it asks you to make connections across subjects and to use the knowledge picked up in the study of history, say, to make sense of the literature you will be asked to read. Typically, you might start with an introduction to the literature, politics, and history of the US before specialising in particular periods or areas of interest. Some universities allow greater scope for the study of contemporary culture through areas such as film studies, popular music or visual arts, while others are more akin to a traditional arts course.

Don't go thinking it's a softer option compared to other humanities courses – you're going to have a range of different areas to get to grips with. It is, however, a useful degree course to keep your options open. Employment prospects are good: as with any arts degree, graduates can try their hands at marketing, advertising or the media. You'll be good on analysis and presentation, and will impress employers with your ability to make connections across subjects instead of having tunnel vision in one specialist area.

Entry requirements tend to be pretty flexible, although humanities A-levels are an advantage. Assessment can be exam- or coursework-based.

Choosing a university can be difficult. The multidisciplinary nature of the course means you'll be conducting a virtual health check of the whole of the humanities side of your universities, since you'll be studying with different departments within it. One lame duck of a department in a discipline important to you could really let you down.

Courses last three or four years. It is possible to spend a year, a semester or no time at all on the other side of the Atlantic: consider how much time you would like to and can afford to spend abroad. And if you are going to hop the pond, remember British universities work in collaboration with different American institutions: if you have a burning desire to soak up the LA sunshine or see politics in action at Washington, then remember when filling out your Ucas form that you are in effect choosing two universities rather than one. And try to find out about the level of support offered while you're away. You don't want to feel isolated while you're out there.

American studies tends to mean the United States of, rather than the continents of North and South America, but many universities now offer options to study and live in Canada or Latin America and at least one university has merged its American and Latin American studies department, so it's worth investigating if you don't want to be confined to the US.

---

66 I have enjoyed my American studies degree, as it combines aspects of the different subjects I studied at A-level: we focus on literature, history, and politics, as well as film studies and other disciplines. Additionally, the final year allows us to choose exactly what we want to study and therefore is really enjoyable. University is definitely a step up from sixth form, but the relaxed atmosphere of the American studies department here and the structure of the degree programme has made the transition easy.

Michael Mill, *fourth-year American studies student, University of Leicester*

↗ Online reading

The British Association of American Studies www.baas.ac.uk
49th Parallel www.49thparallel.bham.ac.uk
American Memory www.memory.loc.gov/ammem/amhome.html
ARNet www.americansc.org.uk
New York Times www.nytimes.com
Washington Post www.washingtonpost.com
The Center for the Study of the Presidency www.thepresidency.org
Smithsonian Institution www.si.edu

American studies

		Guardian score	Satisfied with teaching %	Satisfied with assessment %	Spend per student score /10	Student:staff ratio	Job prospects %	Value added score /10	Average entry tariff
1	Warwick	100.0	89	65	10	14			429
2	Leicester	88.5	97	85	5	15	68	8	322
3	Manchester	78.1	85	61	8	14	47	8	379
4	Birmingham	75.0	86	75	9	18	42	7	372
5	Lancaster	74.9	88	62	7	15			402
6	Liverpool	72.8	92	67	6	17			305
7	King's College London	72.5	93	57	8	12		2	371
8	Sussex	71.1	85	54	4	20	71	8	391
9	Hull	66.3	96	71	3	21	70	7	287
10	Essex	62.0	89	63	4	12			259
11	Canterbury Christ Church	59.7	94	76	5	17		3	236
12	Kent	59.4	91	76	4	18			279
13	UEA	58.8	86	55	7	23	47	7	361
14	Aberystwyth	58.0	93	72	2	14			258
15	Nottingham	57.3	87	63	5	20	53	5	366
16	Plymouth	46.0	86	69	3	20			210
17	Winchester	39.2	92	71	2	20	23		293
18	Liverpool John Moores	33.8	87	68	5	24			215
19	Swansea	31.6	90	59	3	23	30	2	285

Anthropology

❝ Many people think of anthropology as the study of 'other cultures'. Travelling abroad to a foreign society — to Bali, Sri Lanka, Cameroon, Thailand — is frequently a stimulus for students to decide to study the subject, to make sense of their experiences of the 'differences'. But just as importantly, through a comparative approach, it also helps you to see your own society with fresh eyes. Anthropology is a profoundly liberating subject: things that always seemed natural and inevitable turn out to be just one among many ways of doing things, helping you realise that things can be different.

Because anthropology is 'the study of humankind' [from the Greek *anthropos* ('human')], the world is your oyster. Anthropologists learn about cultures and societies across the world and the ways in which they are increasingly connected through global processes, though they may go on to develop expertise about a specific region (say, South Asia, Europe, or Latin America). It's also a broad church. Anthropologists study pretty much anything that human beings do and create: from making music and art to making a living, from healing to migrating to creating virtual worlds on the internet, from making war to working for peace, environmental sustainability, and human rights. What makes anthropology distinctive is that it considers each of these in context, in relation to other areas of people's lives — that is, holistically.

While anthropology opens you to the diverse range of human experience and challenges your prejudices, it also gives you tools to evaluate cultural and social practices critically. For instance, identifying the power relations that underlie them. More than anything, anthropology is a way of seeing, rather than particular subject matter. It can be used to examine and understand any social setting, but at the same time, can help us all to imagine alternative approaches to the complex problems we now face.

Jane K Cowan, *Professor of Social Anthropology, Department of Anthropology, University of Sussex*

Do you prefer bones or beliefs? There are few subjects that can offer you specialisms as far apart as the evolution of human beings and the big contemporary issues, such as how universal human rights fit into a multicultural world. But, somehow, anthropology manages it.

There's no aspect of human life that is not touched on by the subject to some degree: you'll cover language, physiology, art, and the way we (or others) organise our societies. You'll start by studying all these different areas before moving on to specialise, usually in one of two areas: social and cultural anthropology or biological anthropology (which is based more in science than in social science). Social and cultural anthropology (related to sociology in many ways) looks at the organisation of societies and their politics, economics and religions, and tries to place those in context.

Biological anthropologists, on the other hand, start from the evolution of mankind and the human race's differing genetics and concern themselves with physical differences between people: skin, blood groups, the shape of the head and so on, and therefore draw on a different range of disciplines — including anatomy, physiology, and biochemistry.

Some courses do lump the two together, but you're more likely to specialise in one side of the subject — so think hard before applying. You'll start by learning the basic theories that cover the mechanics of human societies, before moving on to specialisations, such as moral and ritual systems, kinship, or ethnography. You'll also be expected to do a certain amount of fieldwork, usually as part of your own research project, and often out of term-time. At some places the fieldwork can last a week, at others it can be 20 weeks. Find out what the options are and how much assistance you'll be given.

Those projects can play an important part in the assessment process, otherwise it's a case of large amounts of continuous assessment (often in the newer universities) or the traditional end-of-year exams (the older institutions).

Given its close ties with other social sciences courses, you'd do well to check the relative health of those departments. Where the teaching and facilities cross over, a healthy "partner" department can indicate the health of the one you're entering.

Look at who will be teaching you and what their specialisations are: if you're taught by someone at the leading edge of research, you'll feel right on top of the game. When you make your trip to the open day, try to ask whether that heroic figure you long to learn from will actually have time to be teaching.

Once you've graduated, there are many careers outside academe in which you can use your anthropological knowledge and skills – marketing, international development, consultancy, business, healthcare, law, local government, and the media.

Anthropologists' professional organisations help to keep close contacts between the university world and working anthropologists, and offer training at different stages of your career.

---

66 Anthropology, broadly speaking, is the study of humans, and I've found the course to be a varied and challenging degree programme. From economic and political organisation, nutrition and health, evolution and religion, it provides an exciting view of the world's diverse populations. I have particularly enjoyed studying the new directions anthropology is taking, linking insights into human behaviour with success in the business world. Hence, anthropology provides a fantastic opportunity to explore the world through many eyes.

Krystyna Lesniak, *third-year anthropology student, Durham University*

⟫ Further information

The Royal Anthropological Institute
50 Fitzroy Street
London W1T 5BT

t 020 7387 0455
↗ www.therai.org.uk

↗ Online reading

Anthropology matters www.anthropologymatters.com
The American Anthropological Association www.aaanet.org
American Association of Physical Anthropologists www.physanth.org
Intute: Social Science www.intute.ac.uk/socialsciences
Anthrobase www.anthrobase.com
Experience Rich Anthropology era.anthropology.ac.uk
Max Planck Institute for Social Anthropology www.eth.mpg.de
Internet Anthropologist www.vts.rdn.ac.uk/tutorial/anthroplogist

Anthropology

		Guardian score	Satisfied with teaching %	Satisfied with assessment %	Spend per student score /10	Student:staff ratio	Job prospects %	Value added score /10	Average entry tariff
1	Oxford	100.0	96	60	10	11			501
2	UCL	90.2	99	65	8	16	66	7	424
3	London School of Economics	78.3	74	54	7	13		4	415
4	Soas	75.4	96	57	5	14		8	358
5	Cambridge	73.7			8	16		2	483
6	Kent	71.6	92	67	4	17	45	10	288
7	Edinburgh	70.7	83	39	8	16	42	8	406
8	St Andrews	67.5	96	74	4	19		4	454
9	Queen's, Belfast	65.2	92	66	4	20		7	345
10	Nottingham Trent	63.6	83	60	6	17			273
11	Durham	62.3	92	53	5	19	58	3	359
12	Brunel	61.2	83	61	3	17			322
13	Sussex	60.9	78	49	3	18	60	6	381
14	Aberdeen	59.5	95	81	4	21			272
15	Goldsmiths	54.8	89	75	3	15			301
16	Manchester	53.6	91	39	6	19	23	4	383
17	Oxford Brookes	47.8	90	65	3	19			263
18	Roehampton	33.1	86	56	3	29	55	3	206

Archaeology

> Archaeology is much more than just fun in the mud! Imagine turning over in your hand a chipped stone axe made 80,000 years ago, or scraping the dirt away from ancient foundations, whether in Egyptian sun or British drizzle. Think about walking across landscapes from the Neolithic to 18th-century gardens, or clambering through the attics of a half-timbered Tudor house.
>
> Archaeology is about understanding human beings over a timespan of many thousands of years, of reconstructing past ways of life from the bones, pots, and metal left behind. It's about the big questions — why humans evolved, why gatherers and hunters settled down to agriculture, the origins of the great civilisations, and of the modern world.
>
> Archaeology can also be political. Entire nations, like Zimbabwe, have named themselves after archaeological sites; the Nazis excavated 'Aryan' sites in eastern Europe. Even simply visiting the Acropolis or Stonehenge tells us about who we think we are. Archaeology students don't just study stones and bones, they think critically about the way the past is used today for political and cultural ends.
>
> On courses like ours, students get to work on projects around the world, from the Caribbean to Hampshire to Egypt. Back on campus, as well as essays and individual and group projects (for example, museum and heritage displays), students handle, draw and classify materials ranging from human and animal bones to Stone Age hand-axes to Roman pottery.
>
> In addition to being highly literate and numerate, archaeologists know all about teamwork — a skill you learn to value when you need to finish digging and recording a trench with three hours to go before the developers' bulldozers move in. But most importantly, students acquire a passion for understanding the material world around them, skills which serve them well regardless of whether they go on to be professional archaeologists. The excitement and relevance of archaeology to the modern world is one of its best-kept secrets.

Professor Matthew Johnson, *Head of Archaeology, University of Southampton*

Archaeology is the study of the human past from its physical remains. It's a combination of the heady fresh air and excitement of an excavation and the forensic attention to detail needed to piece together the evidence uncovered. Put broadly, it is the study of human artefacts and remains, in an attempt to see how humans originated, spread across the world, developed tools and technology, and lived and died over the past few million years.

As a subject, it has never been more popular, and it's significant that there are a relatively large number of mature students on archaeology degrees — many opt out of work to study it. But if you're still not sure whether it's for you, try your local museum, which will doubtless be delighted to help you find a short course or dig nearby to give you the chance to see if it's what you want.

After graduation, many find archaeology to be a tough profession — researchers are sometimes desk- and usually budget-bound, while poorly paid field archaeologists are often engaged on high-pressure, short-term developer-funded rescue excavations — the quick dig before the car-park people move in.

Saying that, the employment prospects are pretty good, although students don't by all means end up still working in the profession. Archaeological careers can land you in academia, in a museum, in some form of landscape management, or in work as a consultant.

Consider too the more glamorous (thanks to CSI and the like) world of forensic archaeology – working for the police or for human rights organisations, trying to piece together incidents of murder or genocide. The chances are, though, that you'll end up outside the field (as it were) working in the civil service, banking, the media – anywhere where there is a need for critical and analytical thinking in areas both scientific and human.

Most courses include the opportunity to develop excavation skills, but the approaches vary, from degrees based in the theoretical and documentary to those specialising in particular periods or geographical areas. Most courses offer a range of choices, and students have to take a number of options, including general (that is, theory and methods) and specific (such as human remains or Far Eastern). As ever, check the modules available to see if they cover the areas you are interested in. If you have a talent for languages, you might consider a joint honours degree – someone's got to make sense of all those inscriptions. And check too that the balance between classroom theory and actual digging is how you'd prefer.

While this country's rich historical heritage makes it an excellent place to study the subject, many are keen – for understandable reasons – to travel abroad. Many digs are in remote and fascinating places, so ask about the possibilities of joining an excavation or research programme abroad if you're interested in this.

But for most of your degree, you'll more than likely be in the UK, so check out the city you'll be studying in as well as the institution. See what libraries and museums are around to help broaden your study, and even what local sites of importance there are if you want to go that extra yard.

If you're sure you want to be a field archaeologist, makes sure your course meets the national professional requirements for membership of the Institute of Field Archaeology.

Also investigate whether the institution has a field unit or centre for applied archaeology. Not only is this good for facilitating field trips, it's also handy for consultancy work, from which students might make contacts for a future career.

---

66 Archaeology is a vibrant subject, there are constantly new discoveries and theories to reflect upon. I don't think I could have chosen a more interesting area of study. It combines theory and learning with hands-on work and good muddy fun. I have even been able to do field work in Albania and Kazakhstan. I've found the department here to be welcoming, friendly, and the staff always have time for me. I've enjoyed the course so much I'm staying on for an MA.

Peggy Gilje, *third-year archaeology student, University of Exeter*

》 Further information

Council for British Archaeology
St Mary's House, 66 Bootham
York YO30 7BZ

t 01904 671417
e info@britarch.ac.uk
↗ www.britarch.ac.uk

Institute of Field Archaeologists
SHES, University of Reading
Whiteknights, PO Box 227
Reading RG6 6AB

t 0118 378 6446
e admin@archaeologists.net
↗ www.archaeologists.net

English Heritage
PO Box 569
Swindon SN2 2YP

t 0870 333 1182
e members@english-heritage.org.uk
↗ www.english-heritage.org.uk

The Association of Archaeological Illustrators & Surveyors
SHES, University of Reading
Whiteknights, PO Box 227
Reading RG6 6AB

e admin@aais.org.uk
↗ www.aais.org.uk

 Online reading

The Society of Museum Archaeologists www.socmusarch.org.uk
Internet archaeology intarch.ac.uk
European Association of Archaeologists www.e-a-a.org
Archaeology www.archaeology.org
Archaeologica www.archaeologica.org
The Archaeology Channel www.archaeologychannel.org
The Ashmolean Museum www.ashmolean.org
Current Archaeology www.archaeology.co.uk
Time Team www.channel4.com/history/timeteam

Archaeology

		Guardian score	Satisfied with teaching %	Satisfied with assessment %	Spend per student score /10	Student:staff ratio	Job prospects %	Value added score /10	Average entry tariff
1	UCL	100.0	90	76	9	8	81	8	383
2	Cambridge	94.9			10	7		6	483
3	Oxford	84.7	95	61	9	15			497
4	Durham	81.7	93	64	4	10	62	9	412
5	Glasgow	73.8	94	77	4	10			339
6	York	73.7	96	77	4	13	58	5	377
7	Queen's, Belfast	73.3	91	68	9	13		7	290
8	Reading	70.0	92	70	3	10	62	8	313
9	Leicester	69.9	95	73	5	12	60	4	345
10	Southampton	69.3	94	75	3	13	50	7	354
11	Manchester	69.0	89	55	10	15	39	8	334
12	Bristol	66.1	96	76	4	22	50	10	374
13	Bournemouth	65.0	87	70	9	9	52	4	241
14	Exeter	64.3	96	80	4	14	34	7	356
15	Liverpool	63.6	89	69	4	12	41	7	361
16	Sheffield	61.9	91	70	4	11	50	4	361
17	Cardiff	59.9	83	61	5	11	46	5	305
18	Newcastle	58.3	87	58	3	11	45	8	323
19	Nottingham	58.2	88	46	7	14		7	350
20	Edinburgh	57.9	91	58	5	20		5	430
21	Birmingham	57.3	88	58	3	11	41	4	372
22	Bradford	56.7	89	54	6	12	63	3	257
23	Lampeter	53.9	84	59	3			2	257
24	Kent	50.2	95	70	3	21			239
25	Lincoln	37.9	82	46	4	22	50	5	270
26	De Montfort	34.3			4	14		1	191
27	Winchester	32.9	91	62	3	17	30	3	230
28	Teesside	31.2	78	57	6	20	41	2	260

Classics

❝ Classics is the study of ancient Greece and Rome in its broadest sense: language, literature, history, philosophy, art, and archaeology. Athens and Italy are just part of the picture: classics covers the Black Sea, North Africa, Spain, Roman Britain. It is about where we have come from and who we are today. Ever wondered why Washington has a capitol and a senate? Where democracy comes from, or our ideas about law, beauty, justice? The answer is the classical world.

Like some other universities, at Cambridge, we think it important for every classics student to learn Latin and Greek. English translations are a wonderful introduction to the classical past but do not provide the same degree of direct engagement. While it is obviously helpful to start these languages early, a large number of our students are studying one or both of them from scratch.

But language is the tip of the iceberg. Few degrees offer the opportunity of acquiring language skills alongside such a wide range of other expertise from essay-writing to critical thinking, from visual analysis to digging. No wonder that classicists are amongst the most employable graduates, and in fields that you might not expect – accountancy, the civil service, law, journalism, banking, media. If you enjoy Plato's Republic, Peterson's Troy, or Shakespeare's Antony and Cleopatra, visiting museums and art galleries or Hadrian's Wall, classics will help you work out why. If you want a truly interdisciplinary experience with plenty of excuses to travel, then classics is the course for you.

Dr Caroline Vout, *University Lecturer, Faculty of Classics, Fellow of Christ's College, University of Cambridge*

When picking your subject, it's crucial to choose one you'll enjoy studying and will enhance your employment prospects later on. While classics can seem like a determinedly obscure approach – the dry, dusty path that leads on to a career in academia – this is far from the case.

The course – loosely defined as the study of ancient civilisations – combines a variety of disciplines, including language (particularly Latin and ancient Greek), literature, philosophy, art, history, and archaeology. It's about the interlinking of all these aspects in a particular historical context, making the connections between them and thereby developing a variety of analytical skills (which are always appreciated by employers). What's more, your study may not be based exclusively in the ancient world – you can also study how the classical world has been represented in later media.

So a classics degree equips you for far more than simply teaching or academia. Graduates go into law, accountancy, public relations, and many other careers not associated with Cicero and his chums.

There's a huge range of options available to you in a classics department, and as study is often through translation you don't have to have a private school background. There is now less emphasis on the study of languages in university classics departments because Latin and Greek are not generally offered in state schools.

As with any subject, it's worth asking some rigorous questions about what you want from your degree. You could take straight classics, which means a degree with particular focus on the study of Greek and Latin languages. Or you could take classical studies/civilisation or an ancient history course and study through translation, though studying at least some Greek and/or Latin may, however, be a compulsory part of a classical studies/civilisation and ancient history degree in some institutions. If you feel that language study is not your strength, then you need to bear this in mind – it would be beneficial to do some language work if you are aiming to undertake postgraduate work or become a teacher.

There may also be opportunities to travel abroad. The chance to study the classics in Italy or Greece is a valuable one, and if you're combining the course with archaeology, it could offer fascinating possibilities. Pay attention to the wider institution and the city you will be studying in. The older universities tend to have classics as part of their very fabric and so will have the libraries and teaching to match. And investigate the wider city for galleries and museums.

The opportunity to look at genuine artefacts from the period you're studying can make the subject more worthwhile and also offers the possibility of work placements if you fancy curatorial work. Try to get a feel for how the subject is regarded by the institution. Check out the number of teaching staff, their specialisations and the facilities. If you're interviewed in a shed at the back, it could be time to look elsewhere.

---

66 From Homer to Hume, classics is the ultimate degree. I chose my course because it gave me the chance to begin both Latin and Greek from scratch in intense but captivating classes. There's nothing like the satisfaction of reading Plato in the Greek or Roman comedies in Latin, and the sheer variety of choice on the course opens up huge new areas of study and texts to explore and devour. There's something for everyone, whether you're into languages, literature, philosophy, history or archaeology.

Rebecca Rigby, *final-year classics student, Jesus College, University of Oxford*

» Further information

The Classical Association
Senate House, Malet Street
London WC1E 7HU

t 020 7862 8706
↗ www.classicalassociation.org

The Society for the Promotion of Roman Studies
Senate House, Malet Street
London WC1E 7HU

t 020 7862 8727
e office@romansociety.org
↗ www.romansociety.org

The Society for the Promotion of Hellenic Studies
Senate House, Malet Street
London WC1E 7HU

t 020 7862 8730
e office@hellenicsociety.org.uk
↗ www.hellenicsociety.org

↗ Online reading

Classics Web www.classics.ac.uk
The British Epigraphy Society www.csad.ox.ac.uk/BES
The Perseus Digital Library www.perseus.tufts.edu
The Classical Pages www.classicspage.com
Vroma www.vroma.org

Classics

		Guardian score	Satisfied with teaching %	Satisfied with assessment %	Spend per student score /10	Student-staff ratio	Job prospects %	Value added score /10	Average entry tariff
1	Oxford	100.0	96	73	10	15	73	8	493
2	Cambridge	97.2			10	14	84	7	522
3	Warwick	85.5	91	69	9	14	68		439
4	St Andrews	82.0	93	81	5	14			445
5	Edinburgh	78.2	88	48	7	16		9	439
6	UCL	78.0	87	64	7	12	71	5	430
7	Durham	74.6	86	75	3	16	77	8	451
8	Bristol	72.8	84	70	4	19	77	8	442
9	Exeter	72.5	95	86	4	16		4	393
9	King's College London	72.5	90	75	6	12	59	4	418
11	Glasgow	69.5	92	62	5	17			361
12	Liverpool	68.7	88	63	5	17			325
13	Manchester	64.3	86	40	7	14		4	426
14	Royal Holloway	63.5	93	77	4	15	54	5	337
15	Birmingham	62.5	92	67	7	18	47	4	373
16	Kent	61.3	94	70	3	18			255
17	Leeds	61.1	88	67	4	16	53	5	367
18	Nottingham	54.3	94	62	4	20	47	5	399
19	Reading	50.6	83	65	3	17			302
20	Swansea	49.5	86	69	3	23			323
21	Roehampton	40.0	71	54	3	18			221
22	Newcastle	33.6	80	49	3	25		1	403

English

❝ For many sixth-formers and college students, undergraduates, and even academics with decades of teaching and research behind them, English literature is the dream subject. It offers intimate access to the experiences, imaginations, and laughter of people who have lived in many parts of the world, over many centuries.

It is always familiar: your favourite poems, novels, short stories, and plays are always at hand to let you into their special worlds. It is always new: the questions you ask can lead you to an unending series of exciting texts and topics, including children's literature, Beowulf, letters, travel books and Gothic in many varieties. Even your old favourites are never quite the same the next time you read them.

Search out programmes that give you some grounding in every period from the Middle Ages to the present day, but also offer you flexibility: it is a principle in the school where I teach that every student who is passionate about a specific topic in English literature should have the opportunity to study it. Small group teaching and essay tutorials are also very helpful. Since no essay is expected to be exactly like any other, all essays require a lot of individual attention.

You will find yourself encouraged to explore beyond the range of the printed page in many fascinating directions: drama studies may take a practical turn, for those with an interest in theatre. Many programmes offer you the chance to enhance your own creative skills, perhaps with a career in the media in mind. What you get out of English literature is very much a reflection of your energy: employers will appreciate your ability to process written data, weigh up evidence, think independently, and put your ideas across, in speech and writing. You will appreciate a lifelong joy.

Carolyn Lyle, *Lecturer and Undergraduate Admissions Tutor, School of English & American Literature, University of Reading*

One of the great attractions of studying English is that most of it was written to give pleasure. The same cannot be said of – say – geography or sociology. The other great attraction is that it cultivates individuality of response. In a maths class, all 30 students can come up with the same answer and get A+. In an English class, 30 students can each get an A+ with wholly different essays.

But while conversing with some of the most imaginative minds in world history (the authors you're reading) is a fine way to pass a few years, you may find the experience quite different from your previous experiences of studying English. For one thing, no book is duller than the one you have to read, and for another, you may well be daunted by the length of the reading list and the fact that you will be much more on your own than ever before – much more so than most students. You'll spend many lonely hours poring over books and criticism as you try to work through your own responses to the material.

Your course should consist of a few lectures per week, plus seminars or tutorials, where you and a number of other students gather with a tutor to discuss a topic. The exchange of views is absolutely central to the degree.

English courses tend to cross-reference politics, the broader arts, philosophy or psychology. There are few barriers to the interests you can develop: you are as likely to find yourself learning about Shakespearean theatre audiences as examining the influence of Trainspotting on contemporary Scottish dialects.

There are few subjects where the possibilities within it vary so much. You might touch on linguistics, cultural studies, the history of ideas and theory, women's writing, as well as the different literary periods, such as Anglo Saxon or Middle English.

An English degree can teach you to respond, think, and articulate thought as one act. You'll be able to present ideas well and formulate your own opinions, and (rightly or wrongly) an English degree is still valued more highly than a BA in media or cultural studies. Graduates with a 2:1 or higher should have no trouble getting on to one of the major graduate training schemes for marketing or business management, or a law conversion course, and plenty go on to do a master's degree or teacher training.

There can be huge differences between the various choices of department on your Ucas form, so look carefully at the prospectus for each of your selections. What you learn, how you learn it, and how you're assessed (most employ a mixture of exams and coursework) can be vastly different things in each institution.

The easy option is often to pick the course with the more contemporary feel – the idea that Hemingway is an easier read than Chaucer. For one thing, that may lead you to apply for vastly oversubscribed courses, as others think the same. And for another, do you really want to be ploughing the same literary furrow for three or four years? This is your chance to expand your mind, so with all that choice out there, you'd be mad to waste it.

Tread carefully through course titles too. Similar-sounding courses can have very different content, but generally you can assume that English language and English literature are quite separate fields of study.

English language looks at syntax, the development of the language from its Old English origins, and how and why it is manipulated by writers. English literature takes literary texts as its main focus, studies their forms and modes, often in relation to literary periods or movements, and studies them in broader contexts, such as social history, philosophy, and politics.

English studies is different again: it adopts a more socio-cultural perspective, and also often uses a broader approach – more theoretical, perhaps involving literature in translation ("literary studies" is also used for this), or an emphasis on modern/contemporary literature.

To confuse matters further, you can take modules in both. So choose carefully, and also check the institution itself. Are the staff well known in their fields? And does it have a good library? If not, does the town have good secondhand bookshops? As always, it pays to do a lot of research before you commit to a course.

If you like English at A-level then you'll enjoy the degree, but they are very different. The biggest change is the focus on independence — you will be expected to have your own opinions and be original. Seminars take in a huge range of literature, from medieval ballads to 21st-century television, so don't expect three years of Shakespeare. Most of all, the course teaches you to think critically and to form an argument coherently, useful skills for almost any job you choose afterwards.

Lucy Taylor, *final-year English and related literature student, University of York*

》 Further information

The English Association
University of Leicester   **t** 0116 252 3982
University Road, Leicester LE1 7RH **↗** www.le.ac.uk/engassoc

Institute of English Studies
Room NG18, Senate House **t** 020 7862 8675
Malet Street   **e** ies@sas.ac.uk
London WC1E 7HU   **↗** www.ies.sas.ac.uk

↗ Online reading

Guardian.co.uk Books books.guardian.co.uk
The London Review of Books ww.lrb.co.uk
New York Review of Books www.nybooks.com
Janus Head www.janushead.org
Eclat (Essential Comparative Literature and Theory) ccat.sas.upenn.edu/Complit/Eclat
Online Literary Criticism www.ipl.org/div/litcrit
The Council for College and University English www.ccue.ac.uk

English

		Guardian score	Satisfied with teaching %	Satisfied with assessment %	Spend per student score /10	Student:staff ratio	Job prospects %	Value added score /10	Average entry tariff
1	Oxford	100.0	93	72	10	15	70	7	496
2	Cambridge	92.8			10	14	71	5	493
3	UCL	92.5	95	83	9	12	74	7	484
4	Warwick	83.8	89	65	10	14	61	7	453
5	St Andrews	83.4	95	80	7	14	60	8	466
6	Durham	81.0	94	78	4	16	74	7	500
7	Dundee	78.4	93	79	6	15	59	10	337
8	Queen Mary	78.2	93	78	8	19	61	9	365
9	Exeter	77.5	96	77	6	16	60	8	426
10	Edinburgh	77.2	94	57	9	16	58	8	423
11	Aberdeen	76.7	99	70	6	16	69		327
12	Glasgow	75.2	91	73	8	17	62	8	395
13	York	74.8	91	55	6	17	67	7	479
14	Bristol	74.5	88	64	7	19	66	7	470
15	Leicester	74.3	97	85	6	15	59	6	373
16	Leeds	72.7	93	68	6	16	59	6	444
17	King's College London	72.6	92	58	8	12	47	7	416
18	Royal Holloway	72.2	93	66	6	15	60	5	416
19	Liverpool	71.8	92	68	7	17	55	8	422
20	Loughborough	70.9	96	82	6	21	61	7	366
21	Stirling	70.5			4	16	63	9	312
22	Manchester	67.8	87	51	8	14	45	6	431
22	UEA	67.8	93	69	7	23	57	7	384
24	Anglia Ruskin	67.7	78	57	10	12	56	5	264

	Guardian score	Satisfied with teaching %	Satisfied with assessment %	Spend per student score /10	Student:staff ratio	Job prospects %	Value added score /10	Average entry tariff
24 Cardiff	67.7	94	68	7	21	55	7	408
26 Kent	67.3	91	76	5	18	60	7	333
27 Birmingham	67.1	85	50	9	18	54	6	411
28 Oxford Brookes	66.0	89	71	4	15	60	7	312
29 Gloucestershire	65.8	87	75	8	14	42	9	268
30 Hull	64.7	92	67	3	21	66	8	316
31 Essex	64.6	91	60	5	12	55	6	313
32 Sussex	64.5	84	51	5	20	58	8	428
33 Lancaster	64.1	87	61	4	16	53	6	403
34 Newman University College	63.9	91	72	3	21	86	7	244
35 Nottingham	63.3	89	52	5	20	59	5	443
36 Hertfordshire	62.8	84	61	7	16	60	6	267
37 UWE Bristol	62.2	87	73	3	18	62	8	276
38 Sheffield	61.3	89	61	4	20	50	7	439
39 Reading	61.1	91	75	4	17	43	6	355
40 Nottingham Trent	61.0			8	15	62	3	255
41 Brunel	60.9	85	57	8	17	50	6	303
42 Goldsmiths	60.8	88	77	3	17	58	4	344
43 Birmingham City	60.7	84	70	4	17	61	7	260
44 Sunderland	60.4	87	66	7	15	51	7	239
45 Queen's, Belfast	60.2	90	62	5	16	60	3	345
46 Southampton	59.9	95	75	3	26	54	7	386
47 Northampton	59.2	88	70	3	12	40	10	230
48 Newcastle	59.0	88	47	5	25	61	6	425
49 Northumbria	58.4	86	63	6	19	51	7	305
50 De Montfort	58.2	92	75	3	17	52	7	260
51 Kingston	58.0	90	67	5	19	45	8	237
52 Leeds Trinity & All Saints	57.7	90	73	2	18	56	3	378
53 Glamorgan	57.3	94	65	4	10	41	5	241
54 Chichester	56.0	96	87	4	16	41	4	246
55 Strathclyde	55.8	82	61	4	19	48	8	287
56 Aberystwyth	55.7	94	72	3	14	41	4	325
57 Marjon (St Mark and St John)	54.0	95	78		22	46	8	220
58 Bath Spa	53.9	91	71	3	22	42	8	294
59 Teesside	53.7	90	79	5	16	44	2	281
60 Cumbria	53.6	78	60	7	20	69	2	276
61 Westminster	53.4	85	69	5	14	44	5	237
62 Worcester	52.8	90	65	5	15	46	3	262
63 Chester	52.5			2	23	42	6	302
64 Bedfordshire	52.4	82	74	3	25		5	252
65 Liverpool John Moores	52.3	89	69	6	24	43	7	244
66 Winchester	52.1	92	70	2	20	43	7	266
67 Huddersfield	51.8	85	62	7	16	44	2	287
68 Roehampton	51.2	84	66	4	18	55	3	241
69 Ulster	50.4	76	63	6	17	46	5	246

		Guardian score	Satisfied with teaching %	Satisfied with assessment %	Spend per student score /10	Student:staff ratio	Job prospects %	Value added score /10	Average entry tariff
70	Bangor	49.8	87	61	4	20	44	4	322
71	Lampeter	49.5	84	53	2	28		8	274
72	Canterbury Christ Church	48.9	90	71	5	17	39	2	253
73	York St John	48.6	86	59	6	23	53	3	276
74	St Mary's UC, Twickenham	48.5	92	69	2	21	47		237
75	Swansea	48.4	91	70	4	23	43	3	320
76	UC Falmouth	47.9			5	36	54		267
77	Staffordshire	47.5	67	44	8	16	46	3	240
78	North East Wales Institute	47.2	85	75	2	31	56		202
79	Central Lancashire	46.5	84	69	7	26	55	1	263
80	Edge Hill	46.0	92	73	3	22	47	2	262
81	Middlesex	45.9	90	79	7	19		1	229
82	Manchester Met	45.5	90	61	3	26	42	4	314
83	Derby	44.4	85	76	6	26	31	5	244
84	Leeds Met	43.7	85	61	5	16	36	1	281
85	Sheffield Hallam	41.8	86	60	5	25	35	2	290
86	Greenwich	40.7	74	68	3	27			203
87	Lincoln	38.5	88	65	3	30	37	4	275
88	Plymouth	37.1	83	68	4	20	24	1	284
89	Salford	33.3	85	66	3	34	31	3	281
90	Wolverhampton	30.1	80	69	3	27	45	1	189

History and history of art

> History is as popular a hobby today as it has ever been — the growing number of documentaries on television and books in the shops are ample proof of that. We are clearly fascinated with the lives of people in the past, whether famous rulers, politicians or generals, or the ordinary men, women, and children whose lives were so different from our own. And of course, it must be a truism that knowing about the past helps us to develop empathy and a moral compass, to understand different people and societies, and to realise how our own world has come into being, thus defining our own sense of identity.
>
> Yet studying history at university involves far more than passively receiving the fruits of historical research, that is to say the books and television programmes that our modern society consumes so voraciously.
>
> Knowing what happened in the past does not make you a historian, any more than being able to use a computer makes you a computer technician. History degrees aim to teach students how to reconstruct the past by interpreting the surviving documents and physical evidence of our ancestors and to sort through diverse and often conflicting interpretations of past events and societies in the history books that we read. These are skills that have enormous practical benefit in society at large, which is why the study of history is such a central component of the school curriculum — and also why employers are so keen to recruit history graduates! But ultimately, the real reason for studying history at university must be personal: the joy of exploration and discovery, of peeking behind the curtain and understanding how and why our societies tell stories about the past.

Dr Craig Taylor, *Senior Lecturer in History, University of York*

To start with "straight" history: the possibilities of studying the history of the world are so vast that most history degrees begin with general outline courses in the first year and become gradually more specialised from then on. The intention of such broad surveys is to acquaint students with as wide a range of materials and approaches to history as possible in order for you to make informed decisions when it comes to choosing options in subsequent years — during which you might focus on a particular place, period or theme. Those based around the study of foreign countries or earlier periods may encourage you to learn a language; those based around particular methodologies or historical approaches may draw on theories from other branches of the human and social sciences or may encourage a knowledge of statistics.

The standard method of teaching is by a combination of lectures and small group tutorials. The purpose of tutorials is the discussion of assigned reading, and short student presentations may be encouraged. Essays are required at regular intervals and these are included in an element of continuous assessment on some degree courses. Otherwise assessment generally remains weighted towards examinations.

Partly because it has become such a broad discipline, a history degree is widely respected by employers as fostering the ability to read critically and think independently, to gather information and analyse data, and to present ideas both orally and on paper. History graduates go on to pursue a wide variety of careers, including teaching and researching, administration and management, and the media.

When applying, pay attention to the choice of modules and who will be teaching them. Look into related departments as there's often some teaching crossover, and into what scope there is for joint degrees.

History of art

History of art, meanwhile, is an altogether different degree. It's a valuable inter-disciplinary course that studies how visual art and expression have changed through history, developing a high degree of visual literacy and an awareness of the close relationship between art and its wider historical context. Students use a wide range of historical, theoretical, and critical approaches, developing the skills involved in critical analysis and the critical reading of texts.

There is no doubt that history of art suffers from an image problem as the course of choice for toffs, but things are changing for the better. Institutions are broadening their recruitment strategies and looking to open up the scope of the course to wider influences than the narrow white Eurocentric view of (often painted) art that has traditionally dominated the subject. There is also a growing move away from seeing the subject as connoisseurship towards a more interdisciplinary and academically rigorous approach.

Teaching will be a mixture of classes and lectures, and assessment is nearly always conducted on the basis of analytical essays – either in coursework or exams. A dissertation is also likely to form part of the course.

As with straight history, look closely at the modules on offer and the reputation of the individual staff in the department. There may also be the possibility of spending a year of your degree abroad – this opens up some exciting opportunities and improves employability prospects no end.

Studying in a city that is home to a range of galleries and museums is an obvious advantage, and they can also be valuable for work placements. Look out for these as they are a good chance to get work experience if you want a career in that direction. Also, check if the department has its own slide library. They mostly do, but some are better and easier to use than others.

After graduation you will be ripe for careers in writing, publishing, arts administration, and conservation or teaching.

❝ The main difference between undergraduate and A-level history is the level of independence you are granted. Here, for example, contact with tutors is limited to a maximum of ten hours per week; the rest of the time you are on your own – allowing students to develop their time-management skills and take their work in an independent direction. The range of modules on offer is one of the most enjoyable aspects – you can be studying the Middle Ages in the morning and contemporary US politics in the afternoon.

Dan Richardson, *third-year history student, Durham University*

>> Further information

The British Academy
10 Carlton House Terrace
London SW1Y 5AH

t 020 7969 5200
↗ www.britac.ac.uk

The Institute of Historical Research
Senate House, Malet Street
London WC1E 7HU

t 020 7862 8740
e ihr.reception@sas.ac.uk
↗ www.history.ac.uk

Association of Art Historians
Cowcross Court, 70 Cowcross Street
Clerkenwell
London EC1M 6EJ

t 020 7490 3211
e admin@aah.org.uk
↗ www.aah.org.uk

Museums Association
24 Calvin Street
London E1 6NW

t 020 7426 6910
e info@museumsassociation.org
↗ www.museumsassociation.org

The British Association of Paintings Conservator-Restorers
PO Box 258
Blofield
Norwich NR13 4WY

t 01603 858 129
e secretary@bapcr.org.uk
↗ www.bapcr.org.uk

↗ Online reading

Arlis www.arlis.net
Economic History Services eh.net
Arts Council (of England) www.artscouncil.org.uk
History Today www.historytoday.com
The Women's Library www.thewomenslibrary.ac.uk
The History Channel www.thehistorychannel.co.uk

History and history of art

		Guardian score	Satisfied with teaching %	Satisfied with assessment %	Spend per student score /10	Student:staff ratio	Job prospects %	Value added score /10	Average entry tariff
1	Oxford	100.0	94	67	10	15	79	7	490
2	Courtauld Institute	99.6	91	69	10	13		7	414
3	Cambridge	95.7			10	14	72	7	500
4	King's College London	87.2	97	76	7	12	69	6	454
5	Warwick	85.4	92	65	9	14	64	7	444
6	Durham	85.3	95	86	4	16	73	7	478
7	UCL	85.2	91	64	8	12	70	7	441
8	St Andrews	82.8	95	80	7	14	61	7	444
9	London School of Economics	81.9	80	67	8	13	82	5	426
10	Queen Mary	79.1	96	83	7	19	63	8	368
11	York	78.9	92	73	6	17	65	7	451
12	Exeter	78.8	95	79	5	16	67	7	413
13	Bristol	77.3	89	69	6	19	70	8	432

	Guardian score	Satisfied with teaching %	Satisfied with assessment %	Spend per student score /10	Student:staff ratio	Job prospects %	Value added score /10	Average entry tariff
14 Dundee	75.3	93	78	5	15	45	9	354
15 Leicester	75.2	94	73	5	15	58	8	357
16 Soas	74.0	94	62	7	10	47	6	355
17 Edinburgh	73.8	87	57	8	16	60	7	423
18 Glasgow	73.2	95	81	7	17	51	4	408
19 Royal Holloway	72.9	87	70	6	15	60	7	385
20 Leeds	72.7	92	69	6	16	55	7	411
20 UEA	72.7	95	84	7	23	52	8	377
22 Birmingham	72.2	91	72	8	18	53	5	401
23 Manchester	70.1	88	53	8	14	43	7	411
24 Kent	70.0	92	74	4	18	62	7	333
25 Liverpool	69.9	95	80	6	17	45	6	377
26 Teesside	69.5	94	88	5	16	26	10	249
27 Aberdeen	68.9	92	72	5	16	52		331
27 Essex	68.9	89	71	5	12	58	5	325
29 Nottingham	68.8	91	62	5	20	56	7	419
30 Huddersfield	68.7	95	82	6	16	55	5	290
31 Chichester	68.5	96	88	4	16		9	234
32 Lancaster	68.4	93	79	4	16	45	6	379
32 Sheffield	68.4	92	67	4	20	58	6	436
34 Plymouth	66.2	93	76	4	20	41	10	276
35 Gloucestershire	65.9	91	66	8	14	33		257
36 Anglia Ruskin	65.6	89	76	9	12		5	224
36 Cardiff	65.6	92	69	6	21	49	6	399
38 Sussex	65.5	90	68	5	20	38	9	388
39 Southampton	65.4	94	75	4	26	57	8	383
40 Bath Spa	65.1	95	75	3	22	58	8	269
41 Reading	64.8	93	69	4	17	50	6	328
42 Bradford	64.5	87	66	10	24			264
43 Brunel	64.3	89	67	7	17		5	309
44 Hull	63.7	96	81	4	21	63	5	295
45 Goldsmiths	63.3	87	69	3	17	52	7	311
46 Aberystwyth	63.2	93	75	3	14	45	5	310
47 Newman University College	62.8	99	79	3	21			235
48 Oxford Brookes	61.5	89	71	4	15	36	6	335
49 Newcastle	61.0	86	56	4	25	61	7	405
50 De Montfort	60.6	91	83	3	17		8	257
51 Glamorgan	60.1	89	74	4	10		6	216
51 Northampton	60.1			3	12	24		241
53 Queen's, Belfast	59.5	89	64	5	16	49	3	340
54 Nottingham Trent	59.0	83	71	7	15	54	2	273
55 Sunderland	58.5	86	81	6	15	46		255
56 Leeds Trinity & All Saints	57.6	75	61	3	18		3	379
57 Hertfordshire	57.2	89	72	6	16	40	3	267
58 Staffordshire	56.9	80	74	7	16			252

	Guardian score	Satisfied with teaching %	Satisfied with assessment %	Spend per student score /10	Student:staff ratio	Job prospects %	Value added score /10	Average entry tariff
58 Strathclyde	56.9	87	70	4	19	39	6	295
58 Ulster	56.9			5	17	48	3	254
61 Kingston	56.4	82	68	4	19	50	8	231
62 Roehampton	56.3	89	70	4	18	35	7	235
63 Worcester	56.2	86	70	5	15			242
64 Newport	55.5	85	70	4	22			189
65 Canterbury Christ Church	55.3	94	83	5	17	39	2	244
66 St Mary's UC, Twickenham	54.5	93	71	3	21			240
67 Central Lancashire	53.8	90	76	7	26	57	2	268
68 Brighton	53.6	81	66	4	20	44	7	229
69 Bangor	52.7	90	70	4	20	52	2	265
69 Stirling	52.7			4	16	48	1	269
71 Chester	52.6	95	82	3	23		5	280
71 Northumbria	52.6	83	68	5	19	38	5	301
73 Winchester	51.9	87	78	3	20	42	4	257
74 UWE Bristol	51.2	91	79	3	18	29	3	261
75 Sheffield Hallam	50.9	88	66	5	25	44	5	276
76 Cumbria	50.8	83	53	6	20	47		273
77 York St John	49.8	90	68	5	23	40	4	210
78 Swansea	49.0	92	68	4	23	41	2	299
79 Wolverhampton	48.6	92	79	4	27		5	194
80 Edge Hill	44.0	95	81	3	22	37	1	216
81 Greenwich	43.3			3	27		5	198
82 Lampeter	42.1	85	67	3	28	33	5	247
83 Manchester Met	39.3	81	67	3	26	29	3	283
84 Lincoln	37.0	83	78	3	30	43	1	251
85 Liverpool John Moores	36.4	76	52	5	24	32	2	231
86 Salford	32.0	83	66	3	34	49	1	250

Philosophy

❝ Studying philosophy gives you a chance to think in depth about the big questions: what is justice? What is morality? What is truth? How are we to understand the mind (perception, experience, belief, desire, imagination, emotion)? When is it reasonable to believe? Is faith opposed to reason? What is an explanation? What is the status of a scientific theory? What is a number? What is a language? What is art?

But while philosophy is abstract in its content, it is concrete in its benefits. Studying philosophy at university is uniquely able to equip you with the kinds of skills that employers look for: clarity of thought and expression, an ability to reason and analyse arguments, an ability for abstract thought, and an ability to write in a clear and concise way. This combination of abstract content and concrete skills will engender a greater appreciation for the world and your place within it. Philosophy looks at foundations: the foundations of science, of mathematics, of society, of morality, and of humanity. It is quite simply the most fundamental of academic disciplines.

Dr Sarah Sawyer, *Senior Lecturer and Head of the Department of Philosophy, University of Sussex*

Philosophy is the perfect subject for those who wonder what on earth it's all about. Don't listen to the sneerers, asking whether you'll find it all worthwhile the moment you have to start repaying your tuition fees, just let them know that philosophy involves a critical examination of our most basic beliefs about truth and reality, right and wrong, interpretation, explanation, and morality. It looks at basic assumptions about what we know and how we should live, and it teaches you how to think and how to argue. Added to that, you might also study the history of philosophy, business or medical ethics, elements of law, and the philosophers themselves, including Plato, Kant, Russell, Descartes, and Locke.

There are four main branches to the study of philosophy: the logic and philosophy of language; ontology and metaphysics (abstract stuff such as being and knowing, and the nature of life); epistemology and methodology (the theory and nature of knowledge); and ethics. Within these groupings there's even further room for specialisation.

It's not, of course, a directly vocational subject. Instead it gives you the opportunity – perhaps the only chance many people will have in their lives – for extended reflection on and discussion of, as the cliché has it, "life, the universe and everything".

The academic rigour isn't for everyone, but during a philosophy degree you'll learn transferable skills of thought, analysis, and problem-solving and the ability to think logically and to present your thoughts cogently. Employers value such attributes, so your chances of a good job are pretty high, especially in areas such as journalism, publishing, and management consultancy. Some specialisations can help ease the move into the real world; philosophy of law is a good link to a legal career, while business ethics is valued in many areas of commerce.

There are no specific A-level requirements for a course in philosophy, and you shouldn't be at any disadvantage if you have not studied the subject at A-level – nor advantage if you did. If you want to hedge your bets, you could do the course as part of a joint honours degree. Philosophy is often done jointly with English language and linguistics, Greek, German, maths, economics (for those into business ethics), and law.

You might also want to look into the specialisations of the staff, whether you'll get to spend a year abroad, and also investigate how the course is assessed – there's a variety of combinations of exams, coursework, and dissertation, so have an idea which suits you best.

---

66 The biggest difference between the A-level and the degree is that philosophy at university has so much more discussion. The great thing about this is that you hear others' views and learn new things – taking your thoughts to new places. Philosophy could be described as the search for knowledge, and through the reading of key thinkers coupled with good discussions, it's a deeply liberating subject that frees your mind from normal constraints and teaches you to think for yourself.

Edward Rushforth, *first-year philosophy student, University of Greenwich*

» Further information

The Royal Institute of Philosophy
14 Gordon Square
London WC1H 0AG

t 020 7387 4130
↗ www.royalinstitutephilosophy.org

↗ Online reading

The Philosopher's Magazine www.philosophersnet.com
Episteme Links www.epistemelinks.com
Archelogos Projects www.archelogos.com
Philosophy News Service www.philosophynews.com
The Secular Web www.infidels.org

Philosophy

		Guardian score	Satisfied with teaching %	Satisfied with assessment %	Spend per student score /10	Student:staff ratio	Job prospects %	Value added score /10	Average entry tariff
1	Oxford	100.0	93	64	10	15	73	8	515
2	Cambridge	93.2			10	14	75	6	532
3	St Andrews	81.6	98	85	6	14			438
4	UCL	78.9	80	56	8	12	63	8	431
5	Warwick	77.8	81	54	9	14	58	7	455
6	Aberdeen	76.7	97	67	5	16			315
7	London School of Economics	75.7	80	65	8	13		3	459
8	Anglia Ruskin	75.2	90	75	9	12			211
9	Durham	74.2	87	54	3	16	76	7	478
10	Edinburgh	73.8	87	54	8	16	73	4	419
11	King's College London	73.6	91	74	7	12	50	4	439
12	Dundee	73.3	92	76	5	15			296
13	Glasgow	71.7	96	63	6	17	44	8	402
14	Bristol	69.9	89	60	5	19	62	6	455
15	York	69.5	90	49	5	17	62	5	452
16	Manchester	68.5	88	63	7	19	44	8	422

	Guardian score	Satisfied with teaching %	Satisfied with assessment %	Spend per student score /10	Student:staff ratio	Job prospects %	Value added score /10	Average entry tariff
17 Exeter	67.6	92	71	4	16			381
18 Sheffield	66.7	90	70	3	20	55	6	437
19 Cardiff	66.4	94	81	5	21	56	5	383
20 Hull	65.0	90	62	3	21	67	8	294
21 Lancaster	64.2	89	60	6	15	45	5	348
22 Oxford Brookes	64.0	91	73	7	21			290
23 Newcastle	63.3	87	58	4	25		10	383
24 Sussex	62.7	80	47	4	20	53	9	387
25 Kent	61.5	89	56	4	18	63	4	300
26 Roehampton	61.2	88	57	3	18			251
27 Essex	60.9	90	71	4	12		3	309
28 Central Lancashire	60.5	90	77	6	26			267
29 Hertfordshire	60.3	85	69	6	16		7	244
30 Nottingham	60.1	90	46	4	20	63	3	398
31 Leeds	59.9	89	56	5	16	53	2	398
32 Middlesex	59.6	81	73	6	19			187
33 Liverpool	59.5	89	48	5	17	48	3	361
34 Birmingham	59.4	80	51	8	18	65	1	376
35 Southampton	58.5	91	59	3	26	63	7	379
36 UEA	58.3	93	66	6	23	39	6	325
37 UWE Bristol	57.7	91	79	3	18			226
38 Queen's, Belfast	57.6	90	60	4	16			315
39 Heythrop College	57.3			3	17		3	334
40 Reading	56.7	88	65	3	17	40	5	351
41 Brighton	55.6	84	69	3	20		6	258
42 Newport	51.2	83	72	4	22			207
43 Manchester Met	36.3	82	66	2	26	32		251
44 Wolverhampton	32.8	76	57	3	27			170

Religious studies and theology

> Although some atheists describe God as a 'delusion', religious belief continues to thrive. Why? Reports of the death of religion are much exaggerated, even in so-called 'secular' Europe. Again, why? Institutional Christianity may be in decline, but religion is not. Novelist Philip Pullman may question religion, yet religious themes are evident in many places — from Harry Potter to Doctor Who. What's more, religious traditions continue to make headlines: Buddhist monks resisting Chinese authorities in Tibet, a British archbishop supporting the inclusion of Islamic or Sharia law into UK law.
>
> You'll find the influence of religious traditions everywhere, sometimes in a conservative way and sometimes in a progressive fashion. Because they are attentive to human needs and limitations, religious groups are today at the forefront of debates in medical ethics and genetic manipulation as well as promoting care of the earth in the face of climate change.
>
> 'Why do you do that? What do you hope for? What consoles you?' If you have ever wanted to pose these questions to religious communities, then the study of religion is for you. To appreciate the power of religion — for good and ill — you need to understand religious traditions in all their depth, variety, and complexity. Religious studies and theology enables you to do that. As you study, you also acquire many life skills: from an ability to empathise to the facility to analyse, discuss, and present controversial topics.
>
> Our world is a religious world — to understand how this world is religious prepares you to work in this world. So study religion — you won't regret it!
>
> **Dr Peter M Scott**, *Senior Lecturer in Christian Social Thought and Director of the Lincoln Theological Institute, University of Manchester*

One glance at the newspapers or TV should be enough to convince anyone that religion is an extraordinarily powerful force in the world, used to justify an array of actions, for good and ill. All the more important, then, that we should understand the beliefs and value systems that drive the major faiths.

The teaching of religion at universities has been rapidly transformed in the past few years. Many courses have widened their remit to include a variety of religious traditions, while the profile of students arriving in theology and religious studies departments is very different from even ten years ago. Most noticeably the proportion of female students has risen. Gender studies is now an important part of most theology and religious studies courses.

Students can study for undergraduate degrees in religious studies, world religions, divinity, theology, and biblical studies. Academics are keen to stress that none of these are courses simply for the religiously committed, and that the basic questions about human existence are studied without privileging any single viewpoint. If you are committed to one particular faith, though, you need to be sure you are open to that faith being tested and criticised in an academic setting.

Typically, religious studies courses look at the human phenomenon of religion in all its variety, while theology (or divinity) departments tend to focus on Christianity and the way it understands itself — so be careful to choose the right one. However most departments offer some experience of both types of study. Undertaking theological studies may suggest that you have more than a passing interest in Christianity, but does not require any religious commitment.

Theology students go on to a wide variety of careers and certainly do not all work within religious organisations, although clerical training is part of some theological degree courses, and some departments are linked to colleges that train people for the ministry. Graduates emerge not just with analytical and textual skills, but also skills in language, field research, historical and archaeological methods, philosophy, ethics and sociology, literature, art and music – all hugely valuable assets to any employer.

Be aware of the ever-widening scope of courses available – you could find yourself looking at the philosophy of religion and ethics, the sociology and practice of religion, or even anthropology. There may even be the chance to study abroad or head off on field trips, which is always worthwhile, and the chance to visit holy sites or see religions in their context can add a whole new dimension to your studies.

---

66 Doing theology is a wonderfully mind-expanding experience, which has completely changed both my approach to life and my outlook on everything. Even in my final year as an under-graduate, I feel that I am still barely past the beginning of an incredible journey of discovery which has no foreseeable end.

Pete Forest, *third-year theology student, University of Hull*

» Further information

British Association for the Study of Religions
Arts Faculty, The Open University   e basr.open.ac.uk
Walton Hall, Milton Keynes MK7 6AA

↗ Online reading

Association for the Sociology of Religion www.sociologyofreligion.com
MultiFaithnet www.multifaithcentre.org
Internet for Religious Studies www.vts.rdn.ac.uk/tutorial/religion
Centre for Reception History of the Bible www.crhb.org
Al-Islam www.al-islam.org
Bible Gateway www.biblegateway.com
Center for the Study of New Religions www.cesnur.org
The Pluralism Project www.pluralism.org
Society for the Study of Theology www.exeter.ac.uk/theology/sst

↗ Faith sites

Baptist Union of Great Britain www.baptist.org.uk
Buddhism www.buddhism.org
Church of England www.cofe.anglican.org
Church of Scotland www.churchofscotland.org.uk
Hinduism Today www.hinduismtoday.org
Al-Islam www.al-islam.org
Judaism www.jewish.co.uk
Methodist Church www.methodist.org.uk
Roman Catholic Church in England and Wales www.catholic-ew.org.uk
Roman Catholic Church in Scotland www.catholic-scotland.org.uk
Sikhism www.sikh.org

Theology

		Guardian score	Satisfied with teaching %	Satisfied with assessment %	Spend per student score /10	Student-staff ratio	Job prospects %	Value added score /10	Average entry tariff
1	Oxford	100.0	94	65	10	15	77	7	477
2	St Andrews	91.1	98	85	7	14		9	422
3	Cambridge	89.7			10	14	71	5	467
4	Edinburgh	77.2	95	60	8	16	70	8	407
5	Soas	75.9	84	60	7	10		8	315
6	Aberdeen	73.1	97	67	5	16			310
7	Glasgow	72.1	95	65	7	17		9	
8	Durham	71.3	96	77	4	16	74	3	438
9	King's College London	66.3	87	63	7	12		3	376
10	Heythrop College	65.9			3	17		9	321
11	Manchester	64.7	92	67	8	14	36	5	396
12	Bristol	63.2	93	64	6	19	66	5	402
13	Cardiff	63.0	92	78	6	21	77	5	341
14	Lancaster	62.8	97	79	7	15		4	342
15	Gloucestershire	62.4	91	66	8	14		8	283
15	Newman University College	62.4	98	80	3	21			231
17	Sheffield	60.9	91	72	4	20			368
18	Oxford Brookes	59.8	91	73	4	15			291
19	Leeds	59.4	92	61	6	16	59	5	362
19	Queen's, Belfast	59.4	91	60	5	16	59	7	318
21	Kent	58.2	87	58	4	18		9	282
22	Bath Spa	57.9	93	78	3	22			280
23	Exeter	57.3	92	71	5	16		3	385
23	Nottingham	57.3	96	62	5	20	65	4	382
25	Hull	56.0	92	65	3	21			254
26	York St John	53.2	96	86	5	23	61	4	290
27	Bangor	52.5	94	71	4	20		5	258
28	St Mary's UC, Twickenham	52.0	93	77	3	21			244
29	Leeds Trinity & All Saints	51.3	77	66	3	18			353
30	Roehampton	49.7	88	57	4	18			253
31	Chester	47.3	93	74	3	23	71	4	256
31	Cumbria	47.3	83	57	5	15			252
33	Birmingham	44.9	83	50	8	18	39	2	353
34	Winchester	42.6	88	72	3	20			269
35	Canterbury Christ Church	40.3	94	65	5	17		1	239
36	Lampeter	30.1	91	47	3	28		4	296

Medical sciences

Anatomy and physiology

" Human anatomy is concerned with the study of the structure of our bodies, both at the macro-scopic and the microscopic levels. It provides an understanding of the relationship between the structure and function of organs and tissues 'beneath the skin'.

Anatomy has a glorious tradition and anatomists can count amongst their number such illustrious historical figures as Galen, Vesalius, Leonardo da Vinci, Michelangelo, William Harvey, Leeuwenhoek, and, more recently, JZ Young and Solly Zuckerman. Of course, the work of these important anatomists continues to be central for the teaching of biomedical sciences – whether for medical and associated healthcare disciplines or for those who are primarily studying anatomy as a scientific subject.

Anatomy is not just of historical importance, as it continues to move with the times and remains a key area for research in contemporary biomedical science. Many advances are being made in our understanding of microscopic structure (using such technologies as electron microscopy and confocal laser-scanning microscopy) and, in the 'post-genomic era', we need to know not just about the human genome but, more significantly, when and where certain genes are being expressed – this is where contemporary anatomists have a crucial role to play.

Furthermore, new imaging technologies, like MRI, rely upon anatomical information. Important discoveries are also being made in neuroanatomy and developmental biology.

So, if you are intrigued by the complexity of the human body, in awe of the wonder and the spectacle of anatomical images, and want a discipline with good vocational and scientific prospects, studying anatomy at university is for you!

Professor Bernard Moxham, *School of Biosciences, Cardiff University*

Anatomy and physiology, contrary to popular belief, do not represent easy options for those who can't last the course to become a doctor. While the subjects are, obviously, closely allied with medicine, they are actually of a completely different bent to most other branches of medical study, interesting those who are into the academic side of medicine, but don't wish to become doctors.

Those who do want to stay in the "sector" after graduating are more likely to see themselves as scientists, researchers, paramedical staff or working in the pharmaceutical industry. Of course, they also have the knowledge and skills to enter a whole range of careers, including teaching, scientific journalism, or perhaps less traditional areas of medicine, such as osteopathy or reflexology – although further training would be required.

Anatomy (the structure of the body) and its close cousin physiology (how living organisms and their parts function) are both life sciences, concerned with the study of the body and the relationship between its structure and its functions. Human development, ageing, and response to dysfunction are all likely areas of study, and you'll spend most of that study time in the lab, the lecture hall, and tutorials.

Assessment tends to be largely exam-based, with some emphasis on coursework, practical and research projects or presentations. Most courses also include a significant research project, which is generally in the last year, and occasionally this can lead to those crucial academic publications that will look so fabulous on your CV.

If you want to do anatomy, there is a limited number of institutions to choose from, and these are usually going to be the older universities. It can be combined with developmental biology, biomedical science or cellular science; or included as an option in some biological science or human biology courses.

Physiology is rather more widely offered. Some courses allow for focus on humans, mammals, or areas such as neuroscience, so investigate the possibilities thoroughly. Physiology courses will vary from department to department: there may be focus on how individual organs or tissues work, or on complete systems. Alternatively, you might study how systems interact or how life functions at the cellular level. Where courses do vary is in their number of compulsory study modules, or how much of a free hand you are given to bolt together your own physiology degree.

Also, in many universities the physiology department has come to be closely allied with psychology. Most universities will let you take papers from fields related to physiology, such as biochemistry and psychology, in the course of your degree.

Look carefully at who will be teaching you and what their specialisations are – and those of staff in related departments. There's a great deal of crossover with the teaching staff, so a decent medical school will be of great benefit.

Some universities offer a year abroad or working in industry, so investigate the possibilities – it'll be a challenging experience and look great on your CV.

“ For some reason, anatomy is a subject that a lot of people are unfamiliar with. I was once accused of learning about space! It is a hands-on approach to learning about the human body. The captivating sessions in the dissection room are, not surprisingly, the favourite aspect for most people as they put lecture theory into practice with real cadavers. Although challenging and accompanied by plenty of work, I have yet to meet anybody who doesn't have a genuine passion for this subject.

Charlotte Johnston, *second-year anatomy student, University of Bristol*

» Further information

The Academy of Medical Sciences
10 Carlton House Terrace
London SW1Y 5AH

t   020 7969 5288
e   info@acmedsci.ac.uk
↗   www.acmedsci.ac.uk

British Medical Association
BMA House, Tavistock Square
London WC1H 9JP

t 020 7387 4499
↗ www.bma.org.uk

The Royal Society of Medicine
1 Wimpole Street
London W1G 0AE

t 020 7290 2900
↗ www.rsm.ac.uk

 Online reading

The Center for Human Simulation www.uchsc.edu/sm/chs
MedBioWorld www.sciencekomm.at
The Royal Society www.royalsoc.ac.uk
The Virtual Autopsy www.le.ac.uk/pathology/teach/va
Virtual Creatures k-2.stanford.edu/creatures

Anatomy and physiology

		Guardian score	Satisfied with teaching %	Satisfied with assessment %	Spend per student score /10	Student:staff ratio	Job prospects %	Value added score /10	Average entry tariff
1	Oxford	100.0	86	57	10	14	73	7	496
2	Cardiff	92.4	90	51	9	11	84	8	408
3	Liverpool	80.4	93	68	9	9	74	5	357
4	Plymouth	78.3	95	70	8	12		9	301
5	Aston	77.6	93	78	7	15	93	4	371
6	UCL	77.3	89	55	8	12	67	8	393
7	Manchester	74.1	78	50			79	6	417
8	Queen's, Belfast	72.5	91	67	7	10	82	7	326
9	Bristol	66.6	89	58	6	14	78	6	372
10	Bradford	65.4	88	64	4	12	86	5	340
11	Newcastle	64.5	86	55	5	16	74	7	433
12	Glasgow Caledonian	63.9	88	60	5	16	70	6	443
13	City	62.0	85	43	6	14	92	4	359
14	Aberdeen	58.4	92	66	3	14	72		345
15	Hertfordshire	57.8	91	57	4	12	83	6	299
15	King's College London	57.8	82	45	8	15	67	7	380
17	Brunel	57.4	96	70	3	18	56	9	377
18	Birmingham	57.1	83	47	4	13	73	6	408
19	Ulster	56.3	80	54	4	11	73	7	335
20	Leeds	44.9	94	70	4	21	58	5	381
21	De Montfort	40.9	70	53	4	15	85	7	287
22	Anglia Ruskin	40.1	83	54	4	23	92	7	295
23	Manchester Met	37.8	81	63	3	18	53		334
24	Robert Gordon	35.9			3	18	58	3	426
25	Cumbria	34.0			2	21	100	2	304
26	Birmingham City	29.4	80	61	3	17	58	3	369
27	Bedfordshire	29.2	93	56	3	21	94	1	332

Dentistry

❝ The dental undergraduate degree course is action packed. Within the five years students have the opportunity to change peoples' lives, become team leaders, use the latest technology and techniques, and develop skills for business or academia. The course challenges students in many ways: developing skills to carry out very precise procedures including implants and aesthetic restorative dentistry (as seen on makeover shows), teaching an anxious seven-year-old how to clean their teeth or examining a patient with oral cancer.

Students learn the importance of the role they are set to take in the community. Learning does not solely take place within dental schools. Students widen their experience by going on elective studies, often to other parts of the world, and gain work-based learning in local outreach centres. The dental graduate therefore has an understanding of the differing dental needs of patients and has the management skills to provide appropriate treatment.

This degree is the stepping stone to wide-ranging career options – general dental practice, community care, hospital dentistry, specialising in a particular aspect of dentistry (orthodontics, oral surgery, oral medicine, restorative dentistry, to name a few), academic dentistry carrying out research, dentistry in the armed forces or work abroad with charities providing dental care to people in third-world countries.

New techniques and procedures are developing rapidly, expanding the scope and ability of dentists to diagnose and treat disease and gain greater understanding of health education and management. Using scientific knowledge, manual dexterity, interpersonal skills, and a professional attitude dentists can take their skills all over the world and feel fulfilled in their work. Dentistry is a very popular career choice as it offers so many challenges and opportunities.

Dr Angela Fairclough, *Director of Learning and Teaching, School of Clinical Dentistry, University of Sheffield*

Dentistry is one of the youngest (more than half of all dentists are in their 20s and 30s) and most progressive professions in the UK. Equally, it can be one of the best paid. Even in the NHS, net earnings can be around £80,000 a year, with private practitioners able to set their own fees. So although it's not a licence to print money (most dentistry graduates emerge with a large debt burden, for one thing), it is an extremely popular course to choose – and competition is hot.

You'll be expected to have excellent A-levels – chemistry is a requirement, and while biology is sometimes not specified, it is usually preferred. In any case, a second science A-level is required and usually an AS-level in biology as a minimum. It helps if you've had some work experience too – your school or college might run or know of a scheme whereby you can do some observation and work experience at a local practice.

The majority of students are interviewed, and some dental schools also require you to sit the Ukcat (UK Clinical Aptitude Test) before you fill in your Ucas form. For more information on this, including a list of the institutions that currently require it, see the Medical sciences section in this guide.

Once you're in, the form of degree is determined by the General Dental Council, which also sets the minimum standard a dental student must reach upon graduation. After that, what variation there is depends on the individual dental school. The course will involve five years of academic work – two years of pre-clinical study and three years of clinical work. In that five years of study you should gain a thorough scientific knowledge and the necessary clinical and practical skills to care for and treat your patients and run a practice. There may also be the option of an intercalated year, in which you will be encouraged to take a science-related course before returning to dentistry.

Teaching includes a wide range of methods from lectures to tutorials, from computer-assisted learning to practical classes as well as the problem-based learning approach favoured by some courses. Exams are generally held at the end of every year, and a percentage of the marks for each exam may be derived from in-course assessment, which may take the form of essays, practical tests or project work.

Remember that the closing date for applications to dentistry courses is earlier than that for most other courses – usually around mid-October. Competition is stiff, and as a safety net for the many who fail to get in, Ucas insists that no more than four of the five choices on your form should be to schools of dentistry. The others can be used to bid for alternative courses, including medicine, without prejudicing your perceived commitment to dentistry.

However, when sizing up the dental options, consider the course carefully. Many courses now introduce you to patients almost at the beginning, while others start with up to two years of pre-clinical work. If you have plans for the intercalated year, consider the wider institution and the courses on offer. Elective periods – which offer the opportunity to extend experience and study elsewhere, either at home or abroad – can also offer invaluable experience, and should be investigated. Look too at the availability and state of the library, IT, laboratory, and clinical facilities.

Specialisations begin after you qualify. Those who wish to concentrate on areas such as orthodontics, restorative dentistry, endodontics, prosthodontics, periodontics, and paediatric dentistry can do so under training and qualifications schemes run by the dental schools. But if you want to go on to postgraduate study, that will be organised by the local postgraduate institute. Investigate the school's links to postgraduate vocational training – the obligatory learning you will have to take on once you start in your practice will, more than likely, start from there. It may seem like a long way away, but it'll soon come around.

---

66 I wanted to enter a profession combining my interests in the sciences and arts with the opportunity to help others. It wasn't until I started dental school that I realised how dentistry brings additional challenges. This includes self-directed learning, professional development, and assuming responsibility for standards of patient care. The most enjoyable aspect of my training at Leeds has been the early patient contact. Clinical and operative skills are taught in new 'phantom head' suites alongside relevant theory, making learning fun and interactive.

Stacey Clough, *fourth-year dentistry student, University of Leeds*

» Further information

The General Dental Council
37 Wimpole Street
London W1G 8DQ

t   020 7887 3800
↗ www.gdc-uk.org

British Dental Association
64 Wimpole Street
London W1G 8YS

t   020 7935 0875
e   enquiries@bda.org
↗ www.bda-dentistry.org.uk

↗ Online reading

Dentistry www.dentistry.co.uk
The British Fluoridation Society www.bfsweb.org
Dentistry On-Line www.priory.com/dent.htm
Dental Update www.dental-update.co.uk
Dental Cyberweb www.dentalcyberweb.com

Dentistry

		Guardian score	Satisfied with teaching %	Satisfied with assessment %	Spend per student score /10	Student:staff ratio	Job prospects %	Value added score /10	Average entry tariff
1	Dundee	100.0	96	55	8	5	100		454
2	Leeds	84.9	89	46	10	9	100		440
3	Queen's, Belfast	82.9	96	71	4	7	100		455
4	Sheffield	79.9	96	69	5	9	100		449
5	Cardiff	72.5	91	37	6	6	100		445
6	Glasgow	71.7	94	76	2	9	100		451
7	King's College London	70.1	82	26	7	7	100		450
8	Manchester	64.6	75	41	7	8	100		442
9	Newcastle	63.4	92	55	3	12	98		465
10	Birmingham	57.3	87	61	3	9	94		438
11	Liverpool	50.1	91	57	4	10	100		422
12	Queen Mary	38.6	83	47	5	9	100		402
13	Bristol	32.9	84	24	6	17	100		441

Medicine

“ Ask most doctors about their work and they are quite likely to moan about the NHS or the pressures. Ask them what else they would like to do as a job and most are struggling to find a comparison with medicine. Despite recent problems with job applications and career plans for young doctors, medicine remains an immensely rewarding career. It has huge variety, everything from regular patient contact to research, teaching, and administration. Medicine combines the great privilege of dealing with people's problems, often helping them at their most vulnerable times; at the same time it has the stimulating challenge of keeping up to date with ever-increasing advances in technology and treatments. What could be better than to train for a job that keeps you interested, challenged, and rewarded, while entering a profession that the public still trusts more than any other.

Professor John Rees, *Dean of Undergraduate Education, Head of Division, Medical Education, King's College London, School of Medicine*

Each year, thousands of students with lots of As in sciences at A-level sign up for five years of unpaid training. Once qualified, they will work long, long hours for little money. They make life and death decisions without much supervision and there's a high risk of suicide, drug addiction or alcoholism, with potential for high earnings after, oh, 20 years. Yet each year, many of the UK's finest 18-year-old minds decide this is the career for them, leaving Britain's medical schools oversubscribed and able to pick and choose the crème de la crème of the applicants. These applicants know that, despite the pitfalls, medicine can be a uniquely rewarding profession, impacting practically and emotionally on people's lives in a way that only doctors can.

The medical school business is booming, with new schools being launched and established places enrolling both mature and even former arts degree students in response to demand.

The institutions are looking for candidates who are ready for a world of pain (their own as well as their patients'), aware of the daily crises that make up the NHS, and have the inner robustness that means they won't go to pieces at the first sight of blood.

You'll be up against the very best, so in addition to excellent A-levels (which must include chemistry and biology) and GCSEs, achievements in several areas – music, sport, languages, Duke of Edinburgh awards, being head of school, or anything else that shows you have initiative and drive – will all be an important advantage, as will work experience.

Medical courses are changing. Typically they involve five years of academic work, with an optional intercalated year (studying a science course for 12 months before returning to medicine). In the early 1990s, medical schools attracted criticism from the General Medical Council for spending too long on lectures, and so each changed their curriculum to put more emphasis on communication skills, understanding cultural issues, and more patient interaction.

Although the government has promised to pay tuition fees for medical students in their fifth and sixth years (or in years two, three and four of fast-track courses) as one of a number of schemes to attract young people from poor families and ethnic minority communities to train as doctors, the average medical student is still likely to graduate with debts of between £20,000 and £60,000.

Some medical schools run integrated courses, which means that instead of spending a couple of years in university doing your pre-clinical training and being a normal undergraduate in lectures and laboratories you will be seeing patients from the very first term and applying your knowledge to real-life problems. This can be daunting but invaluable, and whether you prefer this is dependent on whether you see yourself as learning a trade or a science.

Location should be a big factor. You'll be attached to the institution for longer than the normal undergraduate's three or four years, so try to establish whether you'll be happy there. A visit, preferably to an open day, is essential. Investigate the social side, and try to find out how supportive the student environment is – things are likely to get very tough over the five years.

Check the options for the intercalated year, where you can study a subject in depth or pursue research, and also for elective periods, which offer the opportunity to extend experience and study elsewhere, either at home or abroad. Look too at the learning resources – what is the availability and state of the library, IT, laboratory, and clinical facilities?

Remember that the closing date for medicine courses is earlier than for most – October 15, and that you can only pick medicine for four of your five allocated Ucas choices. And finally, two words of warning:

As with dentistry, some medical schools may insist that you sit a new aptitude test before you apply. The clinical aptitude test (Ukcat) has been developed by a consortium of universities and has been in place since 2006. The difference between the Ukcat and similar admissions tests that are currently in use to help universities decide between top medical candidates is that it is taken before students fill in their Ucas forms. The consortium hopes to give candidates and admissions officers a better idea of the suitability of the former to a medical career before they apply for courses. The 90-minute Ukcat exam will test candidates' mental abilities and assesses how they might respond to patients. Scientific knowledge is not tested.

The full list of dental and medical schools currently using Ukcat is:

University of Aberdeen
Brighton and Sussex Medical School
Cardiff University
University of Dundee
University of Durham
University of East Anglia
University of Edinburgh
University of Glasgow
Hull York Medical School
Imperial College, London
Keele University
King's College London
University of Leeds

University of Leicester
University of Manchester
Newcastle University
University of Nottingham
University of Oxford (graduate entry)
Peninsula College of Medicine and Dentistry
Queen Mary, University of London
Queen's University Belfast
University of Sheffield
University of Southampton
University of St Andrews
St George's, University of London
Warwick University (graduate entry)

If your university of choice isn't up there, don't think you've got away with it. A number of universities use the BioMedical Admission Test (Bmat). This is aimed at testing students' thinking skills as opposed to subject knowledge. It is not a pass or fail test but admissions tutors will have the results available alongside candidates' AS-level results and predicted A-level results. You have to register separately for the tests. For dates and more information, check www.bmat.org.uk. The universities who use the Bmat are:

University of Cambridge
Imperial College London
University of Oxford Medical School
Royal Veterinary College
University College London

❝ I love studying medicine, it's the best decision I ever made. You need real drive to keep up with the work, so it's important to know before you start that it's what you want to do. The first couple of years — learning about the physiology of the body (basic medical sciences) — were on a similar level to A-levels; after that you enter clinical teaching, where the workload increases and you're on the wards — effectively preparing to become a doctor.

Cayetano Rebora, *fourth-year medical student, University of Sheffield*

» Further information

British Medical Association
BMA House, Tavistock Square
London WC1H 9JP

t 020 7387 4499
↗ www.bma.org.uk

General Medical Council
Regent's Place, 350 Euston Road
London NW1 3JN

t 0845 357 8001
e gmc@gmc-uk.org
↗ www.gmc-uk.org

The Academy of Medical Sciences
10 Carlton House Terrace
London SW1Y 5AH

t 020 7969 5288
e infor@acmedsci.ac.uk
↗ www.acmedsci.ac.uk

» Online reading

SocietyGuardian.co.uk health section SocietyGuardian.co.uk/health
The British Medical Journal www.bmj.com
Department of Health www.dh.gov.uk

Medicine

		Guardian score	Satisfied with teaching %	Satisfied with assessment %	Spend per student score /10	Student:staff ratio	Job prospects %	Value added score /10	Average entry tariff
1	Dundee	100.0	94	45	10	3	100		476
2	Cambridge	98.0			9	7	99		548
3	Oxford	87.7				7	98		525
4	Edinburgh	83.9	89	38		6	99		497
5	UCL	79.8	83	42	7	4	100		485
6	Imperial College	79.2	87	28	9	7	100		500
7	Leicester	77.6	92	56	4	7	99		465
8	King's College London	74.7	86	44	8	7	99		450
9	Newcastle	70.5	91	42	5	8	100		485
10	Leeds	70.1	91	48	7	8	99		458
11	Warwick	69.5	87	35	8	10	100		
12	Manchester	69.2	80	37	9	9	98		468
13	Aberdeen	69.0	87	57	4	7	97		468
14	Glasgow	65.9	83	34	6	7	100		471
15	Nottingham	63.9	85	33	4	7	99		485
16	Peninsula Medical School	63.0	80	48	10	10			396
17	Hull York Medical School	59.6			5	9			449
18	Southampton	56.5	92	48	3	11	98		445
19	Queen Mary	56.2	83	47	5	9	100		416
20	St Andrews	55.6	96	55	2	14	97		483
21	Sheffield	54.5	82	33	3	8	99		468
22	UEA	52.1	93	49	2	12			439
23	St George's Medical School	52.0	85	40	5	12	100		443
24	Liverpool	51.4	81	37	3	10	100		466
25	Birmingham	50.5	82	24	4	10	100		490
26	Queen's, Belfast	48.6	88	36	2	10	99		438
27	Swansea	45.6			7	5			241
28	Bristol	44.7	84	20	5	13	99		461
29	Cardiff	43.7	71	19	3	8	100		467
30	Brighton Sussex Medical School	31.6			3	17			457

Nursing

❝ Every day, nurses make a difference to people's lives. The three-year course equips you with the confidence and qualifications needed to work in many interesting areas of healthcare, such as supporting patients with cancer, caring for sick children, giving health advice for parents or helping people with mental health problems.

The course equips you with skills to deliver high-quality care, preparing you for a varied and challenging career that makes a real difference to people's lives. This rewarding profession is highly respected and has many opportunities for career advancement into specialist roles both in hospitals and in the community.

Students are encouraged to develop as caring and competent practitioners who can adopt an enquiring, analytical, and creative approach to their work. They develop the ability to critically appraise research literature and link this to clinical practice, working in a multidisciplinary, multi-agency and inter-professional team as part of a dynamic health and social care system.

The course covers many interesting areas of study from psychology, sociology and management, anatomy and physiology, to communication skills and how to assess your client's needs.

Clinical placements — abroad and in the UK — allow students to apply the knowledge they have acquired in the preceding modules to different client groups.

If you want to work in an environment that's interesting, rewarding, and challenging, a career in nursing will give you plenty of scope to do that. Nurses form the largest group of staff in the NHS and are a crucial part of the healthcare team. Nurses work in every sort of health setting, from intensive care units to working in patients' homes, with people of all ages and backgrounds.

If you've got an interest in caring for people, you'll find a role that suits you in nursing.

Gillian A Hilton, *Principal Lecturer, School of Nursing & Midwifery, University of Brighton*

Nursing is a profession that requires a wide range of skills and aptitudes. Caring and compassion, for instance, share equal importance with theoretical knowledge, and communication and teamwork skills are as important as technical expertise. Nursing degree programmes offer the opportunity to develop these abilities, as well as many others, in a variety of practice settings, ranging from NHS Trust hospitals to the patient's own home.

There are four different nursing degree programmes that you can choose from. They all share a common first year and then you follow your chosen branch of nursing: adult, child health, learning disability or mental health. Both diplomas and degrees in nursing lead to state registration.

In England, most student nurses take a three-year diploma course, which requires five GCSEs or equivalent qualifications, but nursing students with A-levels or equivalent qualifications can take a degree course (on which our tables are based), also lasting three years.

All these courses are run by universities, in partnership with local hospitals. Courses are divided into half theory and half practice. Recent changes mean students now go out to hospitals earlier – usually in the first three months of the course, instead of at six months or later. And the placements are longer – eight weeks instead of three.

In theory, this should be a boom time to enter nursing. The government has increased spending in the NHS, employing more nurses and paying them better. Students of all health-related courses can be reasonably confident they are heading into an industry that wants them badly.

But – and it is a big but to bear in mind – a quarter of student nurses drop out of training before they qualify, according to figures published in early 2006. Financial pressures, the burden of childcare, and bad experiences of ward rounds are thought to be the main reasons why students leave early. The government is attempting to deal with the financial pressures, offering bursaries for living costs, and tuition fees are now paid in full by the NHS.

The downside to the increase in places and applications to nursing is the pressure it puts on university departments. Students over the next few years may pay the price in crowded lecture theatres and inadequate supervision. Don't be afraid to ask awkward questions about how well staffed and equipped a department is.

Nurses do most of their training on placements in hospitals, so it is crucial to ask where the placements will be. Does the hospital have a good reputation and is it near enough to make the travel manageable? You may want to have a quick look around the university's hospital "partners" as well as the university itself.

You should also enquire whether the university is good at teaching the type of nursing you want to specialise in (such as children's nursing or mental health). Check also the way students are assessed. If you prefer continuous assessment to an exam-based system, choose universities taking that approach, and vice versa.

---

66 A nursing degree is extremely time-consuming – the combination of working shifts, writing assignments, and trying to fit in a social life can be difficult. However, all these aspects are outweighed by the rewarding nature of the work.

The parts of the course I have enjoyed most are the placements, as it is here that you learn the reality of nursing. The course is well structured, as it ensures you spend time in a variety of clinical situations.

Annie Lowe, *final-year adult health nursing student, Leeds Metropolitan University*

» Further information

Royal College of Nursing
20 Cavendish Square
London W1G 0RN
⤴ www.rcn.org.uk

Nursing and Midwifery Council
23 Portland Place
London W1B 1PZ
t 020 7637 7181
e advice@nmc-uk.org
⤴ www.nmc-uk.org

Health Professions Council
Park House
184 Kennington Park Road
London SE11 4BU
t 020 7582 0866
e info@hpc-uk.org
⤴ www.hpc-uk.org

⤴ Online reading

SocietyGuardian.co.uk www.SocietyGuardian.co.uk/health
Health Service Journal www.hsj.co.uk
Nursing Standard www.nursing-standard.co.uk
Nursing Times www.nursingtimes.net
Department of Health www.dh.gov.uk

Nursing and paramedical studies

		Guardian score	Satisfied with teaching %	Satisfied with assessment %	Spend per student score /10	Student:staff ratio	Job prospects %	Value added score /10	Average entry tariff
1	Edinburgh	100.0	98	77	10			8	414
2	St George's Medical School	80.5	91	57	10		88	3	300
3	UEA	76.4	90	43	8	12	92	7	325
4	Marjon (St Mark and St John)	75.5	87	32	3	10		10	322
5	Nottingham	74.4	86	46	7	15	96	8	340
6	Southampton	73.0	88	61	6	17	85	9	372
7	Leeds	71.9	77	62	10	16	97	2	323
8	Thames Valley	71.5	96	89	4	15	98	6	
9	Bradford	71.3	82	66	5	12	90	6	339
10	Kent	70.3	94	62	9	11		7	272
11	Bangor	68.1	88	72	5	13		7	247
11	Ulster	68.1	78	53	6	14	91	9	313
13	Glasgow	67.2	85	59	5	11			313
13	King's College London	67.2			7	15	98	5	300
15	Northampton	67.1	92	52	4	12	96	7	253
16	Cardiff	66.7	83	59	7	11	92	3	311
16	Queen's, Belfast	66.7	89	74	4	18	99	9	
18	Liverpool	65.7	81	51	8	12	93	2	316
19	Manchester	65.5			7	18	91	6	333
20	Sheffield Hallam	65.0	91	46	4	11	93	6	262
21	Swansea	63.9	78	59	8	12	94	6	251
22	Glasgow Caledonian	63.7	90	71	3	20	86	8	365
23	Surrey	63.2	90	55	6	21	100	6	337
24	Robert Gordon	63.1			4	17	92	8	304
25	Glamorgan	63.0	85	73	5	13	96	6	233
26	Derby	61.9			4	12	78	6	338
27	City	61.8	82	52	7	14	90	4	271
28	Essex	61.7			5	15		8	262
29	Birmingham	60.3	82	43	6	13	79	4	358
30	Staffordshire	60.1	78	62	6	14	95	8	210
31	Plymouth	59.9	85	52	8	20	85	9	262
32	Brighton	59.4	77	51	4	16	81	9	322
33	Salford	59.0	86	67	5	14	79	5	272
34	York	58.9			7	13		1	301
35	Dundee	58.3	81	56	4	19	99		325
36	Leeds Met	58.2	88	71	8	16	74	4	263
37	Oxford Brookes	57.9			4	15	87	4	294
38	Bedfordshire	57.5	94	66	5	21	91	8	229
39	Middlesex	56.2	80	53	8	11	85	3	195
40	Coventry	55.8			4	16	84	6	265
40	Queen Margaret	55.8			4	17	86	6	286
42	Manchester Met	55.7	71	60	3	18	94	5	324
43	Abertay Dundee	54.6			4	17	100		234
43	Edge Hill	54.6	92	66	4	17	83	7	232
45	UWE Bristol	54.5	83	60	4	14	92	3	253
46	Central Lancashire	54.4	80	66	4	21	89	7	301

	Guardian score	Satisfied with teaching %	Satisfied with assessment %	Spend per student score /10	Student:staff ratio	Job prospects %	Value added score /10	Average entry tariff
47 Brunel	53.8	73	54	4	18	76	9	320
48 Cumbria	53.4			4	19	88	4	316
49 Hertfordshire	52.5	77	48	5	14	87	5	244
50 Birmingham City	51.6	80	61	4	17	90	5	268
51 London South Bank	51.5	87	69	4	18	95	4	217
52 Hull	51.2			4	16	98	3	211
53 Huddersfield	51.0	78	66	4	16	73	6	267
54 North East Wales Institute	50.6	90	79	3	17	88	1	293
55 Teesside	50.0	87	78	3	19	83	4	280
56 Bournemouth	49.7	70	58	6	19	93	7	243
57 Anglia Ruskin	49.6	83	53	7	21	90	5	245
58 Chester	48.9	85	70	2	18	82	7	240
59 Northumbria	47.6	81	72	4	19	67	7	290
60 St Mary's UC, Twickenham	44.5	90	66	3	18	58		274
61 De Montfort	44.2	83	63	5	17	72	3	266
62 Liverpool John Moores	42.2	76	65	5	18	77	4	222
63 Canterbury Christ Church	42.1	79	46	5	17	86	2	228
64 Wolverhampton	41.1	77	56	4	16	75	3	197
65 York St John	40.7	85	70	3	19	61	6	254
66 Greenwich	37.6	88	70	4	19	63	3	223
66 Lincoln	37.6	80	62	3	18	56	7	224
66 Worcester	37.6			3	16	79	1	
69 Kingston	34.4	84	58	5	21	49	5	243
70 East London	28.8	83	58	6			1	167

Pharmacology and pharmacy

Lumping these two subjects together is a bit of a problem, as they're very different and, quite frankly, don't belong in the same chapter. But because of the way they are aggregated in university statistics, we can't do anything else. We can't separate them out in the tables (well, we could, and others do, but that wouldn't make any sense statistically speaking), so we've got to consider them together. But you don't have to. They are two different subjects and you should treat them as such.

Pharmacology

> Pharmacology is both exciting and challenging. There are few other subjects where you can appreciate the impact that it is making on medical advances, and the enormous benefits to human health and society. Pharmacology is a highly integrative biomedical science, requiring a wide understanding of chemistry, biochemistry, physiology, and genomics. In a nutshell, pharmacology is about understanding how drugs act on biological systems. It is also about using drugs as tools so that we can better understand how cellular systems of the body work.
>
> Pharmacologists are responsible for the discovery of the hundreds of compounds that are used today in the treatment of disease in both humans and animals. Around a quarter of the world's top medicines were discovered in the UK. These include, for example, new drugs for the treatment of asthma; the management of pain; antibacterial and anticancer drugs; and cardiovascular and neuropsychiatric disorders. As well as the discovery of wholly novel drugs, pharmacology has enabled the development of better drugs with far fewer side effects than were used before.
>
> Where is pharmacology going in the next decades, and where are the frontiers of knowledge? In the post-genomic era, the discipline has made extraordinary strides forward.
>
> Career opportunities for pharmacology graduates are vast: many are so enthused by the excitement of the subject, particularly if they have taken a programme with a sandwich year in industry, that they go on to carry out research for a PhD and ultimately join teams in the pharmaceutical industry or academia. Employment prospects for pharmacologists, within the big pharmaceutical companies and biotechnology enterprises, are excellent. The need by industry for pharmacologists goes far beyond laboratory-based research and development, and many may be found involved in clinical trials and drug safety; regulatory affairs; post-marketing drug surveillance; and sales and marketing.
>
> The study of pharmacology provides great opportunities for challenging and rewarding careers, and it is a particularly exciting time to be setting out on this path.
>
> **Peter Roberts**, *Professor of Pharmacology and Chairman of the Committee of Heads of Pharmacology Departments, University of Bristol*

Pharmacology is concerned with medicinal drugs: the ways they are administered, how the body distributes and eliminates them and their actual effects – it's where chemistry meets medicine. Pharmacologists study right down to single cell level and learn how cells combine in an organ such as the liver or kidney, and how disease changes the normal condition, plus the effect of drugs on those different conditions. For such a narrow discipline, it can touch on a remarkably wide variety of topics, including physiology, cell biology, bio-molecular chemistry, zoology, immunology, medicinal chemistry, and biochemistry.

As most drugs are used to treat or prevent disease, pharmacology has a close association with medicine and the pharmaceutical industry, which not only plays an important role in drug discovery and development, but is also a major contributor to the economy, both in the UK and worldwide.

The job prospects for graduates are good, with careers in postgraduate research, teaching, forensic science, health laboratories, or of course the pharmaceutical industry, where there are also non-lab-based jobs such as marketing, quality auditing or product registration.

More than 25 universities run a course in pharmacology, although some run it only in association with other courses. Some provide modules on pharmacology as part of other biological science degrees. You'll need at least two A-levels in the science subjects and a good science background at GCSE level. Most courses combine practical and tutorial sessions with a lecture programme.

---

66 I first came across the basic principles that lead to the understanding of pharmacology while studying biology at A-level. The subject is largely based around physiology, rather than chemistry, so a good grasp of how the body works at the molecular and cellular level is needed. When physiological systems go wrong, the really challenging part is discovering how exactly they went wrong and how to put it right. And it's great being kept up to date with the very latest research information.

Charlotte Mann, *third-year pharmacology student, King's College London*

Pharmacy

66 Pharmacy is an ideal career choice if you wish to combine a broad-based science degree and vocational training leading to flexible and well-remunerated career options. It is an exciting time to study pharmacy and enter a profession whose role as the experts in medicines is expanding as a result of new scientific advances and recent developments like pharmacist prescribing.

Undergraduate curricula integrate key areas of the physical and biological sciences to enable you to critically evaluate and problem-solve both scientific and professional issues, applying these to clinical practice. Subjects taught will include: pharmaceutical and medicinal chemistry, pharmaceutics (the formulation of active molecules into medicines that patients can take), pharmacology (the interaction of chemical substances with biological systems), molecular biology, leading to topics including stem-cell research, pharmacy law and ethics, and health policy. All MPharm courses include a supervised final-year research project. Placements and formal teaching are organised in both hospital and community pharmacies during the course, in preparation for your pre-registration year of 'on the job' training.

Career opportunities in pharmacy are increasing; pharmacists work in community pharmacies, on hospital wards, in GPs' surgeries, in NHS management, in industry, and in teaching and research at universities. If you are good at science and have sound communication skills then consider pharmacy as an excellent career option!

Dr Philip Rogers, *Director of Undergraduate Studies in the Department of Pharmacy & Pharmacology, University of Bath*

Pharmacy is seeing a healthy rise in applicants, partly because the unemployment levels for the industry are very low, but also because the perception of the role of the pharmacist is changing.

Whether it be in a community or hospital setting, the government is increasingly acknowledging that pharmacy is one of the primary health professions in the NHS, and that pharmacists are an integral part of most people's experience of NHS care.

Schools of pharmacy teach the study of medicinal substances and the application of their therapeutic uses in the practice of the profession.

The course is a broad-based four-year affair, leading to an MPharm degree, producing graduates for careers in community, hospital, and industry or research pharmacy.

All UK pharmacy degree courses are accredited by the Royal Pharmaceutical Society of Great Britain. In almost all cases, graduates follow their degree with a pre-registration year of professional training in community, hospital or industrial pharmacy before qualifying to join the society's register of professional pharmacists.

Teaching is by a combination of formal lectures and lab-based classes, which may be supplemented by computer-assisted learning, video demonstrations, and tutorials. You will be assessed by a combination of written examinations and coursework.

If you want to study pharmacy, you'll almost certainly need three A-levels, including chemistry, with two subjects from biology/human biology, maths, and physics. Work experience is also a big help, but if you lack the contacts to arrange this, get in touch with the pharmacy school yourself to see if they can help.

Check the learning and teaching facilities – the labs, the state of the medical library, and the IT facilities are all important to your everyday work, so you'll need to be happy with the availability and quality.

Check too the methods of teaching on the course you're considering. Many courses are moving away from the traditional lecture-based approach, and the balance between that and more modern methods (computer simulations, or video-based learning, for example) should also be a consideration. Assessment methods can also vary – it won't just be exams, and it'll pay to consider whether a high number of project-based assignments or dissertations are to your taste.

❝ Pharmacy was an ideal choice of degree course for me after completing science subjects at A-level. I have found the vocational course both challenging and enjoyable, and the blend of science and practice-based course material has prepared me well for my future career as a pharmacist. The excellent academic and research standards here combined with the friendly department atmosphere has provided a fantastic learning environment for me.

Catherine Golics, *final-year pharmacy student, Cardiff University*

》 Further information

British Pharmacological Society
16 Angel Gate, City Road
London EC1V 2SG

t 020 7417 0113
↗ www.bps.ac.uk   **》**

Pharmacology and pharmacy

		Guardian score	Satisfied with teaching %	Satisfied with assessment %	Spend per student score /10	Student:staff ratio	Job prospects %	Value added score /10	Average entry tariff
1	UCL	100.0	92	61	9	13		9	429
2	Leeds	89.6	94	70	8	11		7	380
3	Cardiff	89.0	87	49	9	16	99	6	403
4	Strathclyde	88.2	86	54	5	14	91	10	362
5	Nottingham	85.0	77	32	9	12	99	5	398
6	Queen's, Belfast	84.4	95	68	4	20	100	8	394
7	Liverpool	81.4	92	65	10		83	5	341
8	Bath	79.7	84	46	4	17	97	7	433
9	School of Pharmacy	78.2	84	48	5	18	100	6	381
10	Bristol	78.1	89	61	6	13		3	377
11	Dundee	76.6	86	56	3	8			374
12	Aston	75.6	78	49	4	14	100	5	387
13	UEA	73.1	93	67	7	20		4	346
14	Southampton	70.3	93	59	5	21			365
15	Robert Gordon	70.1			3	20	100		383
16	Newcastle	69.7	83	45	7	15		4	
17	Manchester	67.8	78	50		22	96	5	425
18	Sunderland	66.8	86	65	3	15	92	8	307
19	Hertfordshire	65.1	95	68	6			4	274
20	Brighton	59.0	76	31	4	18	100	4	337
21	King's College London	58.9	83	41	4	17	93	4	369
22	De Montfort	54.3	88	70	3	14	90	4	278
23	Greenwich	50.7	86	69	8	22			248
24	Bradford	49.4	77	61	4	19	93	3	312
25	Liverpool John Moores	43.6	82	39	2	28	99	7	317
26	Kingston	36.0	84	54	3	21		4	240
27	Portsmouth	35.2	86	47	3	20	95	1	269

Psychology

❝ There is nothing as fascinating as people. So what could be more enjoyable than spending three years studying them? The differences between people give the world its character, its complexity, as well as its problems. All the problems — and the solutions — to world issues have a psychological foundation because people are at the core of them. That explains the enduring fascination — and usefulness — of studying psychology. Psychologists cut through common sense to take an objective and scientific look at the myriad of human behaviours. From precise brain mechanisms to the broadest patterns of social behaviour, no other subject offers such breadth and diversity.

A psychology graduate will know how to ask the right questions. They'll be skilled at knowing the best way to investigate issues. They'll have the critical thinking skills and methods to quantify and test ideas. Plus, they'll be able to communicate the answers in the most effective manner. With a broad knowledge of animal and human behaviour and thinking, psychologists can understand why things go wrong, what makes people ill, behave in unexpected ways, or contribute to problems in society.

A psychology degree is the first step to becoming a practising psychologist. Graduates can go on to help people make changes for the better in clinical, occupational, sports, forensic, educational, health, environmental, and counselling settings. But because psychology is about understanding human thinking, performance, and behaviour, it's a degree that is valuable in any future career.

Professor Ben Fletcher, *Head of School of Psychology, University of Hertfordshire*

Tell someone you do psychology, and people tend to get a bit twitchy, worrying that you're going to psychoanalyse them and reveal the hidden horrors of their twisted minds. Luckily for them, it's not quite like that.

These days, you're less likely to dabble with Freud than with the everyday workings of the human mind, both normal and abnormal, calculating why people think as they do.

Psychology is a relatively young scientific discipline, and is fairly flexible in its approach. Those who study it don't necessarily need science A-levels (but it certainly helps), and you don't necessarily need psychology A-level either. It is possible to find a university to take you if you have an arts background, although a mixture of both art and science is best, and most will require at least a good GCSE maths pass or equivalent.

Once you're in, you'll be studying subject areas such as personality types (introvert/extrovert, that sort of thing), defining and testing intelligence (and working out whether that's a valid thing to do in the first place), perception, memory, and developmental psychology. Slightly more left-field options could include environmental, consumer, or paranormal psychology. Across all areas, much of the experimental work is computer-controlled so there are plenty of opportunities for computer fiends to develop their skills.

Courses are usually modular with a wide-ranging, scene-setting first year, before settling down to some serious choice in the following years. Most courses are accredited by the British Psychological Society; you'll have the possibility to take further training to become a professional psychologist if you complete an accredited course. You'll be assessed through a mixture of exams and coursework.

The employment rates for graduates are high. You've gained some excellent experience in problem-solving, so if you don't opt to move on to further clinical or forensic psychology, you can head for educational, health or occupational psychology, counselling or neuropsychology – perfect for the physicists amongst you with all that complex technical equipment (MRIs and MEGs). Alternatively you could find work in advertising, marketing or social work, or perhaps the probation and prison services.

When deciding on a course, investigate the modular options that open up in the second and third years. If you know you want to do face perception, visual processing or memory, then make sure they're on offer and try to find out if the tutors specialise in those areas.

Students are often taken by surprise when they realise the scientific nature of the subject. All psychology degrees involve training in statistics, and all require the writing of essays, dissertations, and projects, so ensure that these appeal.

---

66 The course here has really suited me, as the teaching is of an extremely high quality, and the department has very good facilities, as it's a working research department. Most of the lectures are given by staff at the cutting edge of new and exciting psychological research. I have found the course to be exciting, challenging, and thought-provoking and it has really helped me develop my own ideas and enabled me to do some exciting psychological research.

Rosa Hunn, *second-year psychology student, Goldsmiths*

» Further information

British Psychological Society
St Andrews House   t   0116 254 9568
48 Princess Road East   ↗   www.bps.org.uk
Leicester LE1 7DR

↗ Online reading
Association for Humanistic Psychology www.ahpweb.org
Experimental Psychological Society www.eps.ac.uk
Psychweb www.psywww.com
American Psychological Association www.apa.org
Encyclopedia of Psychology www.psychology.org

Psychology

		Guardian score	Satisfied with teaching %	Satisfied with assessment %	Spend per student score /10	Student:staff ratio	Job prospects %	Value added score /10	Average entry tariff
1	Oxford	100.0	96	68	10	15	70	8	498
2	UCL	85.1	79	67	10	11	58	9	474
3	St Andrews	83.4	93	68	9	13	60	8	428
4	Exeter	81.3	93	64	9	14	64	8	411
5	Glasgow	80.9	88	53	8	15	77	9	382
6	York	80.1	91	57	9	13	63	6	462
7	Bristol	77.2	86	47	7	14	70	8	426

		Guardian score	Satisfied with teaching %	Satisfied with assessment %	Spend per student score /10	Student:staff ratio	Job prospects %	Value added score /10	Average entry tariff
8	Kent	75.1	89	68	6	15	69	9	355
9	Bath	74.2	84	50	7	16	73	7	436
10	Birmingham	73.7	88	45	10	15	54	6	412
11	Nottingham	72.5	87	37	10	15	53	7	428
12	Warwick	72.4	77	42	9	13	65	6	419
13	Southampton	70.7	92	60	7	16	56	7	408
13	Surrey	70.7	85	50	8	15	53	9	382
15	Stirling	70.2			6	12	57	9	287
16	Cardiff	69.9	86	63	8	17	51	6	425
17	Sheffield	69.2	88	55	6	15	62	4	430
18	Heriot-Watt	68.4	87	59	6	10			276
18	Leicester	68.4	80	51	8	16	61	7	370
20	Manchester	68.0	82	45	9	14	48	7	408
21	Loughborough	67.7	88	70	5	24	57	8	399
22	Aberdeen	67.0	87	69	5	18	66		295
23	Lancaster	66.9	90	61	6	17	55	4	394
24	Leeds	66.6	88	50	8	20	52	7	423
25	Bournemouth	66.5			8	13	50	8	240
25	Nottingham Trent	66.5	82	53	6	13	60	7	293
27	Reading	66.1	86	51	5	13	51	7	384
28	Edinburgh	66.0	82	43	7	15	42	8	426
29	Royal Holloway	65.8	83	43	6	13	44	8	376
30	Hull	65.2	86	62	3	20	73	7	318
31	Liverpool	65.1	86	60	6	16	53	7	378
32	Portsmouth	64.7	86	52	4	18	65	8	320
33	Goldsmiths	64.5	80	63	4	12	52	8	302
34	Sussex	63.8	87	54	4	16	52	6	391
35	Essex	63.3	76	62	5	16	63	7	330
36	Queen's, Belfast	63.2	89	40	8	19	38	9	360
37	Napier	63.1			4	15	58	6	
38	Plymouth	62.9	87	52	9	17	31	9	297
39	Newman University College	62.8	90	79	3	20			234
40	Durham	61.6	84	44	5	19	45	7	416
41	City	60.8	87	62	4	20	55	5	347
42	Middlesex	60.6	79	61	9	20	67	4	186
43	Brunel	60.4	76	68	3	20	58	9	318
44	Strathclyde	60.0	81	54	5	17	58	6	
45	Bangor	59.6	87	44	8	20	57	3	309
45	Newcastle	59.6	81	38	6	24	60	6	409
47	Teesside	59.2	86	77	5	16	43	6	253
48	Westminster	59.0	82	56	3	18	42	10	315
49	Canterbury Christ Church	58.6	84	60	10	11	51	1	241
50	Coventry	58.5	82	71	6	19	54	5	279
51	Northumbria	58.1	84	49	4	18	62	5	325
52	UWE Bristol	57.3	91	73	4	26	36	9	281
53	Anglia Ruskin	55.9	88	57	8	21	35	6	269

	Guardian score	Satisfied with teaching %	Satisfied with assessment %	Spend per student score /10	Student:staff ratio	Job prospects %	Value added score /10	Average entry tariff
54 Edge Hill	55.7	86	62	3	14	34	7	261
55 Hertfordshire	55.6	82	57	3	15	51	5	289
56 Aston	55.1	81	46	3	19	53	4	360
56 Worcester	55.1	85	71	4	17	38	7	242
58 Glasgow Caledonian	55.0	85	61	4	16	30	7	349
59 Gloucestershire	54.8	90	68	4	20	40	5	277
60 Northampton	54.7	87	64	3	13	42	4	239
61 Staffordshire	54.0	84	64	6	17	39	5	258
62 Thames Valley	53.7	86	78	4	23		3	176
63 Dundee	52.6	88	59	3	21	45	3	344
64 Oxford Brookes	52.5	83	52	4	16	35	4	339
65 Bedfordshire	51.9	84	68	3	25	50	6	211
66 Central Lancashire	51.7	83	65	6	23	55	2	298
67 East London	51.4	81	62	6	17	52	2	181
68 Chester	51.1	90	65	3	21	45	4	272
68 St Mary's UC, Twickenham	51.1	84	73	3	20			233
70 Bath Spa	51.0	89	76		25	45	6	258
71 Wolverhampton	50.6	72	53	7	16	54	2	247
72 Queen Margaret	50.2			3	20	40		250
73 Sunderland	49.0	77	64	4	18	44	3	258
74 Swansea	48.7	84	54	4	27	43	5	333
75 Ulster	48.1	84	54	5	21	20	7	275
76 Huddersfield	47.8	80	68	4	21	30	6	265
77 Abertay Dundee	47.7			5	21	38	5	222
78 Kingston	47.2	81	48	3	18	44	2	251
79 Roehampton	47.0	79	47	6	25	43	6	217
79 Leeds Trinity & All Saints	47.0	82	55	2	23	43	4	310
81 Southampton Solent	46.9	71	54	4	19	43	4	241
82 Liverpool John Moores	46.7	75	62	3	22	46	4	274
83 Bucks New University	46.3	82	57	4	22	36	8	206
84 Manchester Met	45.6	76	51	3	19	33	4	306
84 Winchester	45.6	85	65	2	17	38	1	276
86 Derby	45.5	89	59	3	23	34	3	260
87 Sheffield Hallam	45.1	80	59	4	27	38	4	299
88 York St John	44.6	75	62	2	17	51	1	261
89 Glamorgan	44.4	86	54	3	18	43	2	224
90 Salford	44.3	76	51	4	30	37	7	302
91 Bradford	44.1	85	61	3	38			228
92 Greenwich	43.8	76	59	5	19	48	1	211
92 Lincoln	43.8	80	60	3	25	36	3	300
94 De Montfort	39.8	77	64	3	22	41	1	244
95 London South Bank	39.2	76	53	3	26	46	2	221
96 Leeds Met	36.5	67	46	3	36	43	6	305
97 Bolton	29.3	69	50	2	29	21	3	230

Sports and exercise science

❝ Throughout history and across cultures, sport and human performance has always held an important position in society. Through studying a sports and exercise science degree you not only learn about the function and limitations of the human body but also about how sport and exercise influence both personal and societal health and wellbeing. You will get to study physiology, psychology, biomechanics, health, and nutrition as well as sociology of sport. Alongside these you will also gain practical experience in not just playing sports but also how to coach, manage, and develop your own, and others', sporting potential.

From a purely pragmatic viewpoint, the degree leads to a greater understanding of the multi-billion pound industries that surround sport, exercise, and health and gives you the background for employment within them. This multi-disciplinary course with both its theoretical and applied aspects, and the fact that employers universally understand what sport and exercise is, also opens up a wealth of job opportunities where employers are looking for well-rounded graduates.

However, sports and exercise science offers more than this as it allows you to investigate what makes us strive to be the best, to push ourselves to the limits, and what those limits are and why. It also allows you to understand why we watch others push themselves, why we have the joy and excitement of shared experiences with thousands of others when our team wins, and why, as a society and as individuals, we invest so much of our recreational time into sport and exercise. The study of sports and exercise science can lead not only to a rewarding career but also gives a window into what it is to be human.

Dr Matt Pain, *Senior Lecturer, School of Sport and Exercise Sciences, Loughborough University*

First thing out of the way – you don't have to be good at sports to do this course. However, it helps and if you aren't a natural athlete you do, at least, need to be interested in sport. You should also be careful which sport and exercise course you select as some require participation in a range of sports while others are more theory-based.

Sports science degrees – those concerned with the science of exercise, health, and sport – have blossomed, with the use of increasingly sophisticated techniques to improve performance and training in the sporting world. For further proof of this booming world, just look at the size of the growth of specialists in professional sport – from peripheral vision experts in football to bio-mechanical bowling coaches in cricket.

Sports science courses are, first and foremost, academic programmes of study and are very strongly science-based. The degree courses involve the application of scientific principles through three major areas – biomechanics, physiology, psychology, or an interdisciplinary combination. You will learn how the body responds and adapts to exercise, how and why different energy systems are deployed at different exercise intensities, how the principles of mechanics determine both the flight of a javelin and the gyrations of a gymnast, and how mind and body interact to influence performance.

The other branch of the industry – exercise science – has a central role in physical activity programmes aimed at improving general health, and how sport and exercise fit into the context of the society in which we live. The very fact that the NHS is now keen on physical activity as a form of preventative care means that there is increasing scope in work opportunities for exercise scientists in clinical settings – hospitals, nursing homes, and the like.

The tendency for sports science students is to head for specialisation through module choice or projects. After that, graduates have various career paths. Some head for teaching and research, while others apply their knowledge through related areas such as coaching and sports management. One of the problems with sport scientists is that graduates enter sports-related jobs at quite a low level – jobs such as personal instructor, fitness trainer, and leisure services manager: ones that can be done without a degree. The key to success with a sports-related career is much longer term, so you may need to keep your eye more on the horizon than on the nearest landmark.

There are basically three types of sports and exercise courses. Those with an emphasis on sport, those that focus on science and those that give equal priority to both. Check that the emphasis is in an area that suits you. Similarly, the more broadly based courses that try to cover all options may lack the depth you want in certain areas.

Look, too, at the departments around sports science. Such a multidisciplinary course brings in a lot from other areas, so see how strong the institution is in biochemistry, physiology, and so on, since those departments will feed into the teaching on your course.

The facilities – both sporting and scientific – are obviously essential. A university with good sporting and clinical facilities is a must for sports science. Sporting arenas and facilities get tatty pretty quickly, so see how well it has been maintained: it's an issue of constant investment and that also gives an idea as to how highly they value the course.

---

66 Applied sports science was a subject that was not available at my school, so coming to study the subject at university was a new and exciting prospect. I've found the degree very challenging – helping to develop a deeper understanding of sport and the science that underpins human sports performance. The highlight of the course has been the regular practical sessions where knowledge from the lectures is put into relevant practical situations.

Andrew King, *fourth-year applied sports science student, University of Edinburgh*

❯❯ Further information

British Association of Sports and Exercise Sciences
Leeds Metropolitan University
Carnegie Faculty of Sport and Education
Fairfax Hall, Headingley Campus
Beckett Park, Leeds LS6 3QS

t 0113 283 6162
↗ www.bases.org.uk

British Association of Sport and Exercise Medicine
Central Office, 15 Hawthorne Avenue
Norton, Doncaster DN6 9HR

e basemcentral@basem.co.uk
↗ www.basem.co.uk

National Sports Medicine Institute
32 Devonshire Street
London W1G 6PX

t 020 7251 0583
e enquiry@nsmi.org.uk

The Centre for Sport and Exercise Science
Sheffield Hallam University
Collegiate Campus
Sheffield S10 2BP

t 0114 225 2544
e cses@shu.ac.uk
↗ www.shu.ac.uk/cses

Sports science

		Guardian score	Satisfied with teaching %	Satisfied with assessment %	Spend per student score /10	Student:staff ratio	Job prospects %	Value added score /10	Average entry tariff
1	Bath	100.0	77	52	10	22	54	10	405
2	Loughborough	98.3	94	71	7	17	63	8	411
3	Exeter	95.7	99	90	5	21	57	10	355
4	Bournemouth	91.8				13	83	8	275
5	Essex	88.5	94	61	8	17	68	7	305
6	Birmingham	88.4	89	57	9	21	56	8	377
7	Edinburgh	87.7	88	42	10	17		8	363
8	Heriot-Watt	87.1	87	59	10	8			206
9	Ulster	85.2	89	73	5	22	65	9	333
10	Bangor	83.0	94	81	8	20	68	6	245
11	Kingston	79.8	70	57	10	15			196
12	Durham	77.7	86	48	4	17	66	5	362
13	Newman University College	77.2	88	81	3	20		9	214
14	Bedfordshire	76.7	88	69	5	16	67	8	206
15	Brunel	75.8	80	55	6	15	60	5	316
16	Nottingham Trent	75.1	85	57	6	18	61	7	259
17	Chester	74.4			6	16	61	3	255
17	Portsmouth	74.4	99	80	5	23	52	8	244
19	Leeds	73.0	78	47	8	35	62	9	347
20	Sunderland	71.2	85	69	7	15	48	8	210
21	Brighton	69.2	85	62	5	21	58	5	299
22	Napier	68.2			7	27	73	6	213
23	Sheffield Hallam	66.5	85	60	5	23	52	7	293
24	Aberystwyth	66.4	97	83	6	23	47	4	258
25	Staffordshire	66.0	93	79	7	19	47	6	195
26	Southampton	65.6	90	55	3	24	60	4	334
27	Swansea	64.9	90	73	5	23	56	6	252
28	Manchester Met	64.6	84	68	5	14	56	3	233
29	Stirling	64.5			3	28	65	8	274
30	Plymouth	64.3	71	50	9	20	34	8	281
31	Worcester	62.4	89	64	5	19	52	5	226
32	Hull	61.8	86	62	4	24	68	3	245
33	Teesside	61.7	90	72	4	23	40	8	245
34	Liverpool John Moores	61.5	84	62	3	31	59	9	273
35	UWIC	60.9	81	54	4	23	55	7	269
36	Leeds Met	60.3	70	54	6	30	59	8	287

	Guardian score	Satisfied with teaching %	Satisfied with assessment %	Spend per student score /10	Student-staff ratio	Job prospects %	Value added score /10	Average entry tariff
37 Greenwich	60.0	74	61	7	24	70	4	190
38 Coventry	59.9	83	71	4	22	59	4	249
39 Leeds Trinity & All Saints	58.3	90	64	2	23	59	4	269
40 Kent	57.3	90	87	4	17		2	182
41 Roehampton	57.2	80	57	6	20	59	3	198
42 North East Wales Institute	57.0	83	69	6	14	34	7	162
43 East London	56.9	83	60	7	21			160
44 Northumbria	56.6	85	49	4	22		4	285
45 Northampton	56.3	83	75	3	22	47	8	193
46 St Mary's UC, Twickenham	55.9	85	73	3	24	52	7	212
47 Chichester	55.7	93	80	3	26	52	4	229
48 Middlesex	53.9	81	58	7	28		4	209
49 Southampton Solent	53.1	64	54	4	11			191
50 Cumbria	51.2	69	46	7	27	67	1	251
51 Hertfordshire	50.7	85	52	4	22	38	4	280
52 Newport	50.2	85	70	3		57		168
52 Winchester	50.2	84	58	2	23	58	4	221
54 Canterbury Christ Church	46.0	87	58	3	23	57	2	195
55 Gloucestershire	45.3	76	57	7	30	42	4	241
56 York St John	44.9	86	64	4	30	52	2	235
57 Lincoln	41.5	86	66	3		40	3	210
58 Edge Hill	41.1	83	63	3	25	41	2	229
59 Derby	35.3	57	41	6	20	35	2	218
60 Bucks New University	34.8	68	58	3	24	55	2	161
61 Wolverhampton	33.2	76	60	3	32	52	2	177
62 Marjon (St Mark and St John)	32.2	83	68	2	32	38	3	193

Veterinary science

❝ Veterinary science is a challenging programme, be in no doubt, but the rewards of a degree in the subject more than repay the effort. Not only does it equip graduates to enter veterinary practice in all its varied forms, it also provides a fantastic applied biology degree. So for those with a passion for all things biological it provides the opportunity to indulge those passions within a secure career framework. Most graduates enter general practice, which can involve work with any species in any country of the world. But there are also opportunities to contribute to human society and animal welfare in other more fundamental ways, such as the control of international disease threats, research into new vaccines and treatments, and in the safeguarding of public health. With a rapidly growing world population demanding more food, with the increasing infectious disease threats posed by climate change and instant travel, and the need for the humane and sustainable production of wholesome food in a volatile world, veterinary graduates are well placed to help address these global challenges to human society.

Professor Sandy Trees, *Dean of Veterinary Science, University of Liverpool*

Veterinary science is the diagnosis and treatment of disease and injury in animals. In addition to veterinary medicine – which we're mostly concerned with here – it also includes dentistry and pre-clinical veterinary medicine. Though getting a place on a veterinary degree course is not easy, competition is not as fierce as you might expect. Naturally, the quality of applicants each year is high, so a strong academic background is essential if you want to apply, but you also need to convince the admissions tutors that you want to be a vet, so make sure you can demonstrate a significant level of commitment to the cause (such as relevant work experience), as well as evidence of a robust, well-rounded personality. While job prospects for graduates from all the veterinary schools are strong, the working life of a vet can be very stressful indeed and you need to able to cope with it.

For most students, a veterinary degree is preparation for an attractive (and sometimes lucrative) career in private practice, but the broad, scientifically based curriculum provides an outstanding background for a wide range of careers in biological and medical fields, in research and in agricultural and food policy roles nationally.

At a time when there is increasing concern about the health and welfare of farm and companion animals, all the schools are giving a higher profile to public health issues, such as BSE, foot-and-mouth disease and avian flu.

A lecture-free final year is common, allowing greater scope for wider study and clinical experience, and more time for teamwork and problem-based learning.

If you plan to study veterinary medicine at Cambridge or the Royal Veterinary College then you face the joys of the BioMedical Admission Test (Bmat), which is aimed at testing students' thinking skills as opposed to subject knowledge and to help universities choose between many high-calibre candidates. The deadline for registering for a Bmat is usually just before the deadline for applying to courses – which, for veterinary sciences is October 15 – but check on www.bmat.org.uk for exact details.

Ucas insists that prospective students include only four veterinary courses among the five choices on their form, in order to give you a safety net if you fail to gain a place.

A few of the universities offering the vet degree are recognised by foreign veterinary associations, such as the American Veterinary Medical Association (AVMA). This means that graduates from those schools can more easily practise abroad. If working overseas is part of your long-term plan, then include this in your criteria for picking a school.

There have been spectacular investments in some veterinary schools recently, so check the facilities, and see if they tally with your own interests, whether it be a new equine centre, new laboratory facilities or a clinical skills centre.

Find out what the student:staff ratios mean at each university. Veterinary faculties often draw staff from other departments to teach on the vet course, particularly in pre-clinical subjects and this can account for apparent variations in staff:student ratios.

❝ The transition from A-level to university for a vet student is quite a shock! I achieved good science A-levels, but nothing can prepare you for the sheer volume of information thrown at you every day of your degree. Thankfully, you quickly learn to adapt to what is required, and before long I was enjoying the demands of my new subjects. It is challenging keeping on top of the work, but time spent doing sport or socialising with friends completes the university experience.

Ben Hanning, *second-year veterinary medicine student, Magdalene College, University of Cambridge*

❱❱ Further information

Royal College of Veterinary Surgeons
Belgravia House
62-4 Horseferry Road
London SW1P 2AF

t 020 7222 2001
e admin@rcvs.org.uk
↗ www.rcvs.org.uk

The British Veterinary Association
7 Mansfield Street
London W1G 9NQ

t 020 7636 6541
e bvahq@bva.co.uk
↗ www.bva.co.uk

Society of Practising Veterinary Surgeons
The Governor's House
Cape Road, Warwick
Warwickshire CV34 5DL

t 01926 410454
e office@spvs.org.uk
↗ www.spvs.org.uk

British Equine Veterinary Association
Mulberry House, 31 Market Street
Fordham, Ely
Cambridgeshire CB7 5LQ

t 01638 723 555
e info@beva.org.uk
↗ www.beva.org.uk

British Small Animals Veterinary Association
Woodrow House, 1 Telford Way
Waterwells Business Park
Quedgeley, Gloucester GL2 2AB

t 01452 726700
↗ www.bsava.com

↗ Online reading

Vetweb www.vetweb.co.uk
European Association of Establishments for Veterinary Education www.eaeve.org
Federation of Veterinarians of Europe www.fve.org

Veterinary science

		Guardian score	Satisfied with teaching %	Satisfied with assessment %	Spend per student score /10	Student:staff ratio	Job prospects %	Value added score /10	Average entry tariff
1	Cambridge	100.0			6	4	95		535
2	Edinburgh	86.2	90	32	9	8	96		478
3	Liverpool	73.8	92	42	3	7	100		459
4	Glasgow	68.0	88	46	4	8	97		454
5	Royal Veterinary College	59.6	82	29	8	11	99		444
6	Bristol	34.7	85	32	3	15	86		434

Modern languages

" After almost 20 years teaching languages here I think I could summarise my students' views as, 'Yes, it can be tough learning a foreign language, but the rewards are amazing.'

Apart from developing excellent communication and interpersonal skills, students gain maturity and self-reliance during placements spent abroad, as well as the sheer thrill and excitement of actually being able to talk to someone from another culture in their own language. Then there is the pride they feel when they can act as an interpreter, switching from one language to another to order a meal or buy some train tickets. Students have told me that the recognition and respect this gives them more than justifies the hard work they put in to learning the language.

It is often only once students graduate and start a job that they realise that the wide range of academic and personal skills they have acquired gives them far more opportunities for exciting and rewarding careers than people who have not studied a language. Prospective employers not only recognise the value of employing a linguist who can take their business into new markets and deal confidently with overseas clients and suppliers, they also acknowledge the additional maturity and perspective that our language graduates have from their period abroad and the cultural issues they have dealt with.

Most of the rest of the world may want to learn English but this only increases the effect it has on any foreigner when an English person greets them and chats to them in their own language. Lifelong friendships have been forged just as a result of a few words exchanged in an airport lounge between someone returning to Spain or Japan and one of our students, who has ventured to communicate with them in their own language.

I think I agree with my students — yes it can be tough, but the rewards are amazing.

Graham Webb, *Principal Lecturer in Languages, Leeds Metropolitan University*

Modern languages is about a whole lot more than learning to order a coffee on holiday – you'll gain an intimate knowledge of another country's literature, culture, history, politics, and people.

As well as the obvious choices – French, German, Italian – you can learn Latin American or Middle Eastern languages, or Serbian and Croatian, or Japanese or Mandarin. The possibilities are as wide as the globe, but whatever you choose, an affection for the country or region linked to your language is rather important.

Most prospective applicants will already be studying a language at A-level, though it is not always necessary to be studying the one you take to degree level, especially for less mainstream languages. Generally speaking, this is a very good time to be aspiring to study languages at university. The number of applicants to language courses has been falling steadily over recent years. Although this is very worrying for universities, it is good news for you if you fail to get the grades they were asking for. You may be able to negotiate your way on to the course, or go elsewhere through Clearing.

Once there, you can study a single language or opt for joint honours in two languages; a few places will let you take three. Alternatively, you can combine a language with almost any other subject imaginable: French with music, Spanish with molecular biology, and so on. Most UK universities offer courses in French, German, and Spanish. For less common languages, such as Dutch, Danish, and modern Greek, your choice of institution will be more limited.

Integrated studies, in which the study of a language is one component of, say, a science or technology degree, are also increasingly available. This might well involve you spending a year in France studying, for example, engineering – but in French.

A modern languages degree makes you eminently employable and not just as a teacher or a translator, so don't feel you need to combine a language with a vocational subject merely to improve your job prospects. More than 50 per cent of jobs are open to graduates from any discipline and modern languages graduates have lower rates of unemployment than almost all others. You'll emerge at the end of your degree with highly developed linguistic, analytical, and communication skills – helped greatly by your year abroad.

Before you pick a course, decide what you are hoping to learn. Do you want a literature-based course? If your main interest is in Italian art or Russian politics, does the course cater for this? How much emphasis is given to acquiring language skills? How much of the course is taught in the language? If you are applying for joint honours, can you vary the mix? Are the two timetables really compatible? How is the course taught – is the emphasis on lectures, tutorials or seminars? Will you have to write a dissertation? Read the prospectus and speak to undergraduates to make sure you know exactly what is on offer.

Most places offer a year abroad, so give careful consideration to this. Here are a few questions you'll want to ask: how much help will the university give you with planning your year? Will you be required to produce a dissertation while you are away? Will you be working or studying? Many UK universities have formal exchange links with universities abroad – find out if yours does. Joint language honours applicants should find out if they will be able to split the year between the two countries. Many students spend the year as English language assistants in schools abroad in a scheme organised by the British Council (full details at www.britishcouncil.org/education).

But four years of study might strike you as rather expensive, so bear in mind the (admittedly few) universities, mainly new ones, that have introduced three-year language-related degrees in a bid to address the problem of student debt, and which may involve spending only one term abroad.

---

66 At university you can study independently and choose your own methods for learning, including watching films. I do classes flexible to my needs, with others of similar ability and experience, and there is a wide range of cultural options to choose from. My biggest challenge was my year abroad in South America, which turned out to be the best year of my life. It gave me the opportunity to experience a completely new and amazing culture in one of the most diverse and beautiful parts of the world.

Alexander Crook, *fourth-year French and Spanish student, University of Southampton*

↗ Online reading

European Centre for Modern Languages www.ecml.at
University Council of Modern Languages www.ucml.org.uk
Your dictionary www.yourdictionary.com
The web journal of modern language linguistics wjmll.ncl.ac.uk
British Association for Applied Linguistics www.baal.org.uk

Modern languages

		Guardian score	Satisfied with teaching %	Satisfied with assessment %	Spend per student score /10	Student:staff ratio	Job prospects %	Value added score /10	Average entry tariff
1	Oxford	100.0	90	73	10	10	72	8	498
2	Cambridge	96.8	95	86	8	11	79	7	511
3	Southampton	77.5	95	66	9	10	61	8	383
4	St Andrews	76.7	92	82	4	12	64	9	445
5	Bath	76.4	89	67	7	16	74	8	411
6	Soas	74.5	86	59	6	10	68	10	362
6	UCL	74.5	86	62	9	11	62	7	432
8	Warwick	73.6	93	71	7	22	73	8	438
9	Queen Mary	70.0	91	70	9	10	61	6	338
10	Birmingham	68.0	93	68	7	13	65	5	385
11	Cardiff	67.9	88	60	10		54	4	378
12	Nottingham	67.7	90	59	7	11	65	6	387
13	Aston	67.4	90	67	4	14	73	7	346
14	Edinburgh	66.2	80	49	7	16	72	6	438
15	King's College London	66.1	89	56	8	13	61	7	397
16	Queen's, Belfast	65.6	85	58	7	9	70	5	369
17	Bristol	65.4	92	63	7	22	72	6	415
18	Lancaster	64.7	88	62	8	9	58	5	366
19	Leeds	63.8	88	65	9	13	59	4	390
20	Heriot-Watt	63.6	98	79	9	11			367
21	Exeter	63.1	88	71	4	17	67	6	411
22	Durham	62.9	90	56	3	15	68	4	469
23	Sheffield	62.6	91	69	4	13	60	7	406
24	Surrey	62.1	78	48	7	9	59	4	359
25	Kent	60.9	94	70	4	14	59	9	301
26	Sussex	59.3	85	55	3	9	49	9	397
27	Leicester	59.0	93	84	7	15	57	3	335
28	Royal Holloway	58.7	92	77	3	13	65	3	369
29	Liverpool	58.2	88	63	6	13	66	4	346
30	Glasgow	57.7	93	61	3	13	54	7	400
31	Strathclyde	57.3	86	68	7	14	65	4	304
32	Essex	57.1	84	63	3	13		7	304
33	Coventry	56.8	92	81	5	16			259
34	York St John	56.1	94	76	2			10	288
35	Hull	54.5	94	75		23	65	8	296
36	Nottingham Trent	53.0	79	68	6	9	67	4	238

		Guardian score	Satisfied with teaching %	Satisfied with assessment %	Spend per student score /10	Student:staff ratio	Job prospects %	Value added score /10	Average entry tariff
37	Swansea	52.6	86	68	3	13	65	4	287
38	Manchester	52.1	82	50		15	50	7	407
39	Anglia Ruskin	49.3	80	62	4	10		2	319
40	Westminster	48.6	74	63	5	11		7	236
41	Portsmouth	48.4	90	73	5	13	59	3	254
42	Reading	47.9	83	64	3	14	58	5	323
43	UEA	47.3	81	65	3		61	6	343
44	Salford	46.1	78	61	8	11	49	2	320
45	Newcastle	45.5	78	56	4	19	56	3	425
46	Brighton	45.2	69	67	4	17	52	9	290
47	Northumbria	44.3	80	62	3	23	69	5	296
48	Aberystwyth	42.4	89	78	3	32		3	298
49	Bangor	41.0	83	54	3	20	62	4	292
49	Ulster	41.0	67	56	7			3	281
51	Leeds Met	40.7	85	63	5	33			274
52	Oxford Brookes	38.6	74	64	4	17	48	4	312
53	Middlesex	36.3	75	63	4	26		7	226
54	Manchester Met	33.7	89	63	3	11		1	261
55	Greenwich	32.9	72	53	2	18		7	208
56	Liverpool John Moores	32.8	67	57	4	11	57	1	223
57	UWE Bristol	32.4	84	67	3	18	43	4	267
58	Roehampton	29.1	71	54	3	29			217
59	Sheffield Hallam	28.4	70	65	5	30			264

Physical sciences

Agriculture and forestry

> Agriculture is the study of how we make the best use of land and other resources to produce crops and animals. It is an exciting time to take a degree in the subject: growing demand for food and biofuels, together with concerns about how agriculture interacts with the environment, have renewed our interest in the problem of how to manage land effectively and sustainably. An agriculture degree gives you knowledge of these exciting areas and equips you for a range of professional careers.
>
> One of the best things about the subject is its breadth. You learn about how crops respond to their environment and how to manage the crop between sowing and harvest to get the best yields. You learn how animals grow, how growth relates to nutrition and about different systems for producing livestock and livestock products. Agriculture is also a great subject to take at a higher level because it is linked to so many other interesting areas of study. It is one of the few degrees that combines science and business management teaching: you learn how to market your produce, draw up business plans and make effective decisions about labour and machinery. You are out in the field, visiting farms, making presentations to business leaders — as well as learning about soils, crop and animal production, business management, and IT.
>
> Agriculture has strong links to the environment. Producing food (and fuel) for a developing world, within environmental limits, is an important and fascinating challenge. An agriculture degree will develop your ability to meet this challenge — and you don't have to come from a farm to apply!
>
> **Dr Stephen Ramsden**, *Associate Professor, Management Division of Agricultural and Environmental sciences, University of Nottingham*

The public perception of agricultural courses is that they are finishing schools for ruddy-faced toffs before they drive off in the Range Rover to manage the family estate. Some places may still be like that, but the subject now involves the increasingly complex scientific issues that characterise modern farming and forestry: from genetically modified produce and the use of pesticides to conservation issues and environmental science.

Quality of life, conservation, and "alternatives" such as organic farming are now serious issues for what might be termed rural degrees. Food production may play only a small part, compared with issues of flooding and landscape conservation.

New developments in agriculture increasingly have a strong scientific basis, and biotechnology (such as genetic engineering of crops), embryo transfer in cattle and bio-control of plant diseases are taking their place on the courses, as well as continuing developments of the technology involved in food production. Course content can, therefore, range from cell biochemistry and molecular biology to plant breeding, plant and animal nutrition, and even engineering and computing. The degree has grown up and in many ways leads environmental and political debate – think of GM crops, BSE, and foot-and-mouth.

The course – a three-year BSc – is of use to those who wish to join the agribusiness, run a farm or get involved with research and development or overseas development, or even to environmentalists who want to understand the issues. Employment rates are good, so if those options aren't to your taste, there's always seed or feed companies, or estate and park management.

Those who are looking for land management skills should head for the more vocational courses where you'll learn the skills you'll need, which may also include the now customary fallback for the post-BSE- and foot-and-mouth farmer – rural tourism and marketing. The traditional farming colleges may well be for you.

However if you're more interested in the applied science side of the subject you should head for the more academically biased courses at the universities. Generally, the older institutions teach the more conventional courses and assess work in the same way, with exams and a level of continuous assessment. The newer places go for a more flexible modular approach and a wider range of assessment options – so check if they're offering the areas you're interested in.

The level of debate about the future of farming has not gone unnoticed in the agri-business world and it is apparent that some departments are linking themselves ever more closely to companies whose agenda may be narrow, to put it kindly. If you have strong opinions on the future roles of agriculture and forestry in this country's ecosystem, then make sure that the department isn't in thrall to a multinational you can't abide. Three years of arguing with your tutors can be exhausting and is unlikely to be rewarded.

And it's worth giving some consideration to the exact location of the course. Some agricultural schools are based in lovely old buildings on acres of land and can be fantastic places to be – or rather isolating.

---

66 The degree is balanced in relation to all aspects of the agricultural industry as well as teaching the underlying principles behind the subject, and challenges students by teaching more complex business and financial techniques as well. It puts us into the shoes of someone within the industry, asking for scheme and policy applications, or farm business analyses and future proposals. I particularly enjoy the personal contact with lecturing staff and practical aspects like regular visits to nearby farm businesses.

George Hood, *second-year agricultural business management student, University of Reading*

» Further information

UK Agriculture
Antrobus House, 18 College Street
Petersfield, Hampshire GU31 4AD

t 02392 410000
↗ www.ukagriculture.com

The Forestry Commission
Silvan House, 231 Corstorphine Road
Edinburgh EH12 7AT

t 0131 334 0303
e enquiries@forestry.gsi.gov.uk
↗ www.forestry.gov.uk

Natural England
1 East Parade
Sheffield S1 2ET

t 0114 241 8920
↗ www.naturalengland.org.uk

↗ Online reading

Department of Environment, Food and Rural Affairs www.defra.gov.uk
Institute for Animal Health www.iah.bbsrc.ac.uk
Environmental News Service www.ens-newswire.com
National Environment Research Council www.nerc.ac.uk
Growing careers www.growing-careers.com

Agriculture and forestry

		Guardian score	Satisfied with teaching %	Satisfied with assessment %	Spend per student score /10	Student:staff ratio	Job prospects %	Value added score /10	Average entry tariff
1	Reading	100.0	89	59	9	11	56	9	294
2	Nottingham	94.8	88	57		8		5	336
3	Central Lancashire	82.6	81	61			47	7	279
4	Queen's, Belfast	80.9			3	11	60	8	306
5	Harper Adams UC	77.8	89	73	4	20	82	6	276
6	Newcastle	77.5	81	72	6	11	62	2	307
7	Royal Agricultural College	59.6	79	65	8	12	31	2	292
8	Aberystwyth	53.5	88	66	7	16	34	3	256
9	Lincoln	49.2	90	62	5	22	36	6	261
10	Nottingham Trent	48.8	78	60	3	17	48	8	257
11	Writtle College	33.4			3	22	41	5	218

Biosciences

" To study how living things work is a truly fascinating experience. It's to be able to understand the very nature of life itself — the molecular mechanisms and processes that interact to create a living entity that can grow and divide, to understand how a cell survives in its environment, how it finds energy, how it resists attack from viruses, and how it communicates with its neighbours to build larger, more sophisticated organisms.

Life can seem extremely fragile — but on the other hand living systems have an ability to adapt and repair unlike any human-built device. Cells can carry out the most amazing chemistry with the most basic requirements and at a fraction of the cost of existing technologies. The potential of harnessing living systems is immense and we are only just beginning to realise it.

Living systems have the potential to provide new solutions to a range of challenges that currently face us. For example, living systems will provide alternative forms of energy to avoid the carbon crisis, new treatments to cure human disease and control pests, new materials with self-assembly or repair properties, crops capable of producing more food in poorly fertile or arid regions of the world, and detoxification of harmful waste.

We are now entering a new era of using molecular machines based on living systems to produce greener, non-polluting technologies — an almost limitless potential. It is clear that bioscientists can expect meaningful and rewarding careers for many years to come.

Dr Richard Williamson, *Lecturer in Protein Biochemistry, Department of Biosciences, University of Kent*

The science of living things has blossomed in universities over the past 50 or so years as the subject has been transformed by momentous events. From the discovery of DNA to the relatively recent decoding of the human genome, the biosciences truly are at the forefront of human research, with perhaps the greatest excitements lying in the knowledge that we have barely touched the surface. There is so much out there for you to discover.

Put simply, bioscience is the study of the research, development, and manufacture of molecules and biological processes that perform key functions in animals and humans. It is the key to animal life on earth.

There are a number of choices to be made right from the off — more than a hundred universities offer courses, covering an increasingly broad discipline, including biology, botany, zoology, genetics, microbiology, molecular biology and biophysics, biochemistry and biotechnology. And that's just the titles — within those courses there are a whole new set of choices for specialisations you might want to consider.

Once you're there, be prepared for a lot of practical work in the laboratory, as with most science degrees, although before you do any serious work in a white coat there is also a fairly large amount of theoretical work required to understand the processes and latest developments. Most universities encourage some independent study through dissertations and projects, which can be an excellent way to develop your research and presentation skills and give you the confidence in your own original thought.

A BSc in the biosciences is often a good prelude to a more specialised MSc — food biotechnology, virology, and biochemical engineering perhaps, although the options are manifold — or a research degree at MPhil or PhD level. There is increasing demand for biosciences in the job market, and many graduates do move straight into industry —

into the fields of pharmaceuticals, food, hospitals, laboratories or medical research. Science A-levels are virtually a necessity, of course, particularly biology and chemistry.

The majority of universities offer a specialised aspect of bioscience, such as human, marine or applied study – so keep one eye on the employment it might provide when you've graduated.

Within applied bioscience there are even more specialised areas that might be more appealing than a general study, related to agriculture, animals, and the environment. If you want to study a more flexible course, look carefully at the options that are offered, especially in the third and fourth years, when a greater emphasis will be on your individual study and research interests.

The level of laboratory provision and facilities for practical work varies across institutions, so investigate thoroughly and try to get an idea of the amount of time you'll be able to spend doing hands-on work, either in classes or in your own time.

If you're specifically interested in applied bioscience look out for work placement opportunities or links with local industries as these will greatly enhance your career prospects after graduation.

And with this being a particularly fast-moving science, look at who will be teaching you and what their specialisations are – if you're taught by someone at the leading edge of research, you'll feel right on top of the game, although you'll also need to factor in whether all that research means they will be too busy to teach. Don't be afraid to ask questions at the open day.

---

66 The obvious difference between school and university study is the complexity of the work and the increased reading around lectures and lab sessions that a degree requires. Taking lecture notes is a skill you need to acquire rapidly; fortunately, it does come quickly. There weren't too many surprises upon coming to university, although the deadlines are more strictly enforced than at A-level and missing them can have subsequent effects on your grades – but that's a good life lesson.

Joanne Turner, *first-year biomedical sciences student, Leeds Metropolitan University*

》 Further information

The Institute of Biology
9 Red Lion Court
London EC4A 3EF

t 020 7936 5900
↗ www.iob.org

The Biosciences Federation
PO Box 502
Cambridge CB1 0AL

t info@bsf.ac.uk
↗ www.bsf.ac.uk

↗ Online reading

Guardian Unlimited Science www.guardian.co.uk/science
The Association of Applied Biologists www.aab.org.uk
The British Society for Cell Biology www.bscb.org
Faculty of 1000 (Biological reports) www.facultyof1000.com
The Biological Inventory Database www.ice.ucdavis.edu/bioinventory/bioinventory.html

Biosciences

		Guardian score	Satisfied with teaching %	Satisfied with assessment %	Spend per student score /10	Student:staff ratio	Job prospects %	Value added score /10	Average entry tariff
1	Cambridge	100.0	94	74	10	13	83	5	546
2	Oxford	88.6	92	67		12	81	6	501
3	Leicester	87.8	96	70	10	8	70	4	369
4	Imperial College	84.9	86	51	10	11	85	5	440
5	York	83.3	95	63	10	9	61	6	409
6	Surrey	83.1	89	49	10	11	85	7	341
7	St Andrews	79.2	93	54	8	9	58	8	402
8	Bristol	78.2	89	54	7	9	77	6	428
8	Ulster	78.2	88	62	6	10	81	10	290
10	Warwick	78.1	89	57		7	65	6	409
11	Bath	74.2	90	47	6	15	78	8	427
12	UCL	73.2	84	52	7	13	70	6	438
13	Sheffield	72.2	93	62	5	13	62	7	418
14	Edinburgh	71.9	89	41	9	15	61	7	436
15	Reading	71.8	91	55		14	58	9	325
16	Sussex	71.7	89	56	8	11	50	10	356
17	Portsmouth	71.4	96	69	9	16	65	7	245
18	Manchester	70.8	90	51	10	15	62	3	419
19	Loughborough	68.8	95	65	4	13	56	7	353
20	Nottingham	68.1	88	48	7	14	73	6	361
21	Aberdeen	68.0	93	59	7	11	65		295
22	Exeter	67.0	91	55	6	16	66	8	332
23	Abertay Dundee	66.6			6	9	67		262
24	Nottingham Trent	66.3	94	70	4	10	85	4	192
25	UEA	65.5	96	64	7	16	52	6	343
26	Liverpool	65.0	88	54	5	14	65	6	350
27	UWE Bristol	64.6	89	65	3	18	72	9	233
28	Newcastle	64.5	82	57	8	15	67	4	368
29	Durham	64.3	85	49	5	16	70	4	452
30	Leeds	64.0	90	51	10	13	55	2	348
31	Kent	62.9	91	58	5	14	68	4	271
32	Cardiff	62.8	93	48	5	18	64	6	374
33	Queen's, Belfast	62.5	91	54	7	14	58	7	329
34	Aston	61.3	81	58	3	21	70	10	290
35	Glasgow	61.0	92	63	7	15	54	2	366
36	Central Lancashire	60.6	79	68	4	18	83	5	253
37	Robert Gordon	60.5			3	19		7	331
38	Lancaster	60.2	91	58	8	12	61	2	338
38	Southampton	60.2	88	50	5	21	61	7	395
40	King's College London	59.5	82	58	5	17	65	5	362
41	Royal Holloway	59.2	89	53	5	14	78	2	313
42	Birmingham	58.7	88	53	8	18	58	2	379
43	Queen Margaret	57.7			3	15	67		261
44	Dundee	57.5	91	59	6	16	45	4	344
45	Hull	57.1	81	64	6	21	62	8	269

	Guardian score	Satisfied with teaching %	Satisfied with assessment %	Spend per student score /10	Student:staff ratio	Job prospects %	Value added score /10	Average entry tariff
45 UWIC	57.1	81	54	3	17	66	10	240
47 Napier	56.9			4	17	63	8	231
48 Brighton	56.8	82	47	7	18	59	8	231
49 Chester	55.8	77	61	7	14		5	278
49 Queen Mary	55.8	85	58	7	17	55	4	335
51 Coventry	55.7	83	71	2	22	65	9	309
52 Essex	55.3	94	67	4	17	64	3	266
53 Staffordshire	52.8	88	73	4	18		6	213
54 Bath Spa	52.2	91	78	2	20			255
55 Bradford	52.1	76	65	5	12			261
56 Greenwich	51.9	85	66	9	22		6	164
57 Glasgow Caledonian	51.6	83	56	4	18	46	7	345
57 Plymouth	51.6	87	55	4	20	43	9	293
59 Brunel	51.2	81	51	5	16	62	3	306
60 Swansea	50.9	84	36	4	14	56	4	291
61 Aberystwyth	50.5	89	59	6	19	46	7	272
62 Northumbria	50.4	87	48	2	19	58	8	255
63 Leeds Met	50.1	74	59	4	19	67	7	248
64 Anglia Ruskin	49.7	96	61	4	13	35	6	224
65 Oxford Brookes	49.3	84	47	5	17	48	7	245
66 St Mary's UC, Twickenham	48.6	84	64	2	15			225
67 Sheffield Hallam	48.2	82	50	4	21	65	5	274
68 Worcester	47.9	87	66	4	15			199
69 Manchester Met	47.2	84	66	3	17	53	4	239
70 Derby	46.8	83	59	3	22			287
71 Salford	46.1	83	60	4	17	54	4	225
72 Heriot-Watt	45.9	87	55	5	24	58	3	289
73 Teesside	45.5	88	74	4	25			243
74 Glamorgan	44.8	82	59	3	21			220
75 Bangor	44.5	78	45	6	22	54	4	301
76 Bolton	44.2	90	75	2	27		9	168
77 Hertfordshire	43.5	69	54	2	22		7	248
78 Wolverhampton	43.2	74	59	4	18		3	187
79 Strathclyde	41.6	86	51	6	19	56	1	237
80 Roehampton	41.4	80	67	3	26	70	3	206
81 London South Bank	40.2	78	52	2		59		144
82 Westminster	37.4	75	57	4	19	47	3	210
83 Kingston	35.8	76	53	3	23		4	199
84 East London	34.6	77	46	3	13		1	166
85 Stirling	34.4			3	27	52	2	274
86 Liverpool John Moores	33.4	85	62	3	19	41	1	223
87 Huddersfield	29.4	77	62	3	30	48	4	236

Chemistry

❝ A student of chemistry enters a rapidly changing world of new ideas, theories, and proofs. Your subject will lead you towards developing new molecules and materials designed to solve modern-day problems, or towards a better understanding of complex biological systems, or reaching towards the solution to the world's pressing energy problems.

You will come to understand the nanoscale world of atoms and molecules and how to control their synthesis and properties. Ideas that seem abstract at the early stage of learning will become clear and you will have the opportunity to combine your intellectual skills with laboratory research in your pursuit of understanding.

In my early days as a chemist I was energised by the endless opportunities to innovate at all levels. Some people do so through original thinking, some through their skill in converting ideas into reality. All build on the knowledge of past practitioners and benefit from the opinions of the experts around them.

Along with the ability to innovate comes the capacity to contribute. Chemists of the future will work in a multidisciplinary scientific community where their skills will influence the quality of life in tomorrow's world. Not a bad outcome from studies that might well have started with a test-tube and a Bunsen burner. It's certainly a subject that holds as much fascination for me now as it did when I started on my studies a good few years ago!

Dr Jeremy Hinks, *School of Chemistry, University of Southampton*

Whether it's why leaves turn red in autumn, why diamonds are hard or even why soap gets us clean, you won't find a better way to explain it than through the study of chemistry. Atoms, molecules, and ions – the fundamental building blocks – are the key actors in the chaotic theatre that is the world in which we live.

Chemistry is the broadest of the traditional physical sciences and covers areas more usually associated with biological, medical or geological studies. It's a challenging degree, requiring a foundation of broad scientific knowledge, as well as an ability to appreciate how different processes interrelate – and an eagerness to conduct investigations and experiments for yourself.

To study it as an undergraduate, chemistry at A-level or equivalent is, as you'd expect, an absolute must, but some universities will also recommend that you have maths, physics or biology – especially if you intend to apply for a more specialised field related to that subject. However, most general courses will provide students with support in these areas if it is needed, so entry can still be pretty flexible.

By and large, chemistry courses build on what you'll already have done at school or college, so you'll work on organic, inorganic, and physical chemistry, and move on to more areas of theoretical and analytical chemistry – and then on to more particular specialisations in areas such as medicinal, biological or pharmaceutical chemistry.

The specialised knowledge required for this degree is such that many graduates decide to stay in scientific fields, either continuing on to higher and research courses or going straight into industry and laboratory work – this could be anything from pharmaceuticals to oceanography. But with the breadth of study you'd be expected to undertake, chemistry students leave university with many of the numerical, IT, problem-solving, and analytical skills appreciated by employers, and are therefore sought after by employers in a very wide range of professions, including, for example, the City, in government or in commerce.

Although there have been a number of closures in recent years, chemistry departments across the country are starting to show signs of recovery – helped partly by the re-branding of certain courses as, for example, forensics.

As well as straight chemistry courses, there are a whole host of chemical science degree courses available that you might like to consider, such as environmental, marine, medicinal or biological chemistry. In addition you can choose to study chemistry with another related science, such as pharmaceutical sciences or drug design, or as a combined degree if you want to keep your options open.

Most chemistry departments now offer a four-year degree leading to a master's qualification, the MChem – which is fast becoming the desirable qualification for practising chemists.

Alternatively, you could choose to study for a BSc qualification. This three-year programme may be ideal for those unsure whether they wish to spend their career in the discipline. Whichever version takes your fancy, be sure to find out what sort of opportunities for jobs and travel a university offers, as well as the extent of its laboratory and research facilities. Many of the UK's universities are at the cutting edge of chemical research and are, therefore, exciting places to study.

Don't be fooled by appearances when you visit for an open day: an older lab could offer great facilities and a flash new-looking one might not be at all well equipped. Ask the students who are already there.

And as with almost any subject, be aware of the assessment levels used at the institutions you apply for. On modular courses, assessment can be more regular than the old-style end-of-year exams, but there is most likely to be a mixture of exams, coursework, and a dissertation.

---

66 The course feels like a natural progression from what I have studied before. Helpful and enthusiastic staff recap and build on previous knowledge to broaden your understanding of chemistry. It maintains a good balance between practical lab work and lectures, involves more experiments than you would have had at A-level – and clear links between lab projects and lecture courses are made. The course is stimulating and challenging, improving not only your chemistry but your critical thinking, numeracy, and communication skills

Fiona McBride, *fourth-year chemistry student, University of Liverpool*

» Further information

Royal Society of Chemistry
Burlington House, Piccadilly
London W1J 0BA

t 020 7440 3344
e education@rsc.org
↗ www.rsc.org/studentzone

Chemical Industries Association
Kings Buildings, Smith Square
London SW1P 3JJ

t 020 7834 3399
e enquiries@cia.org.uk
↗ www.cia.org.uk

Society of Chemical Industry
14-15 Belgrave Square
London SW1X 8PS

t 020 7598 1500
e secretariat@soci.org
↗ www.soci.org

↗ Online reading

ChemSoc www.rsc.org/chemsoc
Chemistry Visualisation education.ncsa.uiuc.edu
Royal Society www.royalsoc.ac.uk
Chemical Abstracts www.cas.org
Web Elements Periodic Table www.webelements.com
Delights of Chemistry www.chem.leeds.ac.uk/delights

Chemistry

		Guardian score	Satisfied with teaching %	Satisfied with assessment %	Spend per student score /10	Student:staff ratio	Job prospects %	Value added score /10	Average entry tariff
1	St Andrews	100.0	90	55	10	11		10	450
2	Imperial College	98.7	90	60	10	11	83	4	467
3	Oxford	98.1	89	69	10	20	82	7	529
3	Sussex	98.1	92	57	8	8			391
5	York	94.9	92	86	9	10	75	4	408
6	Liverpool	93.4	87	69		10		8	333
7	Queen's, Belfast	92.8	81	65	8	12		9	337
8	Sheffield	92.3	93	71	4	12	93	5	390
9	Southampton	91.5	90	72	6	12	78	6	413
10	Warwick	88.4	90	55		14	80	4	429
11	Hull	86.0	91	65	7	14	79	7	286
12	Reading	85.9	86	69	5	12		6	320
13	Aberdeen	83.3	88	71	3	14			324
13	Leicester	83.3	88	78	8	12	74	5	336
15	Loughborough	83.1	94	84	4	15	82	3	302
16	Leeds	83.0	75	62	8	12	78	5	360
17	Durham	82.6	87	63	4	14	79	3	483
18	Nottingham	82.5	85	42	8	12	80	4	358
18	Surrey	82.5	85	44	6	14		6	305
20	Manchester	82.0	78	59	9	11	70	4	404
21	UEA	81.3	91	63	7	9			341
22	Bath	81.1	94	46	3	14	83	4	373
23	Bristol	80.7	83	53	6	15	82	4	391
24	Plymouth	80.2	88	57	4	16			303
25	Newcastle	79.2	94	73	3	14	76	5	332
26	UCL	78.0	81	52	5	13	72	4	405
27	Glasgow	77.6	82	50	4	16	85		379
28	Cardiff	77.4	84	48	7	12	81	2	324
29	Robert Gordon	75.7			2	19	78	9	319
30	Edinburgh	75.1	83	53	9	16	56	5	419

	Guardian score	Satisfied with teaching %	Satisfied with assessment %	Spend per student score /10	Student:staff ratio	Job prospects %	Value added score /10	Average entry tariff
31 Bangor	74.9	89	62	4	14			262
32 Queen Mary	73.3			6	15	75		282
33 Strathclyde	72.7	85	62	4	17	81	2	
34 Birmingham	71.8	75	40	7	15	82	1	372
35 Huddersfield	70.6	85	69	3	14	65	9	227
36 Northumbria	70.2	84	49	3	18	73	8	274
37 Nottingham Trent	69.5	73	50	3	10			210
38 Brighton	69.1	74	47	3	20		10	240
39 Heriot-Watt	68.7	76	56	3	13		5	310
40 Liverpool John Moores	66.1	77	68	2	11			206
41 Manchester Met	65.9	87	68	3	15		5	221
42 Bradford	64.3	89	53	2	19			259
43 Kingston	40.0	79	42	3	37			214

Computer sciences and IT

> Try to imagine a world without computers. There would be no PCs or laptops, and so no word processing or spreadsheets, no communication using the web, no online shopping or photo enhancement. There would be no mobile phones or digital cameras, because these are computers at heart. There would be no internet or phone system. There would be no modern cars, trains or aircraft: computers control how they work and guide their safety on rails or in the air. There would be empty shops: all their stock is computer-controlled. There would be very few goods: many are made by robots, which themselves are computers. Food would be scarce: supermarkets' distribution systems rely on computers and computers often control food production itself.
>
> Computer science teaches you how to use computers to make the world work as it does. You will learn how to make a computer behave how you want – this might be making a robot move something from one end of a room to another, it might be making a calculation which saves someone's life in a medical ward, or it could be creating a whole new world through building pictures or sound or building a computer system so that other people can do this.
>
> You will learn how computers work together in building networks like the internet, how teams of people build systems worth hundreds of millions of pounds, and how computers can be made to behave like people, among many other topics. You will also learn about how to work together in groups, and what your professional responsibilities are to your colleagues, clients, and society.
>
> Many of you will join universities' industrial partners on sandwich placement schemes, where you work with a company for a year during your degree, putting the theory into practice.
>
> At the end of your degree you will be equipped with lifelong skills that you can use in a whole variety of jobs: from management to consulting, from programming to information systems administration, from IT companies to any company, large or small.

Professor Simon Thompson, *Head of Computing Laboratory, University of Kent*

Computer sciences courses are often rather misunderstood, even by those who apply for them. Many are attracted because of their own interest in computers, but the courses are more likely to be about software engineering than the use of information technology and the attractions of gaming and software packages. While some courses can veer towards electronic engineering and some towards pure maths, all students will be expected to have the ability to work through tasks set in a logical manner and should have an overall flair for problem-solving.

The conventional computing science degree (of software engineering) typically embraces computer systems, both hardware and software, algorithm development, networked systems, numerical methods, and database design. You'll start by learning the basics – machine architecture, programming languages, algorithms, computer systems, and general theory. Depending on the particular establishment, the mathematical and theoretical foundations of computer science are studied to varying degrees of complexity, hence the need for good mathematical grades for entry to some institutions.

Beyond that, there is a whole range of options under the computing sciences umbrella, including information systems, artificial intelligence, cybernetics, multimedia, and the internet.

Most modules are taught through a series of lectures, tutorials, and practical sessions. Assessment in the majority of cases is through continuous coursework and a formal examination.

Many universities offer computing science programmes in combination with other subjects. Typically maths, electronic engineering, and business are linked with computing science. Teaching methods generally centre around a lot of practical work, often on a mainframe system and, hopefully, some hi-tech workstations. You'll also work on a number of projects involved with either hardware or software, often as part of a group (as you would in an employment situation).

Computer sciences and IT may not be the most outwardly glamorous of subjects, but graduates will work in a wide field of industrial, governmental, educational or research establishments – often starting with decent salaries. Graduates find employment as programmers, systems analysts, software engineers or IT consultants.

Do plenty of research when choosing your course. To some extent, you are committing yourself to a future career, so ask some serious questions about what, ideally, you want to head towards – although around 50 per cent of IT graduates find employment outside of the sector.

And remember that courses with similar names may not have similar content – there's a wide variation among the different institutions, so look into what compulsory modules you'll be doing and what the discretionary choices are. Also look into lab and workstation availability and the ratio of computers to students.

The university may offer sandwich courses, an intercalated year (where you take time to pursue other studies), or perhaps a period studying abroad.

Find out how many employers the department has regular contact with, and the work recent graduates have gone into. Details are available from individual departments or the university careers service.

Also, a number of courses are increasingly incorporating entrepreneurship skills into the curriculum, reflecting the fact that a large number of graduates set up their own business or undertake freelance work and need to understand the issues involved.

❝ Stepping from the safe world of A-levels to the freedom of an undergraduate degree seemed daunting. However, being given freedom with my A-level project put me in good stead for academic life. The course pushes and challenges, allowing me to develop my skills, while never leaving me without the help and support I need. I've especially appreciated the friendly staff and strong links with industry, which have allowed me to gain a placement with a top investment bank.

Callam McMillan, *second-year computer science student, Loughborough University*

》 Further information

British Computer Society
First Floor, Block D, North Star House
North Star Avenue, Swindon SN2 1FA

t 01793 417417
↗ www.bcs.org.uk

The Institute for the Management of Information Systems

5 Kingfisher House
New Mill Road, Orpington
Kent BR5 3QG

t 0700 0023456
e central@imis.org.uk
↗ www.imis.org.uk

The Institute of Engineering and Technology

Savoy Place
London WC2R 0BL

t 020 7240 1871
e postmaster@theiet.org
↗ www.theiet.org

↗ Online reading

Guardian Unlimited Technology technology.guardian.co.uk
IEE Computer Society www.computer.org
Software Engineering Association sea.co.umist.ac.uk
Wired magazine www.wired.com
Scientific Computing www.scientific-computing.com
Computer Weekly www.computerweekly.com

Computer sciences and IT

		Guardian score	Satisfied with teaching %	Satisfied with assessment %	Spend per student score /10	Student:staff ratio	Job prospects %	Value added score /10	Average entry tariff
1	Oxford	100.0			10	12	80		531
2	Imperial College	92.0	83	63	10	14	83	6	475
3	Southampton	90.8	87	56	10	10	80	8	393
4	Edinburgh	85.1	78	47		9	84	8	398
5	York	84.2	81	45	10	10	88	4	423
6	Cambridge	83.8			8	10	79	3	535
7	Glasgow	81.9	94	61	7	8	87	4	363
8	Lancaster	80.6	86	56	10		65	7	346
9	Sheffield	77.7	69	57	7	10	90	7	362
10	Newcastle	77.2	86	62	8	10	75	8	318
11	Dundee	77.0	90	67	8	11	60	8	381
12	Warwick	76.8	79	61	8	13	71	5	434
13	Strathclyde	75.0	88	64	5	13	77	8	
14	Surrey	74.5	82	51	8	17	88	8	350
14	UCL	74.5	70	53	8	9	79	4	407
16	Reading	73.7	78	60	7	12	73	8	325
17	Birmingham	73.6	81	56	8	13	72	7	367
18	Leicester	73.1	66	71	6	8	73	8	287
19	Bristol	72.5	88	43	5	16	75	7	434
20	Aberdeen	72.3			5	12	86		336
21	Kent	70.6	80	53	7	12	75	8	276
22	Sussex	70.0	75	46	8	11	75	6	361
23	Essex	69.6	77	67	8		68	6	297
24	King's College London	69.3	81	63	8	15	60	8	345
25	Loughborough	69.2	88	73	5	18	74	7	322
26	Nottingham	68.8			9	12	78	4	335

	Guardian score	Satisfied with teaching %	Satisfied with assessment %	Spend per student score /10	Student:staff ratio	Job prospects %	Value added score /10	Average entry tariff
27 Plymouth	68.5	75	57	8	16	59	10	260
28 Leeds	67.3	81	55	9	16	73	3	360
29 Manchester	66.8	70	53	9	15	76	3	373
30 Queen Mary	64.5	66	55	9	9	65	3	257
31 Durham	63.4	65	36	4		91	3	391
31 Royal Holloway	63.4			4		79	4	275
33 Bath	63.1	80	65	6	17	71	3	417
34 Robert Gordon	62.1			3	14	80	8	217
35 Cardiff	62.0	69	65	6	15	76	5	327
36 Bournemouth	61.4	70	53	7	14	77	6	230
37 Queen's, Belfast	61.1	65	47	6	16	83	7	311
38 UEA	60.9	83	71	6	18	66	4	297
39 Anglia Ruskin	60.5	81	62	5	10	54	9	213
40 UWE Bristol	60.4	73	55	4	16	71	9	216
41 Oxford Brookes	60.1	71	52	5	15	72	8	230
42 Heriot-Watt	59.8	79	68	4	12	63	5	299
43 Ulster	59.7	77	61	4	14	67	7	266
43 Central Lancashire	59.7	83	68	4	20	79	6	244
45 Glasgow Caledonian	58.8			3	19	54	10	349
46 Exeter	58.0	82	70	4	18	76	3	310
47 Hull	57.6	80	59	6	16	72	4	228
48 Derby	56.5			3	15	68	4	271
49 Swansea	56.2	73	45	5	11	69	3	287
50 Chester	56.0	76	66	4	16	60	9	221
51 Gloucestershire	55.8	81	71	5	17	63	5	222
52 Napier	55.4			3	14	63	9	209
53 Brunel	55.0	72	59	4	16	56	7	298
54 Stirling	54.6			5	14	60		261
55 Aberystwyth	53.9	85	51	5	20	67	4	243
56 Aston	52.8	73	59	3	19	74	4	283
56 Nottingham Trent	52.8			4	21	80	7	226
58 Staffordshire	50.4	75	51	5	18	69	4	240
59 Hertfordshire	49.5	65	53	4	13	60	5	191
60 Worcester	49.4	80	64	3	14	69	2	207
61 Swansea Met	49.2	87	71		18	59	5	191
62 Brighton	48.7	72	63	3	16	68	3	262
62 Coventry	48.7			4	17	53	5	237
64 Bradford	48.5	61	49	4	17	56	9	212
65 City	48.3	59	40	5	19	68	7	251
66 Roehampton	47.8	72	59	3	23	58	9	176
66 Salford	47.8	74	59	5	25	57	8	229
68 Sheffield Hallam	47.7	74	58	3	18	58	7	204
69 Cumbria	47.1	86	61	3	21			235
70 Abertay Dundee	46.8			3	26	55	8	308
71 Kingston	46.7	70	53	5	16	59	4	203
71 Northampton	46.7	70	63	2	18	54	9	208

		Satisfied with teaching %	Satisfied with assessment %	Spend per student score /10	Student:staff ratio	Job prospects %	Value added score /10	Average entry tariff
73	Goldsmiths	45.8	70	47	4	14	57	4	202
73	Portsmouth	45.8	74	52	4	22	69	3	242
75	Sunderland	44.8	67	56	7	15	45	3	240
76	Glamorgan	44.3	74	65	4		59	3	205
77	De Montfort	43.7	72	61	4	21	61	4	182
78	Northumbria	43.2	76	62	3	22	62	3	253
79	Huddersfield	42.7	73	62	4	21	56	4	229
79	Teesside	42.7	73	59	4	20	50	4	255
81	Bolton	41.7	69	53		22	37	10	177
82	London South Bank	40.3	78	65		21	32	9	129
82	Southampton Solent	40.3	75	66	5	22	59	2	167
84	Edge Hill	39.8	68	53	2	19	61	4	205
85	Canterbury Christ Church	39.1	79	52	5	17		1	203
86	Liverpool John Moores	38.9	56	52	3	20	71	3	201
87	Wolverhampton	38.2			3	18	50	5	165
88	East London	37.9	71	59	4	18	54	2	163
89	Bedfordshire	36.8	71	59	3	18	51	3	137
90	Manchester Met	36.6	71	60	3	22	62	2	235
90	Newport	36.6	60	58	2		58	7	149
92	Birmingham City	36.1	68	47	4	16	40	2	187
93	Westminster	35.3	61	54	3	13	45	2	160
94	Bucks New University	34.4	72	72	3	23	51	3	195
95	Lincoln	34.2	66	71	4	24	40	3	237
96	Greenwich	34.1	75	58	4	27	58	2	163
97	Middlesex	31.3	59	46	4	20	49	3	152
98	Leeds Met	28.4	61	42	3	37	52	9	212

Earth and marine science

❝ Why study earth sciences? Well, it's a great way to combine other sciences (chemistry, physics, biology) in the natural laboratory of the earth. Students of earth sciences are equally at home at a computer screen, looking down a microscope, in an analytical laboratory or in the field. I have spent many weeks on remote volcanoes in the Andes, Russia, and Iran. Many of my colleagues are involved in fieldwork examining ancient rocks more than two billion years old from the continents, or young rocks recently deformed in earthquake zones, or participating in research cruises across the world's oceans. It's not bad being paid to study the planet's wonders! Most of our students get jobs with industry, including oil and mineral exploration. There is a lot more appreciation for environmental concerns these days, and students want to be assured that they can make a positive difference before they take up these jobs. A large number also go on to do further research at universities, volcano observatories or geological surveys.

The start of the 21st century is a great time to be an earth scientist. The theory of plate tectonics has been established to the point where it underlies most of our understanding of how the earth works, and the exploration of other worlds has increased our knowledge of how the earth formed and evolved. New technologies enable us to work over a range of scales – to investigate the interior of the planet, or to determine the compositions of tiny parts of minerals. And from a practical perspective, an appreciation of the earth and how it works is critical in making a contribution to mitigating climate change and responsible stewardship of our natural resources.

Jon Davidson, *Professor of Earth Sciences, Durham University*

It's a big thing, Planet Earth, and the bits of it that aren't made up purely of rocks tend to be covered with sea, so earth and marine sciences are pretty fundamental to our very existence. The two disciplines – rocks or water – are very different, but either way you'll be interested in the environment and the evolution of the planet and its oceans.

Students tend to be the outdoors type, and as environmental awareness increases, so does interest in the courses – so applications are rising and competition for places is growing.

The major earth science is geology and is concerned primarily with rocks and derivative materials that make up the outer part of the planet earth. As is increasingly the case with most sciences, you'll be taking a multidisciplinary approach, making use of knowledge gleaned from other fields, such as physics, chemistry, and biology, and even looking for clues from other planets as to how the earth has ended up as it has.

You'll study landforms and other surface features of the earth, but also be concerned with the structure and inner parts of the planet, all highly valuable if you're searching for useful minerals or looking for stable environments to build on, or trying to predict earthquakes or the eruptions of volcanoes.

The ocean sciences, meanwhile, are similarly multidisciplinary, as they search for the factors that drive these mind-bogglingly complex masses of water, and can be roughly divided into four disciplines: marine biology (the study of marine plants and animals), marine geology (the study of the composition and formation of the seabed), marine chemistry (the chemical composition of seawater, pollutants, and so on), and marine physics (the study of wave formation, ocean currents, water temperature, density, and tides).

For both courses, you'll spend time skipping between the sciences, before really hitting the specialisations in the final run-in.

Once you've chosen between earth and marine sciences, check how the subject is taught. There will certainly be lectures, but how much practical work? How many field trips? Some courses can be stretched to four years to provide an instant science master's (MSc), while others can be that long in order to incorporate a year of foreign study. Fancy a year of tectonics on the San Andreas fault in California?

Some courses also offer work placement, which may be especially useful if you're planning to move into a particular industry afterwards (oil, for example), so check whether that is possible and, if so, what links the university has with the private sector.

As with all multidisciplinary courses, investigate the related departments – you'll likely be sharing facilities and teaching staff. And if it's cutting-edge research you're into, don't forget to check out the specialisations of whoever's going to be teaching you.

---

66 Studying earth sciences is a hands-on learning experience combining geological theory with lots of fieldwork. I'm taking an MGeol (International) degree, which includes a year studying abroad. My year in New Zealand was a fantastic experience with amazing field trips, and really pushed me to fulfil my potential. Others on the course have studied in the US and Australia – and the course has given us the chance to experience real geology while learning from experts at the forefront of their field.

Rob Lednor, *fourth-year geological sciences student, University of Leeds*

» Further information

Geological Society
Burlington House, Piccadilly
London W1J 0BG

t   020 7434 9944
e   enquiries@geolsoc.org.uk
↗   www.geolsoc.org.uk

British Geological Survey
Kingsley Dunham Centre
Keyworth, Nottingham NG12 5GG

t   0115 936 3143
↗   www.bgs.ac.uk

Natural Environment Research Council
Polaris House, North Star Avenue
Swindon SN2 1EU

t   01793 411500
↗   www.nerc.ac.uk

↗ Online reading

Geologists' Association www.geologist.demon.co.uk
British Association for the Advancement of Science www.the-ba.net
Jurassic Coast www.jurassiccoast.com
Geology: An Introduction www.go4uni.ac.uk/tasters/jigsaw/faq.htm
Society for Underwater Technology www.sut.org.uk
Proudman Oceanographic Laboratory www.pol.ac.uk

Earth and marine sciences

		Guardian score	Satisfied with teaching %	Satisfied with assessment %	Spend per student score /10	Student:staff ratio	Job prospects %	Value added score /10	Average entry tariff
1	UCL	100.0	85	60	8	8		9	395
2	Liverpool	97.4	94	77	9	9	82	7	338
3	Manchester	86.1	91	57	10	9	68	5	351
4	Royal Holloway	86.0	88	62	6	11	78	9	341
5	Imperial College	84.7	82	59		12	80	4	443
6	UEA	81.2	91	63	7	12			395
7	York	80.7	98	71	3	12		8	341
8	Leicester	79.7	97	78	7	11	59	5	348
9	Edinburgh	75.7	81	47	9	15	80	4	392
10	Leeds	74.5	84	44	7	12	74	7	355
11	Aberdeen	72.4	88	71	4	11	87		275
12	Southampton	72.3	90	63	8	16	63	7	374
12	St Andrews	72.3	90	55	4	16			384
14	Bristol	71.9	83	53	5	12	68	6	410
15	Durham	71.8	87	55	3	12	71	7	403
16	Bangor	69.8	89	57	6	14	86	4	245
17	Plymouth	59.1	87	54	5	16	56	9	251
18	Cardiff	58.4	90	46	4	14	65	4	323
19	Hertfordshire	58.3	88	72	3	9	62	2	255
20	Aberystwyth	56.9	94	70	4	17			292
21	Birmingham	52.8	88	64	5	16	64	1	319
22	Kingston	49.4	79	42	4	13			197
23	Brighton	48.5	89	69		21	48	9	266
24	Wolverhampton	44.1	68	55	4	11		3	180
25	Portsmouth	43.1	79	52	3	17	68	2	221
26	Liverpool John Moores	34.3	77	68	1	16			207

Geography and environmental sciences

> Let's face it. Geography still has quite a public image problem – capital cities, rivers, and chief imports/exports – handy for Trivial Pursuit, but what else? Even worse is the persistent idea that geographers are all rugged, outdoors types with a secret hankering to be an explorer. We've got those too, but most urban or cultural geographers I know would prefer a cappuccino in Berlin or a chai in Mumbai.
>
> One positive development for the discipline over the last few years has been the growing public appreciation of the environmental challenges that the world faces, and the growing awareness that geography is ideally suited to examining both the scientific and social dimensions of ecological change and human risk and vulnerability. The impacts of climate change are going to demand political, economic, cultural, and historical knowledge – all of which is covered by contemporary human geography – as well as physical geography subjects like climatology, glaciology, biogeography, and oceanography.
>
> Although most students and academics specialise, the ability to see an integrated picture is a tremendous strength. But geography today isn't just about the environment. It is a discipline that allows extraordinary freedom to explore a huge range of subjects. In my own department, we have people working (and teaching) on volcanoes, ice sheets, and coastal erosion; as well as street culture, the history of the American West, indigenous knowledge, and the economic impact of China and India. Students can follow their interests and enthusiasms across a real spectrum of issues. They emerge with an enviable range of skills, and ready to take up job opportunities in everything from climate science to development NGOs, business, and the media. Geography's public image is gradually changing, and it is about time – it is a fabulous subject that has never been more interesting or important.
>
> **Dr Emma Mawdsley**, *Lecturer in Geography, Fellow of Newnham College, University of Cambridge*

Geography

Geography has, in the past decade, been given a makeover by cultural and political trends that have seen it shake off the traditional perception of a degree based on precipitation cycles and plate tectonics to become a multidisciplinary subject tackling fundamental questions about the environment, the movement of peoples around the globe, and population patterns.

Geography is unique in bridging the social sciences and the earth sciences. In fact, you can emerge with a BA or a BSc from different institutions with no discernable difference in the course. Like many of the older subjects, it is taking an increasingly multidisciplinary approach, encompassing ecology, geology, economics, and politics to create an applied science with skills of interpretation and analysis, which are invaluable to future employers, and which make geography one of the top courses in terms of graduate recruitment.

The career options available are extremely wide-ranging. You can head off to pursue jobs directly related to geography – such as in town and transport planning or environmental consultancy – or you could use your skills in more general careers, such as IT or marketing. The third option is to continue with full-time study and training to develop a career in teaching or research, or to gain further qualifications for entry into more specialist professions.

The options for modules are pretty vast, so look carefully at what the course offers. There are a number of key common geographical concepts taught across all the institutions, but after that the choice is wider. The options tend to be based around the research interests and specialisations of departmental staff – so see if they tally with your own interests and career plans.

Fieldwork – perhaps including some abroad – is an appealing and integral part of most geography degrees. Check what the options are, and whether they coincide with the course choices you are making.

Environmental sciences

Everyone tells us the world is going to hell in a deep-fried handbasket, as global warming, the hole in the ozone layer, GM foods, and pollution take an increasingly fevered hold over the public imagination and the end of the world gets more and more nigh. Environmental scientists are generally the ones who think they can do something about it, saving us from ourselves, and taking a degree can be the first step in that process.

The issues facing environmental science have a variety of causes and solutions, so the degree is increasingly multidisciplinary. You'll be studying the principles of (deep breath) ecology, population biology, environmental chemistry, physiology, physical geography, statistics, sociology, law, economics, microbial ecology, energy and biological survey, assessment and conservation (and ... breathe out). In addition, you'll need to be able to produce concise accounts of complex problems and communicate them effectively to others.

The degree is generally a three-year BSc. You'll not have come across anything quite like it at school or college, so the first year is often spent building the foundations of the course, before moving on to a more modular format where you venture into deeper waters following particular interests. It's here that the shape of your degree, and perhaps your future career, becomes clearer. That future career may involve working in local government (planning perhaps), environmental agencies, water authorities, industry, consultancy or even the law.

Teaching is a mixture of the traditional lectures and seminars, with a measure of fieldwork thrown in. Assessment is done by varying amounts of coursework and formal exams. The ratio of one to the other can make a difference, so think about what's best for you.

Course content also varies considerably. Some contain mostly science, and no elements of political or social science, while others are at the opposite extreme. Also check the quality of related departments for any area you're particularly interested in studying.

Look too at the detail of the courses and who will be teaching you. Some universities will be better than others at teaching climate change, global warming or environmental chemistry – staff may be at the forefront of research in these fields.

Some courses last four years and include a year studying abroad – a valuable opportunity. Local field trips will also be a possibility, so consider your location carefully – you could end up on the doorstep of the Pennines, for example.

66 Geography is exciting, challenging, and varied, covering both human and physical aspects. The human side is quite sociological, with elements of psychology, but I particularly enjoy the physical side, looking at hot topics like global warming and the weather. The fieldwork we do is fantastic and has taken me to a Californian desert and to Magaluf to study its unique rock structure. I have enjoyed my geography course so much, I have been inspired to teach the subject when I graduate!

Anthony Wood, *final-year geography student, University of Northampton*

》 Further information

Geographical Association
160 Solly Street, Sheffield S1 4BF

t 01142 960088
↗ www.geography.org.uk

The British Ecological Society
26 Blades Court, Putney
London SW15 2NU

t 020 8871 9797
↗ www.britishecologicalsociety.org

Royal Geographical Society (with The Institute of British Geographers)
1 Kensington Gore
London SW7 2AR

t 020 7591 3000
↗ www.rgs.org

Natural Environment Research Council
Polaris House, North Star Avenue
Swindon SN2 1EU

t 01793 411500
↗ www.nerc.ac.uk

↗ Online reading

Internet Geography www.internetgeography.co.uk
GeoExplorer www.geoexplorer.co.uk
Natural Environment Research Council www.nerc.ac.uk
The Center for International Earth Science Information Network (CIESIN)
    www.ciesin.columbia.edu
The Global Site www.theglobalsite.ac.uk

Geography and environmental studies

		Guardian score	Satisfied with teaching %	Satisfied with assessment %	Spend per student score /10	Student:staff ratio	Job prospects %	Value added score /10	Average entry tariff
1	Cambridge	100.0	99	77	10	13	79	6	509
2	Oxford	99.8	92	62	10	14	70	7	492
3	Edinburgh	88.0	85	45	10	10	73	6	408
4	Bristol	86.2	82	49	8	12	72	8	459
5	UCL	83.6	88	65	10	13	64	4	436
6	Durham	80.6	89	52	6	13	72	7	451
6	Royal Holloway	80.6	95	72	7	11	73	3	358

	Guardian score	Satisfied with teaching %	Satisfied with assessment %	Spend per student score /10	Student:staff ratio	Job prospects %	Value added score /10	Average entry tariff
8 UEA	78.7	93	60	6	15	68	8	384
9 Leicester	78.5	92	76	8	12	62	5	327
10 St Andrews	77.6	92	66	3	12	66	6	423
11 Aberystwyth	77.2	95	78	7	15	62	7	305
12 London School of Economics	75.2	75	54	5	13	81	3	432
13 Nottingham	74.2	88	41	6	17	68	8	425
14 Staffordshire	73.5	89	67	9	9			254
15 Reading	72.8	87	61	9	21	63	8	352
16 Leeds	71.5	84	58	7	18	67	8	365
17 Plymouth	70.8	89	68	5	14	46	10	279
18 Bradford	70.4	84	57	7	12			215
19 Southampton	69.2	87	54	5	20	70	6	404
19 UWE Bristol	69.2	89	74	4	16	55	9	259
21 Birmingham	68.9	89	63	6	20	63	6	379
22 Exeter	68.6	90	73	4	23	65	8	368
23 Hull	68.5	91	62	7	12	63	2	290
24 Newcastle	68.4	81	52	5	17	70	6	368
25 Glasgow	68.0	97	74	5	21	62	3	361
26 Bath Spa	67.9	91	68	3	16	72		256
27 Queen Mary	67.6	88	54	7	10	60	2	294
27 Sheffield	67.6	90	60	4	18	64	4	398
29 Loughborough	67.1	88	60	5	20	62	6	364
30 Lancaster	66.3	86	65	6	19	59	5	368
30 Liverpool	66.3	88	57	5	18	54	8	345
32 Kingston	64.8	85	66	7		65	5	224
33 Dundee	64.4	88	62	3	16	66	4	336
34 Chester	64.3	97	70	3	18	56	8	269
35 Worcester	63.9	87	71	4	10			218
36 St Mary's UC, Twickenham	63.3	89	73	2	14			244
37 Gloucestershire	63.2	83	66	6	19	67	5	266
38 Aberdeen	62.4	90	66	6	16	62		300
39 Manchester	61.8	91	58	5	22	52	5	400
40 Edge Hill	61.6	91	77	4	17			217
41 Bangor	61.3	81	55	3	13			246
42 Sussex	61.2	80	47	5	16	46	8	381
43 Nottingham Trent	60.4	79	60	5	20	52	10	247
44 Northumbria	58.4	84	63	4	16	46	7	269
45 Glamorgan	58.2	84	59	4	9		4	216
46 Swansea	57.2	88	57	5	17	55	3	303
47 King's College London	56.2	83	43	6	18	53	4	349
48 Strathclyde	56.1	85	64	3	20	56	6	
49 Manchester Met	55.6	86	67	5	15	42	4	257
50 Stirling	54.6			4	27	72	4	271

		Guardian score	Satisfied with teaching %	Satisfied with assessment %	Spend per student score /10	Student:staff ratio	Job prospects %	Value added score /10	Average entry tariff
51	Coventry	54.3			4	18	52	3	265
52	Portsmouth	53.9	90	68	3	23	59	4	282
53	Derby	53.8	79	65	9	17			234
54	Canterbury Christ Church	53.6	94	84	2	17		2	259
55	Northampton	52.7	89	71	2	15	39	7	209
56	Sheffield Hallam	52.4	80	71	3	28	45	10	268
57	Queen's, Belfast	50.4	84	67	5	20	48	1	309
58	Ulster	50.1			3	23	61	3	243
59	Oxford Brookes	49.0	81	49	3	23	53	6	281
60	Cumbria	43.5	74	45	2	21	68	1	242
61	Liverpool John Moores	33.1	78	62	3	20	35	1	206

Mathematics

❝ Few people who have not studied a mathematics or science degree will have much idea what modern mathematics involves. Most of the arithmetic and geometry seen in schools today was known to the Ancient Greeks; the ideas of calculus and probability you may have met at A-level were known in the 17th century. And some very neat ideas are to be found there! But mathematicians have not simply been admiring the work of Newton and Fermat for the last three centuries. Since then the patterns of mathematics have been found more profoundly and broadly than those early mathematicians could ever have imagined. There is no denying it: mathematics is in a golden age, and mathematicians are more in demand today than ever before.

The clearest change of emphasis from A-level to university mathematics is in the need to prove things, especially in pure mathematics. Much mathematics is too abstract or technical to simply rely on intuition, and so it is important that you can write clear and irrefutable arguments, which make plain to you, and others, the soundness of your claims. But pure mathematics is more than an insistence on rigour, arguably involving the most beautiful ideas and theorems in all of mathematics, and including whole new areas, such as topology, untouched at school.

Mathematics, though, would not be the subject it is today if it wasn't for the impact of applied mathematics and statistics. There is much beautiful mathematics to be found here, such as in relativity or in number theory behind the RSA encryption widely used in internet security, or just in the way a wide range of techniques from all reaches of mathematics might be applied to solve a difficult problem.

Also with ever-faster computers, mathematicians can now model highly complex systems such as the human heart, can explain why spotted animals have striped tails, can treat non-deterministic systems like the stock market or Brownian motion. The high technical demands of these models and the prevalence of computers in everyday life are making mathematicians ever more employable after university.

Dr Richard Earl, *Schools Liaison Officer for the Mathematical Institute and Tutor in Mathematics, Worcester College, University of Oxford*

You might expect a subject that's been around since the days of Pythagoras and the Ancient Greeks to have run its course. But no – maths is pushing the boundaries like never before, with ideas such as chaos theory revolutionising the way we view the world.

More than that, maths is about pattern and structure; it is about logical analysis, deduction, and calculation within these patterns and structures. When patterns are found, often in widely different areas of nature, science, and technology, the mathematics of these patterns can be used to explain phenomena and reveal new truths and insights.

Maths at university is much broader and more varied than maths at A-level – it takes subjects like algebra and geometry into new, abstract dimensions, such as analysis, topology, and group theory. So read the prospectus carefully and make sure you know what you're getting into. Work could be done with the help of a computer, or just an old-fashioned paper, pencil, and furrowed brow.

Recent studies have shown that the average maths graduate consistently earns more than graduates of other subjects – employers are always looking for the strong skills in reasoning and problem-solving you'll acquire. Computing, high finance, management consultancy, risk assessment, information security, and industrial research are all sectors that welcome maths graduates.

The courses students are pitching at can vary dramatically in content, but the first year at least should contain common elements such as algebra, differential equations, probability, and statistics.

After that, the field can be wide open, so investigate thoroughly before applying and check the compulsory elements aren't precisely those areas that scare the living daylights out of you.

You might also consider joint honours – maths and computer science is a popular degree choice, and four-year degrees with a placement in industry are also available. Maths and accountancy is also a good option – many accounting firms prefer it to a straight accountancy degree. Combinations such as these, along with work experience, give graduates plenty of relevant ways to increase their employability. If you get the chance of a work placement, you should always take it, so look into the possibilities.

“ A maths degree is different to A-level, in that it's not so much about finding the answer any more, but how you find the answer and proving you are right. It expands your knowledge so you understand why things happen, or why a formula is constructed, rather than just accepting it is right. It's a lot more challenging, and you get to look at other aspects of maths that aren't considered in A-level, such as problem-solving, which is my favourite module.

Dawn Crichton, *second-year mathematics student, University of Leicester*

》 Further information

The Institute of Mathematics
Catherine Richards House
16 Nelson Street, Southend-on-Sea
Essex SS1 1EF

t   01702 354020
e   post@ima.org.uk
↗   www.ima.org.uk

The London Mathematical Society
De Morgan House, 57-8 Russell Square
London WC1B 4HS

t   020 7637 3686
e   lms@lms.ac.uk

The Mathematical Association
259 London Road
Leicester LE2 3BE

t   0116 221 0013
e   office@m-a.org.uk
↗   www.m-a.org.uk

↗ Online reading

The Centre for the Popularisation of Maths www.popmath.org.uk
Mega Mathematics www.c3.lanl.gov/mega-math
Maths careers www.mathscareers.org.uk
Plus magazine www.plus.maths.org
The University of Southampton's cipher challenge www.cipher.maths.soton.ac.uk

Mathematics

		Guardian score	Satisfied with teaching %	Satisfied with assessment %	Spend per student score /10	Student-staff ratio	Job prospects %	Value added score /10	Average entry tariff
1	Oxford	100.0	93	81	10	15	83	7	535
2	Cambridge	91.9			10	14	82	7	552
3	Lancaster	85.5	90	73	10		83	5	411
4	Portsmouth	77.1	83	78	8	10		9	249
5	Durham	74.8	88	78	3	14	78	7	522
6	Warwick	73.7	75	55	9	13	73	5	512
7	Imperial College	72.8	77	60	10	15	75	3	496
8	Leicester	72.0	90	84	6	13	78	4	328
9	Sheffield Hallam	71.9	87	80	4	18		10	239
10	Birmingham	71.8	83	78	6	14	75	5	429
11	St Andrews	70.1	90	68	5	12	65	6	473
12	UCL	68.8	81	66	6	17	81	5	473
13	UEA	66.9	94	77	5	15	57	7	400
14	Southampton	66.7	79	51	6	14	79	6	412
15	Hertfordshire	66.4	84	67	3	11	71	10	229
16	Nottingham	66.1	83	66	5	14	75	5	446
17	Edinburgh	65.7	75	62	8	17	73	6	441
18	Bristol	65.2	82	50	5	16	78	4	470
19	Loughborough	65.0	86	75	6	17	79	4	365
20	Bath	64.4	75	57	4	17	84	5	476
20	Royal Holloway	64.4	85	71	7	12		4	361
22	Surrey	64.2	84	67	7	13		2	394
23	Sheffield	64.1	85	74	4	15	70	7	394
24	Heriot-Watt	63.9	78	60	4	16	76	7	414
25	UWE Bristol	63.8	88	79	5	14			255
26	Leeds	62.4	73	56	8	12	65	3	409
27	Kent	62.2	76	59	4	12		8	281
28	London School of Economics	61.9	68	61	6	20	83	4	500
29	Reading	61.6	82	50	6	14	68	6	343
30	Glasgow	61.5	82	68	6	13	74	2	392
31	Exeter	60.9	89	76	4	16	64	5	374
32	York	60.7	76	57	5	15	74	4	440
33	Cardiff	60.6	76	64	5	17	70	8	394
34	King's College London	59.7			5	15	61	5	421
35	Plymouth	59.5	75	75	2	9		9	261
36	Liverpool	57.7	88	68	5	14	59	5	378
37	Sussex	57.0	78	76	4	17	50	9	392
38	City	54.9	78	49	3	21		9	306
39	Queen's, Belfast	53.7	78	70	2	23	86	6	366
40	Newcastle	53.6	85	58	4	17	73	2	397
41	Glamorgan	53.5	84	70	4	20			227
42	Manchester	53.0			8	17	46	3	449
42	Swansea	53.0			3	15		5	329
44	Strathclyde	52.6	78	66	3	19	75		
45	Essex	51.1	74	56	4	11			320
46	Greenwich	49.2	94	83	4	27			210
47	Brunel	48.8	70	60	5	14	45	8	280
48	Queen Mary	43.8	80	61	4	15	58	1	288
49	Cumbria	43.2	79	62	5	20			237
50	Manchester Met	41.3	81	70	3	26		6	267
51	Northumbria	31.4			2	17		1	260

Physics

❝ Physics is the study of the nature and properties of energy and matter. As a physics under-graduate you will develop an in-depth understanding of the forces and interactions that take in both the microscopic and macroscopic worlds, from ionisation to isotopes, from quarks to quadrupoles, from superconductors to supernovae. In doing so you will also encounter new and cutting-edge concepts in science such as nanotechnology and supersymmetry.

People who study physics have a hunger for understanding how things work. A physics degree satisfies this hunger by introducing students to new concepts which include exploring the world of quantum physics, discovering how mass and time itself changes in Einstein's special and general relativity, studying the fundamental building blocks of matter in particle physics, and learning how physics concepts underpin a diverse range of technologies, including micro-processors, non-drip paints, quantum computers, and the global positioning system.

As well as developing skills as a scientist it is well recognised that a physics graduate possesses a wide range of other competences and skills including numeracy, problem-solving, teamwork, and communication — all of which are greatly sought after by employers. Taking a physics degree opens up a huge range of stimulating and lucrative careers.

Dr Lee Thompson, *Undergraduate Admissions Tutor, Department of Physics and Astronomy, University of Sheffield*

To study physics is to join a great tradition of scientists, from Newton to Faraday and from Watt to Hawking, to study interactions on the largest scale imaginable (between stars and galaxies) to the smallest scale we know of (between subatomic particles). In short, it's the study of the universe. And it doesn't get any bigger (or smaller) than that.

So it's no surprise that the demand for graduates is growing. Physics courses have a strong emphasis on analytical skills (and often require a fair proportion of maths skills too), and the degree is a highly respected qualification. Graduates end up in a whole range of professions, in areas as diverse as research, teaching, computing, medicine, and engineering.

The usual offering is a BSc of three years' duration, although about a third of physics students do a four-year degree known as an MPhys or MSc. These courses give you the opportunity to specialise in the final year, and get a deeper understanding in the areas of your choice. The courses cover a variety of topics, with many institutions offering modules in medical physics, astronomy, space and science, applied physics, and other related topics, so check if these are available — though the modular course structure at many universities means that you should be able to tailor your course to fit your interests and career aspirations if you look hard enough.

The drop in applicants to "traditional" science courses which has affected some subjects has left physics relatively unscathed. Teaching is based on the usual mixture of lectures, tutorials, lab work and seminars, with the mix dependent on the institution you are at. Most courses also demand a dissertation in the final year, which is an excellent opportunity for engaging in your own experimental or theoretical research.

Once qualified, and if you want to stay a scientist, the Institute of Physics (IoP), the professional body for physicists, can help you to obtain recognised professional status, such as chartered physicist (CPhys) and chartered engineer (CEng). The simplest first step to becoming chartered is to do a degree that has been accredited by the IoP, otherwise you have to prove that the course is equivalent to an accredited degree. It's far easier to check the accreditation before you start.

Most universities still specialise within certain areas of physics. While their undergraduates will study across a broad spectrum, you will find that the researchers work in only four or five regions, so you can select an institution where world-class researchers are working at the frontline of scientific discovery that interests you. But remember to check if they are still actively involved in teaching – it may be that they have "better" things to do.

Some universities offer courses (generally the four-year version) where you can incorporate industrial or laboratory-based placements and other work experience into your studies, or study abroad. Investigate whether this is a possibility, since it's a great opportunity for you to try out your chosen career and see if you like it or not.

A high number of universities have a physics society that organises events in addition to your academic course, such as inviting guest speakers, arranging tours of research facilities and industrial sites, and holding social functions that provide an excellent opportunity to meet the more senior physicists at your department. Events for students are also organised by Nexus, the student wing of the IoP; these include an annual conference (with a hefty social programme). This is the sort of thing that can provide an extra dimension to your course and occasionally restore your faith on those wet Tuesdays when you're wondering what on earth you're doing there.

“ Degree-level physics is where you learn to think for yourself and, most importantly, to question. A physicist's most used word is 'why?' (closely followed by 'how?'). Physics is challenging – it's the hard things that are the most memorable and it's the fact that you've overcome them that makes it enjoyable. The 'Oh, wow, that must be difficult!' comments you get from non-scientists when you tell them what you do is also quite good though.

Rachel Ashley, *second-year physics student, University of Liverpool*

》 Further information

Institute of Physics
76 Portland Place
London W1B 1NT

t   020 7470 4800
↗ www.iop.org

Royal Astronomical Society
Burlington House, Piccadilly
London W1J 0BQ

t   020 7734 4582
↗ www.ras.org.uk

↗ Online reading

Science and Technology Facilities Council www.scitech.ac.uk
Physics Web www.physicsweb.org
Royal Society www.royalsoc.ac.uk
WiTEC – the European Association for Women in Science and Engineering and Technology
   www.witec-eu.net

Physics

		Guardian score	Satisfied with teaching %	Satisfied with assessment %	Spend per student score /10	Student:staff ratio	Job prospects %	Value added score /10	Average entry tariff
1	Oxford	100.0	85	72	10	11	84	4	551
2	Imperial College	91.5	78	64	8	8	80	6	509
3	Leeds	89.3	80	63	10	9	74	8	397
4	Liverpool	86.7	87	69	7	9	79	8	348
5	Heriot-Watt	85.0	75	57	4	11		10	350
6	Edinburgh	84.9	84	46	10	10	64	5	442
7	UCL	83.8	79	52	7	8	77	5	427
8	Manchester	82.1	85	58	9	10	70	6	446
9	Lancaster	81.0	82	78	6	7	70	6	389
10	Glasgow	80.4	93	64	5	9	91	1	383
10	Strathclyde	80.4	88	72	6	8	63		
12	Aberystwyth	80.2	94	70	8	10	77		266
13	Southampton	79.7	91	65	7	9	70	6	428
14	Sheffield	79.1	79	75	3	10	76	8	386
15	St Andrews	76.9	85	52	6	10	68	5	484
16	Birmingham	76.8	89	71	5	12	67	6	431
17	Royal Holloway	76.2	90	63	4	7		5	333
18	Sussex	75.5	92	57	4	10		9	379
19	Warwick	74.6	86	74	6	12	65	4	490
20	Swansea	74.5	89	66	4	9			295
21	Durham	73.8	85	73	3	13	71	5	507
21	Leicester	73.8	78	50	9	8	69	4	348
23	Nottingham	72.8	79	50	6	11	79	3	427
24	King's College London	69.0	84	44	5	11			363
25	Bath	65.4	83	72	3	13	68	6	428
26	York	62.3	86	60	4	13	69	4	394
27	Queen's, Belfast	61.4	72	61	4	8	62	5	371
28	Bristol	60.7	79	48	3	15	69	7	433
29	Loughborough	60.2	83	68	3	14		7	332
30	Hull	59.6	89	63	4	16			267
31	Kent	58.5	75	57	3	12	72	8	292
32	Cardiff	56.2	78	60	4	10	62	4	345
33	Surrey	55.1	84	57	4	12	69	1	355
34	Exeter	53.7	91	73	3	14	55	4	361
35	Nottingham Trent	46.5	73	50	2	11			218
36	Glamorgan	36.0	83	57	2	23			225

Social sciences

Business and management studies

> The growth of business education has been a major success story, with many UK business schools featuring amongst the most highly rated in the world. This growth has been driven by the demands of industry and commerce for more candidates with relevant, highly transferable skills. Choosing to embark upon a business degree is a smart career choice: recent research demonstrates that business graduates can achieve starting salaries of over £25,000 per year, but with business schools offering the opportunity for post experience courses such as the MBA, specialist masters' degrees, executive courses, and even doctoral programmes, the possibilities for ongoing career development and increasing earnings potential are all part of the lifelong learning and development package.
>
> The majority of graduates join large multinational organisations, with almost half entering careers related to finance. The next most popular business function is sales and marketing, with management consultancy, IT, and human resources well represented, although increasingly the public sector, such as local government and not-for-profit organisations, are also recruiting business graduates.
>
> A business studies course will also introduce you to networking, an important skill for candidates to acquire, who will be going out into a wide range of organisations all over the world. The contacts and relationships built up, both during the course and through alumni associations, will prove a lasting benefit throughout your career.
>
> **Vincent Hammersley**, *Director of Communications, Warwick Business School, University of Warwick*

More students enrol on business or management courses than any other university degree. So you won't be alone, but you may be bewildered by the choice. Almost all universities will have a programme that falls under the general heading of "business", although the titles of the programmes vary considerably across different institutions – business management, commerce, or business administration. Many degrees also suggest a more specialist focus, such as finance, marketing, retail management, tourism management or international business. And this doesn't take into account joint honours degrees ...

But there are certain common building blocks to all business degrees, such as finance, marketing, and human resource management. Most courses will also touch on business strategy, operations, supply chain and production management. Students are expected to be numerate, so most degrees will have courses in quantitative methods and statistics.

It's a generalisation, but the newer universities tend to be more vocationally orientated, while the older courses are more likely to be based on theory. Whichever you choose, most institutions are pretty flexible about what A-levels you need.

Let's face it, much of the reason for doing a degree like this is to get a job – and finance, management, and marketing certainly do pay well. Remember though, many people who succeed in business do so without a business degree – instead they train afterwards, either on short courses or with an MBA perhaps, so make certain you're interested in the subject for its own sake. No degree is a guarantee of post-graduation success or a licence to print money.

Increasingly in business, technology is key, so make sure a course has more than adequate provision in that area, so you'll be up-to-date with the hardware and software that companies would expect you to use.

Business is a multidisciplinary course – it sits some way between the sciences and the humanities – that can encompass a huge range of extra areas, and the temptation is to take as broad an approach as possible to get to know a little of everything. But this jack-of-all-trades modular approach may not be the best for you in terms of future employment, so consider economics or law or another add-on as a separate degree option entirely.

No matter what you know, it's what you've done that will help impress employers most, so have a look at placement schemes, sandwich courses, and links from the course to employers. If you head off to a job interview with a CV packed with relevant experience, you'll soon be picking out your new suit for work.

For some, reputation is all, so if you're taking the course with a specific goal in mind (working in a City bank, for example), talk to people already employed in that field and find out which institution's graduates are most in demand.

---

66 Business is a very diverse subject to study at university and involves drawing together work from areas as broad as economics, finance, marketing, statistics, and organisational behaviour. Some modules develop practical skills for working in a professional environment, while others study business activities in a more objective, academic way. I've really enjoyed choosing modules to suit my developing interests, and at Bath there's the added value of two different work placements, meaning you gain experience in two organisations and business functions.

Sam Manly, *fourth-year business administration student, University of Bath*

» Further information

British Academy of Management
137 Euston Road
London NW1 2AA
t 020 7383 7770
↗ www.bam.ac.uk

Chartered Institute of Marketing
Moor Hall, Cookham
Maidenhead, Berkshire SL6 9QH
t 01628 427500
↗ www.cim.co.uk   »

Institute of Chartered Accountants in England and Wales
Chartered Accountants' Hall   **t** 020 7920 8100
PO Box 433, London EC2P 2BJ   ↗ www.icaew.co.uk

Institute of Chartered Accountants of Scotland
CA House, 21 Haymarket Yards   **t** 0131 347 0100
Edinburgh EH12 5BH   ↗ www.icas.org.uk

↗ | Online reading

Guardian Unlimited Business business.guardian.co.uk
Bized www.bized.co.uk
British Universities Industrial Relations Association www.buira.org.uk
Confederation of British Industry www.cbi.org.uk
Chartered Institute of Management Accountants www.cima.org.uk

Business and management studies

		Guardian score	Satisfied with teaching %	Satisfied with assessment %	Spend per student score /10	Student:staff ratio	Job prospects %	Value added score /10	Average entry tariff
1	Oxford	100.0	84	63		8	94	9	518
2	Warwick	91.3	80	58	10	16	78	8	450
3	City	83.6	84	64	10	22	69	10	383
4	Exeter	80.1	91	80	7	19	80	7	377
5	Lancaster	78.8	86	59	10	16	68	7	395
6	Strathclyde	77.2	82	67	9	19	72	10	306
7	St Andrews	77.0	86	65	5	16		10	407
8	Bath	76.0	80	54	7	25	86	10	416
9	Manchester	75.8	78	53	10	16	62	7	402
10	Glasgow	73.8	88	62	8	20	77	6	406
11	London School of Economics	73.1	72	60	7	16	90	4	458
12	Imperial College	72.4			10	21		2	403
13	Leicester	72.2	89	77	10	26	64	7	312
14	Loughborough	70.9	89	69	6	25	85	5	400
15	King's College London	70.5			6	22	90	5	407
16	Aston	69.9	84	68	8	27	72	9	385
17	Queen's, Belfast	69.3	77	64	3	13	72	8	370
18	Nottingham	68.5	76	49	8	21	77	7	402
19	Leeds	66.8	73	48	8	17	71	5	397
20	Reading	66.7	73	54	6	18	80	7	350
21	Birmingham	65.5	79	58	8	21	62	6	387
22	Bangor	65.2	79	62	4	13	74	7	252
23	Durham	64.9	76	56	7	22	73	7	346
24	Sussex	64.8	80	60	3	18			364
25	Dundee	64.4	89	60	4	15	65	6	323
26	UCL	64.3	74	48	8	15		1	398
27	Edinburgh	64.2	75	42	8	27	67	9	423
28	Queen Margaret	63.0			9		53	7	223
29	Stirling	62.9			4	15	65	8	274

	Guardian score	Satisfied with teaching %	Satisfied with assessment %	Spend per student score /10	Student:staff ratio	Job prospects %	Value added score /10	Average entry tariff
30 Aberdeen	61.9	75	56	5	18	69		324
31 York	61.2	75	49	5	15	81	3	339
32 Central Lancashire	60.5	81	72	6	16	59	6	252
33 Glamorgan	59.7	80	64	9	16	45	5	236
34 Queen Mary	59.4	78	49	5		61	6	315
35 Sheffield	58.7	75	60	4	22	64	7	362
36 Liverpool	58.5	72	58	7	22	53	7	366
37 Southampton	58.4	76	56	5	31	79	8	373
38 Newcastle	58.3	67	51	5	25	75	7	383
39 Robert Gordon	58.2			4	23	80	6	298
40 Nottingham Trent	57.5	69	54	6	21	80	6	257
40 UEA	57.5	82	74	7	31	67	4	336
42 Heriot-Watt	57.4	77	54	8	28	71	6	322
42 Kent	57.4	77	66	6	20	74	3	296
44 Oxford Brookes	56.9	79	60	6	22	60	6	299
45 Bradford	56.6	76	63	8	20	54	5	232
46 Cardiff	56.4	77	51	5	19	57	4	378
47 Surrey	56.2	66	42	6	24	69	7	345
48 Napier	55.2			3	26	76	9	220
49 Hull	55.0	84	67	5	28	67	7	265
50 St Mary's UC, Twickenham	54.8	84	70	3	18		7	209
51 Essex	54.5	74	53	4	20	60	6	290
52 Chester	54.2			4	21	61	5	259
53 Bournemouth	54.1	79	66	5	28	65	7	275
54 Winchester	53.9	79	62	2	15	45	8	244
55 Canterbury Christ Church	53.7	83	72	2	20	37	10	207
56 Bath Spa	53.5	88	70	3	22	53	6	228
56 Lincoln	53.5	82	67	3	23	55	8	247
56 Northampton	53.5	87	68	3	26	52	9	211
59 Glasgow Caledonian	53.1	79	55	3	24	45	9	335
59 Teesside	53.1	75	70	8	18	41	5	217
61 Brighton	52.9	78	67	3	26	53	9	266
62 Royal Holloway	52.8	66	44	5	23	68	6	336
63 Plymouth	52.6	75	54	8	19	45	5	252
64 UWE Bristol	52.4	78	60	3	23	66	7	242
65 Birmingham City	51.7	81	65	6	24	52	8	230
66 Northumbria	50.9	74	54	5	24	69	3	299
67 Cumbria	50.3	80	72	3	17		5	232
68 De Montfort	49.9	81	65	3	23	52	6	239
69 Brunel	49.8	67	53	4	25	53	8	297
70 Royal Agricultural College	49.4	73	58	5	23	68	2	310
71 Ulster	49.3	79	57	4	26	45	8	274
72 North East Wales Institute	49.2			3	24	44	8	225
73 Gloucestershire	49.0	70	64	4	23	56	6	240
73 Staffordshire	49.0	67	51	8	20	44	6	230

		Guardian score	Satisfied with teaching %	Satisfied with assessment %	Spend per student score /10	Student:staff ratio	Job prospects %	Value added score /10	Average entry tariff
75	Edge Hill	48.4	80	76	3	20	43	4	233
75	Sheffield Hallam	48.4	77	62	4	27	50	8	256
77	Manchester Met	47.8	75	63	3	24	54	5	260
78	Swansea	47.4	77	55	4	26	66	4	285
79	Salford	47.3	68	61	4	18	59	2	258
80	Anglia Ruskin	46.5	74	61	5	20	42	4	219
81	Abertay Dundee	45.6			4	20	42	6	204
82	Huddersfield	45.2	71	65	3	20	30	7	236
83	Aberystwyth	45.1	74	60	4	24	43	5	272
83	Portsmouth	45.1	80	60	4	28	64	3	263
85	University College Birmingham	44.4	79	73			44	4	222
86	Newport	43.7	88	86	3	26	30	3	196
87	Wolverhampton	42.9			4	17	48	2	179
88	Kingston	42.8	76	57	6	26	49	3	228
89	Leeds Met	42.4	67	46	5	23	53	3	252
90	Worcester	42.2	77	63	3	22	48	4	201
91	Coventry	40.8	74	61	4	33	45	8	236
91	Liverpool John Moores	40.8	72	58	3	27	58	3	229
93	Greenwich	40.7	73	58	4	27	52	4	172
94	Westminster	40.4	69	53	4	25	45	5	233
95	UWIC	40.2	66	60	3	18	40	3	214
96	Roehampton	39.6	73	64	4	23	58	2	187
97	University of the Arts London	39.4	57	47	5	23	41	5	234
98	Derby	39.1	74	63	4	24	42	3	231
99	Thames Valley	38.7	82	73	3	25	40	3	176
100	Bucks New University	36.8	74	53	4	27	42	4	192
100	Hertfordshire	36.8	68	54	4	26	47	2	244
102	Leeds Trinity & All Saints	35.6	60	38	2	22	51	3	243
103	Bedfordshire	35.5	83	72	3	32	38	3	161
104	Swansea Met	35.0				16	33	1	173
105	Bolton	34.1	76	69	3	22	29	2	175
105	Sunderland	34.1	80	66	3	31	47	2	219
107	Southampton Solent	33.4	71	57	3	33	60	3	194
108	York St John	32.8	71	57	3	29	41	1	324
109	London South Bank	32.6	81	64	3		28	4	162
110	East London	31.3	74	61	5	25	38	1	155
111	Middlesex	27.1	69	54	5	38	42	4	151

Educational studies

❝ Pursuing a course in educational studies opens up a complex and exciting investigation into the nature of learning, as well as policies and structures to initiate and develop education. This entails developing an understanding of social, psychological, cultural, historical, political, and ethical factors that affect learning and which structure the pursuit of learning (and teaching) within and beyond institutional contexts.

In more detail, educational studies allows students to consider the dynamics of human development and learning in a variety of disciplines and fields and the politics of education within state education systems as well as alternative approaches to mainstream educational practices. It involves a comparative study of the history of educational practices and policies within the UK and other countries. It deals with philosophical and ethical issues that interrogate the aims and purposes of education and pedagogy. It considers the relations between education and power as well as social and cultural factors that impact upon educational policies and practices.

Professor Dennis Atkinson, *Head of Department of Educational Studies and Director of the Research Centre for the Arts and Learning, Goldsmiths College, University of London*

Mention that you're doing educational studies and everyone will think of the classroom, but the subject isn't simply about being a teacher. And if you're just leaving school you might be grateful for that – it seems a bit early to be planning to head right back there. And remember, you'll generally need a PGCE (postgraduate certificate of education) if you want to be a teacher.

As education has come to the forefront of the political spectrum, with tuition fees particularly a recurring area for debate, so there has been a correspondingly dramatic increase in the number of degree programmes in broader educational studies – that is, those that do not lead to qualified teacher status and instead award a BA degree.

These programmes do not view education narrowly. They are concerned not only with schools and children, but with a whole host of other areas, such as the nature of teaching and learning, personal development, the rights of children, law, gender, multiculturalism, and justice, and how these interrelate with education policy and practice. They offer an academic exploration of what governments, organizations, and individuals are doing when they invest – financially, politically, personally – in education.

Students do not simply learn about the history, sociology, philosophy, and psychology of education, but also the portrayal of educational experiences in novels, policy documents, and the findings of important studies.

Teaching methods most commonly involve workshops, seminars, and tutorials. Many programmes take the opportunity to explore matters in practical "real world" contexts and employ collaborative group work activities. There is normally a requirement for students to produce a dissertation, often in the final year of study, which involves the collection and analysis of empirical data associated with, for example, bullying in schools, controversial issues in teaching a school subject or equal opportunities.

Some graduates in educational studies go on to follow education-related careers in the heritage industry, media, management, banking, and administration or of course – following a further year's training – teaching.

How you choose a course depends on what you want to do with it. If you see educational studies as a way of becoming a teacher, check if there is any provision for transfer after graduation to a teacher education programme taught in the same department or institution. It might also be advisable, if you want to teach in a school, to take a joint degree in educational studies and a school subject.

If you want to study education in the broader sense, then look at the topics covered by both your course and the research, specialisations or publications of the teaching staff. The broader the range of choices, the more rounded the degree, but that's no use if there's a particular area you find fascinating that isn't offered. Investigate also whether they have decent computer rooms and can fill you in on the latest developments in e-learning.

---

66 My course has provided an insight into the history of education from the 1800s onwards and how changes in society have developed the education system of today. Students have a choice of two study routes: the humanities, or mathematics and science – the units cover a wide variety of interesting and accessible topics. Being a mature student I was daunted by the idea of returning to study and writing essays, however I've really enjoyed having open and frank discussions about the texts.

Helen Redman, *third-year education student, University of Manchester*

》 Further information

British Educational Research Association
Association House, South Park Road   ↗ www.bera.ac.uk
Macclesfield, Cheshire SK11 6SH

Institute of Education
University of London, 20 Bedford Way   t   020 7612 6000
London WC1H 0AL   e   info@ioe.ac.uk
                                            ↗ www.ioe.ac.uk

↗ Online reading

EducationGuardian.co.uk EducationGuardian.co.uk
The Training and Development Agency for Schools www.tda.gov.uk
NUT (National Union of Teachers) www.teachers.org.uk
National Union of Students www.nusonline.co.uk
University and College Union www.ucu.org.uk
Association of University Administrators www.aua.ac.uk
The Commonwealth of Learning www.col.org

Education

		Guardian score	Satisfied with teaching %	Satisfied with assessment %	Spend per student score /10	Student:staff ratio	Job prospects %	Value added score /10	Average entry tariff
1	Cambridge	100.0	89	73	10	14	93	8	438
2	Warwick	76.6	85	67	10	16	71	7	338
3	Aberdeen	76.2	89	62	10	15	94		349
4	Kingston	75.7	91	70	7	13	85	10	235
5	Dundee	74.1	82	68	4	18	97	10	316
6	Edinburgh	72.2	82	50	9	17	93	6	360
7	Exeter	71.4	90	59	10	19	74	7	338
8	St Mary's UC, Belfast	70.3	81	61	2	16	93	10	348
9	Reading	69.9	87	65	6	19	95	9	295
10	Stirling	69.3			6	11	94	4	282
11	Newport	68.4	83	72	10	12	88	3	228
12	Manchester	65.9	91	70		17		6	351
13	Hertfordshire	65.7	89	69	6	13	73	9	258
14	Durham	63.2	85	48	7	18	88	6	365
14	Leeds Trinity & All Saints	63.2	93	64	3	21	93	5	360
16	Leeds	60.4	83	56	8	15	49	8	356
17	Canterbury Christ Church	57.9	82	59	5	17	88	5	309
18	De Montfort	56.1	82	68		12	86	5	231
19	Swansea Met	55.3	93	83	2	23	95	5	270
20	York St John	54.6	93	71	5	19	74	7	276
21	Worcester	54.2	88	66	6	19	76	6	257
22	Stranmillis UC	53.8	81	58	2	17	77	8	340
22	Sunderland	53.8	81	67	6	20	86	7	258
24	Glasgow	53.3	77	61	4	19	98	3	322
25	Birmingham City	53.2	87	67	4	19	76	5	294
26	Middlesex	52.9	70	56	9	20	91	6	205
27	Goldsmiths	52.6	89	53	5	20	91	5	226
28	Plymouth	52.3	82	69	8	21	70	8	244
29	Leeds Met	52.2	78	63	6	17	70	7	277
30	Brighton	51.9	85	70	4	23	93	4	299
31	Gloucestershire	51.8	79	48	9	20	80	6	263
32	UWIC	50.4	79	61	7	22	81	6	257
33	York	49.5	76	51	8	21		5	344
34	Newman University College	49.0	91	70	3	18	84	4	234
34	St Mary's UC, Twickenham	49.0	90	67	2	26	87	7	284
36	Wolverhampton	48.6	84	76	5	19	81	5	219
37	Northumbria	48.5	85	56	7	20	66	5	298
38	Anglia Ruskin	48.4	76	61	8	19	71	5	278
39	Nottingham Trent	48.2	80	64	6	20	67	7	278
40	Aberystwyth	48.1	92	74	6	24			291
41	Manchester Met	47.8	79	60	6	22	83	4	282
42	Bishop Grosseteste UC	47.5	87	72	2	25	93	4	323
43	Oxford Brookes	46.8	87	72	5	21	71	4	273
44	Bedfordshire	46.1	81	63	6	16		2	250
45	Hull	44.6	83	63	5	24	89	4	250

	Guardian score	Satisfied with teaching %	Satisfied with assessment %	Spend per student score /10	Student:staff ratio	Job prospects %	Value added score /10	Average entry tariff
46 Strathclyde	43.4	83	53	5	18	89	2	245
47 Central Lancashire	43.3	78	70			64	1	240
48 UWE Bristol	42.4	76	51	4	24	71	10	246
49 Winchester	42.3	81	68	2	22	76	6	269
50 Marjon (St Mark and St John)	42.2	90	75	3	25	81	4	246
51 Cumbria	42.1	80	59	4	20	84	2	269
52 North East Wales Institute	41.7	90	78	3	21	60	7	239
53 Bangor	41.0	85	74	4	24	80	3	251
54 Edge Hill	40.3	84	68	4	27	82	4	279
55 Bath Spa	39.9	90	72	3	28	71	7	253
56 Chester	38.8	92	67	4	26	69	4	267
57 Sheffield Hallam	38.1	80	63	3	22	67	5	276
58 Northampton	36.9	83	66	4	23	68	4	241
59 Chichester	36.4	88	67	3	24	78	2	256
60 Roehampton	35.2	86	68	4	20	65	2	231
61 Trinity College, Carmarthen	34.2	82	63	2	17	71	2	232
62 Derby	33.8	75	67	3	20	52	6	252
63 Liverpool John Moores	30.9	72	49	4	18	65	2	243
64 East London	30.7	73	57	5	18	68	4	159
65 Birmingham	29.6	73	62	7	26	47	2	337
66 Greenwich	25.7	70	45	5	24	73	4	207

Economics

❝ Want to understand the world? Want to get to grips with the big issues affecting us all, such as climate change, globalisation, the pensions crisis, meltdown in financial markets, why some countries are rich and others poor? Then economics is for you. Economics provides you with the analytical skills to explore these topics in depth and to dissect issues that are both complex and important. As well as big policy issues, economics can answer more micro-orientated questions including how individuals make choices, how firms compete and even what makes people 'happy'!

Economics touches every facet of our lives and the ability to understand and apply economic concepts provides the tool kit and skills to create insights into the macro and micro issues that affect us all. A combination of theory, quantitative skills, and how they are applied are the key ingredients of the economist's tool kit.

Economics is challenging but, then again, the world is a challenging place. It's a dynamic subject where new issues constantly emerge to which business and governments have to respond. Could we have imagined the liquidity crisis a year ago? Why are oil prices now reaching record highs and what are the implications for the future?

If you want to address how the world works, understand how policy can impact on the big issues that affect us all, and attain the appropriate skills that can be focused on new issues as they emerge, then economics is for you.

Professor Steve McCorriston, *Head of Economics, University of Exeter*

Next time there's a huge demonstration at a world summit, or the anti-capitalists take to the streets of London, remember what usually motivates the protestors – yep, economics. If single-issue politics is what galvanises young people, the (social) science that informs them is economics – whose money is making the world go round, and why they control it.

Whichever angle you come from, it's economics that runs – or ruins – the world. As John Maynard Keynes, the 20th century's greatest economist, elegantly put it: "Practical men who believe themselves to be quite exempt from any intellectual influences are usually the slaves of some defunct economist."

Post-university employment rates of economists are among the highest for graduates. The subject gives students a good intellectual training – sitting somewhere between science and humanities – which employers like. It also, obviously, has lots of practical applications in the world of business.

Once qualified, you'll have transferable skills in problem-solving, quantitative analysis, and communication. Very few economics graduates work as professional economists, but the majority do find work in related areas – finance, banking, insurance, accountancy, and management and consultancy.

On an economics course, you'll often start with a basic grounding in the social sciences generally, before moving on to economics proper. Then you'll be studying both macro- and micro-economics, and the links between them: the millions of small choices that make up the big ones. To understand economic models, you have to understand both. You'll learn about reasoning and methodology – how economic models fit, or not. In some ways, studying economics becomes a little like philosophy – you'll have to be prepared to defend theories and economic ideologies you may have long held dear. You can also view economics as a science – you'll work to basic assumptions about how people, and therefore economies, will behave and make a set of deductions from that.

If you're not keen on number crunching, you could be in for a nasty shock – you're going to need maths to help formulate theories and extrapolate assumptions and you're going to have to provide statistics to back yourself up. Indeed, your attitude to maths may well influence your choice of course. Some universities require A-level maths, while others ask only for a good grade at GCSE. These requirements are often reflected in the courses, some of which involve more figure-juggling than others. Bear in mind that while you may be able to minimise the maths and stats that you encounter, in doing so you may distort your view of modern economics.

Naturally, you must check what specialisations are open to you. Often the most interesting parts of any degree are the specialist subjects – economic thought from Adam Smith to Milton Friedman, or development economics in sub-Sahara Africa might be just your thing. Alternatively, doing economics as part of a joint degree is very popular: politics, philosophy, and economics, perhaps, or history.

Otherwise, do the obvious things – visit the departments you are considering applying to and ask the students there what they think of the courses. Also look at who is on the academic staff. Learning from those at the cutting edge of thought is always far more likely to keep you on your toes, though if you want to study under a particular economist, make sure they're not too busy to teach and take tutorials.

Some universities offer a sandwich course, enabling you to head off for work placements partway through, while others let you study abroad. And, as with any course, make sure you understand the assessment – exam, coursework or dissertation – and have a good idea as to whether that works for you.

---

66 The main difference between A-levels and my degree has been the increased level of self-discipline needed. Tutors proactively encourage attendance and are more than happy to help when approached, but at the end of the day you're an adult now and it's down to you. This teaches personal responsibility and for you to take ownership of your actions. The most enjoyable aspect of the course has been learning about the UK economy and the business world.

Murat Haykir, *first-year business economics with accounting student, University of Plymouth*

» Further information

Royal Economic Society
University of York
Heslington, York YO1 5DD
↗ www.res.org.uk

The Economics Network of the UK's Higher Education Academy
University of Bristol
8-10 Berkeley Square, Bristol BS8 1HH
↗ www.economicsnetwork.ac.uk

The Society of Business Economists
Dean House, Vernham Dean
Andover, Hants SP11 0JZ
t 01264 737552

The Government Economic Service
HM Treasury, 1 Horse Guards Road
London SW1A 2HQ

t 020 7270 4571 / 5073
e ges.int@hm-treasury.gov.uk
⌐ www.ges.gov.uk

The Royal Statistical Society
12 Errol Street
London EC1Y 8LX

t 020 7638 8998
e rss@rss.org.uk
⌐ www.rss.org.uk

⌐ Online reading

Why Study Economics? www.whystudyeconomics.ac.uk
Bized www.bized.co.uk
The Internet Economist www.vts.intute.ac.uk/he/tutorial/economist
Economic History Services www.eh.net
National Statistics Online www.statistics.gov.uk
The Economist www.economist.co.uk
The Financial Times www.ft.com
The Adam Smith Institute www.adamsmith.org
The Fabian Society www.fabian-society.org.uk

Economics

		Guardian score	Satisfied with teaching %	Satisfied with assessment %	Spend per student score /10	Student:staff ratio	Job prospects %	Value added score /10	Average entry tariff
1	Oxford	100.0	89	61	10	11	85	9	516
2	Cambridge	83.7			9	16	93	5	539
3	London School of Economics	80.9	82	63	8	13	87	7	512
4	Birmingham	80.5	89	80	9	17	78	8	408
5	Warwick	79.5	75	51	9	14	85	8	476
6	UCL	74.7	77	58	9	16	86	6	464
7	Durham	73.6	83	59	6	19	79	9	462
8	St Andrews	72.9	79	65	6	16		9	430
9	Lancaster	71.3	88	49	10	16	67	3	398
10	Soas	69.4	83	54	6	14	73	8	366
11	Edinburgh	69.3	79	42	8	16	72	7	437
12	Exeter	69.1	85	71	4	17	71	8	399
13	Nottingham	68.4	77	41	6	17	78	8	456
14	Bristol	68.0	77	47	6	20	88	7	460
15	Bath	66.3	78	45	5	17	81	6	439
16	Sussex	65.9	87	73	3	18		8	352
17	York	65.7	77	41	7	14	69	6	448
18	Glasgow	63.7	82	64	4	18	67	7	413
19	Coventry	62.7	82	82	4	19		10	240
20	Nottingham Trent	61.2	83	62	7	17	75	7	228
20	Strathclyde	61.2	85	64	8	22	61		
22	Queen Mary	60.9	72	47	7	17	77	4	349
23	Loughborough	60.7	92	66	6	20	73	3	376

	Guardian score	Satisfied with teaching %	Satisfied with assessment %	Spend per student score /10	Student:staff ratio	Job prospects %	Value added score /10	Average entry tariff
24 Kent	60.4	88	70	5	17	76	4	284
25 Essex	58.8	78	65	4	15	70	3	344
26 Surrey	58.6	79	49	5	20	81	5	285
27 Ulster	58.5	86	61	4	19	54	10	284
28 Leicester	58.3	83	71	4	22	66	6	325
29 Leeds	57.3	74	47	5	19	63	6	414
30 Manchester	56.7	72	49	7	19	56	6	400
31 Liverpool	56.1	81	55	4	22	63	7	372
32 Southampton	55.2	74	45	4	23	75	6	405
33 Royal Holloway	55.1	76	51	3	20	73	5	349
34 City	53.3	71	43	4	18	56	8	330
35 Aberdeen	52.9	80	58	4	21	61		292
36 Leeds Met	52.8	76	55	10	20		4	234
37 UEA	52.4	95	77	4	27	68	3	329
38 Sheffield	52.2	77	47	4	22	69	4	368
39 UWE Bristol	52.0	87	63	3	20	56	7	242
40 Staffordshire	51.3	83	74	5	25			245
41 Plymouth	51.1	81	62	7	16	42		206
41 Queen's, Belfast	51.1	65	52	4	20	53	8	345
43 Cardiff	50.9	69	57	6	19	57	3	397
43 Oxford Brookes	50.9	72	61	4	19		4	298
45 Hull	50.3	79	63	6	28	74	4	278
46 Bradford	49.9	80	65	6	12		1	203
47 Central Lancashire	48.9	88	67	4	28			311
48 Aberystwyth	48.8	91	71	3	21			281
48 Dundee	48.8	70	61	4	20		5	300
50 Newcastle	48.7	67	45	4	23	70	3	395
51 Manchester Met	48.3	78	65	3	20	67	3	261
52 Portsmouth	48.1	85	63	4	17	63	1	240
53 Brunel	47.3	62	42	3	17	58	6	304
54 East London	47.2	83	63	5	22			200
55 Salford	45.0	73	53	6	22			271
56 Swansea	44.1	86	61	3	24	56	3	276
57 Northumbria	43.3	76	56	4	27	67	3	273
58 Reading	41.7	68	49	3	20	55	3	320
59 Hertfordshire	36.0	66	55	4	26	50	3	218
60 Kingston	32.7	68	48	3	27	43	6	182
61 Greenwich	32.0	63	65	2	31		3	199
62 Middlesex	30.8	65	43	4	40		6	173
63 Liverpool John Moores	28.7	76	61	3	29		1	241

Law

❝ Studying law opens doors beyond the traditional route of qualification as a legal practitioner. The skills law graduates are equipped with make them a welcome addition to many varied professions, including journalism, finance, politics, the public sector, and many more. Our course equips undergraduates with a strong set of intellectual, practical, and transferable key skills, such as analytical, communication, and research skills, to give them a head start in the job market. In order to succeed, law students need to be able to study independently, enjoy problem-solving, and be self-motivated.

Options of study include taking a combined degree, for example law and a language. Students are able to take their law degree to many countries, including Europe and the USA, where minimal conversion might be required.

Lindsay Kelly, *Widening Participation Officer, School of Law, University of Edinburgh*

Law is one of the most sought-after careers, and it's therefore no surprise that it's also one of the most sought-after degrees in British universities, with more than 17,000 students applying to study it in 2007 alone. If that weren't competition enough, anyone with a good first degree can take a law conversion course after graduation and go on to become a lawyer. It is even possible to bypass university, start work in a law firm and take professional exams, although this is hardly a short cut.

However you do it, it's a slog at times; you need dedication during your course, and even after that, it's at least two years before you're fully qualified. So think long and hard about whether you're ready for it.

And once you've done that, brace yourself again for the LNat. The LNat is the national admissions test for law degrees, which is mandatory for all students applying to study law at 11 universities: Birmingham, Bristol, Cambridge, Durham, Exeter, Glasgow, King's, Manchester Metropolitan, Nottingham, Oxford, and UCL. It helps admissions tutors to choose the most able students, or to indicate natural ability that may not be shown in A-levels. More information can be found at www.lnat.ac.uk.

Legal education is split, broadly, into two stages: the academic stage and the vocational stage. The academic stage usually comprises a three- to four-year law degree (normally three years in England and Wales, but four in Scotland; four-year degrees in England and Wales are usually combined with another subject). Students should ensure that they study a qualifying law degree if they wish to proceed directly on to courses that allow them to become barristers and solicitors. (Would-be lawyers who take a different undergraduate degree first then take a year-long conversion course, known as the Common Professional Examination (CPE).)

Then the decisions come. To qualify as a barrister requires a year-long bar vocational course (BVC), followed by another year's pupillage in an approved training organisation, usually barristers' chambers. Solicitors take a Legal Practice Course (LPC), followed by a training contract usually lasting two years, before being admitted to the roll of solicitors.

An increasing number of joint degree courses are now on offer at universities, often combining law with sociology, business or politics. You'll generally be graded by a mixture of continuous assessment and exams, although some do expect a dissertation as well.

Once you've graduated, you will at the very least have a good solid professional qualification that your parents will approve of. From that base, you have a degree that can lead to an interesting career within the profession, which, if you get picked up by one of the big City law firms, can be very lucrative indeed. Some of you may even see it as a noble calling and feel the need to take up the shield of justice and fight for what is right. Most will settle for a comfortable career inside the profession either as a barrister or a solicitor, while some will take their training and skills into different arenas, such as the media, marketing or business consultancy.

Whatever course you choose, you'll end up doing the same core subjects you need to earn your professional exemptions, so you'll be studying criminal law, public law, law of the European Union, contracts and tort, land and property law, and equity and the law of trusts. The choice after that is yours to specialise among a range of options, which you need to check are available at your chosen institution, such as tax, international or family law.

In practice, most students have long decided what area they want to specialise in, as applications for sponsorship by law firms have to be made during the second and third years of undergraduate study. Sponsorship for both the LPC and BVC is available.

So how do you choose between being a barrister or a solicitor? The skills of each profession are different, so research and think what you would enjoy most. The barrister is currently the front person in the law courts, while the solicitor is the person who deals with the client and prepares the evidence.

Another factor may be the cost. Few students are sponsored and both the LPC and BVC can cost between £5,000 and £12,770. Once you've done your bar finals you need a pupillage, but you can then practise. It takes longer to be a solicitor, and that extra time means more money.

---

66 I have found studying law not only enjoyable but also an excellent way to get my foot in the door at a real law firm. The fast-paced, detailed course can be challenging, but hard work and commitment can lead to outstanding results. The opportunity to choose my modules and gain invaluable hands-on experience from mooting programmes and pro bono schemes provides an experience beyond that at A-level. The well-informed staff, helpful careers service, and superb facilities have also made life easier.

Matthew Dalley, *final-year law student, Cardiff University*

》 Further information

The Law Society
The Society's Hall, 113 Chancery Lane
London WC2A 1PL

t 020 7242 1222
↗ www.lawsociety.org.uk

Law Society of Scotland
26 Drumsheugh Gardens
Edinburgh EH3 7YR

t 0131 226 7411
↗ www.lawscot.org.uk

The Association of Women Barristers
3 Bedford Row
London WC1R 4DB

↗ www.womenbarristers.co.uk

The Bar Council
289-93 High Holborn
London WC1V 7HZ

t 020 7242 0082
↗ www.barcouncil.org.uk

Faculty of Advocates
Advocates Library, Parliament House
11 Parliament Square, Edinburgh EH1 1RF

t 0131 226 5071
↗ www.advocates.org.uk

The Association of Women Solicitors
114 Chancery Lane
London WC2A 1PL

t 020 7320 5793
↗ www.womensolicitors.org.uk

↗ Online reading

The Lawyer www.thelawyer.com
The European Lawyer www.europeanlawyer.co.uk
Consilio www.consilio.tv
Bar Standards Board www.barstandardsboard.org.uk
Institute of Legal Executives www.ilex.org.uk
British and Irish Association of Law Librarians www.biall.org.uk
Clarity www.clarity-international.net

Law

		Guardian score	Satisfied with teaching %	Satisfied with assessment %	Spend per student score /10	Student:staff ratio	Job prospects %	Value added score /10	Average entry tariff
1	Oxford	100.0			10	11	85	9	528
2	Cambridge	86.2			10	16	94	8	533
3	London School of Economics	85.8			8	13	95	9	499
4	King's College London	79.8	93	81	8	14	81	9	450
5	UCL	79.3	88	59	9	16	86	8	463
6	Warwick	77.8	89	48	10	14	76	8	466
7	Birmingham	73.6			10	17	81	7	421
8	Edinburgh	73.3	86	39	9	16	74	9	444
9	Durham	71.0	86	58	7	19	85	8	486
10	Soas	70.6	87	53	7	14		7	434
11	Queen Mary	69.2	90	74	8	17	76	6	393
12	Manchester	68.5	87	52	7	19	71	8	457
13	Aberdeen	68.4	90	65	4	21	91		412
14	Strathclyde	67.1	85	53	8	22	73	9	420
15	Glasgow	66.2	84	43	4	18	86	8	460
16	Exeter	65.9	90	59	4	17	68	8	423
17	Bristol	65.2	85	52	7	20	85	6	439
18	Leicester	65.1	93	76	5	22	77	7	397
19	City	64.9	75	35	5	18	85	10	350
19	Nottingham	64.9			7	17	82	3	474
19	Sunderland	64.9	90	91	7	12	74	5	251

		Guardian score	Satisfied with teaching %	Satisfied with assessment %	Spend per student score /10	Student:staff ratio	Job prospects %	Value added score /10	Average entry tariff
22	Cardiff	64.5	82	57	8	19	77	5	406
23	Buckingham	64.1	94	79		13		5	244
24	Napier	63.5			4	17	91		265
25	Lancaster	62.7	86	54	7	15	62	7	400
25	Southampton	62.7	90	74	4	23	73	7	412
27	Sussex	62.5	93	70	4	18	72	7	392
28	Liverpool	62.0	83	53	5	22	83	6	426
28	Newcastle	62.0	88	70	5	23	74	6	437
30	Kent	61.9	87	62	6	17	73	7	348
30	Robert Gordon	61.9			4	24	84	10	289
32	Dundee	61.7	87	64	5	20	80	5	397
33	Loughborough	61.3	83	73	7	20		9	293
34	Queen's, Belfast	60.8	84	40	5	20	80	7	409
35	Leeds	59.9	79	43	5	19	73	7	440
36	Nottingham Trent	58.5			7	17	82	3	299
37	Derby	58.0	97	87	4	26	67	8	271
38	Essex	57.5	79	58	5	15	70	6	329
39	Plymouth	55.8	84	63	8	16	44	8	276
40	UEA	55.6	87	64	4	27	69	7	400
41	Reading	55.2	85	61	3	20	72	5	371
42	Surrey	55.0	89	53	6	20	78	2	352
43	Portsmouth	54.3	80	57	5	17		7	296
44	Brunel	53.9	64	41	4	17	81	7	352
45	Hull	53.7	84	56	4	16	70	3	326
46	Sheffield	53.5	84	47	3	24	72	6	407
47	Bradford	53.3	73	61	10	20	43	8	255
48	Glasgow Caledonian	52.5			3	22	54	7	415
49	Bangor	52.2	93	73	3			7	290
50	Manchester Met	50.9			4	20	69	4	316
51	Birmingham City	50.5	80	55	5	19	56	7	270
52	Leeds Met	50.4	59	38	10	20	57	5	291
53	Oxford Brookes	49.5	81	46	4	19	71	3	343
53	Ulster	49.5	73	60	4	19	54	7	318
53	UWE Bristol	49.5	86	65	4	20	70	3	286
56	Staffordshire	49.2	86	74	6	25	56	6	260
57	Sheffield Hallam	49.1	81	60	4	24	63	7	279
58	Aberystwyth	48.3	82	54	4	21	65	3	321
58	Gloucestershire	48.3	92	83	5	29		4	258
60	Glamorgan	48.2	89	75	4		68	3	243
61	Northumbria	47.1	84	56	5	27	72	2	363
61	Central Lancashire	47.1	84	73	4	28	79	3	274
63	Kingston	46.7	87	65	4	27	66	4	268
64	Bedfordshire	45.7	89	83	4	28		7	176
65	Anglia Ruskin	45.2	81	59	7	20	45	4	261
65	Westminster	45.2	71	59	3	21	66	4	288

		Guardian score	Satisfied with teaching %	Satisfied with assessment %	Spend per student score /10	Student:staff ratio	Job prospects %	Value added score /10	Average entry tariff
67	Liverpool John Moores	45.0	85	65	3	29	68	5	262
68	Swansea	44.9	84	51	4	24	63	3	301
69	Teesside	44.6	87	80	5	27	50	5	250
70	East London	44.3	87	62	6	22	59	2	181
71	Edge Hill	43.5	93	78	3	21	39	5	244
72	De Montfort	42.1	82	67	3	24	62	4	230
73	Thames Valley	41.9	75	60	4	21		5	184
74	Bournemouth	41.8	78	57	5	38	69	8	280
75	Coventry	41.1	84	73	5	19	42	2	260
76	Lincoln	38.2	88	69	2	29	60	4	253
77	Southampton Solent	37.7	80	61	3	25	57	3	171
78	Northampton	37.6	85	64	3	27	45	5	206
79	Canterbury Christ Church	34.5	81	66	2			3	234
80	Huddersfield	33.2	76	55	3	27	56	2	249
81	Bucks New University	31.3			3	20		1	159
82	Hertfordshire	31.1	74	52	3	32	60	2	251
83	Greenwich	30.9	79	54	3	31	54	2	241
84	Wolverhampton	29.2	71	46	4	27	55	1	190
85	Middlesex	28.2	72	49	5	40	59	3	206
86	London South Bank	27.4	75	56	3	37	49	5	198

Media studies

❝ The average person interacts with the media for the majority of their waking hours. For around 12 hours a day, most of us engage with some form of media whether computer, television, film, radio, internet, mobile phone or iPod. It would therefore be irresponsible, having created a media-drenched society, to deny young people the opportunity to engage in the critical and in-depth study of media products, practices, and principles. How we use media, how media inform our lives, and how their contents can mislead or inspire us are crucial questions.

The shift from 'old' to 'new' media has generated profound changes in the way people communicate with one another, globally and locally. Audiences and news producers seem to converge with the rise of citizen journalism by the amateur capturing of events on mobile phone cameras; professional film and TV programme makers draw inspiration from young YouTubers and vice versa in a postmodern exchange of ideas. Are new media signalling a new democratic era? Or are existing popular cultural fashions and quick fixes being recycled through profit-led multinational media organisations? Is al-Jazeera challenging western notions of 'news', or is 'news' now collapsing into entertainment in an 'info-tainment' culture? These are exciting questions and themes that students of media are exploring and finding the answers to.

The kinds of skills media graduates gain ensure a wide range of career options in the media and cultural industries, PR, advertising, government, and education. Media students are not only eminently employable. They are also among the most savvy: analytical, engaging, and knowledgeable, with a flair for keeping ahead of state-of-the-art ideas, social trends, and cultural developments associated with the media.

Professor Deborah Chambers, *Media and Cultural Studies, Newcastle University*

It's been a while coming, but media studies is finally coming out of the shadow of the derision hurled by traditionalists who view the degree as simply three years of watching television. In fact, media and communications courses are concerned with the analysis and understanding of key features of social and cultural life, as well as with creating that cultural life, so remember that if you are interested in drama, or the technical and creative side of the media, a media degree will be an enormous bonus.

Given the power of the mass media in this modern age, the ability to conduct an integrated study of the various tools of the age (newspaper, TV, radio, internet and so on) in social, cultural, and historical context is invaluable. You'll study the way the media represent people and events (and there are rich pickings in these turbulent times), and the way those messages are put over: the use of sound and vision in this information-saturated era.

The courses you can take will vary widely in terms of academic content and vocational intent. In some, you'll be looking more at the sociology, the linguistics, and the cultural hinterland of the media, treating the subject as almost purely academic, with perhaps some practical aspects. Alternatively, you'll be heading for a more job-related course, picking up technical skills that will prepare you for work in journalism, film, photography, production or the interactive media. You could also end up somewhere in between, so look carefully at the modules and make sure you pick the right course.

Whatever the slant of your coursework, you'll be building the skills of research, enquiry, and analysis that older courses have always seen as part of their brief. What's more, media studies graduates still come out as above average in statistics for post-graduate employment, with more than three-quarters finding employment in the first six months after graduating.

But be a little wary. This isn't going to sweep you into the director general's seat at the BBC. For most people, success in the media is still about beating the odds: only those willing to make the tea, do the photocopying, or pick up the phone will survive. But if you can do all that, a media studies degree will stand you in as good stead (maybe better) as any other.

If you want a more direct route into the media, then vocational courses might be right for you. If, for example, you want to do journalism, then look for aspects of the course that study news production, elements of bias and propaganda, or the role of the press. Remember too that there are many good postgraduate journalism courses that may be an option if you want to take a different degree later on.

Other courses can be quite technical and almost scientific. Photography, for example, or digital media production teach both the role of those skills in presenting images or rolling news and the technical aspects of running a darkroom or building a website. Digital in particular is the coming element in the media – the dotcom revolution may have stalled but, while it's slower, it's also far more sure-footed.

Since, as many an old hack will tell you, the best way to gain a job in the media is through experience and contacts, check out what links a department has for work placements and make sure that they're in the area you're hoping to work in. Many departments insist that their staff retain links to the real world and you'll need to exploit them if you're going to land that dream job.

" I found my course to be extremely challenging and engaging – it touched upon a wide range of subjects, from the political and social influences affecting media content to the effect of new technologies on society. By the end of the course, I had become much more analytical and politically aware, and it really affected my outlook as a result. I think media studies prepares you for a wider range of jobs than other arts degrees because it touches upon so many areas of study.

Esther Cornell, *media studies graduate, University of Birmingham*

» Further information

Skillset
Prospect House
80-110 New Oxford Street
London WC1A 1HB

t   020 7520 5757
↗ www.skillset.org

The Institute of Communications Studies
University of Leeds
Leeds LS2 9JT

t   0113 343 7608
↗ www.ics.leeds.ac.uk

National Council for the Training of Journalists
The New Granary, Station Road
Newport, Saffron Walden
Essex CB11 3PL

t   01279 430009
↗ www.nctj.com

»

National Union of Journalists
308 Gray's Inn Road
London WC1X 8DP

t 020 7278 7916
↗ www.nujtraining.org.uk

Broadcast Journalism Training Council
18 Miller's Close
Rippingale, Nr. Bourne
Lincolnshire PE10 0TH

t 01778 440025
e sec@bjtc.org.uk
↗ www.bjtc.org.uk

↗ Online reading

MediaGuardian.co.uk mediaguardian.co.uk
Media, Communications and Cultural Studies Association www.meccsa.org.uk
Periodical Publishers Association www.ppa.co.uk
Skillset Careers www.skillset.org/careers
New Media Studies www.newmediastudies.com
Journalism UK www.journalismuk.co.uk
The International Association for Media and History www.iamhist.org
The Media and Communications site www.aber.ac.uk/media
Media UK www.mediauk.com

Media studies, communications and librarianship

		Guardian score	Satisfied with teaching %	Satisfied with assessment %	Spend per student score /10	Student:staff ratio	Job prospects %	Value added score /10	Average entry tariff
1	Southampton	100.0			10	10		5	364
2	Birmingham	97.4	85	65	10	17	51	9	386
3	Newcastle	97.0	81	63	8	17	70	9	350
4	Warwick	94.4			9	15		8	423
5	Leeds	93.6	87	50	9	19	72	6	373
6	Cardiff	91.9	89	55	9	19	57	6	377
7	Surrey	91.3	82	58	9	14		8	297
8	Bournemouth	91.1	80	57		16	67	5	346
9	Royal Holloway	90.7	81	57	7	15	58	7	366
10	Sheffield	87.6	66	69	5	18	70	7	386
11	Westminster	86.8	76	48	7	13	42	10	327
12	Nottingham Trent	84.7	83	59	8	14	69	4	270
13	Birmingham City	84.4	74	46	9	15	60	6	278
14	City	83.9	74	52	7	16			332
15	Napier	83.7			6	19	59	9	260
16	Loughborough	83.4	90	58	5	18	54	3	372
17	Robert Gordon	81.6			5	15	57	4	339
17	Sussex	81.6	80	46	4	19	45	8	379
19	Central Lancashire	81.5	73	56	6	20	75	4	306
20	Aberystwyth	81.3	81	66	7	28		9	250
20	Goldsmiths	81.3	78	54	6	26	57	8	330
22	Lancaster	80.5			5	12	41	4	325
23	Stirling	79.8			4	22	59	8	297
24	Brunel	79.5			4	32	79		295
25	Middlesex	77.9	79	60	8	17	53	6	204
26	St Mary's UC, Twickenham	77.2	90	73	5	16	37	6	244

	Guardian score	Satisfied with teaching %	Satisfied with assessment %	Spend per student score /10	Student:staff ratio	Job prospects %	Value added score /10	Average entry tariff
27 Kingston	76.0	76	48	6	16	48	7	232
28 Staffordshire	75.8	84	67	3	19	43	8	252
29 UWE Bristol	75.4	86	65	3	17	42	7	285
30 Portsmouth	75.2	89	70	3	19	43	4	301
30 Ulster	75.2	81	62	6	20	42	6	284
32 Sunderland	75.0	78	63	5	16	41	7	262
33 Bath Spa	74.8	86	73	2	28		9	270
33 UC Falmouth	74.8	75	63	4	26	52	8	277
35 Gloucestershire	74.3	74	58	8	24	49	5	265
36 Hertfordshire	74.1	75	56	6	16		3	271
37 Coventry	73.9			7	27	55	9	234
38 Salford	73.3	68	38	4	23	56	7	316
39 Bedfordshire	73.0	79	67	5	24		9	188
40 University of the Arts London	72.6	72	53	8	23	42	6	254
41 Liverpool John Moores	72.5	73	53	5	20	51	7	257
42 University College for the Creative Arts	72.3	76	64	10	38		3	
43 Glamorgan	72.0	74	52	8	15	37	4	239
44 Lincoln	71.8	78	64	3	24	46	7	282
45 Northumbria	71.6	74	54	3	21	40	9	269
46 Sheffield Hallam	71.4	75	63	6	19	33	7	258
47 Huddersfield	70.9			4	19	33	5	259
48 Thames Valley	70.8	66	58	6	17	52	6	210
49 Anglia Ruskin	70.7			8	21		3	234
50 Manchester Met	70.6	67	77	7	19	47	3	228
51 Southampton Solent	69.5	79	54	4	23	58	3	258
52 Leeds Met	69.4	77	49	7	29	50	6	271
53 York St John	69.2	95	68	2	28			240
54 Worcester	69.0	81	55	7	20	34	6	210
55 Queen's, Belfast	68.6	76	45	5	31	31	8	324
56 Chichester	67.4	90	83	2	25	29	5	293
57 Edge Hill	67.2	85	75	3	23	43	3	240
58 Bucks New University	64.6	75	61	3	15			206
59 De Montfort	64.2	81	51	2	19	39	4	241
60 Marjon (St Mark and St John)	63.9	90	70		21	46	2	231
61 Wolverhampton	62.9	87	67	3	24	44	5	176
62 London South Bank	62.8	70	60	3	23	36	7	207
63 Canterbury Christ Church	61.9	85	71	2	22	52	1	225
64 Greenwich	60.8	82	58	3	30	41	4	209
65 Chester	60.2	62	54	4	22	43	2	254
66 Lampeter	59.8			2	24		6	202
67 Queen Margaret	58.5			2		46	3	223
68 Teesside	57.8	71	64	7	23	21	2	225
69 Swansea	57.0	87	55	3	31	40	1	272
70 Leeds Trinity & All Saints	55.2	66	51	3	29	41	2	299
71 Northampton	54.7	74	64	3	27	28	3	211
71 Winchester	54.7	80	65	2	26	25	2	268
73 East London	52.4	74	58	7	37	36	3	197
74 Cumbria	36.9	36	31		35	46	1	231

Politics

❝ There has never been a better or more important time to study politics at university. Climate change, 9/11 and its aftermath (including the wars in Iraq and Afghanistan) and the rise of China and India have all given a new salience to the need to understand developments in global politics. The transition from Tony Blair to Gordon Brown in the UK and the election of a new president in the United States have provided a significant new context to the formation of domestic and foreign policy agenda.

Studying politics gives students the opportunity to develop a detailed awareness of the relationship between political ideas, institutions, and policy choices at home and abroad. Politics may be studied from a contemporary and national perspective and in a comparative and historical context.

Studying politics opens up a host of exciting career opportunities. Aside from a career in politics itself (numerous politics alumni have gone on to become MPs and even cabinet ministers), typical career destinations for politics graduates include the media, broadcast and written journalism, public relations, the civil service, campaigning non-governmental organisations, think tanks, and international organisations.

Simon Lee, *Senior Lecturer in Politics, University of Hull*

Political studies has become somewhat fashionable again, up at the top of the lists when Ucas reveals who applies for what each year. Applications have been rising year on year, which makes it both more competitive to get on a course, and more exciting when you get there. It's a growth in popularity likely to be connected to the increase in single-issue politics amongst the nation's youth. The sight of tens of thousands of people taking to the streets to protest has become a common one again as the war against terror, wars in Afghanistan and Iraq, and the crisis in the Middle East are combined with growing concerns about globalisation and more local worries about tuition fees.

But while you may have been galvanised by single-issue politics, once you get on to a degree course the whole thing of course becomes much, much broader. Most degree courses will first take you on a whirlwind tour of the main philosophers from Plato through to Marx and, more than likely, catch up with the beliefs of the anti-globalisation movement. They will move on to consider the institutions and groupings that make up a political society, including parliamentary and presidential democracies, party politics, electoral behaviour, social and unconventional behaviour, and what happens in every corner of the globe, including military and ethnic dimensions.

From them on, you'll specialise and use your newfound skills to analyse modern-day politics. You could take intelligence studies with international politics, democratic politics, or the environment and Third World development. You'll also come to understand how the public relates to governments, be it via the protest march, revolution, ballot box or focus group.

The chances are, you won't lack for work – the ability to analyse evidence and arguments, oral and written communication, and the knowledge to handle statistics are all in demand by employers not related to the world of party politics. Alternative career choices could include the more apolitical arena of the civil service, or perhaps the ever-growing lobby industry, as well as local authorities, journalism or the public sector.

Look carefully at what options are available to you – there is a wide variance in the ways universities approach the concept and the teaching of politics. But be aware that if your motivation for getting into politics has been single-issue stuff, then the actual nitty-gritty of politics may not be for you – the subject itself (environmental sciences perhaps) may be more pertinent.

How you view politics may help you choose where you study it. If you're a party (political) animal, then you'll want a course with strong elements of parliamentary and democratic studies. If you're more of a theorist, then check the option for political philosophy alternatives, poring over the works of Hobbes or Locke.

Many courses are now taking an increasingly global look at politics and its institutions, so consider those opportunities too – the study of systems entirely different to the western model can add a dimension to your studies which may not have occurred to you at sixth form.

Take note too of the assessment options, and whether it's exams, continuous assessment, dissertations or coursework – different methods work best for different people.

Some universities do four-year courses that include a year working in Westminster, Washington or Ottawa, so try to seize that chance or any other possibilities for vocational work experience. The chances are that it'll be dogsbody stuff for an MP or lobby group, but that experience and the contacts you make could turn out to be invaluable. If you want to stay in politics, it really can be a case of who you know ...

---

66 It's hard not to see politics as just a collection of '-isms': anarchism, conservatism, feminism. But if you take a course involving politics you'll quickly start seeing the 'political' all around you. The world will become this churning sea of institutions, people, and ideas, all open to argument. And you'll use everything from history to philosophy to pick apart the fundamental question of why people interact in the ways they do and whether they can do better.

Vincenzo Rampulla, *final-year politics, philosophy and history student at Birkbeck, University of London*

》 Further information

Political Studies Association
Newcastle University   t 0191 222 8021
Newcastle-upon-Tyne NE1 7RU   ↗ www.psa.ac.uk

Civitas (The Institute for the Study of Civil Society)
77 Great Peter Street   t 020 7799 6677
Westminster   e info@civitas.org.uk
London SW1P 2EZ   ↗ www.civitas.org.uk

Demos
Third Floor, Magdalen House   t 0845 458 5949
136 Tooley Street   e hello@demos.co.uk
London SE1 2TU   ↗ www.demos.co.uk   》

Unlock Democracy
6 Cynthia Street
London N1 9JF

t 020 7278 4443
e info@unlockdemocracy.org.uk
↗ www.unlockdemocracy.org.uk

Policy Network
Third floor, 11 Tufton Street
London SW1P 3QB

t 020 7340 2200
e info@policy-network.net
↗ www.policy-network.net

↗ Online reading

Guardian.co.uk Politics politics.guardian.co.uk
Politics Direct www.politicsdirect.com
Working for an MP www.w4mp.org
The UK Parliament www.parliament.uk
Global Action Plan www.globalactionplan.org.uk

Politics

		Guardian score	Satisfied with teaching %	Satisfied with assessment %	Spend per student score /10	Student:staff ratio	Job prospects %	Value added score /10	Average entry tariff
1	Oxford	100.0	92	59	10	11	81	8	519
2	London School of Economics	80.0	83	69	8	13	86	7	470
3	St Andrews	79.3	96	73	4	19	76	10	487
4	Cambridge	77.6	82	67	10	16		7	494
5	Warwick	75.8	84	60	10	14	74	6	458
6	King's College London	73.4	95	67	7	14	64	6	443
7	Durham	70.4	87	67	7	19	81	7	468
8	Birmingham	69.4	87	71	9	17	58	7	385
9	Edinburgh	68.5	85	54	9	16	66	7	406
10	Soas	67.2	91	64	7	14		4	392
11	York	67.1	86	43	7	14	67	6	456
12	Bristol	66.9	85	62	6	20	81	7	435
13	Bath	66.2	79	49	6	17	77	8	423
14	UCL	65.4	83	61	9	16			382
15	Nottingham	63.6	83	50	6	17	72	7	410
16	Exeter	63.5	90	64	4	17	63	7	394
17	Bradford	63.1	85	59	6	12	65	8	274
18	Essex	60.3	92	83	5	15	62	3	338
19	Dundee	60.2	92	78	5	20	44	9	349
20	Glasgow	59.7	86	63	4	18	59	8	392
21	Queen Mary	59.6	79	62	8	17	69	5	358
22	Leeds	59.3	89	58	5	19	66	7	383
22	Plymouth	59.3	84	66	7	16	32	10	239
24	Brunel	59.2	90	63	4	17		7	309
25	Sussex	58.4	87	57	4	18	58	8	386
26	Leicester	58.1	94	73	5	22	57	8	315
27	Manchester	58.0	90	48	7	19	49	6	422
28	Kent	57.4	90	75	5	17	70	4	280

	Guardian score	Satisfied with teaching %	Satisfied with assessment %	Spend per student score /10	Student:staff ratio	Job prospects %	Value added score /10	Average entry tariff
29 Sheffield	56.6	89	62	3	24	64	8	432
30 Nottingham Trent	56.2	86	71	7	17	64	5	219
31 Leeds Met	54.8	78	57	10	20			227
32 Lancaster	54.3	85	71	6	15	45	3	363
33 Portsmouth	54.2	95	85	5	17		3	263
34 Aston	53.8	86	63	3			3	331
35 Strathclyde	53.5	86	71	8	22	44	6	
36 Surrey	53.4	85	59	6	20			314
37 Aberystwyth	53.2	93	72	3	21	57	5	332
38 Cardiff	52.0	83	61	5	21	58	5	381
39 Hull	51.9	91	74	4	16	70	1	316
40 Newcastle	51.8	79	47	5	23	65	7	391
40 Oxford Brookes	51.8	85	62	4	19		5	301
42 Stirling	51.3			3	19	64	7	269
43 Reading	51.2	88	56	3	20	55	7	338
44 Aberdeen	50.7	88	65	4	21	51		307
45 Southampton	49.4	87	47	4	23	61	5	369
46 UEA	47.4	95	68	4	27	46	7	341
47 Loughborough	47.3	81	74	6	20	58	2	302
48 Queen's, Belfast	46.9	85	48	5	20	46	5	350
49 Liverpool	45.7	80	49	5	22	51	4	360
50 Coventry	45.0	85	84	4	19			227
51 Goldsmiths	44.1	88	64	3	15	61	1	261
52 Swansea	43.7	89	55	4	24	54	4	294
53 UWE Bristol	42.9	89	79	4	20	44	3	250
54 Ulster	41.3	77	70	4	19	41	4	262
55 Royal Holloway	41.0	74	59	4	20		2	335
56 Westminster	40.9	77	56	3	21		8	235
57 Northumbria	40.3	77	53	4	27	54	8	267
58 Kingston	40.1	81	64	3	27		5	205
59 Huddersfield	38.9	96	91	3	27			239
60 Birmingham City	38.7	85	66	5	19	30	3	233
61 Manchester Met	37.8	78	65	4	20	37	3	253
62 De Montfort	31.5	87	76	2	24	37	2	208
63 Lincoln	31.0	77	58	2	29		7	222
64 Salford	30.9	69	52	7	22	35	1	247
65 Liverpool John Moores	29.4	91	61	3	29		2	238
66 Greenwich	27.3	68	59	3	27			221

Social policy

❝ Students of social policy explore some of the most pressing issues facing contemporary society. How do societies organise and manage their welfare systems? Who pays, who benefits and who misses out? Governments in the developed world spend huge resources on health and social care, income support and welfare, but how are these resources divided up between different sections of the population? Most importantly, who decides how much to tax and how much to spend to achieve social objectives?

Questions of this kind go to the heart of how societies operate, but they also take students well beyond policy-related concerns to wider issues involving the key moral choices we all face. Different societies approach welfare in different ways, but every society has to make choices about how to treat the poorest communities and marginalised populations. Should we be aiming at achieving as much 'equality' as possible — and what inequalities should we be prepared to put up with?

In one sense, at every stage of the life cycle we each have a stake in one aspect or other of social policy, whether this is through a desire to be educated, a need for childcare or healthcare, or for a decent pension in old age. Studying social policy not only helps us to understand the social and political contexts and processes of policy making, but also who we are, who our neighbours are (locally or globally), and the nature of other people's lives and experiences. Through its attention to social research methods and different forms of social enquiry, a social policy degree will provide significant research skills, which can improve employability in a range of public and private sector occupations.

Professor Nick Ellison, *School of Sociology and Social Policy, University of Leeds*

Social policy is a very contemporary degree course, addressing issues that have only arisen in the last 50 years. Its main concern is with how "we" as a society, and "they" as a government, treat the members of our society. At its core, therefore, are issues surrounding the welfare state and the alternatives to it. You'll be asking some fundamental questions about how things are, as well as how they ought to be, merging philosophical and political theories with social science.

As you work through these meaty issues, you'll be acquiring the skills to critically analyse contemporary society. You'll consider topics such as NHS reform, tackling poverty and social exclusion, and changes in the criminal justice system, drawing on a multidisciplinary approach that takes in politics, law, economics, sociology, philosophy, and history.

Very few of you will have come across anything quite like this at school or college, so most degree programmes assume no prior knowledge. Your first year, therefore, is likely to be a general introduction to the topics, followed in the next two years by a mixture of the core and mandatory topics, with optional specialisations, which often focus on particular problems and areas of social policy, such as poverty and social security, housing and planning, crime and penal policy — so check the options tally with your own interests when you apply.

Teaching is usually centred around lectures, seminars, and your own private research and reading. Assessment can be based on exams, coursework, and dissertations, the exact combination depending on where you study.

Once you've graduated, the chances of employment are pretty high. You can view it as a vocational course, so feel equipped to work in the public sector, or perhaps in central or local government or social work. You can also view it as an academic course, in which case you'll have the analytical, research, and technical skills to work in a number of areas – think tanks, policy evaluation and planning, and in academic research.

When choosing a course, it's always handy to check whether the department is engaged with research as well as with teaching. On the one hand, it can mean you have an insight into the very latest thought and initiatives and can be learning from the freshest minds. On the other hand, you may be dealing with a department where the best teachers are too busy elsewhere to deal with you.

As with all multidisciplinary courses, check the health of the related departments. You'll often be taught by, and use the facilities of, the departments which feed into your course.

There are some sandwich courses and some universities run work placement schemes, both of which are handy for taking you out of the theory and planting you in the very real, often with voluntary schemes or charities. This is especially useful if you see the degree as a vocational way of entering social work.

That can of course be an emotionally draining, as well as rewarding, career, so any way of forewarning yourself can help. Check with the course tutors what the possibilities are, including those for a period of foreign study.

And take time to think again about your own motivation. If you fancy social policy as a way of getting into social work, consider doing a social work course instead. Social policy has enormous relevance to such a career, but it usually takes in the in the broader picture, equipping you with the analytical rather than the practical skills for such a choice.

"" The most striking thing about the social policy course is the diversity of students it attracts, as demonstrated by the continuous flow of passionate dialogue and discussion. The content allows students to express their personal views and broaden their knowledge of current political affairs through challenging academic and contemporary sources. The course is also novel in its approach to assessment, with preparation undertaken for coursework usefully relating to the final assessed essay as well as equipping students with valuable presentation skills.

Vanessa Mullinder, *final-year politics and modern history student, University of Manchester*

》 Further information

SWAP School of Social Sciences
University of Southampton   **t** 023 8059 7782
Southampton SO17 1BJ   ↗ www.swap.ac.uk

The Academy of Learned Societies for the Social Sciences
Berkshire House   **t** 0115 846 7529
252-6 Kings Road   **e** admin@the-academy.org.uk
Reading RG1 4HP   ↗ www.the-academy.org.uk

Social Research Association
175-85 Gray's Inn Road   **t** 020 7812 0634
London WC1X 8UP   **e** admin@the-sra.org.uk
                                         ↗ www.the-sra.org.uk

↗ Online reading

SocietyGuardian.co.uk SocietyGuardian.co.uk
The UK Social Policy Association www.social-policy.com
International and Comparative Social Policy Group icsp.group.shef.ac.uk
SocialPolicy.net www.socialpolicy.net

Social policy and administration

		Guardian score	Satisfied with teaching %	Satisfied with assessment %	Spend per student score /10	Student:staff ratio	Job prospects %	Value added score /10	Average entry tariff
1	Bristol	100.0	91	60	10	14		5	332
2	London School of Economics	90.6	77	59	8	13		4	413
3	York	83.6	86	44	8	14	61	6	358
4	Nottingham	81.4	86	56	7	17			346
5	Birmingham	81.2	83	64	10	17	48	6	314
6	Leeds	78.8	84	58	5	19		10	309
7	Cardiff	78.5	73	51	8	19			339
8	Bath	76.9	79	46	6	17			376
9	Loughborough	74.0	91	66	6	20	48	5	353
10	Nottingham Trent	72.7	83	60	7	17	48	9	200
11	Glasgow	71.2	88	74	4	18	59	4	
12	Kent	69.2	79	64	5	17	62	6	242
13	Ulster	65.8	92	85	4	19			246
14	Manchester	61.9	78	35	7	19		5	366
15	Sheffield	61.8	89	61	3	24			364
16	Teesside	51.3	84	62	4	27			249
17	Swansea	50.7	86	64	3	24	59	1	271
18	Newport	50.1	85	75	3	27			225
19	Northampton	47.6	92	70	2	27			200
20	Salford	45.9	81	58	7	22			197
21	Bedfordshire	42.2	83	76	3	28			149
22	Roehampton	39.6	86	56	4	29			178
23	Wolverhampton	38.1	83	72	4	27			167
24	Sheffield Hallam	36.0	73	63	4	24	25	4	258
25	London South Bank	32.3	90	73	2	37			150

Social work and community studies

" Most people know that social work involves providing practical help for people with problems in their everyday lives, looking after children affected by family breakdown or arranging care for adults who can't manage alone. But studying social work is about much more. It investigates what makes children and adults vulnerable and what can be done to protect them from abuse — and examines what causes people to behave hurtfully to those around them and how intervening in these situations promotes positive outcomes. Sometimes an individual's behaviour prevents them integrating into society; people may experience discrimination and disadvantage because of their race, gender, sexual orientation, disability, or simply because they are different. So social work means exploring social and individual problems from various perspectives and applying theory to better understand and respond to these problems.

An essential part of the course is the 200 days spent in practice learning — working in a real social work agency, supervised and assessed by a practice teacher. Social work students can select from specialist options: bereavement, spirituality, substance misuse, youth justice, and asylum seekers, as well as receiving a solid grounding in child and family practice and adult services. A range of practice placements is available in social work and social care agencies in the area.

Margaret Holloway, *Professor of Social Work, University of Hull*

The aim of social work is to provide and manage care, support, and protection in partnership with individuals, families, groups, and communities to enable them to function, participate, and develop in society. Social work is different from, but complementary to, social care, in which personal care is provided to individuals in day, residential or community settings.

The degree in social work, which replaced the two-year diploma, puts social work graduates on a par with the professions they work closely with, such as nurses, teachers, and physiotherapists, and is raising the profession's status and public image. Despite the impression given by the media, applications for the degree have actually risen in recent years.

The generic qualification combines theory with practice — you'll spend 200 days in practice during the course, with at least two different client groups, and teaching reflects the core skills which social workers require: problem-solving, communication, working with others, personal and professional development, and information technology and numerical skills.

More than 80 universities are accredited by the General Social Care Council to offer the social work degree and, to further encourage people into the profession, the government offers social work students a non-means-tested bursary worth about £4,000 a year. And once you've graduated, the fact that there is still something of a recruitment problem in the profession means employment prospects after graduation are excellent. In addition, and in order to improve recruitment rates in "crisis" areas, social work graduates could be eligible for the reimbursement of their student loans if they sign up to work in boroughs affected by shortages of suitably qualified workers.

Community studies is a markedly different degree, a more academic and less vocational approach to similar issues. It is mainly concerned with concepts of culture and community and cuts across various disciplines, such as sociology, psychology, and anthropology. As such, it can give analytical and problem-solving skills for a range of jobs post-graduation. A community studies course is rather more reliant on traditional methods of teaching – lectures, seminars, and so on – than the more hands-on approach of the social work degree. It's a qualification for those concerned with the issues of society rather than the practicalities. As such, you'll have analytical and problem-solving skills, and that skill of seeing the bigger picture gives you the ability for strategic thought applicable to management jobs in the public and private sectors, and consultancy and journalism, as well as local and central government and the health service.

If you're dithering about which of the two disciplines suits you better, then stop thinking about the degree and think about the job that follows. Are you cut out for social work? If you have an affinity for the subject, but not for the mental and physical bruises of fieldwork, then the broader base of community studies may well be for you. That's not to say that community studies is social work for cowards – it's a new approach to similar issues, and while two graduates from the disciplines will have a lot to say to each other, they will come from totally different standpoints.

In making that choice, talk not just to those who'll be teaching the course, but try those who have graduated and are now working – how do they feel about their job? Remember though that these can be emotionally charged areas to work in. You may get someone on a bad day ...

As ever with the courses in this book, look at the modules of the course and at the research and publications of those who teach and see if they tally with your own interests. Look also at the work experience opportunities and the links the department has for placements. There may even be the opportunity to work abroad.

Consider whether the full-time degree is for you. More so than for most degrees, there are lots of other part-time and short courses that can equip you for work in this field, so look at those and decide if that may be a better option. This might especially be the case for mature students or for those looking for a complete change of career.

All social workers (and social work students) are required to register with the General Social Care Council (GSCC) and abide by their codes of practice, and once you are qualified, you have to give evidence of a minimum level of continuing professional development (90 hours over three years) to maintain registration. Since April 2005 it has been illegal to describe yourself as a social worker if you are not qualified and registered with GSCC.

---

66 The first year of my social work degree has been challenging and thought-provoking. The lecturers are experienced practitioners who encourage creative thinking and further understanding. Social policy, values and ethics, and social theory have been of particular interest to me, and all of the lectures and seminars have been participatory and varied. It's been a fantastic introduction to university study. The first-year preparation for practice placement was inspiring and made me even more determined to qualify and become a social work practitioner.

Emma Weston, *first-year social work student, University of Kent*

General Social Care Council
Goldings House, 2 Hay's Lane   t   020 7397 5100
London SE1 2HB   ↗   www.gscc.org.uk

Scottish Social Services Council
Compass House   t   01382 207101
11 Riverside Drive   e   enquiries@sssc.uk.com
Dundee DD1 4NY   ↗   www.sssc.uk.com

The Care Council For Wales
6th Floor, South Gate House   t   029 2022 6257
Wood Street   e   info@ccwales.org.uk
Cardiff CF10 1EW   ↗   www.ccwales.org.uk

The Northern Ireland Social Care Council
7th Floor, Millennium House   t   02890 417600
19-25 Great Victoria Street   textphone: 02890 239340
Belfast BT2 7AQ   e   info@niscc.n-i.nhs.uk
    ↗   www.niscc.info

↗ Online reading

SocietyGuardian.co.uk   SocietyGuardian.co.uk
British Association of Social Workers   www.basw.co.uk
Association of Directors of Adult Social Services   www.adss.org.uk
Social Care Association   www.socialcaring.co.uk

Social work

		Guardian score	Satisfied with teaching %	Satisfied with assessment %	Spend per student score /10	Student:staff ratio	Job prospects %	Value added score /10	Average entry tariff
1	Strathclyde	100.0	85	64	10	12	72		
2	Oxford Brookes	98.9	94	81		8		8	254
3	Sheffield	94.1	85	55	7	7			329
4	York	93.8	81	43	8	10			358
5	Kent	89.1	88	70	9	11			238
6	Manchester	85.4	79	50	7	15			354
7	Anglia Ruskin	85.0	94	78	7		78	8	224
8	Portsmouth	84.7	81	58	9	11		8	223
9	Southampton	84.6	92	40	9	22			345
10	Leeds	84.4	82	64			45	8	306
11	Lancaster	84.2	87	63	5	15			304
12	Gloucestershire	82.4	95	55	4	9	85	8	218
13	Brunel	80.8	84	58	8	13		4	288
14	Plymouth	79.5	74	57	10	12	83	5	204
14	Queen's, Belfast	79.5	86	38	3	19	97	6	360
16	Birmingham	79.4	75	55	10	15		2	333
17	Central Lancashire	79.3	74	63	10	12	75	4	236
18	Marjon (St Mark and St John)	75.2	95	81	3	10		7	181
19	Nottingham Trent	73.7	80	57	6			7	237

	Guardian score	Satisfied with teaching %	Satisfied with assessment %	Spend per student score /10	Student:staff ratio	Job prospects %	Value added score /10	Average entry tariff
20 Northumbria	73.2	76	48	5	19	92	8	267
21 Birmingham City	73.1	69	64	3	22	92	10	233
22 London South Bank	72.8	93	87	5		63	5	
23 De Montfort	71.8	87	58	4	14	96	7	184
24 Bradford	71.0	70	53	3	24	83	10	281
25 UEA	70.8	93	66	7	29		6	328
26 Sheffield Hallam	70.3	76	46	4	13	90	8	216
27 Winchester	69.3	83	79	2	11			236
28 Cumbria	68.7	87	64	9	21	45	7	236
29 Staffordshire	68.6	81	73	5	17	71	8	201
30 Bournemouth	68.0	60	43	8	15	79	7	229
31 Middlesex	67.9	75	49	9	17		4	
32 Hertfordshire	67.4	72	48	6	10		5	180
33 Bristol	66.7	54	37	9	14		4	306
33 North East Wales Institute	66.7	97	91	3	17		8	185
35 East London	65.1	81	61		15		6	169
36 Sussex	64.8	76	32	5	24		4	395
36 Wolverhampton	64.8	83	75	4	9	64	3	226
38 Edinburgh	64.5	82	44	7	23			246
39 Royal Holloway	63.9	80	59	3	21			311
40 Coventry	63.7	80	67	4			8	225
41 Ulster	63.4	82	63	4	20	57	6	288
42 Bedfordshire	61.8	71	64	4	15		7	192
43 Lincoln	61.7	74	56	3	18	85	7	212
44 Manchester Met	61.0	77	71	4	16	71	3	225
45 Chichester	60.5	89	70	2	16	49	6	270
46 Hull	60.0	82	66	4	24		4	213
47 Southampton Solent	59.9	83	84	6	22			213
48 Teesside	58.3	82	59	7	22		4	214
49 Huddersfield	56.1	79	68	3	25	77	5	227
50 UWE Bristol	55.6	81	48	3	26	97	6	203
51 Sunderland	53.6	75	68	5	18	55	5	205
52 Derby	53.2	69	58	3	20		7	209
53 Robert Gordon	52.7			3	15	83	1	247
54 Salford	52.4	71	48	4	19	56	4	257
55 Leeds Met	51.7	78	55	7	24	40	7	198
56 Liverpool John Moores	50.1	52	33	7			2	213
57 Brighton	47.6	82	62	3	26	41	5	281
58 Reading	47.4	58	49	3	25		8	245
59 Canterbury Christ Church	45.8	75	51	4	26	43	8	219
60 Kingston	44.9	59	68		22	70	2	228
61 UWIC	43.4	85	70	4	17		2	171
62 Edge Hill	41.0	83	58	4	20	36	3	198
63 Bucks New University	39.8	73	55	3	23			174
64 Newport	39.5	85	75	3		50	3	158
65 Greenwich	39.0	62	49	3	19	69	2	163
66 Roehampton	32.5	92	66	5	32		1	175

Sociology

> 66 Sociology is an exciting and challenging subject that enables students to cultivate a critical approach which takes account of the socio-cultural forces, contexts, and processes that significantly inform individuals' ways of living, group relations, and social institutions in contemporary society. Through studying diverse theories, wide-ranging socio-cultural and geopolitical issues, as well as sophisticated quantitative and qualitative research methods, sociology offers students the knowledge and employable skills to question the familiar, the normative, and the commonsensical. It expands students' horizons in understanding the intricate relationships between individuals and social systems and processes, and the complexity and diversity of social life with its divisions, inequalities, and potential for progressive change. Such engagement equips students with a 'sociological imagination' and important life skills that enable them to live meaningfully as individuals and citizens in an increasingly globalised world.
>
> **Dr Andrew Yip**, *School of Sociology and Social Policy, University of Nottingham*

Sociology's resurgence is due in part to its ability to reinvent itself and broaden its scope of study. The degree is still, essentially, concerned with the way society works, and the way social behaviour and relations and social structures and institutions affect and define people's lives, but more attention is now being paid to what you can study on the fringes of the course.

You'll be introduced to a range of conceptual frameworks, as well as studying issues of social theory, key themes of social change (urbanisation, industrialisation, modernity, postmodernity, globalisation), and social identities and structures. Chances are, you'll also cover the so-called canon of social theory – the birth of sociology and famous historical works of social analysis.

It is important and interesting to look at how people started to formalise social enquiry – to think about what kind of thing "society" is, to ask whether it has coherent rules of organisation, and to consider how we can learn about it.

Some degrees will introduce discussion under the broad area of inequalities – analysing the formation and impact of class, race, and gender. A few places will add consideration of sexuality and sexual identity, religion or youth culture. Related to these debates, there may be consideration of changing local, regional, and national identities – and a larger discussion of how we place ourselves in world. You may also cover social activity – areas such as work, leisure and family, consumption, technology, media, and culture.

Sociology graduates tend to go into social work, teaching, local government, or the civil service, but their analytical skills also come in useful for careers in personnel, marketing, and journalism.

Sociology courses are now much more varied than they once were. One big question is how much quantitative sociology you are prepared to do. This can involve a fair amount of statistics and number crunching, so it doesn't suit all students to have this as a compulsory element.

Furthermore, decide whether you want a more traditional course that centres on theory, or a more applied course, which teaches primarily contemporary issues. You can also find courses that concentrate on a specific area – taking a whole degree on crime and society is now possible and such courses are popular. Alternatively, you could choose one with a modular structure that allows you to change focus.

A bolder option would be to pick a joint honours degree; combinations with media studies or psychology are popular examples. Be aware, though, that this can be a greater commitment – joint honours schools often require higher grades and demand more of students attempting to integrate different disciplinary traditions. Finally, take a careful look at how the course is assessed and choose one that will suit your strengths. Formal exams, coursework, and dissertation can all play a part, just make sure the balance is in line with the way you prefer to work.

And, as with many courses, check the research specialisations of the university teaching staff. If you're being taught by those who are at the leading edge of research in your subject, it can be rewarding and you'll learn a heck of a lot more. The downside could be that some of them might have less time to teach you, so do investigate.

---

66 Studying sociology at university has been quite different from studying it at A-level. There are more module choices, which means you look at a wider variety of topics within the subject, making it a lot more interesting. It can be challenging because you cover topics you might not have done at A-level, but the staff are really friendly and helpful. I'm really enjoying my course, because the content is so varied and taught in an interesting way.

Jo Vaughan, *second-year sociology student, University of Glamorgan*

» Further information

The British Sociological Association
Bailey Suite, Palatine House
Belmont Business Park
Durham DH1 1TW

t   0191 383 0839
↗ www.britsoc.co.uk

The Socio-Legal Studies Association
SLSA Chair, School of Law
Queen's University Belfast
Belfast BT7 1NN

↗ www.kent.ac.uk/slsa

↗ Online reading

SocietyGuardian.co.uk SocietyGuardian.co.uk
Sociology Central www.sociology.org.uk
Intute: Social Sciences www.intute.ac.uk/socialsciences
The British Sociology Journal www.lse.ac.uk/serials/bjs
Internet Sociologist www.vts.rdn.ac.uk/tutorial/sociologist

Sociology

		Guardian score	Satisfied with teaching %	Satisfied with assessment %	Spend per student score /10	Student:staff ratio	Job prospects %	Value added score /10	Average entry tariff
1	Oxford	100.0	95	57	10	11			504
2	Cambridge	91.5	82	67	10	16	82	8	494
3	Warwick	80.3	89	73	10	14	53	8	385
4	Birmingham	78.5	87	69	10	17	58	9	370
5	Surrey	75.4	94	75	6	20	68	9	322
6	Edinburgh	75.2	93	46	9	16	47	9	402
7	Manchester	72.2	90	71	8	19	46	9	400
8	London School of Economics	70.7	77	59	9	13			426
9	Durham	70.2	86	65	7	19	57	8	362
10	Exeter	70.1	91	72	4	17	58	9	356
11	Bath	68.6	79	47	6	17	69	9	346
12	Glasgow	68.0	88	55	5	18	57	8	369
13	Aberdeen	67.6	94	79	4	21	59		301
13	Lancaster	67.6	86	61	7	15	58	7	343
15	Leeds	67.2	87	59	6	19	61	8	337
16	Bristol	66.8	82	55	7	20	66	5	399
17	Cardiff	65.5	77	52	9	19	58	7	347
18	Brunel	65.2	83	61	4	17			304
19	York	64.6	81	45	8	14	46	7	365
20	Nottingham	64.5	86	58	7	17	51	8	326
21	Sussex	64.4	73	55	4	18	57	10	364
22	Essex	62.8	87	74	5	15	45	7	322
23	Leicester	62.2	81	64	6	22	60	8	317
24	Nottingham Trent	62.0	84	55	8	17	57	8	238
25	Loughborough	61.8	90	55	7	20	48	7	343
26	Worcester	59.6	82	70	3	16			265
27	Portsmouth	58.7	92	77	5	17	45	4	281
28	Oxford Brookes	57.7	91	68	4	19		6	296
29	Hull	56.8	89	67	4	16	48	4	262
30	Bath Spa	56.2	94	72		15		6	252
31	Newcastle	56.0	81	59	5	23	58	3	347
32	Kent	55.6	87	64	6	17	46	5	277
33	Bradford	55.5	80	65	7	12			218
33	Southampton	55.5	79	58	4	23	42	8	363
35	Stirling	54.7			4	19	54	5	269
36	City	53.8	75	53	6	18	46	7	282
36	Goldsmiths	53.8	85	53	3	15	46	7	255
38	Coventry	53.6	88	71	5	19	34	7	254
38	Ulster	53.6	94	86	4	19	33	5	280
40	Brighton	51.9	89	77	3	31		6	271
41	Liverpool	51.8	77	54	6	22	49	4	320
41	Queen's, Belfast	51.8	78	58	5	20	45	4	312
43	St Mary's UC, Belfast	51.7	94	80	3	23	46	4	260
44	Sheffield	51.6	79	46	4	24	48	6	345
45	Robert Gordon	51.5			4	24		4	261

	Guardian score	Satisfied with teaching %	Satisfied with assessment %	Spend per student score /10	Student:staff ratio	Job prospects %	Value added score /10	Average entry tariff
46 Birmingham City	51.3	78	57	5	19		8	243
47 Anglia Ruskin	51.2	86	70	7	20			260
48 Napier	50.9			4	17	54		230
49 Leeds Met	50.6	76	56	10	20	38	2	243
49 Plymouth	50.6	76	55	8	16	33	6	243
51 Teesside	48.9	86	65	5	27	54	5	213
52 Bedfordshire	47.1	83	75	4	28		5	200
53 East London	46.9	78	58	6	22		7	186
54 Northumbria	46.6	77	58	5	27	50	4	275
55 Staffordshire	46.4	85	79	6	25		4	234
56 Derby	46.1	77	62	4	26			234
57 Sheffield Hallam	45.4	82	65	4	24	29	8	241
58 Sunderland	44.8	63	51	7	12	32	4	226
59 Northampton	44.6	92	70	3	27			203
60 Edge Hill	44.0	81	53	3	21			234
60 Kingston	44.0	78	56	4	27	44	7	216
60 UWE Bristol	44.0	85	64	4	20	36	2	247
63 UEA	43.5	84	54	4	27		3	325
64 Bangor	43.4	80	54	3		36	5	238
64 Gloucestershire	43.4	87	75	5	29			228
66 Canterbury Christ Church	41.6	88	74	2			6	229
67 Roehampton	41.1	88	54	4	29	40	5	204
68 Westminster	39.7	71	54	3	21	33	6	222
69 Lincoln	39.2	81	67	2	29	43	4	253
70 Salford	38.9	83	56	7	22	32	1	250
71 Central Lancashire	38.8	91	63	4	28	28	3	242
72 Southampton Solent	38.7	89	57	3	25	38	3	200
73 Manchester Met	38.5	73	58	3	26	36	6	251
74 Wolverhampton	36.9	74	68	4	27		2	190
75 Bucks New University	35.6	77	58	3	20	42	1	167
76 Liverpool John Moores	31.6	84	64	3	29	32	2	216
77 Abertay Dundee	29.2			4	31	45	1	199
78 Greenwich	29.0	68	59	3	31	44	1	194
79 London South Bank	27.1	88	70	3	37		1	168
79 Middlesex	27.1	77	46	5	40	42	3	168

Tourism and leisure management

> Tourism is a people industry. It's the world's largest industry, and its range is vast both on the supply side and the demand. It is global in reach and if properly managed offers destinations — both in developed and developing countries — a route to economic growth. It offers graduates career opportunities in all parts of the world in many different arenas, both in the private and public sectors.
>
> How many disciplines offer such a wide range of careers, with employers such as tour operators and travel agents, tourist attractions and transport providers, the accommodation sector, national and regional tourist boards, local authorities, the education sector, and the not-for-profit sector? How many disciplines allow the graduate to work with such a diverse range of consumers as leisure visitors, business tourists, conference and incentive travel consumers, and those visiting friends and relatives, to name just a few?
>
> Tourism is the world's fastest growing industry, it is diverse, vibrant, and exciting, and, above all, it needs new young professionals, well trained and skilled, with good business acumen and management capabilities.
>
> However, tourism needs professionals for another reason — its ability to harm our planet. No other industry has such an impact on our environment, the economic balance of our world, and the social and cultural lives of communities touched by tourism. Tomorrow's world needs people with the skills to manage tourism responsibly, to guarantee sustainability for the industry, and to make sure the benefits from tourism are shared.
>
> Tourism students graduate having had an exciting, enjoyable, and educational experience and are vocationally desirable, with good transferable management skills to enter the global tourism industry.
>
> **Greg Headley**, *Tourism Undergraduate Programme Leader, Leeds Metropolitan University*

Tourism and leisure management is a relatively new course to British universities. It is more likely to be found in former polytechnics and further education colleges than in the more traditional universities, but as the industry grows, so it demands increased professionalism, and with that comes a need for graduates.

The tourism industry is now widely recognised as the world's largest and its growth is creating rapid social, economic, and environmental changes across the globe, which require detailed understanding and measures to manage them.

As a subject, tourism isn't just concerned with how the masses flood towards the Costa del Sol. It has much wider concerns, beyond the developed world, and often looks instead at its global impact.

You'll study how people journey to their destination, how people choose where to go, and what they do when they are there. You'll gain an understanding of how people travel and how that interaction gives rise to changes in society, the economy, and the environment on a global scale.

Leisure management courses cover more practical areas, as befits a vocational degree. In a typical degree, you'll be able to study human resource management, accountancy, computing, and marketing. From there, you can specialise in the specific study of operational issues alongside courses related to strategic development. You might, for example, study topics in tourism and the environment, heritage, public and private sector leisure management or leisure and special needs.

As with many vocational courses, there is always the sandwich option, whereby you can spend a year working in a part of the tourism industry, or else the possibility of a shorter period of work experience. Either is invaluable – experience is key to finding the right kind of future employment: it both impresses your future bosses and gives you a far better idea of the areas you might want to work in. Some courses, international hotel management, for example, have foreign travel as an integral part of the course.

Graduates can look forward to careers with transport providers (airlines, ferry operators), tour operators, hotels, travel agents, and leisure developments. There are also possibilities in sports centre management, both private and public, and a relatively large number head off for teacher training courses each year.

In the tourism and leisure industries, there are a number of professional bodies that validate courses. Graduates of those courses are then entitled to membership of the body and thus professional status. If you're treating this as a vocational degree, then check that the appropriate bodies (the Tourism Society or the Institute of Travel, for example) validate the course. It could save a lot of bother later.

And check the nature of the study. Some courses demand a dissertation, and it can come as a shock to those who think they have opted for a work-based qualification to find that they have to undergo such an academic test. Such things are not for everyone. Similarly, the methods of assessment vary widely – from end-of-term exams to projects to continuous assessment. These all tend to prompt different stress patterns, so work out which is right for you.

Make sure a degree course is best suited to your needs. Many higher education and further education colleges offer excellent higher national diplomas (HNDs) which are usually two-year courses when taken full-time or can be done part-time when you're already working. Think hard – and talk to your careers advisers – before you take on a full degree course.

---

66 I have really enjoyed the course and it has challenged me in many areas. The group assessments, which required us to organise group meetings, assemble information as a group, present our findings, and compile a final report, has been particularly challenging. It has taught me new skills and also made me aware of my own weaknesses and strengths. This has helped me to develop a base for the management skills that I will use in the future and has increased my self-confidence.

Melisa Bertucci, *third-year international tourism management student, University of Brighton*

↗ Online reading

Guardian Unlimited Travel travel.guardian.co.uk
The Tourism Society www.tourismsociety.org
Pro Poor Tourism www.propoortourism.org.uk
Star UK www.staruk.org.uk
Articles in hospitality and tourism libweb.surrey.ac.uk/aht2

Further information

Institute of Travel and Tourism
PO Box 217, Ware
Herts SG12 8WY

t 0870 770 7960
e enquiries@itt.co.uk
↗ www.itt.co.uk

Visit Britain
Thames Tower, Blacks Road
Hammersmith, London W6 9EL

t 020 8846 9000
↗ www.visitbritain.com

Tourism Management Institute
41 Charlton Street
London NW1 1JD

t 01926 641 506
↗ www.tmi.org.uk

Tourism Concern
Stapleton House
277-81 Holloway Road
London N7 8HN

t 020 7133 3330
e info@tourismconcern.org.uk
↗ www.tourismconcern.org.uk

Tourism, transport and travel

		Guardian score	Satisfied with teaching %	Satisfied with assessment %	Spend per student score /10	Student:staff ratio	Job prospects %	Value added score /10	Average entry tariff
1	Bournemouth	100.0	79	64		10	72	7	261
2	Surrey	91.9	72	46	9	23		9	321
3	Brighton	90.4	65	64	10	9	44	8	238
4	Plymouth	90.1	92	71	9	19		5	237
5	Oxford Brookes	89.1	83	75	7	25			303
6	Sunderland	88.5	86	71	8	13			237
7	Napier	83.9			4	20	65	9	
8	Gloucestershire	79.6	87	76	7	16	44	5	241
9	Ulster	76.9	78	65	7	15	34	8	229
10	Central Lancashire	76.3	81	73	8	25	56	5	232
11	Leeds Met	69.0	74	57	7	31	57	6	262
12	Huddersfield	67.8	72	78	5	20		5	239
13	Manchester Met	67.0	75	62	5	20			236
14	Glasgow Caledonian	66.1	73	59	3	28	30	8	318
15	Sheffield Hallam	65.6	83	64	4	27	41	8	232
16	London South Bank	65.4	82	64	5	11		4	199
17	Derby	57.2	75	63	8	19	25		222
18	Lincoln	55.9	80	66	2	23		4	222
19	Greenwich	48.9	53	50	4	27	46	6	215
20	Salford	44.4	82	70	4		44	2	179
21	University College Birmingham	40.5	82	75	2	24	26	3	195
22	Hertfordshire	37.7	67	53	4	26		2	202
23	Wolverhampton	35.9			4		37	2	175
24	Bedfordshire	34.4	61	58	3	32		7	184
25	Liverpool John Moores	33.0	63	62	3	28		1	193
26	Thames Valley	32.3	78	54	4	33	20	5	154

University
profiles

Reading the profiles

What follows are short introductions to more than 150 universities and higher education institutions to help you as you take your first step towards that all-important selection. This book would be too heavy to lift – and far too long to read – if we tried to include exhaustive information on every place. What we provide here is merely a taster, so if something appeals do follow the links to that university's website or drop them an email (contact details are included in our profiles): they'll be happy to do all they can to convince you to give them a whirl.

But in the meantime, with universities from the north of Scotland to the southern tip of England just waiting to welcome you as a potential student, you should get cracking with the job of sifting through them. Enjoy it! And here are a few notes on the profiles to keep things clear …

Accommodation

Usually when we say that accommodation is guaranteed, we mean for young, full-time undergraduates who apply during the normal admissions cycle (rather than through Clearing, say) accept an offer and get their forms in by the deadline. Though often the criteria are much less stringent than that: do check with the accommodation offices for exact details.

Prices

Prices (for accommodation, for example) are generally provided by the university and refer to 2008-09, unless otherwise stated. Bear in mind that a slight rise should be expected for your year of entry. And the cost of university accommodation usually refers to a room in halls, including utility bills. Where private accommodation prices are mentioned, they usually refer to sharing a house or flat and don't include bills.

Statistics

Stats included in the profiles have typically been supplied by the university in question and are the most recent available.

Fees

Unless otherwise stated, the fees quoted here are for full-time home or EU students and refer to courses beginning in 2008-09 – for the very good reason that at the time of researching and writing this book the fees for entry in 2009-10 hadn't been set. Check with the university for the most up-to-date figure and expect a rise on this year. (To give you an idea of how much, the increase from 2007-08 to 2008-09 was from £3,070 to £3,145 – £75.)

Bursaries

Bursaries are non-repayable awards, typically aimed at full-time UK undergraduates. Universities charging the maximum fee must offer some level of bursary support to any student who qualifies for the full maintenance grant or special support grant. But many institutions offer awards well beyond the statutory requirement and to students on less than full grants, too.

As with fees, most bursary packages have yet to be finalised: details here generally refer to 2008-09.

And in the case of bursaries and financial support, it really is worth doing plenty of your own research. We can only give a summary here, not a comprehensive run-down of what's available, so make sure you take a look at the relevant sections of the website or prospectus of any university you are interested in.

>> Useful websites

Ucas www.ucas.com

Aim Higher www.direct.gov.uk/uni

Department for Education and Skills www.dfes.gov.uk/studentsupport

Learning Wales www.learning.wales.gov.uk/students/whats-new-e.htm

Student Awards Agency for Scotland www.student-support-saas.gov.uk

Department for Employment and Learning Northern Ireland www.delni.gov.uk

Student Finance Northern Ireland www.studentfinanceni.co.uk

Student Finance Wales www.studentfinancewales.co.uk

Training and Development Agency for Schools www.tda.gov.uk

National Union of Students www.nusonline.co.uk

Union of Students in Ireland www.nistudents.org

Office for Fair Access www.offa.org.uk

Note on the University of London

The colleges and institutes of this federal university are bound together by the prestigious London degree. As far as central facilities go, students have access to the University of London Union (ULU), some student accommodation in intercollegiate halls and some central sporting facilities. Teaching and social events are collegiate.

The following colleges and schools have individual profiles: Birkbeck, Central School of Speech and Drama, Courtauld Institute of Art, Goldsmiths, Heythrop College, King's, London School of Economics and Political Science, Queen Mary, Royal Academy of Music, Royal Holloway, Royal Veterinary College, St George's, School of Pharmacy, Soas, University College London. Other specialist colleges, institutes and schools that also belong to the University of London: Institute of Education, London Business School, London School of Hygiene and Tropical Medicine.

Note on the University of Wales/Prifysgol Cymru

The University of Wales/Prifysgol Cymru is a large federal university. It was founded by Royal Charter in 1893, bringing together the aims and aspirations of three existing colleges in Aberystwyth, South Wales and Monmouthshire, and Bangor.

The following institutions award University of Wales degrees: Aberystwyth; Bangor; Lampeter; University of Wales, Newport; North-East Wales Institute; Swansea Metropolitan University; Trinity College Carmarthen; and University of Wales Institute Cardiff (UWIC). These institutions all have separate profiles in the guide.

Degrees of the University of Wales are also offered in certain subjects at Cardiff University and the Royal Welsh College of Music and Drama (also profiled separately), as well as other HE institutions in the rest of the UK and overseas.

Key to symbols

The following statistics (in each profile) are drawn from the 2005–06 Higher Education Statistics Agency (Hesa) performance indicators, the most recent publicly available (www.hesa.ac.uk):

 Total number of full-time, first-time degree entrants

 The percentage of entrants from state schools or colleges

 The percentage of young full-time first degree entrants from NS-SEC classes 4, 5, 6 and 7 (the lowest four socio-economic classes in the data)

 Non-continuation rates, as a percentage: the projected outcomes for full-time students starting first degree courses in 2004–05

 Graduate employment rates: these refer to leavers obtaining degrees from full-time courses in 2005–06. The employment indicator is based on the new Destinations of Leavers in Higher Education (DLHE) survey. It expresses the number of graduates who say they are working and/or studying as a percentage of all those who are working, or studying or seeking work, six months after graduation

The profiles also include an (anonymous!) quote from a current student or recent graduate, to give you a tiny flavour of a "real" experience. So they'll be subjective, biased and unreliable. They might just be right though! And there's only one way for you to find out ...

London institutions

1 University of the Arts London
2 Birkbeck, University of London
3 Brunel University
4 Central School of Speech and Drama
5 City University London
6 Conservatoire for Dance and Drama
7 Courtauld Institute of Art
8 University of East London
9 Goldsmiths, University of London
10 University of Greenwich
11 Heythrop College
12 Imperial College London
13 King's College London
14 Kingston University
15 London Metropolitan University
16 London School of Economics
17 London South Bank University

18 Middlesex University
19 Queen Mary, University of London
20 Roehampton University
21 Rose Bruford College
22 Royal Academy of Music
23 Royal College of Music, London
24 Royal Holloway, University of London
25 Royal Veterinary College, University of London
26 St George's, University of London
27 St Mary's University College, Twickenham
28 School of Oriental and African Studies (Soas)
29 School of Pharmacy
30 Thames Valley University
31 Trinity Laban
32 University College London
33 University of Westminster

University of Aberdeen

University Office
King's College
Aberdeen AB24 3FX

t 01224 272090/91
e sras@abdn.ac.uk
↗ www.abdn.ac.uk/sras

》 further links

ACCOMMODATION www.abdn.ac.uk/accommodation
STUDENTS' UNION www.ausa.org.uk

Aberdeen

2160   84.0   25.7   15.9   93.0

Aberdeen is an ancient university with a strong academic reputation. Its picturesque 15th-century King's College campus lies just outside the city centre. The university is investing heavily in new facilities – a new library, student centre and an Olympic sports facility for starters. Aberdeen is a charming, student-friendly city with plenty of good pubs.

Fees Scottish students pay no tuition fees. For other UK students, annual tuition fees of £1,775 from 2007–08 (£2,825 for medicine).

Bursaries Young students' bursaries for Scottish-students under 25 from low-income families. Other grants available. A minimum of 30 entrance awards of £1,000 for every year of study to new undergraduates, plus a range of other scholarships available.

Accommodation Guaranteed for all new first-year students. Weekly prices range from £60.50 to £89.70 for self-catering accommodation and from £103 to £123 for catered halls.

Facilities The library and computing facilities are state of the art. A £23m sports centre is due to open in 2009.

Transport There's an airport, a station that connects directly to Edinburgh and London and plenty of good road links. It's an easy stroll or quick bus ride into town.

❝ STUDENT VIEW ❞

"I'd recommend Aberdeen because it's a proper academic environment and there's plenty to do. There are lots of attractions in town: a good music scene, art galleries, and many random things to do if you ever have time to get bored. The academic staff give passionate lectures that usually fill seats."

University of Abertay Dundee

40 Bell Street
Dundee DD1 1HG

t 01382 308080
e sro@abertay.ac.uk
↗ www.abertay.ac.uk

》 **further links**

ACCOMMODATION accommo@abertay.ac.uk
STUDENTS' UNION www.abertaystudents.com

1040   97.2   37.2   22.4   92.6

Abertay offers world-leading courses in computer arts and computer games technology, has some of the best IT facilities in the UK, and an £8m library. Dundee itself is a bustling city. In 2005, a new £6m student centre with a cinema, coffee shop, nightclub and exhibition space opened. There are good local arts scenes, with a particularly good track record in music.

Fees Fees for all undergraduate courses are £1,735 for new students in 2007–08. Scottish students have their fees paid for them.

Bursaries Means-tested hardship fund, with an average payout of £1,000. Another similar fund for mature students. Other scholarships and bursaries available.

Accommodation Priority is given to first-year students. All university accommodation is in single rooms. Average rent is around £65 a week.

Facilities A higher rate of PCs to students than almost any other university.

Transport The campus is right in the city centre. Dundee is 90 minutes by train from Glasgow and an hour from Edinburgh. There's an airport with direct links to London, too.

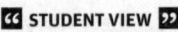 **STUDENT VIEW** 》

"Although studying can be a challenge and sometimes frustrating, the craic you have during your time here makes it really worthwhile."

Aberystwyth, University of Wales

Old College, King Street
Aberystwyth
Ceredigion SY23 2AX

t 01970 622021
e ug-admissions@aber.ac.uk
↗ www.aber.ac.uk

》 further links

ACCOMMODATION accommodation@aber.ac.uk
STUDENTS' UNION www.aberguild.co.uk

2030   92.6   27.6   9.6   90.6

The university is central to life in "Aber": in a town of 12,000 people, the addition of 9,000 students is going to make an impact. It's frequently rated highly in student satisfaction surveys. Encouragingly, more than 90 per cent of the undergraduate population come from the state sector. The town itself, while small, has a lovely, breezy position on the west coast of Wales, and is known for a thriving local music scene.

Fees £3,145 a year for all full-time undergraduate courses in 2008–09. Welsh students will qualify for a fee subsidy paid directly to the institution and will in effect be liable for a fee of about £1,225.

Bursaries Bursaries are means-tested, and range from £1,000 for students on a maximum grant to £200 for students who receive the minimum grant. There are also subject-specific excellence bursaries available of £2,000 over three years, dependent on Ucas points. There is a £500 discount off first-year hall fees for all UK/EU students who hold Aberystwyth as their firm choice through Ucas by June 30. Other awards are also available.

Accommodation Guaranteed for first-years. Accommodation prices start at £42 a week. Catered single rooms are £92.50 a week.

Facilities The university library is very well equipped but should it fall short you can always pay a visit to the National Library of Wales, which is based in Aberystwyth.

Transport Trains will whisk you to Birmingham and beyond. Road links will take you to north or south-west Wales with ease.

⁇ STUDENT VIEW ⁇

"The quality of life is amazing — the town is dominated by students and that gives it a real community feel. I can't imagine not living by the sea once I leave Aber!"

Anglia Ruskin University

Bishop Hall Lane
Chelmsford CM1 1SQ

t 0845 271 3333
e answers@anglia.ac.uk
↗ www.anglia.ac.uk

Cambridge Campus East Road, Cambridge CB1 1PT

》 further links

ACCOMMODATION www.anglia.ac.uk/accommodation
STUDENTS' UNION www.angliastudent.com

2415   98.1   34.5   27.1   91.1

Based at two main campuses in Cambridge and Chelmsford, Anglia Ruskin is fiercely committed to widening access to higher education. The university has 24,000 students, 97 per cent of whom are from state schools.

Fees £3,149 a year for all full-time undergraduate courses in 2008.

Bursaries From 2008, £310 per year to students with a full maintenance grant. Other scholarships are available.

Accommodation The university can accommodate 100 per cent of Chelmsford applicants and more than 95 per cent in Cambridge. Rents £78 to £120 a week.

Facilities Good sports facilities, particularly at Chelmsford. Both sites have bars, computing facilities and libraries.

Transport Both Cambridge and Chelmsford have easy access to motorways, main roads, rails links and Stansted airport.

《 STUDENT VIEW 》

"Everyone is really nice up here: it feels safe and there's a community feeling on campus. Cambridge is made for students and the area is idyllic for work and play."

Arts Institute at Bournemouth

Wallisdown, Poole
Dorset BH 12 5HH

t 01202 533 011
e general@aib.ac.uk
↗ www.aib.ac.uk

》 further links

ACCOMMODATION studentadvice@aib.ac.uk
STUDENTS' UNION www.aib.ac.uk/studentinformation
/studentunion.aspx

540   98.0   25.9   10.0   95.2

Bournemouth

The Arts Institute at Bournemouth is a specialist institution offering undergraduate, foundation degree, postgraduate and further education courses in contemporary arts, design and media. The campus is two miles from Bournemouth and consists of a series of purpose-built studios accommodating approximately 2,000 students on full-time courses.

Fees £3,145 for full-time undergraduate programmes in 2008.

Bursaries All students with the full grant of £2,835 will receive £310. These students will also receive a bonus of £150 on successful completion of their first year, £225 after their second year and a further £425 after their final year. All students who receive a grant of £1,050–£2,834 will receive £160.

Accommodation Halls of residence on campus or in town cost £85-£125 per week, including all bills. The majority of students live in privately rented accommodation during their first year. The average cost is £70–£85 a week.

Facilities A purpose-built library provides material to support the courses. The institute also boasts a contemporary arts gallery.

Transport London is less than two hours away, with regular train and coach services and good road networks.

《 STUDENT VIEW 》

"I would recommend it to anyone. The staff are brilliant and the facilities are great. There is a good social life and I loved living in Bournemouth."

University of the Arts London

Camberwell College of Arts Peckham Road, London SE5 8UF
Central Saint Martins College of Art and Design Southampton Row, London WC1B 4AP
Chelsea College of Art and Design Millbank, London SW1P 4JU
London College of Communication Elephant & Castle, London SE1 6SB
London College of Fashion 20 John Princes' Street, London W1G 0BJ
Wimbledon College of Art Merton Hall Road, London SW19 3QA

t 020 7514 6000
e info@arts.ac.uk
↗ www.arts.ac.uk

》 further links

ACCOMMODATION www.arts.ac.uk/housing
STUDENTS' UNION www.suarts.org

1960   94.3   25.0   12.1   86.5

London

University of the Arts is Europe's largest university for art, design, fashion, communication and the performing arts. It is a federation of six internationally renowned colleges: Camberwell College of Arts, Central Saint Martins College of Art and Design, Chelsea College of Art and Design, London College of Communication, London College of Fashion and Wimbledon College of Art.

Fees For 2008-09, home students will pay up to £3,145 for first degrees.

Bursaries Students in receipt of the full government grant are automatically entitled to a £305 bursary (2007-08). Over 300 access bursaries of £1,000 are awarded, according to need. There is a wide range of other bursaries available, including privately funded scholarships.

Accommodation Costs for 2007-08 in university accommodation range from £72.60 to £159.04 a week. There is accommodation available for 1,754 students. Disabled students and those under 18 at the start of their course are guaranteed accommodation.

Facilities As you'd expect, there are excellent facilities for students in all disciplines and students from each college can access some of the resources at the others.

Transport No problem getting around: all the colleges are close to tube or bus links.

◀◀ STUDENT VIEW ▶▶

"The courses on offer and the people who study here make it one of the leading institutions for art and design in the world. Amazing people teach amazing people and everything about my time at Arts London has been inspirational."

Aston University, Birmingham

Aston Triangle
Birmingham B4 7ED

t 0121 204 3000
e ugenquiries@aston.ac.uk
↗ www.aston.ac.uk

》 further links

ACCOMMODATION www.aston.ac.uk/accommodation
STUDENTS' UNION www.astonguild.org.uk

1780   89.0   35.2   10.3   94.1

Birmingham

Aston offers a broad range of degree courses, with particular success in business, science, engineering, health sciences, social sciences and languages. Some 70 per cent of the 7,000 or so undergraduates take sandwich placement years or years abroad. The university is proud both of its student mix and diversity and of its excellent graduate employment rate (84.1 per cent of 2006 graduates entered "graduate level" jobs, against a national average of 5 per cent). Aston is located on a green, self-contained campus right in the centre of Birmingham.

Fees £3,145 a year for all full-time undergraduate courses in 2008. Sandwich placement-year fees are £1,570.

Bursaries Means-tested bursaries of up to £800 a year. Students on full grant will receive £800, then there's a sliding scale for those receiving a partial grant. All UK/EU students on a placement year will receive a placement bursary of £1,000 for that year.

Accommodation Guaranteed for eligible first-years. Self-catering accommodation ranges from £65 to £101 a week.

Facilities The campus boasts two sports centres and a 25-metre pool. Recent developments include The Loft, a state-of-the-art social space. All student accommodation has internet access.

Transport Excellent road and train links, especially to Manchester, London and the west.

《 STUDENT VIEW 》

"Top of the league tables, and it's the best university in the West Midlands. Superb location next to the city, excellent transport links, low-price housing both on and off campus — there really is nothing that Aston should be ashamed about."

Bangor, University of Wales

Bangor
Gwynedd LL57 2DG

t 01248 382018
e admissions@bangor.ac.uk
↗ www.bangor.ac.uk

》 further links

ACCOMMODATION halls@bangor.ac.uk
STUDENTS' UNION www.undeb.bangor.ac.uk

| 1920 | 93.9 | 32.7 | 22.5 | 91.0 |

It's close to the sea and the mountains. The cost of living is low and part-time work is fairly easy to come by, so it might be easier on your wallet than some places. The town – actually one of the UK's smallest cities – has a significant proportion of Welsh speakers. As for the university itself, major investment is taking place to provide more student accommodation and it is expanding academically, too.

Fees For 2008–09, fees were £3,145 for all undergraduate degrees.

Bursaries Up to £1,000 a year depending on family income. Specific awards for certain subjects, merit scholarships and other awards available.

Accommodation A range is available from £63 to £98 a week.

Facilities One main library each for arts and sciences and numerous satellite libraries. Nine computer rooms are open 24 hours a day.

Transport Most parts of the university are within walking distance of each other. Bangor is on the main rail line between London and Holyhead and has good road links to the motorway network along the A55.

《 STUDENT VIEW 》

"It's such a great community – everyone knows everyone. It's the sort of place that people come to because they want to be here, which is nice. The terrace, which is at the front of the main arts building, has the most stunning, sweeping view over Bangor and across the coast to Llandudno. It makes you want to be a poet or something."

University of Bath

Bath BA2 7AY

t 01225 388388
e admissions@bath.ac.uk
↗ www.bath.ac.uk

University of Bath in Swindon
Oakfield Campus, Marlowe Avenue, Walcot, Swindon SN3 3JR

 further links

ACCOMMODATION www.bath.ac.uk/accommodation
STUDENTS' UNION www.bathstudent.com

1795   75.9   18.7   4.8   93.7

Bath could hardly be more visually charming, and the campus is on a hill overlooking the city. The droves of tourists ensure there's plenty of shopping and leisure activity to join in with, and you can always dash off to neighbouring Bristol for some urban grit. The university boasts impressive student satisfaction results.

Fees £3,145 for all undergraduate courses in 2008-09.

Bursaries Up to £1,200 for students with a family income of £25,000 or less, on a sliding scale after that. Other merit and subject-based awards available.

Accommodation Accommodation is guaranteed for first-years. Prices from £75 to £115 a week.

Facilities The library is one of the few in the country to stay open 24 hours a day, seven days a week. Sports facilities were already some of the best in the country, even without the addition of a £30m training village.

Transport A frequent bus runs into town and takes about 10 minutes. The train to Bristol takes 15 minutes and it's 90 minutes to London.

Bath Spa University

Newton Park, Newton St Loe
Bath BA2 9BN

t 01225 875875
e enquiries@bathspa.ac.uk
↗ www.bathspa.ac.uk

Sion Hill Campus Sion Hill, Bath BA1 5SF
Somerset Place Landsdown, Bath BA1 5HA
Culverhay Rush Hill, Bath BA2 2QL

» further links

ACCOMMODATION accommodation@bathspa.ac.uk
STUDENTS' UNION www.bathspasu.co.uk

1275   95.4   26.5   11.8   94.9

Bath

Bath Spa is a relatively new university and prides itself on its teaching focus and emphasis on employability. The university is split over four sites. Newton Park is a few miles from town, but it's so lovely-looking you couldn't possibly mind.

Fees £3,145 for all full-time undergraduate courses in 2008–09.

Bursaries Means-tested bursary of up to £1,200. An extra £1,000, non-means-tested, for certain science subjects. Further bursaries and emergency financial support are available.

Accommodation A range of accommodation is available, priced from around £55 to £95 a week. The university expects to be able to house all first-years who want accommodation.

Facilities Each campus has a library whose content reflects the courses taught there, as well as study areas and access to computing resources. The students' union is a well-established music venue.

Transport See Bath, previous page.

‹‹ STUDENT VIEW ››

"This is an exciting place to live — from the new Bath Spa complex to the redevelopment of the city centre, Bath is a world heritage site moving into the 21st century. And sports fans can get a kick out of the successful rugby and high-flying football teams."

University of Bedfordshire

University of Bedfordshire

t 01234 400 400
e admission@beds.ac.uk
↗ www.beds.ac.uk

Luton Campus Park Square, Luton, Bedfordshire LU1 3JU
Bedford Campus Polhill Avenue, Bedford MK41 9EA
Putteridge Bury Campus Hitchin Road, Luton, Bedfordshire LU2 8LE

»» further links

ACCOMMODATION accommodation@beds.ac.uk
STUDENTS' UNION www.ubsu.co.uk

1505   99.6   43.0   19.8   88.8

Bedfordshire was born from the merging of the University of Luton with the Bedford campus of De Montfort University. Both towns are within striking distance of London. Luton has a busy social scene and Bedford boasts a nice riverside position. It has an excellent graduate employment record and a diverse student population. A sizeable proportion of students hail from the local area.

Fees Bedfordshire was charging the full £3,145 fee in 2008–09.

Bursaries Range from £310 to £4,180 depending on personal circumstances. All full-time degree students will receive at least £310.

Accommodation All first-years are offered accommodation on the Bedford or Luton campus. A new £20m block has opened in Bedford; a similar £30m development is planned for Luton. Rents are reasonable.

Facilities There are good sports facilities on both campuses, as well as libraries, computers and bars.

Transport The airport is close by, the bus station is a short walk from Park Square and there are regular trains to London.

❝ STUDENT VIEW ❞

"The teaching staff are very committed to students and to providing them with support. I am proud of the diversity of the university and the fact that there are so many people from different cultures, countries, and backgrounds."

Birkbeck College, University of London

Malet Street
Bloomsbury
London WC1E 7HX

t 0845 601 0174 (Bloomsbury); 0845 602 4169 (Stratford)
e info@bbk.ac.uk or info@birkbeckstratford.ac.uk
⌁ www.bbk.ac.uk or www.birkbeckstratford.ac.uk

》 further links

ACCOMMODATION http://housing.london.ac.uk/cms
STUDENTS' UNION www.bbk.ac.uk/su

As well as being a respected teaching and research institution, Birkbeck is unique among the colleges of the University of London for its emphasis on part-time, non-residential teaching. Undergraduate teaching takes place in the evening and a degree takes four years to complete. Fees are competitive and the ability to work while studying makes Birkbeck a good choice for those concerned about debt. Applications are direct to the college and not through Ucas.

Fees Fees vary. For details see the website.

Bursaries Contact the college directly. There is a package of financial support for students.

Accommodation No on-campus accommodation. Students from outside London can use the University of London housing services.

Facilities There is a new library and access to computing facilities. You have access to the University of London students' union.

Transport All campuses are easily accessible by public transport.

❝ STUDENT VIEW ❞

"I'd recommend Birkbeck because it is flexible, the standard of education is high, and the lecturers are dedicated. It was important that I could continue to work full-time. Studying part-time at Birkbeck is affordable and you are not stuck with a large student loan even before your first job!"

University of Birmingham

Edgbaston
Birmingham B15 2TT

t 0121 414 3344
e admissions@bham.ac.uk
⌐ www.bham.ac.uk

» **further links**

ACCOMMODATION www.housing.bham.ac.uk
STUDENTS' UNION www.guildofstudents.com

4530   76.5   19.9   6.2   93.4

Birmingham

Large, prestigious and rather grand – you wouldn't expect anything less from Birmingham's university. Established in 1900, it was the first "red-brick" university to receive its royal charter. The large, leafy campus in Edgbaston comes equipped with bars, cafes, shops, a hair salon, a concert hall, banks, an art gallery, a medical practice, a nursery – even its own train station (only one stop to the city centre). It also has one of the largest students' unions in the country, as well as excellent employment figures.

Fees £3,145 in 2008-09 for all full-time undergraduate programmes.

Bursaries In 2008, there will be £840 available to all students with a household income of less than £34,600. Students who qualify will also be eligible for a scholarship of £1,260 based on academic achievement. Other scholarships in selected subjects and for excellence in music and sport.

Accommodation Guaranteed for first-years. Approximate rents £75 for a standard single, rising to £110 for an ensuite room.

Facilities Great facilities and even an art gallery on campus.

Transport Good for rail, road and air.

❝ STUDENT VIEW ❞

"Our libraries and computer facilities are second to none and academic support is also very good. It's a good campus university where students are very involved. There isn't a typical student that comes here so you'll have a wide circle of friends."

Birmingham City University

Perry Bar
Birmingham   B42 2SU

t 0121 331 5000
e choices@bcu.ac.uk
↗ www.bcu.ac.uk

》 further links

ACCOMMODATION accommodation@bcu.ac.uk
STUDENTS' UNION www.birminghamcitysu.com

3490   97.0   42.8   17.2   91.5

Birmingham

Birmingham City University, formerly the University of Central England, has around 25,000 students spread across seven campuses. Courses have a strong focus on relevance for the job market and there's an excellent careers service. The university prides itself on its reputation for widening participation and you'll find a broad spectrum of cultures, nationalities and ages here. The city itself is similarly diverse, with plenty to see and do.

Fees £3,145 a year for all full-time undergraduate courses in 2008–09.

Bursaries Up to £525 available for students receiving a full or partial maintenance grant.

Accommodation Applicants are guaranteed a room in halls of residence for their first year of study provided they have accepted an offer on a full-time course, do not live in Birmingham and apply by the start of the autumn term. Most halls are self-catering and 2008–09 prices range from £70 to £100 a week.

Facilities Specialist facilities support the different faculties, with the libraries, computers and bars you'd also expect.

Transport Birmingham is easy to get to by road or rail.

《 STUDENT VIEW 》

"I'm proud to have come to Birmingham City University as I've gained so many experiences that I wouldn't have got if I had gone to another university. Birmingham City is an amazingly diverse, dynamic, friendly, and entertaining university that thrives on community and equality of opportunity. I really have had the best time of my life here."

Bishop Grosseteste
University College Lincoln

Lincoln   LN1 3DY

t   01522 527347
e   info@bishopg.ac.uk
↗ www.bishopg.ac.uk

》 further links

ACCOMMODATION   http://www.bishopg.ac.uk/?_id=10155
STUDENTS' UNION   http://www.bishopgsu.co.uk

325   99.6   39.9   9.9   97.0

Robert Grosseteste was a 13th-century bishop of Lincoln. The college bearing his name was established in 1862 and has a reputation as an independent Anglican higher education institution. It also offers courses in arts and education and is firmly committed to diversity and opening access to higher education. Lincoln itself is a charming historical city.

Fees £3,145 for full-time undergraduate students in 2008-09.

Bursaries £1,050 will be paid to students with a household income of £39,250 or less. Further means-tested and discretionary support is available.

Accommodation Accommodation is guaranteed for first-years who have the university as their firm choice. Costs are reasonable.

Facilities A new sports and fitness centre opened in 2006, and there's a good library and IT facilities, too.

Transport One to two hours to London by train. It's a 25-30 minute walk from the station to campus.

《 STUDENT VIEW 》
"The best aspect of my time at BG was the quality of teaching on my course and the support provided by my tutors."

University of Bolton

Deane Road
Bolton   BL3 5AB

t 01204 900800
e enquiries@bolton.ac.uk
↗ www.bolton.ac.uk

》 further links

ACCOMMODATION accomm@bolton.ac.uk
STUDENTS' UNION www.bisu.co.uk

1090   99.2   42.7   31.7   88.2

Of the 9,000 or so students, around three-quarters are north-west natives. Bolton itself may not be massive, but there's a rich cultural heritage and plenty to do – not to mention the fact that Manchester is just a short hop away.

Fees Currently £3,145 for all full-time undergraduate courses.

Bursaries £320 annual bursaries to those receiving a full grant, then support on a sliding scale for those receiving partial grants, down to £70 a year. £730 annual scholarships for those who have completed a preparatory course or period of study at the university or a partner institution, irrespective of financial means.

Accommodation The university is usually able to accommodate all first-years who have requested a place in halls. Self-catering accommodation costs £60 a week.

Facilities There's a range of sports teams to join or classes to take part in at the sports centre. The library opens late and there is 24-hour access to computing facilities.

Transport Bolton station is half a mile away, with frequent connections to Manchester. The motorway network is on the doorstep.

❝ STUDENT VIEW ❞

"Bolton is a town with all the facilities of a city. The university is relatively small, which makes it good in terms of teaching – rather than sitting in large lecture theatres and having the tutor only know you as a name on the register, you often get more individual help and tutors get to know you."

Bournemouth University

Fern Barrow
Talbot Campus, Poole
Dorset BH12 5BB

t 08456 501501
e askBUenquiries@bournemouth.ac.uk
↗ www.bournemouth.ac.uk

》 further links

ACCOMMODATION www.bournemouth.ac.uk/accommodation
STUDENTS' UNION www.subu.org.uk

2995   93.5   25.6   12.8   94.2

Bournemouth

The university is firmly rooted in the professional application of education. It works closely with key employers and courses are designed with future career success in mind. The 15,000 students can also enjoy all the benefits of living in a tourist town, with some of the UK's best beaches.

Fees £3,145 for full-time undergraduate courses in 2008-09.

Bursaries Up to £1,000 a year, based on household income. If you are entitled to a full grant you'll also get an extra £310 a year. Some scholarships are also available.

Accommodation The university expects to offer all new students somewhere to live. Costs average £72 to £88 a week.

Facilities Award-winning learning facilities. There's a Sony HD TV studio (the only one in the UK) and the National Centre for Computer Animation. There's a great cricket ground and unrivalled sailing and watersports.

Transport There's an inter-campus bus, extensive cycle routes in town and there are ferry services and rail and road links.

❝ STUDENT VIEW ❞

"Bournemouth is absolutely the best place to live as a student in the UK. The beach is a favourite with students. In the summertime everyone chills down there and in the winter it's great for relaxing after a night out. Because it's not a massive city the students feel like one large family and the social life is second to none."

University of Bradford

Bradford
West Yorkshire BD7 1DP

t 0800 073 1225
e course-enquiries@bradford.ac.uk
↗ www.bradford.ac.uk

》 further links

ACCOMMODATION halls-of-residence@bradford.ac.uk
STUDENTS' UNION www.ubuonline.co.uk

2020   93.8   43.7   16.7   90.3

Bradford

Bradford is a bustling, diverse, friendly and energetic city — and the university follows suit. It continues to draw large numbers of applicants, drawn by the promise of good employment prospects, a low cost of living and arguably the best curry in the country. The city-centre campus fosters a close-knit student community. The university is committed to sustainable development.

Fees £3,145 for full-time undergraduate courses in 2008-09.

Bursaries Two levels of bursary for 2008-09 means-tested up to £40,000 and £60,005 household income respectively: £400 or £500 in a foundation year; £400 or £500 in the first year, rising to £500 or £700 in the second year and £600 or £900 in the final year and subsequent years.

Accommodation Prices range from £60 a week to £82.40.

Facilities The students' union boasts three nightclubs and the university has one of the highest PC-to-student ratios in the country. There is an art gallery, theatre and music centre on the campus.

Transport Walking to the town centre takes about 15 minutes. Leeds is about 20 minutes away by train and Bradford is within reach of Leeds/Bradford international airport and the M62 motorway.

❝ STUDENT VIEW ❞

"There's such a diverse mix of people and you'll really feel at home. And it's a great feeling to be part of an organisation that takes pride in looking after the environment."

University of Brighton

Mithras House
Lewes Road
Brighton BN2 4AT

t 01273 600900
e admissions@brighton.ac.uk
↗ www.brighton.ac.uk

Moulsecoomb Place Lewes Road, Brighton BN2 4GA
Falmer Campus Village Way, Brighton BN1 9SF
Eastbourne Campus Trevin Towers, Gaudick Road, Eastbourne BN20 73P

》 further links

ACCOMMODATION accommodation@brighton.ac.uk
STUDENTS' UNION www.ubsu.net

3105   92.7   27.4   10.1   93.5

Despite its size (20,000 or so students), Brighton is a laidback university. Its varied degrees have a strong professional focus – 94 per cent of undergraduate courses have opportunities for work-based learning – with good employment rates. The student body is diverse, with many part-time and mature students. The university is split over campuses in Brighton and Eastbourne.

Fees £3,145 for full-time undergraduate students in 2008–09.

Bursaries All full-time undergraduate students with household incomes of up to £39,305 a year are eligible for a bursary of £520 to £1,050 a year. Additional bursaries are available for local students and there are scholarships for exceptional achievement.

Accommodation Guaranteed for non-local first-years. Weekly rents range from £66 to £127.

Facilities Extensive sporting facilities, the students' unions hosts its own club nights and there are good computing resources.

Transport London is less than an hour by train. Gatwick and the Newhaven ferry port are both nearby. Eastbourne is about 40 minutes away from Brighton by car.

❝ STUDENT VIEW ❞

"I would definitely recommend it. Brighton University campuses offer a really safe and friendly city experience with a community full of people from many walks of life that can enhance your perceptions. There is so much to see and do, you will never be bored."

University of Bristol

Senate House
Tyndall Avenue
Bristol BS8 1TH

t 0117 928 9000
e ug-admissions@bristol.ac.uk
↗ www.bristol.ac.uk

》 further links

ACCOMMODATION accom-office@bris.ac.uk
STUDENTS' UNION www.ubu.org.uk

3065   65.1   16.4   4.0   95.2

Bristol has become an internationally respected academic powerhouse with around 12,500 undergraduates and 3,500 postgraduates. The university is one of the most popular in the UK, partly because of its excellent research and teaching and partly because Bristol has a great social scene. Most of the main buildings are located within a few minutes' walk of each other in a lively part of the city centre.

Fees £3,145 for full-time undergraduate students in 2008-09.

Bursaries All new undergraduate students with a household income of £50,000 or less receive a bursary of up to £1,160. There's a top-up bursary of up to £1,050 for local students and other support and awards available.

Accommodation Guaranteed for non-local first-years. Weekly rents range from £47 to £146.

Facilities The library has the largest academic collection in south-west England — 1.4m volumes. The university has invested more than £8m in facilities for sport and exercise in recent years. Drama and music are also well catered for.

Transport Good road and rail links including the M4 and M5. Convenient for Bristol airport.

❰❰ STUDENT VIEW ❱❱
"Bristol has everything you would expect of a city this size. The university is academically strong and has so much more to offer than a campus university."

Brunel University

Uxbridge UB8 3PH

t 01895 274000
e admissions@brunel.ac.uk
↗ www.brunel.ac.uk

》 further links
ACCOMMODATION accom-uxb@brunel.ac.uk
STUDENTS' UNION www.brunel.ac.uk/life/ubs

2835   93.3   37.0   13.1   90.4

London

Since becoming a university in 1966, Brunel's mission has been to combine academic rigour with the practical, entrepreneurial and imaginative approach pioneered by its namesake, Isambard Kingdom Brunel. It's proving successful. All of its 14,000 students are now on a single campus at Uxbridge, west London, which has enjoyed £250m of investment in recent years. Brunel has the rare distinction of being a campus university in London, with all the bars, cafes and facilities you'd expect.

Fees £3,145 for full-time undergraduate students in 2008-09.

Bursaries For students entitled to the full government grant, £1,000. For students who receive a partial grant, £500. Other scholarships are also available.

Accommodation Guaranteed for all first-years. From around £79-£97 a week.

Facilities The library has had recent investment, and there is good access to computing facilities.

Transport Uxbridge is at the end of the Metropolitan underground line, so it's easy to get to London. Heathrow and the motorways are also handy.

❝ STUDENT VIEW ❞

"Brunel is a little concrete utopia. You have ready access to central London but with the addition of trees and little bits of grass. Everything you need is right on your doorstep: nowhere on campus is more than five minutes away."

University of Buckingham

Hunter Street
Buckingham MK18 1EG

t 01280 814080
e info@buckingham.ac.uk
↗ www.buckingham.ac.uk

»» further links

ACCOMMODATION accommodation@buckingham.ac.uk
STUDENTS' UNION www.buckingham.ac.uk/life/social/su

Buckingham is a unique institution: Britain's only private university. Just under 900 students study here and the university offers intensive two-year degree programmes. Even so, a Buckingham degree is still more expensive than your regular kind, though you do get an impressive staff-student ratio and students are among the most satisfied with their experience. The pretty campus is compact, but big enough to boast its own cinema. More than 63 per cent of students are from overseas.

Fees £7,500 a year for most undergraduate courses.

Bursaries A range of scholarships are available.

Accommodation Campus accommodation is guaranteed for all first-years who apply for it. Self-catering accommodation costs between £67 and £111 a week.

Facilities The students' union is based at the hub of students' entertainment in Tanlaw Mill at the Hunter Street campus. Facilities include a bar, refectory, gym, studio and common room.

Transport The town boasts a good public transport service, with regular buses to Oxford, Milton Keynes and Cambridge. Milton Keynes railway station is 20 minutes away and there are regular trains to London, a journey that takes 30 minutes.

«« STUDENT VIEW »»

"We have a motto here: 'Work hard, play hard!' There is a time to study and there is a time to have fun and the University of Buckingham offers both. We have a lot of green spaces. We even have rivers. There is something very healthy about the whole area. It is like heaven in the UK."

Buckinghamshire New University

High Wycombe Campus Queen Alexandra Road, High Wycombe HP11 2JZ
Wellesbourne Campus Kingshill Road, High Wycombe HP13 5BB
Chalfont Campus Gorelands Lane, Chalfont St Giles HP8 4AD

t 0800 0565 660
e advice@bucks.ac.uk
↗ www.bucks.ac.uk

》 further links
ACCOMMODATION www.bcuc.ac.uk/accommodation
STUDENTS' UNION www.bucksstudent.com/student_marketing

1485   97.1   39.2   12.0   91.8

High Wycombe

Buckinghamshire New University, or Bucks, nestles in the beautiful countryside of the Chiltern Hills. The university offers a varied range of vocationally targeted degrees and studying options not widely available in the sector, from commercial pilot training to music management, textiles and furniture. There is a large proportion of mature students. The town centre is within easy walking distance.

Fees £3,145 for full-time undergraduate courses in 2008-09.

Bursaries A package that includes an annual cash bursary paid to all full-time UK and EU students, plus additional faculty-based support.

Accommodation Costs range between £65 and £85 a week. All students living outside a 25-mile radius of the High Wycombe campus are guaranteed an offer of a room in halls.

Facilities The campus boasts a new learning resources centre, including music, drama and sports facilities.

Transport The local main line station connects to the London underground in 40 minutes.

❝ STUDENT VIEW ❞
"When I joined, I had one-to-one support with my studying to help with the move from college. The lecturers are really down to earth; they're really approachable and teach us things we can actually use."

University of Cambridge

Cambridge CB2 1TN

t 01223 333308
e admissions@cam.ac.uk
↗ www.cam.ac.uk

》 further links

ACCOMMODATION See individual college websites for details
STUDENTS' UNION www.cusu.cam.ac.uk

| 2975 | 56.8 | 12.4 | 1.8 | 95.7 | ● Cambridge |

The above data is drawn from the 2004–05 Hesa performance indicators

With a history stretching back 800 years, a solid-gold academic reputation, a wealth of lore and tradition and some truly glorious architecture, Cambridge has plenty of justification for its boast of being one of the best universities in the world. It's made up of 31 colleges – three just for women and two for graduates only – and the college you belong to will be the focus of your university life. Academic pressure is intense, though most students find time to throw themselves into extra-curricular activities.

Fees £3,145 for full-time undergraduate students in 2008.

Bursaries Means-tested and calculated on a sliding scale. Up to £3,150 for eligible students. Further awards and bursaries are also available.

Accommodation Almost all students are housed by their college for the full length of their course. Standard rents are between £70 and £90 a week.

Facilities Extensive resources include access to 149 libraries, eight specialist museums and collections, and the University Botanic Garden. Most student rooms are connected to the university network and wireless hotspots are available.

Transport Cambridge is a small city and almost all the colleges and departments are fairly central – most students walk or cycle everywhere. London is about an hour away by train. Stansted airport is nearby.

❝ STUDENT VIEW ❞

"Contrary to popular perception, anyone can fit in here – and make friends for life. The workload can get a bit heavy, but don't let that put you off: you'll have plenty of free time to do whatever you want."

Cambridge colleges

Christ's College
St Andrew's Street, Cambridge   CB2 3BU
  t 01223 334 900
  ↗ www.christs.cam.ac.uk

Churchill College
Storey's Way, Cambridge   CB3 0DS
  t 01223 336 000
  ↗ www.chu.cam.ac.uk

Clare College
Trinity Lane, Cambridge   CB2 1TL
  t 01223 333 200
  ↗ www.clare.cam.ac.uk

Clare Hall (postgraduates)
Herschel Road, Cambridge   CB3 9AL
  t 01223 332360
  ↗ www.clarehall.cam.ac.uk

Corpus Christi College
Trumpington Street, Cambridge   CB2 1RH
  t 01223 338 000
  ↗ www.corpus.cam.ac.uk

Darwin College (postgraduates)
Silver Street, Cambridge   CB3 9EU
  t 01223 335 660
  ↗ www.dar.cam.ac.uk

Downing College
Regent Street, Cambridge   CB2 1DQ
  t 01223 334 800
  ↗ www.dow.cam.ac.uk

Emmanuel College
St Andrew's Street, Cambridge   CB2 3AP
  t 01223 334200
  ↗ www.emma.cam.ac.uk

Fitzwilliam College
Storey's Way, Cambridge   CB3 0DG
  t 01223 332000
  ↗ www.fitz.cam.ac.uk/index.jsp

Girton College
Huntingdon Road, Cambridge   CB3 0JG
  t 01223 338999
  ↗ www.girton.cam.ac.uk

Gonville & Caius College
Trinity Street, Cambridge   CB2 1TA
  t 01223 332400
  ↗ www.cai.cam.ac.uk

Homerton College
Hills Road, Cambridge   CB2 2PH
  t 01223 507111
  ↗ www.homerton.cam.ac.uk

Hughes Hall
Mortimer Road, Cambridge   CB1 2EW
  t 01223 334898
  ↗ www.hughes.cam.ac.uk

Jesus College
Jesus Lane, Cambridge   CB5 8BL
  t 01223 339339
  ↗ www.jesus.cam.ac.uk

King's College
King's Parade, Cambridge   CB2 1ST
  t 01223 331100
  ↗ www.kings.cam.ac.uk

Lucy Cavendish College (female)
Lady Margaret Road, Cambridge   CB3 0BU
  t 01223 332190
  ↗ www.lucy-cav.cam.ac.uk

Magdalene College
Magdalene Street, Cambridge   CB3 0AG
  t 01223 332100
  ↗ www.magd.cam.ac.uk

New Hall (female)
Huntingdon Road, Cambridge   CB3 0DF
  t 01223 762100
  ↗ www.newhall.cam.ac.uk

Newnham College (female)
Sidgwick Avenue, Cambridge   CB3 9DF
  t 01223 335700
  ↗ www.newn.cam.ac.uk

Pembroke College
Trumpington Street, Cambridge   CB2 1RF
  t 01223 338100
  ↗ www.pem.cam.ac.uk

Peterhouse
Trumpington Street, Cambridge   CB2 1RD
t   01223 338200
↗ www.pet.cam.ac.uk

Queens' College
Silver Street, Cambridge   CB3 9ET
t   01223 335511
↗ www.queens.cam.ac.uk/splash.asp

Robinson College
Grange Road, Cambridge   CB3 9AN
t   01223 339100
↗ www.robinson.cam.ac.uk

St Catharine's College
Trumpington Street, Cambridge   CB2 1RL
t   01223 338300
↗ www.caths.cam.ac.uk

St Edmund's College
Mount Pleasant, Cambridge   CB3 0BN
t   01223 336250
↗ www.st-edmunds.cam.ac.uk

St John's College
St John's Street, Cambridge   CB2 1TP
t   01223 338600
↗ www.joh.cam.ac.uk

Selwyn College
Grange Road, Cambridge   CB3 9DQ
t   01223 335846
↗ www.sel.cam.ac.uk

Sidney Sussex College
Sidney Street, Cambridge   CB2 3HU
t   01223 338800
↗ www.sid.cam.ac.uk

Trinity College
Trinity Street, Cambridge   CB2 1TQ
t   01223 338400
↗ www.trin.cam.ac.uk

Trinity Hall
Trinity Lane, Cambridge   CB2 1TJ
t   01223 332500
↗ www.trinhall.cam.ac.uk

Wolfson College
Barton Road, Cambridge   CB3 9BB
t   01223 335900
↗ www.wolfson.cam.ac.uk

Canterbury Christ Church University

University Centre Folkestone
Mill Bay
Folkestone CT20 1JG

t 01227 782900
e admissions@canterbury.ac.uk
↗ www.canterbury.ac.uk

Canterbury Campus North Holmes Road, Canterbury, Kent CT1 1QU

Broadstairs Campus Northwood Road, Broadstairs, Kent CT10 2WA

Medway Campus Rowan Williams Court, 30 Pembroke Court, Chatham Maritime, Kent ME4 4UF

Salomons Campus David Salomons Estate, Broomhill Road, Southborough, Tunbridge Wells, Kent TN3 0TG

》 further links

ACCOMMODATION accommodation@canterbury.ac.uk
STUDENTS' UNION www.ccsu.co.uk

2030   96.3   35.7   14.1   98.1

Canterbury

Canterbury, yes, but not only there – the university has campuses all over Kent, in Broadstairs, Folkestone, the Medway and Salomons, near Tunbridge Wells. 14,000 students study a broad range of courses. It's the largest centre in the region for training people for careers in the public services such as education, policing, health and social care.

Fees £3,145 for full time undergraduate students in 2008.

Bursaries £820 for students with a household income of less than £25,000. £510 for students with a family income of between £25,001 and £49,305. Sports scholarships also available.

Accommodation Guaranteed for first-years. A range of accommodation is available, most within walking distance of the campuses. Prices start at £80 a week.

Facilities The students' union boasts CTV, its own TV production facility, the Unified student newspaper and CSR Radio, a full FM community radio licence shared with the University of Kent.

Transport London by train or car is one-and-a-half hours away.

《 STUDENT VIEW 》

"As a fun and vibrant place to be, with the opportunity to gain so much more than just a degree. Christ Church is a great place to learn and a brilliant institution for offering a rounded experience."

Cardiff University

Cardiff CF10 3XQ

t 029 2087 4455
e enquiry@cardiff.ac.uk
↗ www.cardiff.ac.uk

》 further links

ACCOMMODATION residences@cardiff.ac.uk
STUDENTS' UNION www.cardiffstudents.com

4365   83.9   21.1   9.8   94.8

Cardiff has grand civic architecture in a breezy waterside location, smart city bars and venues just a short hop from lovely countryside. The university is as confident and forward-looking as the city. It has 26,000 students and an excellent reputation for teaching and research.

Fees £3,145 for all full-time undergraduate courses. Eligible Welsh students can apply for a Welsh Assembly fee grant of £1,890, meaning that students only pay an annual fee of £1,225 and this is not paid "up front" — payment is deferred until after graduation.

Bursaries The bursary scheme is available to full-time undergraduate students from lower-income households, valued at up to around £1,000 per year. Also available are subject-specific scholarships awarded for academic achievement.

Accommodation A place in one of the university's 5,100 single study bedrooms is guaranteed to all first-years applying through the normal Ucas admissions cycle. Prices range from £56 to £84 a week.

Facilities The university's 18 libraries contain 1m books and journals. There are computer rooms with 24/7 access and wireless connections across the campus. The students' union contains a cafe, bookshop, computer shop, general shop, nightclub, bar, and 1,500-capacity concert hall. There are nearly 60 athletic clubs for students.

Transport Good for road and rail; London is two hours by train, Manchester three. Closer in, Swansea takes 40 minutes and Bristol 45.

《 STUDENT VIEW 》

"Although it's not a typical campus university, the schools on the main site near the city centre are so close together it feels like one. There are great pubs, great parks, and nice old university buildings to have lectures in."

University of Central Lancashire

Preston PR1 2HE

t 01772 892400
e cenquiries@uclan.ac.uk
↗ www.uclan.ac.uk

》 further links

ACCOMMODATION saccommodation@uclan.ac.uk
STUDENTS' UNION www.uclansu.co.uk

| 4505 | 97.6 | 37.1 | 18.6 | 95.0 |

UCLan is one of the country's largest universities, with 32,000 students. The recently opened, £15.3m "media factory" will support work in art, design and performing arts as well as providing business facilities for entrepreneurial graduates. All courses have an employability strand.

Fees £3,145 for full-time undergraduate courses in 2008.

Bursaries The Ones to Watch scholarship worth £1,000 a year will be available to all UK full-time undergraduates who come from homes where the principal earner's gross salary is less than £60,000 a year. Other excellence scholarships are also available. Bursary arrangements are likely to change for 2009-10.

Accommodation Weekly costs range from £53 to £75 in university accommodation; slightly more in privately rented accommodation.

Facilities Libraries are open 24 hours a day and there are extensive sports facilities.

Transport A 10-minute walk into town. Less than three hours on the train to London or Glasgow, and an hour from Manchester.

⟨⟨ STUDENT VIEW ⟩⟩

"I would recommend UCLan to anyone who is looking for a varied, fun, and exciting student life and who is interested in meeting new people and gaining varied experience in every way you can think of. UCLan has so much to give, and it has been one of the most effective and positive learning experiences of my life."

Central School of Speech and Drama

Embassy Theatre
Eton Avenue
London NW3 3HY

t 020 7722 8183
e enquiries@cssd.ac.uk
↗ www.cssd.ac.uk

》 further links

ACCOMMODATION accommodation@cssd.ac.uk
STUDENTS' UNION http://www.ulu.co.uk/content/index.php?page=6322

255   87.7   20.5   11.1   96.7

London

Central is a highly regarded drama and theatre school, near Swiss Cottage in north London, and is part of the University of London. Undergraduate courses range from acting to costume, design, lighting, sound, prop making, puppetry and stage management – plus a course in drama, applied theatre and education.

Fees £3,145 for full-time courses in 2008.

Bursaries There are a range of scholarships and bursaries.

Accommodation There is very limited provision for Central students at the University of London's intercollegiate halls. Renting in the private sector will cost from £90 a week.

Facilities Facilities include the £5m, 224-seat Embassy Theatre, plus the Embassy Studio and New Studio.

Transport Located in London with access to good tube, bus and rail services.

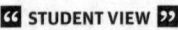 **STUDENT VIEW 》**

"Central is really specialist at what it does. Because it's not huge you form a great relationship with your lecturers. It's got brilliant facilities and a brilliant reputation. I'd thoroughly recommend it."

University of Chester

Chester Campus
Parkgate Road
Chester CH1 4BJ

t 01244 511000
e enquiries@chester.ac.uk
↗ www.chester.ac.uk

Warrington Campus University of Chester, Crab Lane, Warrington WA2 0DB

》 further links

ACCOMMODATION accommodation@chester.ac.uk
STUDENTS' UNION www.chestersu.com

2240 97.4 34.4 20.9 94.7

Chester is a handsome, historical town in the north-west of England. Around a third of the students come from the area. There are two campuses – one in Chester and one in Warrington. A new £2m students' union building has recently opened on the Chester campus. Both centres are close to Liverpool for some big nights out.

Fees £3,145 for students on full-time undergraduate courses in 2008.

Bursaries Bursaries of £1,000 a year available for those with family income of less than £25,000.

Accommodation Approximately 65 per cent of first-years are housed in university halls of residence. Weekly prices range from £53 to £119.

Facilities A new library and learning resources centre has recently opened in Warrington, to complement the rather larger one at Chester. Specialist degrees in sports science are run at both campuses, so facilities are good.

Transport There is a shuttle bus service between campuses and the city centre is walkable from the Chester campus. Good connections to Manchester and Liverpool.

⫷ STUDENT VIEW ⫸

*"Chester is a nice, scenic city, which is very historic, with a student-friendly, community feel.
The teaching staff are really good, very willing to help, and have a good relationship with the students."*

University of Chichester

Bishop Otter Campus
College Lane, Chichester
West Sussex PO19 6PE

t 01243 816000
e admissions@chi.ac.uk
↗ www.chiuni.ac.uk

Bognor Regis Campus
University of Chichester, Upper Bognor Road, West Sussex PO21 1HR

>> **further links**

ACCOMMODATION accommodation@chi.ac.uk
STUDENTS' UNION www.chisu.org

940   97.8   29.6   8.5   95.0

Chichester

Chichester prides itself on its friendly, close-knit feel. It's based on two historic campuses in Chichester and Bognor Regis. They're both relatively small places, so the university feels accessible and integrated. West Sussex boasts some genuinely gorgeous scenery and the coast is within easy reach. As well as good employment rates, Chichester has an excellent student satisfaction rating and some of the best student retention rates in the country.

Fees £3,145 a year for all full-time undergraduate courses in 2008.

Bursaries All students receiving full maintenance grant will receive bursaries of £1,050 a year, then on a sliding scale for those receiving partial grant, down to £250 a year.

Accommodation All first-years who request campus accommodation can be housed. Halls are both catered and self-catering. Prices in 2008–09 range from £73.50 to £126.30 a week.

Facilities Chichester will also be an Olympic training camp for international athletes leading up to the 2012 London Olympic games. The learning resource centre at Bishop Otter campus is award-winning and modern.

Transport Free bus service between Chichester and Bognor Regis campuses. Both are within 10 minutes' walk of the town centre. London is an hour and a half away.

⁶⁶ STUDENT VIEW ⁹⁹

"The staff are enthusiastic and friendly. Both campuses have WiFi so you can study pretty much anywhere on campus. Chichester and Bognor are pleasant places to live as a student. Both campuses are very communal and have a great atmosphere."

City University London

City University
Northampton Square
London EC1V 0HB

t 020 7040 5060
e ugadmissions@city.ac.uk
↗ www.city.ac.uk

》 further links
ACCOMMODATION www.city.ac.uk/accommodation
STUDENTS' UNION www.city.ac.uk/disability/students_union.html

1750   85.9   36.1   14.3   93.1

As the name suggests, City is in the heart of London, but its outlook is truly international. Students are drawn from 157 countries. There are commendable graduate employment rates, state-of-the-art facilities and an extensive public lecture and events programme.

Fees   £3,145 a year for full-time undergraduate courses in 2008.

Bursaries   £750 for students in receipt of full maintenance grants and £350 for students from household incomes of between £25,001 and £30,000. Merit-based scholarships in certain subjects.

Accommodation   Guaranteed for first-years from outside Greater London who apply by May 15. Self-catering accommodation costs from around £100 a week.

Facilities   A brand new students' union venue is set to open in October 2008. It will provide a hub to socialise in during the day between lectures and host a wide range of evening entertainment including club nights, society events and quiz nights.

Transport   City's location ensures that it benefits from London's excellent transport links.

 STUDENT VIEW 》

"Our diversity makes me proud. We have students here from more than 130 countries around the world. I have been able to make friends from places I would never have dreamed of going to."

Conservatoire for Dance and Drama

1-7 Woburn Walk
London WC1H 0JJ

t 020 7387 5101
e info@cdd.ac.uk
↗ www.cdd.ac.uk

》 further links

ACCOMMODATION Contact each affiliate school direct
STUDENTS' UNION www.cdd.ac.uk/student-info/student-support

185 91.7 6.6 89.6

London

The CDD was founded in 2001 and is a higher education institution with a unique structure. It's made up of eight schools around the country – all of them small and all of them specialist providers of education and training in different areas of performance. The constituent schools are: Bristol Old Vic Theatre School, Central School of Ballet, The Circus Space, London Academy of Music and Dramatic Art, London Contemporary Dance School, Northern School of Contemporary Dance, Rambert School of Ballet and Contemporary Dance, and the Royal Academy of Dramatic Art. The CDD doesn't have its own degree-awarding powers so degrees are validated by different universities.

Fees £3,145 for full-time undergraduate courses in 2008.

Bursaries Up to £1,650 a year for students with a household income of £25,000 of less, then on a sliding scale.

Accommodation Depends, naturally, on where you're living and studying.

Facilities The constituent institutions of the CDD are specialist and well-respected: expect their facilities to be of a high standard and tailored for the demands of your course.

Transport Depends on which school you're at: see their individual websites (all listed on the main CDD site) for details.

Courtauld Institute of Art

Somerset House
Strand
London WC2R 0RN

t 020 7848 2645
e ugadmissions@courtauld.ac.uk
↗ www.courtauld.ac.uk

》 further links
ACCOMMODATION www.lon.ac.uk
STUDENTS' UNION www.ulu.co.uk

45   42.9   20.0   9.1   100.0

London

The only BA course offered here is history of art, but the Courtauld is one of Britain's most famous galleries and art institutes and the 400 or so students (of whom undergraduates make up about a third) have unrivalled access to it. Degrees are awarded by the University of London.

Fees £3,070 for undergraduates in 2007–08.

Bursaries There are a range of scholarships on offer.

Accommodation The institute aims to house as many first-years as possible in halls in Bloomsbury or its own residence near Somerset House.

Facilities Students can use outstanding libraries and the gallery collection of paintings, drawings and prints, and sculpture and decorative arts.

Transport Excellent: access to most underground, rail and bus networks.

❝ STUDENT VIEW ❞

"As soon as I was offered a place at the Courtauld I knew I had to go. With an academic reputation that is one of the best in the country, and a chance to live in London, there really was no other choice for me."

Coventry University

Priory Street
Coventry CV1 5FB

t 02476 887688
e studentenquiries@coventry.ac.uk
↗ www.coventry.ac.uk

》 further links

ACCOMMODATION accom.ss@coventry.ac.uk
STUDENTS' UNION www.cusu.org

3270   97.1   40.1   22.9   90.6

The university has a 13-hectare campus in the heart of one of the largest cities in England. A pleasant Cathedral Quarter and city centre showcase 1,000 years of history. The university thinks of itself as modern and forward-looking. Courses have close vocational links with big global corporations and employability is a key concern.

Fees £3,145 a year for all full-time undergraduate courses in 2008.

Bursaries A bursary of £310 is available to all eligible undergraduate students who qualify for a full or partial maintenance grant. A range of excellence scholarships is also available.

Accommodation Guaranteed for eligible first-years. Catered accommodation costs approximately £95 a week; self-catering accommodation £85 (standard) to £90 (ensuite) a week.

Facilities Students benefit from an award-winning library, a new sports centre and a £5m student centre.

Transport Close to the M1/M6 intersection and half an hour from Birmingham by train; an hour-and-a-quarter to London.

⁶⁶ STUDENT VIEW 》

"Coventry's a place that can bring out the best in you, and the city's just the right size to feel at home and part of the local community."

University College for the Creative Arts

New Dover Road
Canterbury CT1 3AN

t 01227 817302
e info@ucreative.ac.uk
↗ www.ucreative.ac.uk

University College for the Creative Arts at Epsom
Ashley Road, Surrey KT18 5BE **t** 01372 728811

University College for the Creative Arts at Farnham
Falkner Road, Surrey GU9 7DS **t** 01252 722441

University College for the Creative Arts at Maidstone
Oakwood Park, Kent ME16 8AG **t** 01622 620000

University College for the Creative Arts at Rochester
Fort Pitt, Kent ME1 1DZ **t** 01634 888702

》 further links

ACCOMMODATION accommodation@ucreative.ac.uk
STUDENTS' UNION www.uccasu.com

1575 96.7 31.6 10.0 89.6

Canterbury

The University College for the Creative Arts at Canterbury, Epsom, Farnham, Maidstone and Rochester, to give it its full title. It's one of the UK's leading providers of specialist education and research in art, design, architecture, media and communication. A diverse community of students, staff and researchers is spread across the south-east in the five constituent colleges. The college has ambitions to win full university status soon.

Fees £3,145 for full-time undergraduate courses in 2008.

Bursaries £305 for students in receipt of the full maintenance grant. Generous excellence scholarships also available.

Accommodation Priority is given to new full-time students who don't live locally.

Facilities Good specialist libraries and active student support networks in place.

Transport All campuses are close to motorways, rail networks and international airports.

❝ STUDENT VIEW ❞

"It's been a challenging and thoroughly rewarding three years. The tutor support has encouraged me to branch out in my own direction and feel confident in my future. It's a versatile qualification, with endless options to put it to use in the 'real world' outside of college."

University of Cumbria

Fusehill Street, Carlisle
Cumbria CA1 2HH

t 01228 616234
e admissions@cumbria.ac.uk
↗ www.cumbria.ac.uk

Carlisle Campuses Brampton Road, Carlisle, Cumbria CA3 9AY
Paternoster Row, Carlisle, Cumbria CA3 8TB
Lancaster Campus Bowerham Road, Lancaster LA1 3JD
London Campus English Street, Bow, London E3 4TA
Penrith Campus Newton Rigg, Penrith, Cumbria CA11 0AH
Ambleside Campus Rydal Road, Ambleside, Cumbria LA22 9BB

》 further links

ACCOMMODATION www.cumbria.ac.uk/accommodation
STUDENTS' UNION www.thestudentsunion.org.uk

1655   97.7   37.6   20.8   94.3

The university has campuses in Carlisle, Penrith, Ambleside and Lancaster and a specialist teacher education centre in London. It prides itself on preparing its students for employment and on its links with local schools, colleges, businesses and the community.

Fees £3,145 for full-time undergraduate courses in 2008.

Bursaries Means-tested grants of between £1,260 and £210 are available to most students and excellence scholarships are also available, worth £1,000.

Accommodation First-year students are likely to find a place in university accommodation, providing they apply by the deadline.

Facilities Sport facilities are extensive and of a high standard. Integrated services for library, media and IT support.

Transport Good links by motorway and rail, and international airports and big cities, including Manchester and Glasgow, are accessible.

ᴳᴳ STUDENT VIEW 》

"When I started searching for my course I found the University of Cumbria and that was it; it just felt right. And when I arrived here I wasn't disappointed either. It was just as I imagined — friendly, supportive, and a great place to study. I love it!"

Dartington College of Arts

Dartington Hall Estate
Totnes
Devon TQ9 6EJ

t 01803 862224
e enquiries@dartington.ac.uk
↗ www.dartington.ac.uk

»» further links

ACCOMMODATION 01803 847137
STUDENTS' UNION www.dartington.ac.uk/information
forstudents/supporting/su/index.asp

220   92.2   28.3   15.2   93.2

Totnes

Based in Totnes in Devon, Dartington College of Arts is one of the few specialist art colleges to offer undergraduate and postgraduate degrees through practice-led learning methods. It offers degrees in all areas of performance and theatre in a quiet rural setting. Degrees are validated by the University of Plymouth. It's a small college with around 500 undergraduates.

Fees £3,145 in 2008 for full-time undergraduates.

Bursaries In 2006–07 Dartington provided a bursary of £600 to students in receipt of the full maintenance grant. Further targeted awards are also available. A travel bursary is available to students who live off campus.

Accommodation Limited to 200 places on the estate. Rent starts at about £60 a week.

Facilities A range of well-equipped studios, a specialist library with a unique collection of resources and leading-edge technical equipment and workshops.

Transport Dartington Hall itself is tucked away, but nearby Totnes is on a main rail line with direct links to London, Birmingham and Bristol.

«« STUDENT VIEW »»

"The supportive lecturers, great facilities, and balance of theory and practice helped me make the most of my degree. It was a unique experience."

De Montfort University

The Gateway
Leicester LE1 9BH

t 08459 454647
e enquiry@dmu.ac.uk
↗ www.dmu.ac.uk

Charles Frears Campus 266 London Road, Leicester LE2 1RQ

》 further links

ACCOMMODATION housing@dmu.ac.uk
STUDENTS' UNION www.demontfortstudents.com

4875 96.6 41.0 15.8 91.8

De Montfort is a dynamic, forward-thinking and sizeable university. The main campus is in Leicester's city centre, with a second — the Charles Frears campus, offering courses in nursing and midwifery — on the outskirts. Leicester is England's 10th largest city, with good transport links and all the facilities you'd expect.

Fees £3,145 for full-time undergraduate courses in 2008.

Bursaries £400 for student in receipt of a full maintenance grant. Further regional bursaries and generous excellence scholarships are available, too.

Accommodation Guaranteed for all first-years on full-time courses. All accommodation is single study bedrooms in halls and ranges from £74 to £90 a week.

Facilities £1.7m has been spent on revamping the library. Good sports and social facilities.

Transport Both campuses are within walking distance of the city centre. Road and rail links to the rest of the UK are excellent.

University of Derby

Kedleston Road
Derby DE22 1GB

t 01332 591167
e askadmissions@derby.ac.uk
↗ www.derby.ac.uk

University of Derby Buxton 1 Devonshire Road, Buxton, Derbyshire SK17 6RY

》 further links

ACCOMMODATION www.derby.ac.uk/accommodation
STUDENTS' UNION www.udsu.co.uk

2735   99.4   40.9   22.8   90.0

Derby invites you to create your own degree, study part-time or choose a fast-track degree. It also emphasises its vocational slant, and 2008 will see the launch of a £12m division dedicated to engaging with employers and businesses, as well as developing enterprise and entrepreneurship. Derby is a pleasant, historical city and Buxton, location of the university's Grade II-listed Devonshire campus, is an equally charming spa town.

Fees £3,145 for all full-time undergraduate courses in 2008.

Bursaries £800 for students eligible for the full government maintenance grant; then on a sliding scale for those eligible for a partial grant, down to £200. Further awards for local students are also available.

Accommodation Guaranteed for first-years. The halls are all close to the campuses. The costs range from £59.99 to £80.01 per week.

Facilities Sir Richard Branson opened the university's new £21m bespoke arts, design and technology site in November 2007.

Transport The university has an excellent sustainable transport plan. Derby is 10 minutes from the M1 and on the main line from London St Pancras.

⁴⁴ STUDENT VIEW ⁴⁴

"A quality place to live, work, and study. You get more than just a degree at Derby and it really shows. A brilliant experience for your entire time here."

University of Dundee

Nethergate
Dundee DD1 4HN

t 01382 384000
e university@dundee.ac.uk
↗ www.dundee.ac.uk

》 further links

ACCOMMODATION residences@dundee.ac.uk
STUDENTS' UNION dusa.co.uk

2310   92.2   26.6   18.5   95.1

Dundee has claimed to be the sunniest city in Scotland. It's large enough to be interesting (and the most densely populated bit of Scotland after Glasgow) but compact enough to be friendly and manageable. And it's close to Edinburgh if you have a surplus of cultural requirements, and also nice countryside and coast.

Fees Currently, Scottish students pay no fees. Other students are liable for £1,735 fees (£2,760 for in medicine) from 2008.

Bursaries Young students' bursaries available for Scottish students under 25 from low-income families. Students applying for and going on to study one of the three-year honours degree programmes can apply for the chancellor's scholarship of £1,000 a year for three years. Additional academic, musical and sporting bursaries available.

Accommodation Guaranteed for applications received by July of the year of entry. Prices range from £56 to £105.

Facilities The main library has excellent modern facilities for silent and group study. The union has bars and clubs over five floors.

Transport The main campus is in the city centre. Transport links to the rest of the country are excellent. Trains are part of the main east-coast route and Edinburgh and Glasgow are both within 90 minutes by car or rail. The airport has a direct link to London City that takes 90 minutes.

❝ STUDENT VIEW ❞

"Though occasionally cold and windy, Dundee is a great place to live as a student. As the city is fairly small, it has a great student-community atmosphere. It also has a good multicultural feel, with many students from all over the world and a great selection of activities and places to visit."

Durham University

University Office
Old Elvet
Durham DH1 3HP

t 0191 334 6128
e admissions@durham.ac.uk
↗ www.durham.ac.uk

Queen's Campus Stockton University Boulevard, Thornaby, Stockton-on-Tees TS17 6BH

》 further links

ACCOMMODATION www.dur.ac.uk/colleges
STUDENTS' UNION www.dsu.org.uk

3395   61.8   16.4   2.8   93.6

Durham

Lovely Durham is home to one of the country's top universities. The city is picturesque, wooded, hilly and aching with heritage. The brooding Norman cathedral dominates the skyline. Durham is a collegiate university, meaning that student life has a real sense of focus and community. The Queen's campus in nearby Stockton-on-Tees boasts plenty of local and mature students. Durham students are well placed for glorious countryside and coastline and there are good transport links.

Fees £3,145 a year for all full-time undergraduate courses in 2008–09.

Bursaries Students with a household income of less than £18,500 are eligible for a Durham grant of up to £1,285 per year (£2,570 if they are local students.)

Accommodation Around 99 per cent of first-years live in college accommodation. Accommodation is provided by colleges and varies accordingly. Prices average around £80 a week in Durham and £64 in Stockton.

Facilities Excellent, well-stocked library in an award-winning building. Good IT facilities and 26 hectares of sports fields. Each college provides its own range of services.

Transport Good road and rail links to the rest of the east coast and country, with two regional airports around half an hour away. A free shuttle bus operates between campuses.

❝ STUDENT VIEW ❞

"Though Durham may just be the size of a postage stamp, it offers all the benefits of a modern city within a beautifully historic setting. It's one of the oldest, most beautiful, and academic universities. In the world!"

University of East Anglia

Norwich NR4 7TJ

t 01603 591515
e admissions@uea.ac.uk
↗ www.uea.ac.uk

»» further links

ACCOMMODATION   www.ueaaccommodation.com
STUDENTS' UNION   www.ueastudent.com

| 2275 | 86.5 | 22.9 | 8.0 | 91.6 |

The UEA campus is just a couple of miles from the centre of Norwich, though you may wonder why anyone would ever venture off campus: the 130 landscaped hectares boast excellent sports facilities, bars and cafes and the excellent Sainsbury centre for visual arts. No wonder, then, that UEA came joint top in the 2006 national student survey and performed well last year, too.

Fees   £3,145 for all full-time undergraduate courses in 2008-09.

Bursaries   £600 for students in receipt of the full grant and £300 for students in receipt of a partial grant. Other scholarships are available.

Accommodation   Guaranteed for eligible first-years. All accommodation is self-catering and most on campus, costing from £52 to £93 a week.

Facilities   The award-winning library has been recently extended and is open seven days a week. The £17.5m sports park has excellent facilities. The union hosts top-name bands.

Transport   The campus is walkable to Norwich city centre, though there's a 24-hour bus service. It's a two-hour trip by road or rail to London. There's nearby Norwich airport and Stansted 90 minutes away.

❝ STUDENT VIEW ❞

"UEA students in general live such an overtly enjoyable life. Teaching staff in all the faculties are often willing to do that little bit extra to help students with work. Norwich is quite out of the way but once you get here you generally find that it has everything you could possibly need."

University of East London

Docklands Campus
4-6 University Way
London E16 2RD

t 020 8223 3000
e admiss@uel.ac.uk
↗ www.uel.ac.uk

Stratford Campus University House, Romford Road, London E15 4LZ
Duncan House Stratford High Street, London E15 2JB

》 further links

ACCOMMODATION www.uel.ac.uk/residential
STUDENTS' UNION www.uelsu.net

2890   98.7   48.8   22.9   94.0

London

UEL has around 20,000 students. The university is centred on the ultra-modern Docklands campus by the Thames, with another base at Stratford in east London, the hub of one of Europe's largest urban regeneration programmes, thanks to the 2012 Olympics. Almost all students come from state schools and a large proportion are from ethnic minorities.

Fees £3,145 for all full-time undergraduate courses in 2008-09.

Bursaries £300 for students in receipt of the full grant, plus a £500 progress bursary to all students who complete the first semester and progress to the second. The progress bursary is also available to students in receipt of a partial grant. Further scholarships for excellence are also available.

Accommodation Available for first-years who live outside the Greater London and Essex area. All rooms are ensuite and range from £92 to £124 a week.

Facilities Modern and inspiring buildings at the Docklands campus, with purpose-built teaching and learning facilities. Good libraries and some unexpected attractions, such as on-site manufacturing facility and two industry-standard television studios.

Transport You've got the overground rail, tube, buses and Docklands Light Railway.

⊠ STUDENT VIEW 》

"The courses are good. They are well thought out and teach skills that will be helpful after you graduate. It's so multicultural and a very modern place to study."

Edge Hill University

St Helens Road
Ormskirk
Lancashire L39 4QP

t 01695 575171
e enquiries@edgehill.ac.uk
↗ www.edgehill.ac.uk

Aintree Campus University Hospital Aintree, Longmoor Lane, Liverpool L9 7AL
Woodlands Campus Woodlands Centre, Southport Road, Chorley, Lancashire PR7 1QR
Gateway House Faculty of Health, Piccadilly South, Manchester M60 7LP
Woodford Lodge Professional Centre Woodford Lane, West Winsford, Cheshire CW7 4EH
Wirral Education Centre Acre Lane, Bromborough, Wirral, Merseyside CH62 7BZ

》 further links

ACCOMMODATION accommodationteam@edgehill.ac.uk
STUDENTS' UNION www.edgehillsu.com

1745   98.0   38.5   20.6   93.1

Ormskirk

Edge Hill only became a university in 2006 but is growing rapidly. It has almost 20,000 students and has experienced a consistent increase in Ucas applications in recent years. Edge Hill is expanding physically, too, and is due to double in size by 2020. The main campus is a 30-hectare site on the outskirts of Ormskirk, Lancashire. It is a small market town, but is close to Liverpool and Manchester. Also worth a mention is Edge Hill's award-winning student finance package.

Fees £3,145 for full-time undergraduate courses in 2008–09. Fees for siblings of those studying at Edge Hill and paying the full amount are reduced by £1,000.

Bursaries £500 if your household income is less than £25,000. £200 "uni card" for all students to spend on study materials. Scholarships are also available.

Accommodation Most first-years live on campus, though it isn't guaranteed. Self-catering costs £49 to £63 a week, and catered halls are £79.

Facilities The campus boasts a lake, piazza area and plenty of green space. The sports centre provides high-quality facilities.

Transport The motorway connections to the rest of the UK are easy enough, but the train journey means a change at Liverpool or Preston.

《 STUDENT VIEW 》

"I've made loads of great friends (living in halls in my first year helped that!) and there's always something going on to get involved in. The sports facilities in particular are really good and the fact that you can use the computers any time can be a god send if you've left something until the final moment!"

University of Edinburgh

Old College
South Bridge
Edinburgh EH8 9YL

t 0131 650 1000
e sra.enquiries@ed.ac.uk
↗ www.ed.ac.uk

》 further links

ACCOMMODATION accommodation@ed.ac.uk
STUDENTS' UNION www.eusa.ed.ac.uk

3970   65.5   17.7   5.1   94.8

Edinburgh

Edinburgh is a venerable institution – founded in the 1580s – and has forged a special position in academia. Its reputation is excellent and it has a large, diverse and multi-national student body. Edinburgh itself is vibrant and cosmopolitan, with stately architecture and green spaces. University buildings are spread throughout the city.

Fees Scottish and EU students from outside the UK pay no tuition fees up front. For other UK students, there is an annual non-means-tested tuition fee of £1,735 (£2,760 for medicine) in 2007–08.

Bursaries Scottish students under 25 receive up to £2,510 a year in 2007–08 depending on parental income. Students from England, Wales and Northern Ireland who are in receipt of a maximum grant are eligible for an additional bursary. There is a large range of other scholarships and bursaries.

Accommodation First-year undergraduates from outside Edinburgh are offered places from £134 a week to £167. Self-catering options cost £78 to £94 a week.

Facilities There are 17 libraries. The sports centre has several state-of-the-art gyms, swimming pool, sports halls and a climbing wall.

Transport The university is spread throughout the city, with the majority of buildings within walking distance. Excellent transport links. Edinburgh airport is eight miles away.

❝ STUDENT VIEW ❞

*"Edinburgh is an excellent all-round city and in many ways an ideal student one too.
There is a great student atmosphere and all the facilities that you would want and expect."*

Edinburgh College of Art

Lauriston Place
Edinburgh EH3 9DF

t 0131 221 6027
e registry@eca.ac.uk
↗ www.eca.ac.uk

» **further links**

ACCOMMODATION ss@eca.ac.uk
STUDENTS' UNION www.eca.ac.uk/index.php?id=335

| 295 | 84.8 | 22.7 | 7.3 | 93.1 |

Edinburgh

Based in the old town of Edinburgh near the famous Grassmarket, the Edinburgh College of Art offers diverse courses in art and design, architecture, and visual and cultural studies. There are just under 2,000 students from all over the world.

Fees Full-time fees for 2007-08 were £1,735 for new entrants, £1,225 for continuing students, and £613 for students taking a sandwich year.

Bursaries Bursaries or grants may also be available to students who meet certain criteria.

Accommodation ECA offers rooms close to the college in self-catering halls from between £350 and £500 per month, including bills. Priority is given to students under the age of 19. The average rent for a room in a shared flat is around £260 to £280 a month.

Facilities The college library lies at the heart of the newly developed Evolution House Learning Zone. It has wireless internet, and laptops may be borrowed for use anywhere within the zone.

Transport Regular trains from London King's Cross, and the airport is less than 10 miles away.

❝ STUDENT VIEW ❞

"Studying at ECA provides a great opportunity to develop your skills: you can get the guidance you need, but also the freedom to figure out what it is you want. For me it has been the perfect start for a professional career, as well as a great experience meeting so many other international students and enjoying the beautiful city of Edinburgh."

University of Essex

Wivenhoe Park
Colchester CO4 3SQ

t 01206 873666
e admit@essex.ac.uk
↗ www.essex.ac.uk

East 15, Loughton Campus Hatfields, Rectory Lane, Loughton IG10 3RY
Southend Campus Elmer Approach, Southend-on-Sea SS1 1LW

» **further links**

ACCOMMODATION accom@essex.ac.uk
STUDENTS' UNION www.essexstudent.com

1715   94.3   32.3   16.5   92.4

Essex is a 1960s university, but it has remained smaller than many of its contemporaries, with just over 6,000 undergraduates. They have plenty of space: 80 hectares of landscaped campus on the outskirts of Colchester. Essex has a consistently strong academic performance, which it hopes to extend to students on the recently opened Southend campus, which boasts state-of-the art facilities.

Fees £3,145 for all full-time undergraduate courses in 2008–09.

Bursaries £310 a year for students with a household income of less than £25,000. Students with household incomes of £25,001 to £32,500 will receive bursaries to top up their partial grants, to bring their overall maintenance support to £3,145. Support is on a sliding scale for students with household incomes of £32,501 to £60,005.

Accommodation From £61 a week for standard accommodation and £90 ensuite. All first-year students are guaranteed accommodation as long as they apply by the deadline.

Facilities The union nightclub has been named the best student venue in the UK and there are three further bars. On the Colchester campus, 16 hectares are devoted to sport.

Transport Colchester campus is two miles from town on major bus routes. Three stations in Colchester; London takes an hour. Excellent road links. Convenient for Stansted. Southend campus is in the middle of town; 50 minutes by train to London.

❝ STUDENT VIEW ❞

"For a different experience, come to Essex. It's a friendly place, the campus atmosphere is brilliant, and there's always loads to do. The campus is its own student mini universe with a real international flavour."

University of Exeter

The Queen's Drive
Exeter, Devon EX4 4QJ

t 01392 263855
e ug-ad@exeter.ac.uk
↗ www.exeter.ac.uk

St Luke's Campus Heavitree Road, Exeter EX1 2LU
Tremough Campus Penryn, Cornwall TR10 9EZ

》 further links

ACCOMMODATION www.exeter.ac.uk/accommodation
STUDENTS' UNION www.exeterguild.org

| 2710 | 72.5 | 18.2 | 5.2 | 93.0 |

Exeter

Exeter has campuses in the cathedral city and also near Falmouth, in Cornwall, as well as plenty of coastline, countryside and glorious weather. Exeter is also rated one of the best universities in the UK for "ents", and it's no wonder that increases in applications far exceed the national average. It has an excellent academic reputation.

Fees £3,145 for full-time undergraduate courses in 2007-08.

Bursaries Means-tested bursaries of up to £1,500 per year are available for students from low-income backgrounds and the south west bursary scheme allows students resident in the region to apply for additional "top-up" awards. Other scholarships are available.

Accommodation Guaranteed for first-year students, as long as they apply by the deadline. Costs range from £60 to £157 a week.

Facilities Users benefit from 24/7 access, self-service machines, state-of-the-art multimedia facilities, enhanced group and silent study areas and an extended WiFi network. Excellent sports facilities, too.

Transport Short walks into town from either campus in Exeter. The Cornwall campus is a 15-minute bus ride into Falmouth. The M5 is handy for Exeter and London is two hours by train.

❝ STUDENT VIEW ❞

"I recommend it to anyone serious about studying. It has great countryside and beaches close by. For those wanting to study somewhere cheap, Exeter is also a winner, but not for those wanting city life or who are active clubbers!"

University College Falmouth

Woodlane
Falmouth
Cornwall TR11 4RH

t 01326 211077
e admissions@falmouth.ac.uk
↗ www.falmouth.ac.uk

Tremough Campus Tremough, Penryn, Cornwall TR10 9EZ

》 further links

ACCOMMODATION www.tremoughservices/accommodation
STUDENTS' UNION www.fxu.org.uk

710   97.5   24.5   9.4   89.5

Falmouth

In 2005, University College Falmouth became the first institution in Cornwall to award its own degrees. Its courses focus on art and design, and they are taught in Falmouth and on the Tremough campus of the Combined Universities in Cornwall. Falmouth is famous for its harbour and as a centre of water-based fun. The rest of Cornwall is no less enticing.

Fees £3,145 for full-time undergraduates in 2008–09.

Bursaries Maximum bursary of £850 to students with a household income of less than £25,000. Around 40 per cent of students qualify for some kind of bursary.

Accommodation University accommodation (rents in the region of £95 a week) is oversubscribed so students have traditionally lived in private accommodation, which is readily available.

Transport Falmouth has easy access to the A39, which will take you to Bath. Regular trains link the town to London and elsewhere, but it's a five-hour journey to the capital.

Facilities A range of specialist IT facilities are on offer.

 STUDENT VIEW 》

"The tutoring and support is very motivating. They really knew how to bring out the best in me, enhancing my skills and helping build my confidence for future success."

Glamorgan University

Pontypridd CF37 1DL

t 0800 716925
e enquiries@glam.ac.uk
↗ www.glam.ac.uk

》 further links

ACCOMMODATION   accom@glam.ac.uk
STUDENTS' UNION   www.glamsu.com

2810   98.2   41.4   29.9   93.4

Pontypridd

The University of Glamorgan boasts three modern campuses, two in Treforest near the town of Pontypridd, and a brand new facility in the heart of Cardiff. The university attracts more than 21,000 students across its campuses and is known for its friendly community atmosphere.

Fees   £3,145 a year for all full-time undergraduate courses. Wales and EU (non-UK) students qualify for a subsidy paid directly to the institution and are liable for a fee of approximately £1,200.

Bursaries   Glamorgan is offering two scholarships for 2008 entry for undergraduate full-time students. The first is an entry scholarship worth £3,000, £1,000 to be paid each year to students who have achieved 300 or more Ucas points. The second is a residential allowance worth £1,500, £500 to be paid each year to students whose home address is more than 45 miles away. Other funding is also available.

Accommodation   Weekly rent for self-catering accommodation ranges from £56.50 to £69. Catered option at £25 a week extra.

Facilities   The campus boasts good IT and sports facilities.

Transport   On the M4 corridor and 20 minutes by train or car to Cardiff.

❝ STUDENT VIEW ❞

"It's a lovely place. Great for a night out. The academic side is also good. But, most of all, the people on and off campus are really friendly."

University of Glasgow

University Avenue
Glasgow G12 8QQ

t 0141 330 2000
e ugenquiries@gla.ac.uk
↗ www.gla.ac.uk

》 further links

ACCOMMODATION accom@gla.ac.uk
STUDENTS' UNION www.theguu.com

3690   85.7   23.7   14.3   95.0

Glasgow is Scotland's second oldest university, the UK's fourth oldest, and an important pillar of Scotland's biggest city. As well as excellent teaching and a worldwide reputation, students enjoy a compact campus at the heart of the city's stylish west end. There's an unusually high proportion of local students: almost half come from west Scotland. Among the rest are representatives of 124 other countries. Facilities for shopping, entertainment and cultural pursuits are excellent, and there is dramatic countryside nearby.

Fees Eligible Scottish students studying full-time are entitled to free tuition. Tuition fees are charged for English, Welsh and Northern Irish students. Currently these are £1,735 (£2,760 for medicine) per year.

Bursaries Young students' bursaries for Scots under 25 from low-income families. Students from England, Wales and Northern Ireland who are in receipt of a maximum maintenance award are eligible for a bursary of £300. A further range of generous scholarships and bursaries is available.

Accommodation Most first-years live in university accommodation; a wide range is available.

Facilities The university library is one of the best academic libraries in Europe, with more than 2m items on 12 floors.

Transport Travel within Glasgow is made easy by an underground system that connects the university to the city centre in 10 minutes. There are bus and overground train services, plus two train stations, good road links and an airport nearby, too.

❝ STUDENT VIEW ❞

"As well as the history, grandeur, and reputation that come with Glasgow, student activism has always been an enduring feature of university life, making it difficult not to get involved and meet new people. The famous architecture of the main building is spectacular and makes my heart soar."

Glasgow Caledonian University

Cowcaddens Road
Glasgow G4 0BA

t 0141 331 3000
e admissions@gcal.ac.uk
↗ www.gcal.ac.uk

》 further links

ACCOMMODATION accommodation@gcal.ac.uk
STUDENTS' UNION www.caledonianstudent.com

3405   96.6   37.1   21.3   92.1

With more than 15,000 students, Glasgow Caledonian University is Scotland's fourth largest in terms of recruitment. Its campus is in the Cowcaddens area, close to the city centre. Key academic strengths are health, the environment, creative culture, business and social justice. Widening access is central to its philosophy.

Fees Scottish students receive free tuition. Students from England, Wales and Northern Ireland are currently liable for tuition fees of £1,775.

Bursaries Young students' bursaries for Scottish students under 25 from low-income families. Other grants, scholarships and bursaries available.

Accommodation Awarded according to criteria that include age, special needs, distance from campus and international status. Self-catering costs £70.40 to £81.20 a week.

Facilities The Saltire Centre, the hub of the campus, is the first university building of its kind to integrate all learning and student services. Innovative teaching facilities, such as the virtual hospital, too.

Transport As you would expect in a big city: extensive public transport and good links. The airport is seven miles away.

❝ STUDENT VIEW ❞

"Glasgow is definitely one of the best cities in the UK. The people are fun and friendly and will tell you the right direction to go when you are suitably inebriated. There's so much to do there aren't enough hours in the day. Surprisingly, even the library is an all right place to hang out."

Glasgow School of Art

167 Renfrew Street
Glasgow G3 6RQ

t 0141 353 4500
e registry@gsa.ac.uk
↗ www.gsa.ac.uk

》 further links

ACCOMMODATION   welfare@gsa.ac.uk
STUDENTS' UNION   www.gsa.ac.uk/gsa.cfm?pid=23

265   84.6   19.6   20.1   92.2

The Glasgow School of Art (GSA) is an internationally recognised independent school of art, design, and architecture, based in the heart of Glasgow. Courses are offered within the schools of architecture, design or fine art, and around 15 per cent of the 1,600-strong student body is international.

Fees Currently £1,735 a year. Scottish students do not pay the fee.

Bursaries The GSA offers a range of scholarships with different eligibility criteria. There is also a hardship fund.

Accommodation The GSA has one purpose-built hall of residence within a couple of minutes' walking distance from the campus and easy reach of all city-centre amenities.

Facilities A digital design studio, a centre for advanced textiles and several galleries and exhibition spaces. The school also boasts a nightclub and venue, The Arts School.

Transport Five hours by train to London. Short walk to the city centre from campus.

 STUDENT VIEW 》

"There's a good social scene at the art school and Glasgow is an excellent place to be a student. There's always someone interesting to talk to at the school and the tutors are really supportive of your ideas."

University of Gloucestershire

The Park
Cheltenham GL50 2RH

t 08707 210210
e admissions@glos.ac.uk
↗ www.glos.ac.uk

Pittville Studios Albert Road, Cheltenham GL52 3JG
Francis Close Hall Campus Swindon Road, Cheltenham GL50 4AZ
Oxstalls Campus Oxstalls Lane, Longlevens, Gloucester GL2 9HW

》 **further links**

ACCOMMODATION accommodation@glos.ac.uk
STUDENTS' UNION www.yourstudentsunion.com

| 1870 | 94.3 | 32.7 | 11.0 | 94.8 |

Students are spread over four campuses — three in Cheltenham and one in Gloucester. Both can support a decent social life and have good links to bigger cities, as well as some appealing rural surroundings. The university is proud of its green credentials and sustainable policies. There are many mature and part-time students, and courses are innovative. There is emphasis on industry links and work placements.

Fees £3,145 for full-time undergraduate courses in 2008-09.

Bursaries Students qualifying for a full grant can get a bursary of £310. A one-off payment of £500 is available to students entering with 360 or more Ucas tariff points. Students from partner colleges are eligible for a payment of £1,000. Further scholarships and support available.

Accommodation There are halls on or near all campuses for 1,000 students. Most students (and some first-years) live in private accommodation. Rooms cost from £67 a week.

Facilities Learning centres on each campus with differing provision.

Transport Good (free) bus links are provided between campuses. Road and rail links are generally pretty good.

❝ STUDENT VIEW ❞

*"It's a unique, rewarding place to study. Everyone seems to know everyone.
It also has some of the most modern learning facilities in the country."*

Goldsmiths, University of London

New Cross
London SE14 6NW

t 020 7919 7766
e admissions@gold.ac.uk
↗ www.goldsmiths.ac.uk

1215   88.0   29.9   17.7   91.9

Goldsmiths is best known for creativity and culture, and has a reputation for producing visual artists. The university is almost entirely based on one site in New Cross, south-east London, which is vibrant, with excellent links to the centre of London, and the cost of living is more reasonable than in many areas. You are, however, deep in the urban sprawl. There is plenty of creative energy flowing among the 8,000 or so students; a high proportion are mature students and a third come from overseas, which makes for a diverse student body.

Fees £3,225 a year for all full-time undergraduate courses in 2009-10.

Bursaries A bursary worth up to £1,000 each year is available to all students who are receiving the full grant and have a household income below £19,000. Those in receipt of a partial grant or special support grant and with a household income of below £25,000 may be eligible for a bursary of up to £500. Students receiving a partial grant and have a household income of between £25,001 and £40,000 may be eligible for a bursary of £315. Other bursaries and scholarships available.

Accommodation Priority is given to new first-years from outside London travel zone 6. Accommodation is self-catering and the average weekly cost is £85 to £109. Catered accommodation in University of London intercollegiate halls costs between £113.40 and £128.50.

Facilities Facilities include an award-winning students' union, a well-equipped library, wireless hotspots, a virtual learning environment and media facilities.

Transport Goldsmiths has great travel connections to central London — by train just 15 minutes. The campus is also well-placed in terms of bus (including night bus) routes and Deptford Bridge DLR station (which links to the tube network) is a 10-minute walk away.

◀◀ STUDENT VIEW ▶▶

"It's a very creative place to be, catering for most interests. It also has a pretty impressive alumni list. Goldsmiths is small so there is a nice community feel about the place. Just like one big family ... "

University of Greenwich

Old Royal Naval College
Park Row
Greenwich SE10 9LS

t 0800 005006
e courseinfo@gre.ac.uk
↗ www.gre.ac.uk

Avery Hill Mansion Site, Bexley Road, Eltham, London SE9 2PQ
Medway Central Avenue, Chatham Maritime, Kent ME4 4TB

》 further links

ACCOMMODATION accommodation@gre.ac.uk
STUDENTS' UNION www.suug.co.uk

3210   97.2   47.1   17.8   87.2

London

There aren't many universities that can boast a World Heritage site, but this is one of them. The main campus is on the banks of the Thames in three baroque buildings designed by Sir Christopher Wren. Other sites are Avery Hill, in an 35-hectare park in Eltham, south-east London, and Medway, another charming campus near Chatham's historic dockyard. As a result, the 30,000 students are spread between city and more rural locations.

Fees £2,835 for full-time undergraduates in 2008–09. (MPharm and osteopathy are £3,145.)

Bursaries Greenwich offers mature student bursaries and scholarships for students with high Ucas points. There are also more specialised scholarhips available for eligible students.

Accommodation Guaranteed for first-years. Prices range from around £77 a week to £151 a week.

Facilities Major libraries, computing facilities, students' union facilities, catering facilities and bars at all campuses. Avery Hill has a gym and sports fields. Medway has a sports centre. Greenwich is near a council-run sports centre.

Transport The Greenwich campus can be reached by Docklands Light Railway, rail and boat. You can be at London Bridge in 20 minutes. Avery Hill to London Bridge involves a 10- to 15-minute walk to the station and 25-minute rail journey. Greenwich provides an inter-campus bus service linking Avery Hill to Greenwich and Medway.

《 STUDENT VIEW 》

"Great links to London, Premiership football round the corner at Charlton, great shopping. Lots of bookshops, great computing facilities, and the libraries are great. The site at Maritime Greenwich is outstanding, a great historic site, and it can fill you with awe the first time you see it."

Harper Adams University College

Newport
Shropshire TF10 8NB

t 01952 820280
e admissions@harper-adams.ac.uk
↗ www.harper-adams.ac.uk

》 further links

ACCOMMODATION 01952 815286
STUDENTS' UNION www.harper-adams.ac.uk/su

315   83.1   59.0   6.6   98.3

This former agricultural college has just 1,800 undergraduate students, giving them the chance to experience living in a close-knit community. The location can only add to that sense – set in the lovely Shropshire countryside, there's little around but peace and quiet and the small town of Newport. Despite this, or perhaps because of it, the on-campus entertainments will easily satisfy the bits of you that thirst for noise, raucous fun and beer. Most of the courses focus on rural and land-based subjects.

Fees £3,145 for full-time undergraduate courses in 2008–09.

Bursaries £1,000 for students with a household income of up to £17,911. £750 to students with a household income between £17,911 and £28,500. £500 to students with a household income between £28,501 and £38,330. Students who do not qualify for the award of a means-tested scholarship can apply for a merit scholarship, which may be from £250–£750.

Accommodation All first-year students are guaranteed a place in university-managed accommodation. Charges in 2008–09 range from £85 to £125 per week.

Facilities The modern library and IT suite are at the heart of the campus, which also contains a working farm. There are also specialist facilities for students studying engineering, animal health and veterinary nursing programmes. There are also a number of sports pitches, a sports hall, gym and swimming pool.

Transport The college is located on a single campus. A bus service is available to take students into the nearby market town of Newport, about three miles away. The larger towns of Shrewsbury and Telford (for the nearest station) are also conveniently located.

❝ STUDENT VIEW ❞
Here, lecturers know your name and you're not just one of the crowd. My time here has been so rewarding and given me the opportunity to make some great friends and gain lots of experience. Everything is here and nothing is beyond your reach."

Heriot-Watt University

Edinburgh EH14 4AS

t 0131 451 3451
e enquiries@hw.ac.uk
↗ www.hw.ac.uk

Dubai Campus Dubai International Academic City, UAE
Scottish Borders Campus Netherdale, Galashiels, Selkirkshire TD1 3HF

》 further links

ACCOMMODATION www.hw.ac.uk/welfare/accommodation
STUDENTS' UNION www.hwusa.org

1160   92.1   30.7   15.6   93.7

Uniquely among Scottish universities, Heriot-Watt can boast near-constant sunshine, a glamorous beachside position and sky-scrapers as far as the eye can see. This, however, is admittedly only if you are studying on the Dubai campus. The Edinburgh campus occupies 155 hectares of meadow and woodland and the Scottish Borders campus in Galashiels, south of Edinburgh, is right in the very heart of the Borders.

Fees If you are from Scotland, you won't have to pay fees. Students from England, Wales and Northern Ireland will pay fees — yet to be set — but with a loan to cover the cost.

Bursaries The Young Students' Bursary is available for Scottish students from low-income families. A wide range of further bursaries and scholarships is also available.

Accommodation Guaranteed for first-years, with rents ranging from £70 to £94 a week.

Facilities The Heriot-Watt University Archive and Museum contains many unique records relating to the history of science, engineering, technology and business going back to 1821. The textile collection at the Scottish Borders campus houses one of the finest collections of textile records and artefacts anywhere in the world.

Transport Edinburgh's the capital, so all the links by road, rail and air are what you would expect.

❝ STUDENT VIEW ❞

"If you live on campus in your first year, you get the whole university experience and then some. Some of the subjects are internationally renowned. The campus is pretty idyllic, with the library overlooking the picturesque Sunken Garden and the Union right next to the loch."

University of Hertfordshire

College Lane
Hatfield
Hertfordshire AL10 9AB

t 01707 284000
e ask@herts.ac.uk
↗ www.herts.ac.uk

Law Studies 7 Hatfield, St Albans, Hertfordshire AL1 3RS

》 further links

ACCOMMODATION accommodation@herts.ac.uk
STUDENTS' UNION uhsu.herts.ac.uk

| 4810 | 97.4 | 39.7 | 20.3 | 92.5 |

The university is located on two sites in Hatfield, and a third in St Albans. The purpose-built De Havilland campus is barely five years old, which accounts for the excellent facilities for sport, 24/7 learning and stylish undergraduate accommodation. It's all fairly close to London, too. Hertfordshire offers possibilities for e-learning and part-time study. The new £10m building at the University in Hatfield houses the latest technology for the teaching of music, animation, film, television and multimedia.

Fees £3,145 for full-time undergraduate courses in 2008–09.

Bursaries The university will pay 50 per cent of the value of your maintenance grant. Students may receive one of two main scholarships: those with at least 360 Ucas points will receive the chancellor's scholarship of £2,500 in their first year; science and engineering scholarships worth up to £3,000 over four years are available for students on specific courses who get at least 280 Ucas points.

Accommodation Accommodation is guaranteed for first-years. Prices range from approximately £61 to £96 a week.

Facilities A pool and climbing wall are among the sports facilites. There's also the Weston Auditorium, for arts events. Two art galleries and one of the best teaching observatories in the UK.

Transport Good transport links to the rest of the UK. Only 25 minutes by train to London King's Cross rail and tube station. A frequent university shuttle bus travels between campuses.

◀◀ STUDENT VIEW ▶▶

"The university has equipped the students with some state-of-the-art facilities. Constantly in development, the university is leading in lots of fields. We can share work and arrange meetings with our peers online, as well as pick up old lecture notes and journals."

Heythrop College

Kensington Square
London W8 5HQ

t 020 7795 6600
e enquiries@heythrop.ac.uk
↗ www.heythrop.ac.uk

》 further links

ACCOMMODATION www.housing.lon.ac.uk
STUDENTS' UNION www.ulu.co.uk

Heythrop is one of the constituent colleges of the University of London and teaches philosophy, theology and psychology. Its teaching is highly specialised and it offers just eight undergraduate degrees, priding itself on its one-to-one teaching: a privilege enjoyed by students at Oxbridge and few other places. Its home is Kensington, in west London — a central and attractive location.

Fees £3,142 for full-time undergraduate studies in 2008.

Bursaries Students in receipt of the full maintenance grant will receive £310.

Accommodation The college can help students find accommodation. Students are also entitled to use the University of London's accommodation service.

Facilities Excellent libraries with specialist collections. You have access to the University of London's students' union facilities too.

Transport The college has ready access to all forms of transport.

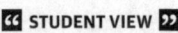 **STUDENT VIEW 》**

"Because it's a small university you get one-to-one attention. The libraries, especially the theology library, are amazing."

University of Huddersfield

Queensgate
Huddersfield HD1 3DH

t 01484 422288
e admissions@hud.ac.uk
↗ www.hud.ac.uk

>> **further links**

ACCOMMODATION accommodation@hud.ac.uk
STUDENTS' UNION www.huddersfieldstudent.com

| 3705 | 97.0 | 38.6 | 18.2 | 89.7 |

Huddersfield is a pleasant town close to Manchester and Leeds with an expanding social scene – thanks, in large part, to the 22,000 or so students. The campus straddles the old canal and there's a new £4m students' union building. Courses are modular, with a strong vocational emphasis, and many offer the option of a year abroad or working in industry. The university rates highly for student satisfaction.

Fees £3,145 for full-time undergraduate courses in 2008-09.

Bursaries The university offers eligible students with a household income of less than £25,000 £500 a year.

Accommodation The university does not have its own accommodation, but recommends a couple of private providers and approves the accommodation they offer.

Facilities The students' union is active, with great facilities including a stylish bar. The five-floor library and computing centre is at the heart of the campus.

Transport Transport from the campus to the town is good, with the M62 and the M1 within striking distance. Good rail links, too.

<< **STUDENT VIEW** >>

"It's got everything. Living in halls in your first year will mean you'll make hundreds of friends and have the absolute time of your life. Huddersfield itself is bursting with life and the university is relaxed yet focused."

University of Hull

Hull HU6 7RX

t 0870 126 2000
e admissions@hull.ac.uk
↗ www.hull.ac.uk

Scarborough Campus Filey Road, Scarborough YO11 3AZ

》 further links

ACCOMMODATION www.hull.ac.uk/accom
STUDENTS' UNION www.hullstudent.com

2895   92.5   30.1   13.4   94.3

Hull is friendly and down to earth, with a diverse population and a very low cost of living. No wonder it rates highly for student satisfaction. It has a strong research reputation and its teaching is very well regarded – two-thirds of students emerge with a first or 2:1. The Hull campus is 15 minutes' walk from the city centre and there are plenty of student-friendly bars and venues to investigate. The smaller campus in Scarborough is close to the faded seaside glamour of the resort. The coastline is marvellous.

Fees £3,145 a year for all full-time undergraduate courses in 2008–09.

Bursaries If your family's annual income is £25,000 or less you will receive a bursary of £1,000 per year. If it is between £25,001 and £40,000 you will receive a bursary of £500 per year. Excellence scholarships of £1,500 are also available, as well as other awards.

Accommodation Guaranteed for all first-years. Weekly prices range from £83 to £119 for catered halls, with self-catered halls and student houses from £52 to £68 a week. Self-catering flats cost around £82 a week. Private accommodation around £42.50 a week.

Facilities There's an award-winning students' union nightclub with good sports provision, too. A £2.4m Enterprise Centre is due to open this month and will provide vital support for start-up businesses run by graduates and students at the university.

Transport Road links are good, but rail links can be slightly bothersome.

❝ STUDENT VIEW ❞
"It's a hidden gem: big enough for you to get the benefits of a city university but small enough to leave your mark. Cheap rent, cheap nightlife, cool people."

Imperial College London

Exhibition Road
South Kensington
London SW7 2AZ

t 020 7589 5111
e info@imperial.ac.uk
↗ www.imperial.ac.uk

Charing Cross Reynolds Building, St Dunstan's Road, London W6 8RP
Chelsea & Westminster 369 Fulham Road SW10 9NH
Hammersmith The Commonwealth Building, The Hammersmith Hospital,
Du Cane Road, London W12 0NN
Northwick Park Watford Road, Harrow, Middlesex HA1 3UJ
Royal Brompton Dovehouse Street, London SW3 6LY
Silwood Park Buckhurst Road, Ascot, Berks SL5 7PY
St Mary's Campus Norfolk Place, London W2 1PG
Wye Campus Ashford, Kent TN25 5AH

》 further links

ACCOMMODATION accommodation@-imperial.ac.uk
STUDENTS' UNION www.imperialcollegeunion.org

London

| 1370 | 61.3 | 17.3 | 4.0 | 94.0 |

Imperial's reputation places it as one of the best academic institutions in the world. Not surprisingly, competition for places is stiff, and there is a certain grandeur about the institution that is only reinforced by its main location among the pomp and circumstance of one of London's swankiest boroughs. Hyde Park, the V&A and the Albert Hall are all on your doorstep.

Fees £3,145 for all full-time undergraduate courses in 2008-09.

Bursaries For 2008 entry, Imperial offered up to £3,000 depending on household income. Those who qualified for the full bursary and also got three As at A-level were awarded a further £300. Scholarships and further bursaries are also available.

Accommodation First-years are guaranteed a place. In the academic year 2007-08, prices started at around £55 a week and can go up well into the mid-hundreds for the swankiest rooms.

Facilities Excellent sporting facilities, predictably good libraries and labs.

Transport The closest tube is South Kensington.

◢◢ STUDENT VIEW ◢◢

"Many of the teaching staff are leaders in their fields, which can be intimidating (and inspiring).
If you want to be worked to within an inch of your life, but have a great time, come here."

Keele University

Keele
Staffordshire ST5 5BG

t 01782 584005
e undergraduate@keele.ac.uk
↗ www.keele.ac.uk

» **further links**

ACCOMMODATION sas@kfm.keele.ac.uk
STUDENTS' UNION www.kusu.net

1900   92.1   26.9   15.0   93.3

Keele

Keele has pioneered the dual honours degree. Many courses include an option for study abroad. There is a friendly atmosphere created by the relatively low student numbers (5,600 full-timers) and a lovely, semi-rural campus. Around 70 per cent of full-time students live on campus.

Fees £3,145 for full-time undergraduate courses in 2008–09.

Bursaries Currently under review, but in 2008 students were given £305 if they were receiving the full grant. There are additional bursaries for students from partner schools and colleges, and for students from rural areas and ethnic minorities. Exellence scholarships (of £4,000 a year) as well as other awards, including subject-specific scholarships, are also available.

Accommodation On-campus accommodation guaranteed for first-years holding Keele as their firm choice, and in fact the majority of students live in university accommodation. Self-catering from £60 to £94 a week.

Facilities Good for sport.

Transport Being between Manchester and Birmingham, Keele has good links to both. It's a 20-minute car journey to the M6. The nearest stations are Stoke-on-Trent and Crewe – both can be reached by bus.

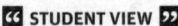

❝ STUDENT VIEW ❞

"Keele is the best: you will meet friends for life. The campus setting and atmosphere really make Keele unique in bringing people together who ordinarily would not have met."

University of Kent

Canterbury
Kent CT2 7NZ

t 01227 764000
e recruitment@kent.ac.uk
↗ www.kent.ac.uk

The Medway Building Chatham Maritime, Kent ME4 4AG
Bridge Wardens' College Clocktower Building, Chatham Historic Dockyard, Kent ME4 4TE
University of Kent at Brussels Boulevard de la Plaine 5, 1050 Bruxelles, Belgium
Tonbridge Centre Avebury Avenue, Tonbridge, Kent TN9 1TG

》 further links

ACCOMMODATION   01227 766660
STUDENTS' UNION   www.kentunion.co.uk

3150   90.9   25.7   12.6   95.1

Canterbury

Many courses offer a foreign language option or a year abroad. It's part of the Franco-British University of the Transmanche and there's even a campus in Brussels. But it also takes its regional role seriously. The leafy main campus (there are also centres at Medway, Chatham, and Tonbridge) is about two miles from Canterbury centre. The university rates highly for student satisfaction. Canterbury is a historic city with plenty of visitor attractions – and good shopping, bars and leisure facilities.

Fees £3,145 for full-time undergraduate courses in 2008-09.

Bursaries Up to £1,000 for students from households with an income of less than £25,000, then on a sliding scale down to £250 a year for students with a family income of up to £40,000. Academic excellence scholarships of £1,000 are also available.

Accommodation All first-years can live in halls providing Kent is their first choice. Price varies.

Facilities Sports facilities include a climbing wall, a beach volleyball court and an artificial "3G" football pitch. There are well-stocked libraries and a good range of social facilities.

Transport The Canterbury campus is a half-hour walk from the city centre. Kent in general is well-served with transport links to London.

⁶⁶ STUDENT VIEW ⁹⁹

"Canterbury is an incredibly scenic city and there is just the right mixture between the historic and modern. Most of the teachers I have encountered are extremely friendly and easy to approach, and many will go out of their way to help you — you only have to ask."

King's College London

Strand
London WC2R 2LS

t 020 7848 2929
e studentenq@kcl.ac.uk
↗ www.kcl.ac.uk

Waterloo Campus The Franklin-Wilkins Building, Stamford Street, London SE1 9NN
Guy's Campus New Hunts House, London SE1 1UL
Hampstead Campus Kidderpore Avenue, London NW3 7ST
King's College Hospital Denmark Hill, London SE5 9RS

》 further links

ACCOMMODATION accomm@kcl.ac.uk
STUDENTS' UNION www.kclsu.org

2640   70.3   21.3   6.4   96.2

London

London is quite literally on your doorstep. Four of the five campuses are clustered together on a landmark-packed stretch of the Thames. The London Eye? The Houses of Parliament? People fly across the world to see these things; you'll pass them on the way to your lectures. The fifth campus is the college's own hospital in Denmark Hill, a quick trip on the overland train. King's also boasts an impeccable reputation for its teaching and research. Graduates have an employment record much higher than the national average.

Fees £3,145 for all full-time undergraduate courses in 2008–09.

Bursaries For all new full-time undergraduate students in receipt of a maintenance grant, King's will award a bursary linked to this amount. Various scholarships are also available.

Accommodation Full-time undergraduates are guaranteed one year – though not necessarily their first – in either a college or an intercollegiate residence. Single room in self-catering from around £98 per week. Single room in college-catered accommodation just over £100 a week. Catered accommodation in University of London intercollegiate halls costs between £113.40 and £120.40 a week for a single room; shared rooms cost £98. Couples from £152 to £227.50. Shared private accommodation costs from around £80–£95 a week.

Facilities The main Maughan Library is the largest new university library in Britain since the second world war. Lots of computers, and wireless, too. Good sports facilities include a rifle range.

Transport It's close to many forms of transport – tubes, bus, trains and even the river.

❝ STUDENT VIEW ❞

"Pro: top-class tuition and research facilities. Con: smog. Pro: a never-ending list of things to do and see. Con: no time for an education. Pro: best three years of your life. Con: most expensive three years of your life. But when you weigh it all up, it stands to reason: you'd be stupid not to enjoy three years here and live the experience of a lifetime."

Kingston University

River House
53-57 High Street
Kingston upon Thames KT1 1LQ

t 08700 841 347
e admissions-info@kingston.ac.uk
↗ www.kingston.ac.uk

Kingston Hill Campus Kingston Hill, Kingston upon Thames, Surrey KT2 7LB
Penrhyn Road Campus Penrhyn Road, Kingston upon Thames, Surrey KT1 2EE
Knights Park Campus Grange Road, Kingston upon Thames, Surrey KT1 2QJ
Roehampton Vale Campus 104 Friars Avenue, Roehampton Vale, London SW15 3DW

》 further links

ACCOMMODATION accommodation@kingston.ac.uk
STUDENTS' UNION www.kusu.co.uk

4400   95.0   36.4   17.1   90.3

Kingston is based on four campuses scattered around the rather swanky town of Kingston upon Thames. It's close to London, though you might have to go through the even swankier areas of Richmond and Twickenham to get there. Around 19,000 students study in seven schools, with more at partner colleges abroad. Its portfolio of foundation degree programmes has recently been extended and includes plenty of interesting vocational options. The university has invested in cutting-edge e-learning systems, too, with students now able to access at least 80 per cent of course modules online.

Fees £3,145 for full-time undergraduate courses starting in 2008.

Bursaries All students eligible for a full or partial maintenance grant will be entitled to some level of bursary, ranging from £1,000 a year down to £310. Every student who enters the university as a member of the local "compact scheme" will receive an extra £300 per year.

Accommodation The university is able to offer self-catering accommodation to most first-years who make Kingston their firm or insurance choice. Weekly prices are £83.75 to £105.

Facilities There are specialist Learning Resources Centres at each campus with 24-hour opening at the two larger campuses during term time. There is a newly refurbished fitness centre.

Transport Two campuses are based within the town centre, with the other two a 10-minute bus ride away. Central London is less than half an hour away by train. There is a frequent and free bus service for students.

❝ STUDENT VIEW ❞
"It's so close to London — literally 20 minutes and you're in the centre of the amazing capital!"

Lampeter, University of Wales

Ceredigion SA48 7ED

t 01570 422351
e recruit@lamp.ac.uk
↗ www.lamp.ac.uk

》 further links

ACCOMMODATION p.thomas@lamp.ac.uk
STUDENTS' UNION www.lamp.ac.uk/su

335   92.7   27.5   21.1   94.9

Lampeter is the oldest degree-awarding institution in Wales and also the smallest, with around 1,000 students. The campus has a beautiful setting in the Ceredigion hills, on the river Teifi and boasts some handsome old buildings. Town/gown relations are excellent and the students' union's entertainment officers work tirelessly to ensure campus life has its fair share of fun. Academically, the university rates highly in theology and religious studies, and English language and literature. Around a third of first-year students are over 21.

Fees £3,145 a year for full-time under-graduates.

Bursaries Bursaries of around £300. There are 20 scholarships of up to £2,000 and 18 departmental scholarships of up to £1,000 a year. Numerous small scholarships and prizes.

Accommodation Guaranteed for first-years. Weekly prices from around £55 to £65.

Facilities Significant investment in online library resources means Lampeter now holds one of the largest collections of e-books in Wales.

Transport Everything is within walking distance. Bus to Carmarthen or Aberystwth stations.

❝ STUDENT VIEW ❞

"Lampeter is an extremely beautiful town. Being so rural, it's very quiet here. This means studying is peaceful. The university is situated in the middle of town, close to everything, and the best part of all is that it's only a two-minute walk to the lecture rooms from halls."

Lancaster University

Bailrigg
Lancaster LA1 4YW

t 01524 65201
e ugadmissions@lancaster.ac.uk
⌐ www.lancaster.ac.uk

》 further links

ACCOMMODATION cro@lancaster.ac.uk
STUDENTS' UNION www.lusu.co.uk

2400   90.6   22.0   7.5   93.9

Lancaster is a collegiate university with eight undergraduate colleges (and a ninth for graduates). Colleges provide accommodation and have their own bars and common rooms, giving a sense of community. Academic staff are also affiliated with a college. The campus is located outside Lancaster and students make up about a fifth of the population. The coast, Lake District, Manchester and Liverpool are within reach. Academic standards are high.

Fees £3,145 for full-time undergraduate courses in 2008.

Bursaries Students with a household income of below £18,360 are eligible for £1,315. Students with a household income of up to £27,800 are eligible for £500. Excellence scholarships of £1,000 are also available.

Accommodation Accommodation is guaranteed to all students who accept an offer and apply. Self-catering accommodation from £65 to £124.

Facilities Include the Ruskin library, the Peter Scott art gallery and the Nuffield theatre plus a sports centre and computing facilities.

Transport There are direct trains to the major cities and good bus and coach networks, with the M6 within spitting distance.

❝ STUDENT VIEW ❞

"Lancaster has a beautiful campus, with acres of grass — perfect for barbecues and Frisbee in the summer. In freezing winter, students run between the bars, halls, and lecture theatres. The close proximity to Blackpool, Preston, Manchester, and Liverpool allows students to get away and spend nights out, but for a campus university it doesn't get much better than this."

University of Leeds

Woodhouse Lane
Leeds LS2 9JT

t 0113 343 2336
e ask@.leeds.ac.uk
↗ www.leeds.ac.uk

》 further links

ACCOMMODATION www.leeds.ac.uk/accommodation
STUDENTS' UNION www.luuonline.com

6250   74.2   18.9   7.9   95.9

Leeds is a top red-brick university – in fact a top university of any colour brick – and one of the giants of the higher education system. The student population is 31,000, drawn by the excellent standards for teaching and research and the chance to live in Leeds itself. A large, dynamic city, Leeds is student-friendly and buzzy, and opportunities for going out and having fun abound. There's also some impressive civic architecture and it's the regional centre for the arts. Students have the benefit of a campus between the city centre and Headingley, where many students live. There's an active union, and an award-winning student newspaper and radio station.

Fees £3,145 a year for all full-time undergraduate courses in 2008.

Bursaries £1,500 to students receiving a full maintenance grant. Bursaries from £1,300 to £325 for students receiving partial grants. Many additional scholarships and awards of £3,000 a year for eligible entrants from under-represented groups.

Accommodation Guaranteed for eligible single first-years. Catered rooms from £90 to £126 a week, with self-catering accommodation costing between £83 and £100 a week.

Facilities Some of the best computing resources in the country and a renowned library with more than 2.5m books. The student union provides clubs, a theatre, bars and live music.

Transport London is two and a half hours away by train, and there are good links to the rest of the country. Leeds Bradford airport takes you further afield.

❝ STUDENT VIEW ❞

"It's got everything for everyone. If in coming to uni your main objective it to get trolleyed nightly, then Leeds will definitely serve that purpose, but equally if you want to get as diverse an experience as possible, surrounded by a variety of people, then it's perfect too."

Leeds College of Music

3 Quarry Hill
Leeds LS2 7PD

t   0113 222 3400
e   enquiries@lcm.ac.uk
↗   www.lcm.ac.uk

》 further links

ACCOMMODATION   0113 222 3514
STUDENTS' UNION   www.lcm.ac.uk/about-lcm
/student-life/student-union.htm

230   86.3   21.8   95.7

Leeds College of Music is the UK's largest music college, with more than 1,000 full-time and 1,500 part-time students. Undergraduate courses include music, jazz, music production, sound design and pop music studies. Students can progress from BTEC courses through to degree-level. LCM is situated on Quarry Hill, at the very heart of the city's emerging arts and cultural quarter, where its neighbours include the West Yorkshire Playhouse, the live music venue the Wardrobe, South Asian Arts UK, Yorkshire Dance and BBC Yorkshire.

Fees   £3,145 for full-time undergraduate courses in 2008.

Bursaries   Annual bursary for students whose household income is below £39,305, ranging from £500 to £1,000. Other scholarships available — including for people who play instruments of which there is a shortage.

Accommodation   Many first-years live in Joseph Stones House, which has 190 study bedrooms. Prices start from £79 a week. The average private-sector rent is around £60 a week.

Facilities   The Venue, a 350-seat performance space, hosts an annual concert season. The Centre for Jazz Studies was established in 2005. The 13 studios are designed to meet a variety of needs from live recording and multi-track recording through to sound design, sampling, production of sound for moving image, digital editing and mastering. There is a specialist library.

Transport   The bus and coach station is opposite LCM. Leeds station is a 10-minutes walk. A bus to the main student areas of Hyde Park and Headingley takes about 20 minutes.

❝ STUDENT VIEW ❞

"At times being surrounded by so many talented people and great facilities in one place can feel a little overwhelming; a kind smile from a fellow student or a reassuring word from a friendly tutor soon banishes those thoughts and reminds me what a fantastic opportunity studying here really is!"

Leeds Metropolitan University

Civic Quarter
Leeds LS1 3HE

t 0113 812 3113
e course-enquiries@leedsmet.ac.uk
↗ www.leedsmet.ac.uk

Headingley Campus Beckett Park, Leeds LS6 3QS
Harrogate Campus Hornbeam Park, Harrogate, North Yorkshire HG2 8QT

>> **further links**

ACCOMMODATION accommodation@leedsmet.ac.uk
STUDENTS' UNION www.lmusu.org.uk

5310   93.5   33.3   14.9   92.3

Leeds Met is a university with a lot of clout. It has over 50,000 students and is lauded for its local contributions. The majority of students are from the region and the university puts its money where its mouth is on widening participation by electing to charge well under the maximum fees. The university has a charming parkland campus in Headingley and a cluster of buildings in central Leeds.

Fees Well below the maximum — currently £2,000 a year for undergraduates.

Bursaries Leeds Met says it prefers the approach of overall lower fees to redistributing money through bursaries. Sports and other scholarships are available.

Accommodation Guaranteed for eligible first-year undergraduates. Prices from £63 to £120 a week.

Facilities Excellent sports facilities, good access to IT resources and libraries with 24-hour access during term-time weekdays.

Transport Handy for just about anywhere, Leeds is well served by road and rail links.

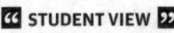 **STUDENT VIEW** >>

"Leeds is a great stepping-stone for getting used to living away from home, having that freedom that all students want, without being in a city that is overwhelming and daunting. You can have the time of your life here."

Leeds Trinity and All Saints

Brownberrie Lane
Horsforth
Leeds LS18 5HD

t 0113 283 7150
e enquiries@leedstrinity.ac.uk
↗ www.leedstrinity.ac.uk

» **further links**

ACCOMMODATION accommodation@leedstrinity.ac.uk
STUDENTS' UNION www.leedstrinity.ac.uk/services/su

710   94.4   37.9   12.9   95.3

Leeds Trinity has offered degrees validated by the University of Leeds since 1974 — mainly in vocational or humanities courses, especially business, media, health and education. All courses include a work placement and graduate employment rates are good. The college is six miles from Leeds city centre, on the edge of the Yorkshire Dales, and attracts around 2,500 students. Leeds Trinity is investing heavily in accommodation and facilities.

Fees Full-time undergraduates pay fees of £2,390 in 2008–09.

Bursaries Students who receive a maintenance grant may qualify for a top-up bursary, equivalent to 10 per cent of the maintenance grant.

Accommodation Leeds Trinity can normally accommodate all first-years. Students can apply for self-catering or part-catered accommodation, and many rooms have internet access. Prices vary.

Facilities A state-of-the-art sports and fitness centre opened in 2007. The modern purpose-built learning centre has the study resources you'll need, plus you can use Leeds University's libraries.

Transport There is a local station at Horsforth and access to the A1, M1 and M62.

❝ STUDENT VIEW ❞

"I have thoroughly enjoyed my time at Leeds Trinity. The atmosphere is very friendly and welcoming and my confidence in my abilities has grown due to my chosen course and the support of staff. The professional work placements were great preparation for life after graduation and helped me confirm my career choice."

University of Leicester

University Road
Leicester LE1 7RH

t 0116 252 2522
e admissions@le.ac.uk
↗ www.le.ac.uk

>> **further links**

ACCOMMODATION accommodation@le.ac.uk
STUDENTS' UNION www.le.ac.uk/su

2115   87.9   25.3   7.0   93.4

Leicester

Leicester came joint top for teaching quality and overall satisfaction in the national student survey two years in a row. The appeal might lie in the friendly and compact campus – a 10-minute walk from one end to the other. Victoria Park next door is a popular place to relax. Leicester puts up a consistently strong academic performance across all subject areas. It's understandably proud of its most famous research achievement: the development of DNA genetic finger-printing. Leicester is a lively, multicultural city.

Fees £3,145 a year for all full-time undergraduate courses in 2008.

Bursaries Annual £1,310 bursary for those with a household income of up to £20,000. Between £100 and £1,010 for students with a household income of up to £39,305. Entrance scholarships of £1,000 for students achieving ABB or above at A-level.

Accommodation Guaranteed for first-years. Costs vary. Basic rooms start at around £60 a week, up to £130 a week.

Facilities A new library has just opened, with access to computer facilities, bookshop and cafe.

Transport Direct rail services to all parts of the country and access to the M1 and M69.

ᴋ STUDENT VIEW ᴋ

"The University of Leicester has it all. An excellent academic pedigree, a fantastic social scene built around an award-winning students' union, a city small enough to get around easily but that has everything you could ever need as a student, and a very central location too that means you can easily access friends around the country. You'd be mad not to apply!"

University of Lincoln

Brayford Pool
Lincoln LN6 7TS

t 01522 882000
e enquiries@lincoln.ac.uk
↗ www.lincoln.ac.uk

》 further links

ACCOMMODATION 01522 886195
STUDENTS' UNION www.lincolnsu.com

2840   96.9   35.6   14.3   92.3

Lincoln is a cathedral city that attracts a million tourists a year. The main campus offers great views, though you may be too busy to look: the waterfront developments include a cinema, restaurants, clubs, accommodation and a new union building with great concert space and bars. The university's city-centre buildings are known as the Cathedral Quarter and there's a lovely rural campus, Riseholme Park. A new arts centre opened in 2007, with excellent facilities for students and the public.

Fees £3,145 for full-time undergraduates.

Bursaries Students receiving a maintenance grant of up to £2,835 will be eligible for up to £600, then on a sliding scale. Other scholarships and support available.

Accommodation Guaranteed for first-years. Costs between £80 and £130 a week.

Facilities The media, humanities and computing building is fully equipped to industry standards with media suites providing TV, radio and sound equipment. The award-wining library is located in the Great Central Warehouse building. The Engine Shed is the region's largest live music venue and home to the union. The conversion from railway engine shed cost £6m.

Transport Train services to London, Birmingham, Newcastle and more and the A1 isn't far.

❝ STUDENT VIEW ❞

"The campus is central and has a real sense of community. The staff are really passionate and innovative in their styles of teaching. It's a growing university that will offer an all-round experience in a friendly, buzzing little city."

University of Liverpool

Liverpool L69 3BX

t 0151 794 2000
e ugrecruitment@liv.ac.uk
↗ www.liv.ac.uk

》 further links

ACCOMMODATION accommodation@liv.ac.uk
STUDENTS' UNION www.lgos.org

3995   86.4   23.6   8.8   95.4

Liverpool

It has everything you'd expect from a classic red-brick university: excellent ratings in teaching and research, a large, diverse student body, a strong sense of self and a city location — and 2008 sees it becoming the European Capital of Culture. In 2006, the university opened the first independent Anglo-Asian university in China in partnership with Xi'an Jiaotong University in Suzhou. The cost of living is low and there is a real commitment to community and open access.

Fees £3,145 for full-time undergraduate courses in 2008.

Bursaries Students eligible for a full maintenance grant receive a further £1,330 a year. Students with a partial maintenance grant will receive £1,025. These figures may rise slightly. Further scholarships and awards for academic excellence are also available.

Accommodation Guaranteed for eligible first-years. Self-catered from £70 to £100 a week. Catered ranges from around £98 to £111.

Facilities Two main libraries. Extensive sports grounds, and the union offers three bars.

Transport The campus is situated about 10 minutes walk from the city centre. Good for trains and coaches and motorway access.

❝ STUDENT VIEW ❞

"It's an awesome city as a first step to independent living. It is quite beautiful. Feeling that you're part of the uni makes you feel part of the city — I get very defensive if people try to criticise Liverpool!"

Liverpool Hope University

Hope Park
Liverpool L16 9JD

t 0151 291 3000
e course-enquiry@hope.ac.uk
↗ www.hope.ac.uk

Everton Campus Hope at Everton, Haigh Street, Liverpool L3 8QB

>> **further links**

ACCOMMODATION accommodation@hope.ac.uk
STUDENTS' UNION www.hopesu.co.uk

1625   97.8   40.0   26.3   92.5

Hope is the only ecumenical university in Europe, with a significant female population, and is strong in teacher training. The number of applications continues to rise, and it gained full university status in 2005. It has two campuses, where 7,500 students are taught. Hope has a high-quality careers service and opportunities for part-time work and work experience are plentiful, including the chance to work overseas with the university's award-winning charity, Hope One World.

Fees £3,145 a year for full-time undergraduates.

Bursaries Every undergraduate will receive a bursary of no less than £400 a year irrespective of family income. Those receiving a full maintenance grant will be given an annual bursary averaging £1,000 a year. Those on partial grant will get £700 a year. Scholarships awarded for academic achievement.

Accommodation All first-years are guaranteed accommodation. Prices vary.

Facilities Moodle is the fastest growing and most used virtual learning environment in the UK. The library has extended opening hours and claims to be the most flexible of any university. Hope aims to provide the most up-to-date computer facilities, with access to email and virtual learning environment from anywhere in the world.

Transport Excellent transport links — even an international airport.

❝ STUDENT VIEW ❯❯

"Hope University is a really relaxed and comfortable place to study. Liverpool is a fantastic place to live. It's one of the most student-orientated cities in the country. There is a great mix of things to do both in the daytime and at night. Everything a student could want!"

Liverpool John Moores University

Roscoe Court
4 Rodney Street
Liverpool L1 2TZ

t 0151 231 5090
e recruitment@ljmu.ac.uk
↗ www.ljmu.ac.uk

》 further links

ACCOMMODATION accommodation@ljmu.ac.uk
STUDENTS' UNION www.l-s-u.com

4495   95.6   36.7   21.0   91.4

Liverpool

At LJMU, graduate skills development and work-related learning are now integral to all undergraduate degrees. Backed by an advisory panel of leading employers, students are encouraged to develop work skills. The graduate development centre offers an extensive range of "ready for work" training courses. The university remains a popular choice internationally. Liverpool's a fun city and it's fairly cheap for a big urban centre. With three large campuses in the city, you're never far from an LJMU base.

Fees £3,145 a year for full-time undergraduates.

Bursaries Students with a household income below £25,000 receive a bursary of £1,050. Students with a household income of up to £50,000 receive £420. Six awards of £10,000 a year are available for gifted students who can demonstrate achievement in areas such as volunteering, citizenship or the arts. Other awards are available.

Accommodation Guaranteed for first-years, including those who apply through clearing. Self-catering halls range from £61 to £96 a week.

Facilities Sporting facilities include a swimming pool, hockey and football pitches, a gym, dance studios and climbing walls.

Transport Two campuses are in the middle of town, a third is a 15-minute bus ride away.

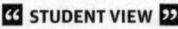 **STUDENT VIEW 》**

"There's a real buzz about the city and it does live up to its claim to be 'the world in one city'. If you want to have fun and meet great people, then LJMU is for you."

Liverpool Institute for Performing Arts

Mount Street
Liverpool L1 9HF

t 0151 330 3000
e admissions@lipa.ac.uk
↗ www.lipa.ac.uk

》 further links

ACCOMMODATION 0151 330 3084

LIPA was the brainchild of Sir Paul McCartney, who wanted to save the site of his former school, and Mark Featherstone-Witty, who wanted to provide training for people intent on entering showbusiness. Together, they poured seven years and £20m into the institute, which opened in 1996. It currently offers nine undergraduate degrees in the performing arts and its curriculum is designed to give graduates a sense of the business side of the industry as much as the creative aspects.

Fees Contact LIPA for most up-to-date information.

Bursaries Contact LIPA for most up-to-date information.

Accommodation The institute doesn't have any of its own accommodation but has partnerships with local providers meaning first-years can usually have a choice of halls-style accommodation. Prices range from £50 to £100 a week.

Facilities The grand Grade II listed building houses world-class facilities, including two performance spaces. There are recording studios and music practice rooms, dance studios and classrooms.

Transport Liverpool is a transport hub with good access to road, rail and air links.

❝ STUDENT VIEW ❱❱
"LIPA was everything I had been looking for in a college.
The attention to the business of being a professional performer made it really special."

London Metropolitan University

31 Jewry Street
London   EC3N 2EY

t   020 7133 4200
e   admissions@londonmet.ac.uk
↗   www.londonmet.ac.uk

London City Campus   Calcutta House, Old Castle Street, London   E1 7NT
London North Campus   Student Services, London Metropolitan University,
Tower Building, 166-220 Holloway Road, London   N7 8DB

》 further links

ACCOMMODATION   accommodation@londonmet.ac.uk
STUDENTS' UNION   www.londonmetsu.org.uk

4120   97.5   40.9   21.2   80.7

London Met is London's largest single university, with one campus near trendy
Brick Lane and another just north of Islington. Of the 34,000 students, almost a third
are international. Courses have a professional and vocational bent. Last year, the
four business departments merged, creating Europe's largest business school.

Fees   £3,145 a year for full-time undergraduates.

Bursaries   University bursaries of up to £1,000 are available to all eligible home students.
There is a wide range of scholarships, including sports and excellence scholarships.

Accommodation   Accommodation is guaranteed for all eligible first-years as long as they live
farther than 25 miles from the university, have accepted an offer and have applied in time.
Catered costs around £100 a week. Self-catering costs £80 to £100 a week.

Facilities   Extensive libraries, including the specialist Women's Library and TUC collections.
There's an ultra-modern science centre, sound and recording studios, a mock courtroom,
a lightning lab and seven floors of IT facilities at the Technology Tower.

Transport   London's usual embarrassment of transport riches is on offer.

❝ STUDENT VIEW ❞

*"Who could ask for more than to be part of the vibrant, busy, and culturally packed city of London.
Everything you can imagine is right at your fingertips, as the city is plentifully supplied with museums,
libraries, resources, and news swimming round you at all times!"*

London School of Economics and Political Science

Houghton Street
London WC2A 2AE

t 020 7405 7686
e ug-admissions@lse.ac.uk
↗ www.lse.ac.uk

>> further links

ACCOMMODATION accommodation@lse.ac.uk
STUDENTS' UNION www.lsesu.com

595   59.4   17.5   3.1   94.0

The LSE is the only university in the UK specialising in the study of social sciences, and has a worldwide reputation. Of the 8,000 or so students, half are postgraduates and around a third are from the UK, making for the largest proportion of overseas students at any university in the world. Students have a reputation for being academic and determined. Graduates enjoy top employment rates and starting salaries. The school is located in the heart of London, close to the West End and Bloomsbury.

Fees £3,145 a year for all full-time undergraduate courses in 2008.

Bursaries A maximum bursary of £2,500 a year for students with the lowest household income, and then on a downwards sliding scale. Other forms of financial support available. There are also scholarships.

Accommodation Guaranteed for all first-years. Prices vary. LSE can offer rooms to 45 per cent of students.

Facilities Excellent. Great libraries and other learning resources. The students' union is so well-regarded it attracts plenty of non-students.

Transport All roads lead to London and so do quite a lot of train tracks and flight paths. LSE is central: walk or cycle most places.

<< STUDENT VIEW >>

"LSE is different, to say the least. You meet so many different people from every corner and background in the world. LSE teaches you a hell of a lot of life skills while you gain a sought-after degree that employers will value highly. You will come out of LSE a different person, but usually for the better."

London South Bank University

90 London Road
London SE1 6LN

t 020 7815 7815
e enquiry@lsbu.ac.uk
↗ www.lsbu.ac.uk

>> **further links**

ACCOMMODATION accommodation@lsbu.ac.uk
STUDENTS' UNION www.lsbsu.org

2205   98.0   41.9   25.3   89.5

LSBU is based at Elephant & Castle in south London. Major investment is planned for the area. LSBU is doing its bit, with £47m being put into its campus. It's hard to beat the location – within easy reach of London Bridge, Southwark, the South Bank, Waterloo and Westminster. The 21,000-strong student body is diverse and culturally rich. Half are from ethnic minorities, 3,000 come from outside the UK. A large proportion are mature students. Courses are built with future careers in mind, and graduate salaries are very good.

Fees £3,145 for full-time undergraduates.

Bursaries Bursaries currently worth £2,250 over three years available to all students. Other financial assistance available.

Accommodation LSBU offers a range of self-catering halls and flats. The cost per week is between £86 and £106. Low-cost private accommodation is also available nearby.

Facilities Good on-site sports facilities and access to libraries and computing resources.

Transport Easy access to the tube, plentiful bus routes and overland rail services.

Loughborough University

Loughborough
Leicestershire LE11 3TU

t 01509 263171
e admissions@lboro.ac.uk
↗ www.lboro.ac.uk

» further links

ACCOMMODATION sac@lboro.ac.uk
STUDENTS' UNION www.lufbra.net

3075   82.9   23.6   4.9   95.4   Loughborough

Academically strong across the board, but Loughborough is still famous for sport. The Midlands market town is about a mile away. The university is the town's biggest employer and students are a major part of the population. Uniquely, the students' union is physically owned by the students. The 175-hectare campus has good facilities for all aspects of student life.

Fees £3,145 for full-time undergraduates.

Bursaries £1,360 for students with a household income up to £25,000, then calculated on a sliding scale. Merit-based scholarships are also available in some subjects.

Accommodation Loughborough encourages first-years to live in halls. Self-catering from around £62 to £130 per week. Catered options cost from around £118 to £145 per week.

Facilities The university has the country's largest concentration of world-class training facilities across a wide range of sports. The campus is home to two of the town's major performance venues. The Sir Robert Martin theatre and Cope auditorium regularly host concerts, dance and drama productions, both by visiting artists and students.

Transport A 20-minute walk from the town centre, or take the shuttle bus. Train to Nottingham, Derby or Leicester in 30 minutes.

‹‹ STUDENT VIEW ››

"I'd recommend Loughborough for a work-hard, play-harder lifestyle and an unbeatable sense of belonging and community. Students thrive on the campus atmosphere, enjoying the feeling of community and the open environment for making friends."

The University of Manchester

Oxford Road
Manchester M13 9PL

t 0161 306 6000
e ug.admissions@manchester.ac.uk
↗ www.manchester.ac.uk

》 further links

ACCOMMODATION accommodation@ manchester.ac.uk
STUDENTS' UNION www.umsu.manchester.ac.uk

6015   77.7   20.7   7.6   93.4

Manchester is massive: almost 30,000 students and 10,000 staff make it the biggest university in the UK bar the Open University. It's often the most popular among Ucas applicants, and is heavily targeted by the UK's top graduate employers. The city is also a big draw – down to earth and friendly, but ever-increasingly hip and happening. Shopping, bars and the epic architecture of the city's industrial past and vibrant present are all a short walk away.

Fees £3,145 for full-time undergraduate courses in 2008–09.

Bursaries £1,000 a year for all UK students with an annual household income of up to £27,120. Further awards and scholarships for eligible students.

Accommodation Guaranteed for first-years. Prices range from around £60 a week for a single, self-catered room to about £120 for a catered, single ensuite room near the city centre.

Facilities Access to one of the UK's largest academic libraries, more than 10,000 PCs across campus, e-learning facilities and excellent teaching resources for both arts and sciences.

Transport There are two mainline stations, an international airport and good motorway connections.

❝ STUDENT VIEW ❞

"Manchester is the next best thing to London, with an array of shops, restaurants, bars, and nightclubs. You are always guaranteed a good night out. It offers a great selection of courses and the teaching staff are friendly, helpful, and approachable."

Manchester Metropolitan University

All Saints Building	**t** 0161 247 2000
All Saints	**e** enquiries@mmu.ac.uk
Manchester M15 6BH	↗ www.mmu.ac.uk

Alsager Campus Hassall Road, Alsager ST7 2HL

Aytoun Campus Aytoun Street, Manchester M1 3GH

Crewe Campus Crewe Green Road, Crewe CW1 5DU

Didsbury Campus Wilmslow Road, Didsbury, Manchester M20 2RR

Elizabeth Gaskell Campus Hathersage Road, Manchester M13 0JA

Hollings Campus Old Hall Lane, Manchester M14 6HR

》 further links

ACCOMMODATION accommodation@mmu.ac.uk
STUDENTS' UNION www.mmunion.co.uk

7550	94.0	34.0	23.6	92.3

MMU is one of Britain's largest universities, offering some 700 courses and the opportunity for industry placements and international exchange programmes. The social scene is great, and Diva magazine voted it the best place to be a gay student, ahead of London and Brighton.

Fees £3,145 for full-time undergraduates in 2008.

Bursaries £1,000 a year for students receiving full grant, then on a sliding scale, to those with a family income of £39,920, who get £100.

Accommodation All first-years will be housed in university or privately owned halls of residence. Costs range from £66.50 to £93 per week.

Facilities The Manchester Aquatics Centre on the Manchester campus has two Olympic-standard main pools. The Sugden sports centre has a 100-station state-of-the-art fitness suite. High-spec engineering and science labs, and good arts facilities, too.

Transport Transport round Manchester or Cheshire is easy. Free bus between Cheshire campuses.

◄◄ STUDENT VIEW ►►

"There is so much to get involved in and you can take advantage of so much, whether it's politics, sports, a society, job opportunities, or just the shopping! You really will love this city!"

Marjon (University College Plymouth St Mark and St John)

Derriford Road
Plymouth
Devon PL6 8BH

t 01752 636700
e admissions@marjon.ac.uk
↗ www.marjon.com

》 further links

ACCOMMODATION 01752 636711
STUDENTS' UNION www.marjonsu.co.uk

640   95.5   39.5   20.5   90.8

Plymouth

Marjon, on Plymouth's outskirts, is a small, welcoming, single-campus higher education institution with about 5,000 students. Courses are mostly humanities-based, and include media, PR, community work, applied sports science and coaching.

Fees Marjon charges £2,300 or £2,825, depending on the course.

Bursaries A hardship fund is available; new students get a free laptop.

Accommodation There are places on campus for around 500 students and priority is given to first-years. Accommodation is around £65 a week.

Facilities The sports centre has a 25-metre pool, gym, squash courts, two sports halls, a fitness suite and outdoor pitches. The library is at the heart of the campus and there is 24-hour access to computing facilites.

Transport Rail and road links to most big cities, plus ferries. Plymouth airport is very close.

❝ STUDENT VIEW ❞

"I chose UCP Marjon as I felt they had a good balance of academic and social life. The campus is small and friendly and Plymouth is a great city, close to the coast and moors. For a small university college, there is a wide selection of courses. The lecturers are helpful and approachable. I am really happy with my choice."

Middlesex University

The Burroughs
Hendon
London NW4 4BT

t 020 8411 5000
e enquiries@mdx.ac.uk
↗ www.mdx.ac.uk

Cat Hill Campus Chase Side, Barnet, Herts EN4 8HT
Enfield Campus Queensway, Enfield, Middlesex EN3 4SA
Trent Park Campus Bramley Road, London N14 4YZ
Middlesex University Dubai Knowledge Village, P O Box 500697, Block 16, Dubai, United Arab Emirates

》 further links
ACCOMMODATION accomm@mdx.ac.uk
STUDENTS' UNION www.musu.mdx.ac.uk

3720   98.2   44.6   26.5   90.1

Middlesex is spreads over five north London campuses, though Enfield will close in 2008; Hendon is the focus. All are less than an hour from central London. A fifth of its students are from outside the UK.

Fees £3,145 for all full-time undergraduate courses in 2008-09.

Bursaries £310 for all students who qualify for a maintenance grant. Other scholarships too.

Bursaries Middlesex prioritises first-years who have made the university their first choice and those from furthest away. International students are most likely to get university accommodation. There are nine halls. Rents are around £80–£90 a week.

Facilities The Sheppard library has fantastic views of London. Its Museum of Domestic Design and Architecture has an important collection of decorative art and design. Each campus has learning resources and there are facilities for the study of sport.

Transport It's virtually in London, with all the transport benefits (and problems) that implies.

❝ STUDENT VIEW 》
"The campuses are scenic. There are good teaching facilities and excellent tutors with courses recognised by professional bodies. The fact that there are so many mature and international students creates a diverse student body. Most lecturers are extremely helpful and go out of their way to enrich the lives of their students."

Napier University

Craiglockhart Campus
Edinburgh EH14 1DJ

t 08452 606040
e info@napier.ac.uk
↗ www.napier.ac.uk

Merchiston Edinburgh EH10 5DT
Craighouse Campus Craighouse road, Edinburgh EH10 5LB
Canaan Lane Edinburgh EH9 2TB
Comely Bank Edinburgh EH4 2LD
Marchmont Campus Edinburgh EH9 1HU
Morningside Campus Edinburgh EH10 4BY

》 further links

ACCOMMODATION accommodation@-napier.ac.uk
STUDENTS' UNION www.napierstudents.com

| 1780 | 94.0 | 33.9 | 16.5 | 93.8 |

Napier is a modern university with more than 14,000 students on seven campuses in Edinburgh. It arranges work placements for many students; modular courses allow students to customise their courses.

Fees Scottish and EU students from outside the UK pay no tuition fees. For other UK students, annual tuition fee is £1,775 in 2008.

Bursaries A range of scholarships and trust funds for new students, particularly those in need, also for mature students, overseas students, or those with dependents. Students from the UK (not Scotland) paying fees and claiming a full maintenance grant are entitled to a bursary of around £300.

Accommodation Available to most, though not all, new students from outside the area. A room in a university flat is about £80 a week.

Facilities Fully networked libraries on each campus with seven-day-a-week opening. The Craiglockhart campus has a new fitness suite.

Transport Good train links from Edinburgh to London via Newcastle and York. Access to motorways and a nearby airport.

⟪ STUDENT VIEW ⟫

"Edinburgh is absolutely fantastic. Especially during August, if you can tolerate tourists holding coins up at belligerent bus drivers and shouting, 'Castle!'. I have to say my lecturers are all absolutely brilliant. Some of them are barmy, which is also brilliant."

Newcastle University

Newcastle upon Tyne   NE1 7RU

t 0191 222 5594
e enquiries@ncl.ac.uk
↗ www.ncl.ac.uk

》 further links

ACCOMMODATION accommodation-enquiries@ncl.ac.uk
STUDENTS' UNION www.unionsociety.co.uk

4050   68.4   20.3   7.7   93.6

Newcastle upon Tyne

Newcastle has got an impressive academic track record and is located in a city that inspires immense affection. The city is famous for its nightlife, but is also a regional centre for the arts, theatre and live music. Living costs are relatively low. The university has a modern outlook — it has Fair Trade status, is a smoke-free campus, was the only university to formally back the Jubilee Debt Campaign for the cancellation of debt in developing countries, and has a strong commitment to the Make Poverty History campaign.

Fees £3,145 for all full-time undergraduate courses in 2008.

Bursaries £1,240 for students whose family income is up to £18,360; £930 where family income is £18,361 to £26,222; and £620 where family income is between £26,223 and £31,466. Hundreds of excellence scholarships.

Accommodation Guaranteed for eligible non-local first-years. Prices from £65 to £115 a week.

Facilities The library has several specialist collections. There's a £5.5m sports centre and an online service for submitting work or checking lectures.

Transport The campus is in the middle of the city and close to the Metro. There are links to London and Edinburgh, and an airport.

❝ STUDENT VIEW ❞

"Newcastle is friendly, vibrant and full of opportunities. The city is a perfect size — big enough to offer everything you want, but small enough that you feel part of the community. The university is really friendly too; my course was interactive and lecturers were always supportive. The careers service is outstanding and staff were fully committed to helping me decide what to do after university, which gave me confidence in my final year."

Newman University College

Genners Lane
Bartley Green
Birmingham B32 3NT

t 0121 476 1181
e registry@newman.ac.uk
↗ www.newman.ac.uk

》 further links

ACCOMMODATION 0121 483 2219
STUDENTS' UNION www.newmansu.org

475   99.3   44.3   14.7   98.3

Birmingham

Founded in 1968 by the Catholic Education Council, Newman is located in a purpose-built campus eight miles from Birmingham. Once a teacher-training college, it now has a small portfolio of degrees awarded by the University of Leicester. All students take a work placement module and there are European placement opportunities. Newman has one of the best graduate employment records in the country.

Fees £3,145 for full-time undergraduates in 2008–09.

Bursaries Means-tested bursary available, starting at £1,100 if your family income is under £17,910, and then on a sliding scale.

Accommodation First-years get priority; about £70 a week.

Facilities A big sports centre, a library with computing resources, and a lively students' union.

Transport Birmingham is well served by transport.

University of Wales, Newport

Caerleon Campus
Lodge Road
Newport NP20 5DA

t 01633 432432
e uic@newport.ac.uk
↗ www.newport.ac.uk

》 further links

ACCOMMODATION accommodation@newport.ac.uk
STUDENTS' UNION www.newportunion.com

1150   99.2   39.3   23.2   90.5

The university is on two campuses, one near the city centre, another in Caerleon. Accommodation and the union are on the latter. In 2010 a new campus will open in central Newport. The university has been highly rated in the national student survey and applications are leaping.

Fees £3,145 for full-time undergraduate courses in 2008.

Bursaries £1,000 for students with a household income of up to £20,000, then calculated in a downward sliding scale. The university also offers a further range of bursaries and scholarships.

Accommodation Guaranteed for eligible first-years. Self-catered accommodation costs between £62 and £75 a week.

Facilities A good sports centre and an elite School of Golf. Also a useful online learning scheme.

Transport It's two hours' drive to London on the M4 with direct train links too.

❝ STUDENT VIEW ❞
"It's a friendly little place to live where you are guaranteed friends and a good time all year long. Come here if you want to be part of a unique university ... and to learn a tiny bit of Welsh."

North East Wales Institute of Higher Education

Plas Coch Campus
Mold Road
Wrexham LL11 2AW

t 01978 290666
e sid@newi.ac.uk
↗ www.newi.ac.uk

》 further links

ACCOMMODATION accommodation@newi.ac.uk
STUDENTS' UNION www.newisu.com

775   97.9   49.2   25.0   86.8

Situated in Wrexham, north Wales, Newi is based at two campuses: Plas Coch, with the students' union, student village and new sports centre; and the school of art and design nearer the town centre.

Fees £3,145 for full-time undergraduate courses in 2008, but Welsh students are eligible for a fee remission grant of £1,890.

Bursaries Means-tested and up to £500 for Welsh students or £1,400 for students from the rest of the UK.

Accommodation Most first-years are housed by the university. Costs are from £50 to £72 a week.

Facilities Interesting teaching facilities include the Human Performance Lab, the Terry Hands Theatre, radio and recording studios.

Transport The nearest stations are in Wrexham, five to 15 minutes' walk away. Manchester International and Liverpool airports are both a 45-minute drive away.

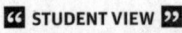 **STUDENT VIEW 》**

"The facilities and the accommodation are close together and give us the opportunity to meet different people and build up relationships. Newi is a nice place for student life."

University of Northampton

Avenue Campus
St Georges Avenue
Northampton NN2 6JD

t 0800 358 2232
e study@northampton.ac.uk
↗ www.northampton.ac.uk

Park Campus Boughton Green Road, Northampton NN2 7AL

>> **further links**

ACCOMMODATION accommodation@northampton.ac.uk
STUDENTS' UNION www.northamptonunion.com

2120   97.3   37.5   19.3   92.9

Ten thousand students attend courses on two city campuses, many of them locals. The university has seen a substantial investment in campus facilities in the past few years, with a further £80m planned. The students' union regularly has live entertainment. Northampton is a big market town with some attractive green spaces and architecture.

Fees £3,145 for full-time undergraduate courses in 2008.

Bursaries Undergraduate students from the UK with household incomes of up to £40,000 get a bursary of £500 to £1,000 a year.

Accommodation Guaranteed for first-years who make Northampton their first choice. Prices range from £37.50 a week for a small twin to £79.75 for an ensuite room. All halls are self-catering.

Facilities Park campus has a nightclub and Avenue campus also has a student union bar, as well as dance and drama studios and computer-aided design suites. There is 24-hour access to IT resources.

Transport Northampton town centre is close by and easily accessible.The city is one hour by train to Birmingham and London and is accessible via three junctions on the M1.

◀◀ STUDENT VIEW ▶▶

"It's a fun-loving, social place to live, with a good opportunity to gain a good degree and friendships. The teaching staff are very nice and pleasant and you can even have a laugh and a joke with most of them."

Northumbria University

Newcastle City Campus
Ellison Place
Newcastle upon Tyne NE1 8ST

t 0191 232 6002
e er.admissions@northumbria.ac.uk
↗ www.northumbria.ac.uk

Coach Lane Campus Coach Lane, Benton, Newcastle upon Tyne NE7 7XA

》 further links

ACCOMMODATION rc.accommodation@northumbria.ac.uk
STUDENTS' UNION www.mynsu.co.uk

4695   91.7   31.6   16.4   94.9

Newcastle
upon Tyne

Northumbria is in the top 10 for growth in terms of applications – no surprise when you consider it's based in a city renowned for its culture, friendliness and nightlife. Northumbria's teaching has a good reputation, and courses allow for flexibility.

Fees £3,145 a year for full-time undergraduate courses in 2008.

Bursaries Around £300 a year to those receiving full maintenance grant. Awards of between £250 and £1,000 in the first year, depending on subject studied. The amount received in subsequent years will depend on academic performance.

Accommodation The university can accommodate all first-years. Self-catering is from £59 to £94 a week, catered from £99 a week.

Facilities The City Campus East has won numerous awards. Sports facilities keep the university in the top 10 UK sporting institutions.

Transport The train station is a short walk from the university; it's under three hours to London or one and a half to Edinburgh. There's a Metro and an international airport.

Norwich School of Art and Design

Francis House
3-7 Redwell Street
Norwich NR2 4SN UK

t 01603 610561
e info@nsad.ac.uk
↗ www.nsad.ac.uk

》 further links

ACCOMMODATION accommodation@nsad.ac.uk
STUDENTS' UNION www.nsad.ac.uk/abouttheschool
/studentunion.php

435   98.7   31.5   7.5   90.9

The Norwich School of Art and Design is in central Norwich, with about 1,000 full-time students. All undergraduates do critical studies. Based at the school is the Norwich Gallery, which runs the Aurora Festival.

Fees £3,145 for full-time undergraduate courses in 2008.

Bursaries Tied to the amount of maintenance support you receive and between £113 and £567 a year.

Accommodation There are a couple of residences charging £74 to £98 a week. Allocation is based, for instance, on how far away your home is.

Facilities The library has good specialist resources.

Transport The train station is a short walk away and it's less than two hours to London.

❝ STUDENT VIEW ❞

"NSAD offered me the invaluable insight and experience that I craved. It has always had a strong reputation for creative excellence — which was what lured me in the first place. I know I made the right decision. It's a fantastic campus in a beautiful part of a fine city."

University of Nottingham

University Park
Nottingham NG7 2RD

t 0115 951 5151
e undergraduate-enquiries@nottingham.ac.uk
↗ www.nottingham.ac.uk

Sutton Bonington Campus
  Sutton Bonington, Near Loughborough, Leicestershire LE12 5RD
Jubilee Campus Wollaton Road, Nottingham NG8 1BB
Kings Meadow Campus Lenton Lane, Nottingham NG7 2NA
The University of Nottingham China Campus
  199 Taikang East Road, Ningbo, 315100, China
The University of Nottingham Malaysia Campus
  Jalan Broga, 43500 Semenyih, Selangor Darul Ehsan, Malaysia

》 further links

ACCOMMODATION ugaccommodation@nottingham.ac.uk
STUDENTS' UNION www.su.nottingham.ac.uk

4495   66.1   16.9   3.0   95.1

Nottingham is one of the most popular universities for British and overseas students.
It has campuses in Malaysia and China so UK students can spend part of their degrees
there. The attractive campus is a short distance from town, and the union is active.
There's an award-winning student radio station.

Fees £3,145 for full-time undergraduate courses in 2008.

Bursaries Between £260 and £1,050 for each year of an undergraduate degree, dependant on
residual household income. Students may also be eligible for additional bursaries.

Accommodation Guaranteed for eligible first-years. In 2008–09 weekly prices ranged from
£101.25 (double) to £164.75 (ensuite single) for a room in catered halls of residence, and started
at around £78.75 for a standard room in a self-catering flat.

Facilities Library facilities include the new Hallward Library Learning Hub.

Transport A free bus, good rail and road links and an international airport nearby.

‹‹ STUDENT VIEW ››

*"The university is known for excellence in academia, and it's fair to say that you'll be worked quite hard
in the later years of your course. Nottingham delivers exactly what you want from a city. That is unless
you are looking for a quiet and uneventful university experience — then it's probably not for you!"*

Nottingham Trent University

Burton Street
Nottingham NG1 4BU

t 0115 941 8418
e admissions@ntu.ac.uk
↗ www.ntu.ac.uk

Clifton Campus Clifton Lane, Nottingham NG11 8NS
Brackenhurst Nottingham Roadm Southwell NG25 0QF

》 further links

Accommodationsas.general.enquiries@ntu.ac.uk
STUDENTS' UNION www.trentstudents.org

4700 91.8 31.8 9.4 97.2

NTU is one of the largest "new" universities, with 25,000 students. It has three campuses: one in the city centre, one five miles away, one 12 miles out of town. The university has one of the best records in the country for graduate employment. Most courses are vocational. Students may spend up to a year on placements.

Fees £3,145 for full-time undergraduates in 2008.

Bursaries £1,050 a year for those on full maintenance grants, then on a sliding scale between £650 and £350 for those on partial grant. Those whose family lives in Nottinghamshire get an extra £110 to £260. Scholarship bursaries of £2,000 a year go to at least 25 students on full grant.

Accommodation All new students get university-allocated accommodation. Self-catering accommodation is from £69 to £105 a week

Facilities Some 24-hour computing facilities.

Transport The city centre is easily accessible. Nottingham has great transport links.

◄◄ STUDENT VIEW ►►

"It's a great place to spend your university years and the extensive range of clubs, shops, and gigs will have you blowing your loan before you have time to be homesick. Tutors are always happy to talk to you and many still practise in their area so their expertise is fresh even if their jokes are stale."

Open University

PO Box 197
Milton Keynes MK7 6BJ

t 0845 300 6090
e general-enquiries@open.ac.uk
↗ www.open.ac.uk

The Open is the UK's largest university, a world leader in distance learning, achieves high standards in teaching and research, and came top for student satisfaction in the national student survey three years running. Undergraduate degrees have no entry requirements. Teaching is via online resources and interactive DVDs; students are supported by staff at regional centres. The average cost of an OU undergraduate degree is under £3,860.

Fees Vary. See the website for more details.

❝ STUDENT VIEW ❞

"The OU is a fantastic place to study. I have been able to work and earn money at the same time as completing my degree. The teachers are enthusiastic and committed and it's an option more young people should consider when they look at universities."

University of Oxford

University Offices
Wellington Square
Oxford OX1 2JD

t 01865 288000
e undergraduate.admissions@admin.ox.ac.uk
⌕ www.ox.ac.uk

》 further links

ACCOMMODATION   contact individual colleges
STUDENTS' UNION   www.ousu.org

2920   53.7   11.4   1.4   94.4

Oxford

Oxford's history – all 900 years of it – may be present in its centuries-old buildings and traditions, but it's also a modern university: at, or near, the top of national and global rankings and at the forefront of research and teaching. Whichever of the 39 colleges or six private halls you call home will be the focus of your university life: where you'll live, eat, party and have the one-to-one tutorials that are the keystone of Oxford teaching. You can step out of your college to get involved in university-wide drama, sport, politics, journalism or whatever else takes your fancy.

Fees   £3,145 for full-time undergraduate courses in 2008.

Bursaries   Oxford has a generous bursary scheme. Students with a household income under £25,000 get £3,150; those under £18,000 also qualify for an extra £850 in year one. Students with a household income of between £25,001 and £49,999 get a partial award.

Accommodation   All colleges house first-years; many can house students for subsequent years. Standard accommodation in most colleges is approximately £116 a week over 27 (term-time) weeks.

Facilities   Oxford has the largest university library system in the UK, with more than 100 libraries. There are four major museums in the university as well as botanic gardens. Great for sport. University provision is supplemented by colleges' own libraries, sports grounds and IT facilities.

Transport   Within Oxford, everything is walkable or bikeable. Good links to London by train or coach.

❝ STUDENT VIEW ❞

"It's a completely different experience to almost anywhere else in the world, probably. If you think you could get in and don't give it a shot, do you really want to regret it for the rest of your life? Whatever you want to do here there's so much support and expertise to help you that time and your own potential are the only limitations."

Oxford colleges

All Souls College
High Street, Oxford   OX1 4AL
 t   01865 279379

Balliol College
Broad Street, Oxford   OX1 3BJ
 t   01865 277777

Blackfriars
St Giles, Oxford   OX1 3LY
 t   01865 278400

Brasenose College
Radcliffe Square, Oxford   OX1 4AJ
 t   01865 277830

Campion Hall
Brewer Street, Oxford   OX1 1QS
 t   01865 286100
 ↗ www.campion.ox.ac.uk

Christ Church
St Aldate's, Oxford   OX1 1DP
 t   01865 276150
 ↗ www.chch.ox.ac.uk

Corpus Christi College
Merton, Oxford   OX1 4JF
 t   01865 276700
 ↗ www.ccc.ox.ac.uk

Exeter College
Turl Street, Oxford   OX1 3DP
 t   01865 279600
 ↗ www.exeter.ox.ac.uk

Green Templeton College
At the Radcliffe Observatory
Woodstock Road, Oxford   OX2 6HG
 ↗ www.gtc.ox.ac.uk

Harris Manchester College
Mansfield Road, Oxford   OX1 3TD
 t   01865 271006
 ↗ www.hmc.ox.ac.uk

Hertford College
Catte Street, Oxford   OX1 3BW
 t   01865 279400
 ↗ www.hertford.ox.ac.uk

Jesus College
Turl Street, Oxford   OX1 3DW
 t   01865 279700
 ↗ www.jesus.ox.ac.uk

Keble College
Parks Road, Oxford   OX1 3PG
 t   01865 272727
 ↗ www.keble.ox.ac.uk

Kellogg College
62 Banbury Road, Oxford   OX2 6PN
 t   01865 612000
 ↗ www.kellogg.ox.ac.uk

Lady Margaret Hall
Norham Gardens, Oxford   OX2 6QA
 t   01865 274300
 ↗ www.lmh.ox.ac.uk

Linacre College
St Cross Road, Oxford   OX1 3JA
 t   01865 271650
 ↗ www.linacre.ox.ac.uk

Lincoln College
Turl Street, Oxford   OX1 3DR
 t   01865 279800
 ↗ www.lincoln.ox.ac.uk

Magdalen College
High Street, Oxford   OX1 4AU
 t   01865 276000
 ↗ www.magd.ox.ac.uk

Mansfield College
Mansfield Road, Oxford   OX1 3TF
 t   01865 270999
 ↗ www.mansfield.ox.ac.uk

Merton College
Merton Street, Oxford   OX1 4JD
 t   01865 276310
 ↗ www.merton.ox.ac.uk

New College
Holywell Street, Oxford   OX1 3BN
 t   01865 279555
 ↗ www.new.ox.ac.uk

Nuffield College
New Road, Oxford   OX1 1NF
t   01865 278500
↗ www.nuffield.ox.ac.uk

Oriel College
Oriel Square, Oxford   OX1 4EW
t   01865 276555
↗ www.oriel.ox.ac.uk

Pembroke College
St Aldate's, Oxford   OX1 1DW
t   01865 276444
↗ www.pmb.ox.ac.uk

The Queen's College
High Street, Oxford   OX1 4AW
t   01865 279120
↗ www.queens.ox.ac.uk

Regent's Park College
Pusey Street, Oxford   OX1 2LB
t   01865 288120
↗ www.rpc.ox.ac.u

St Anne's College
Woodstock Road, Oxford   OX2 6HS
t   01865 274800
↗ www.st-annes.ox.ac.uk

St Antony's College
Woodstock Road, Oxford   OX2 6FJ
t   01865 284 700
↗ www.sant.ox.ac.uk

St Catherine's College
Manor Road, Oxford   OX1 3UJ
t   01865 271700
↗ www.stcatz.ox.ac.uk

St Cross College
St Giles, Oxford   OX1 3LZ
t   01865 278490
↗ www.stx.ox.ac.uk

St Edmund Hall
Queen's Lane, Oxford   OX1 4AR
t   01865 279000
↗ www.seh.ox.ac.uk

St Hilda's College
Cowley Place, Oxford   OX4 1DY
t   01865 276884
↗ www.sthildas.ox.ac.uk

St Hugh's College
St Margaret's Road, Oxford   OX2 6LE
t   01865 274910
↗ www.st-hughs.ox.ac.uk

St John's College
St Giles, Oxford   OX1 3JP
t   01865 277300
↗ www.sjc.ox.ac.uk

St Peter's College
New Inn Hall Street, Oxford   OX1 2DL
t   01865 278900
↗ www.spc.ox.ac.uk

Somerville College
Woodstock Road
Oxford   OX2 6HD
t   01865 270600

Trinity College
Broad Street, Oxford   OX1 3BH
t   01865 279900
↗ www.trinity.ox.ac.uk

University College
High Street, Oxford   OX1 4BH
t   01865 276601
↗ www.univ.ox.ac.uk

Wadham College
Parks Road, Oxford   OX1 3PN
t   01865 277545
↗ www.wadham.ox.ac.uk

Wolfson College
Linton Road, Oxford   OX2 6UD
t   01865 274100
↗ www.wolfson.ox.ac.uk

Worcester College
Walton Street, Oxford   OX1 2HB
t   01865 278300
↗ www.worcester.ox.ac.uk

Oxford Brookes University

Headington Campus
Gipsy Lane, Headington
Oxford OX3 0BP

t 01865 484848
e query@brookes.ac.uk
↗ www.brookes.ac.uk

Westminster Institute of Education Harcourt Hill Campus, Oxford OX2 9AT
School of Health & Social Care Jack Straw Lane, Oxford OX3 0FL
Wheatley Campus Wheatley, Oxford OX33 1HX

» **further links**

ACCOMMODATION accomm@brookes.ac.uk
STUDENTS' UNION www.thesu.com

3015   71.3   37.0   11.9   92.0

Oxford

Brookes is rated one of the best newer universities. Its students are spread over three campuses: Headington and Harcourt Hill just out of the the city centre; Wheatley is seven miles away in the countryside. The modular degree system gives the opportunity to tailor-make your own course.

Fees £3,145 for full-time undergraduate courses in 2008–09.

Bursaries Awarded on a sliding scale according to family income, from £150 to £1,800.

Accommodation Not guaranteed for first-years – but last year all requests were met.

Facilities Separate facilities on each campus.

Transport A bus connects campuses. A bike or a bus pass will come in handy.

◀◀ STUDENT VIEW ▶▶

"Come to Brookes to live in a beautiful and buzzing city, to make great friends and have lots of fun, and to actually learn something that might be useful to you!"

University of Plymouth

Drake Circus
Plymouth PL4 8AA

t 01752 585858
e prospectus@plymouth.ac.uk
✎ www.plymouth.ac.uk

》 further links

ACCOMMODATION accommodation@plymouth.ac.uk
STUDENTS' UNION www.upsu.com

4480   93.0   31.8   16.4   90.8

Plymouth

Plymouth is one of the largest UK universities. A £35m complex housing the arts faculty opened recently. The main campus is a great seaside spot. Courses relating to the oceans are well-regarded. Where else could you find a degree in surf science?

Fees £3,145 for full-time undergraduate courses in 2008–09.

Bursaries £815 for those on a full grant, £300 for those with a household income from £25,001 to £37,000. Other bursaries and scholarships are also available.

Accommodation The university guarantees accommodation. All accommodation is managed or inspected by the university. Weekly cost in self-catered halls is £74 to £114, in private accommodation, £55 to £125.

Facilities Students have 24/7 access to computing and media areas and a new sports centre. Plymouth is the only UK university to have a diving and marine centre, and an internationally recognised diving qualification.

Transport The campus is in the city centre, with everything you need — including the coast — a short walk away. About three hours on the train to London; slightly longer by road.

❝ STUDENT VIEW ❞

"Plymouth is one of the most modern and innovative universities in the country, situated in arguably the most beautiful region in the country. The campus is not only trendy but practical and from a walk on the moors to a swim in the sea, Plymouth has it all."

University of Portsmouth

University House
Winston Churchill Avenue
Portsmouth PO1 2UP

t 02392 848484
e info-centre@port.ac.uk
↗ www.port.ac.uk

》 further links

ACCOMMODATION student.housing@port.ac.uk
STUDENTS' UNION www.upsu.net

3590   93.8   28.0   17.8   91.7

Portsmouth

Portsmouth is based on two sites: the Langstone campus is on the eastern edge of Portsea Island, and the University Quarter is the name given to the grouping of university buildings in the city centre, which include impressive modern buildings and green park space. Portsmouth is compact and easy to navigate, and the seaside location is a real plus. There are good opportunities for part-time and vacation work, not to mention an active careers service.

Fees £3,145 for full-time undergraduate courses in 2008–09.

Bursaries Up to £900 a year, means-tested. A further £300 is available to students from eligible local colleges. Other bursaries are also available.

Accommodation Most new students are able to find a place in halls for their first year. The weekly cost of self-catered accommodation is currently between £74 and £111.

Facilities Include a state-of-the-art newsroom for the journalism course and the new Expert centre, equipped with computerised mannequins that breathe, bleed and react to drugs (for people on health courses, not just for fun). The students' union is award-winning.

Transport London is just over an hour away. The station is near the university, so there's easy access to much of the rest of the south too.

❝ STUDENT VIEW ❞

"Portsmouth is large enough to supply the variety students want but small enough to feel like you know the place. The huge seafront draws a lot of people and it's a favourite with students who want to hang out on the beach or have long, lazy Saturdays on one of the many green seaside areas."

Queen Margaret University

Queen Margaret University Drive
Musselburgh EH21 6UU

t 0131 474 0000
e admissions@qmu.ac.uk
↗ www.qmu.ac.uk

》》 further links

ACCOMMODATION accommodation@qmu.ac.uk
STUDENTS' UNION www.qmusu.org.uk

950   91.9   28.4   19.6   94.1

Edinburgh

Edinburgh's fourth university, granted full status in 2007, is on a new, purpose-built campus in Musselburgh, just to the east of the city. There are some 6,000 students, almost 80 per cent of them women. There's an emphasis on vocational education and good graduate employment rates. The university values its supportive atmosphere and engagement with the community.

Fees Arrangements differ for students from Scotland and the rest of the UK.

Bursaries Young students' bursaries available for Scottish students under 25 from low-income families. Other funds available.

Accommodation Allocated by year of study, age and geographical distance from the university. Prices range from £91 to £96 a week.

Facilities The new campus has an innovative learning resource centre and sports facilities.

Transport The airport is eight miles away.

❝ STUDENT VIEW ❞

"The unique selling point about Queen Margaret is its size. It's small and friendly so it feels like everyone knows each other. It is also a new campus so the facilities are ultra-modern and eco-friendly!"

Queen Mary, University of London

327 Mile End Road
Poplar
London E1 4NS

t 020 7882 5555
e admissions@qmul.ac.uk
✐ www.qmul.ac.uk

》 **further links**

ACCOMMODATION residences@qmul.ac.uk
STUDENTS' UNION www.qmsu.org

2460   83.6   32.4   11.4   93.9

London

Queen Mary offers life on a contained campus, but in the middle of a huge city. The main campus is in London's Mile End. It's a multicultural area, and fittingly a fifth of students are from overseas. Beside good teaching and research, it is one of the best universities for student employability – and graduate starting salaries.

Fees £3,145 for full-time undergraduate courses in 2008-09.

Bursaries Around £1,000 for students with a full grant, and £800 for those on a partial grant. Further scholarships available.

Accommodation 2,355 places in university-owned accommodation, and more in University of London halls. £64 to £113 a week.

Facilities A state-of-the-art gym and fitness centre opens in September 2008.

Transport Easy access to the London transport system for travel between campuses, around the city and beyond.

❝ STUDENT VIEW ❞

"It's one of the few campus universities in London. It combines the appeal of being in the city with the idea that you are at university for more than just an academic education."

Queen's University Belfast

University Road
Belfast BT7 1NN

t 028 9024 5133
e comms.office@qub.ac.uk
↗ www.qub.ac.uk

》 further links

ACCOMMODATION accommodation@qub.ac.uk
STUDENTS' UNION www.qubsu.org

3995   99.5   34.4   12.9   96.9

Queen's has a good academic reputation. The campus is a 15-minute walk from the city centre, by the lovely botanical gardens and the Ulster Museum. Queen's takes its role in the community seriously: there's the annual Belfast festival, a film festival, art gallery and Northern Ireland's only arthouse cinema.

Fees £3,145 for full-time undergraduate courses in 2008-09.

Bursaries £1,025 for students on a full grant, £515 for with a partial grant. Other support too.

Accommodation Guaranteed for first-years, from £60 to £86 a week.

Facilities The students' union features a new WiFi-enabled social space. It hosts concerts and club nights. New sports facilities, too.

Transport Handy for the city centre. Most major British cities are within an hour's flying time from one of Belfast's two airports. These offer flights to many locations in Ireland and mainland Europe, and some direct services to North America. Regular ferry services to Scotland and England.

❝ STUDENT VIEW ❞
"A good education as well as a good social life to go with it. If you are willing to get involved, it's excellent."

Ravensbourne College of Design and Communication

Walden Road
Chislehurst
Kent BR7 5SN

t 020 8289 4900
e info@rave.ac.uk
↗ www.rave.ac.uk

》 further links

ACCOMMODATION info@rave.ac.uk
STUDENTS' UNION www.rave.ac.uk/life/student_union.htm

245　　96.6　　32.6　　15.4　　95.0

London

Apart from being the institution with the most memorable web address – www.rave.ac.uk – Ravensbourne is a single-campus college based in 7 hectares of parkland south-east of London, near Chislehurst in Kent. Courses are offered within two faculties – design, which includes fashion, interior design and product design, and communications media, where courses include broadcasting, graphic and sound design and animation. Degrees are validated by the University of Sussex.

Fees £3,145 for full-time undergraduate courses in 2008.

Bursaries £310 for students receiving a full grant. Other awards and support are available.

Accommodation 100 students can be accommodated. Rent is from £66 to £77 a week.

Facilities Students enjoy large open-plan studios and high-standard individual workspaces.

Transport Central London is just 20 minutes away by train, and there is easy access to Europe.

《 STUDENT VIEW 》

"Ravensbourne is really helpful in preparing you for a career. We are taught to really plan and think through what we're doing and follow up on our ideas."

University of Reading

Whiteknights
PO Box 217, Reading
Berkshire RG6 6AH

t 0118 987 5123
e student.recruitment@reading.ac.uk
↗ www.reading.ac.uk

》 further links

ACCOMMODATION accommodation@reading.ac.uk
STUDENTS' UNION www.rusu.co.uk

Reading

2490	83.6	24.0	7.4	93.0

Reading is a popular choice and claims to receive eight applications for each place. It's academically sound with an innovative slant to its course portfolio. Reading is an easy, liveable town with excellent facilities for shopping and leisure. It's about 45 miles west of London and transport links are good. The main Whiteknights campus has a lake, woodland and even meadows.

Fees £3,145 for full-time undergraduate courses in 2008.

Bursaries £1,350 bursary if household income less that £25,000; £900 if less than £35,000; £450 if less than £45,000. A wide range of other support and awards is available, including entrance scholarships of £2,000.

Accommodation Accommodation comprises both self-catered and catered halls and most first-years can be accommodated. Costs range from around £65 to £150 a week.

Facilities The library contains more than a million volumes, there's advanced electronic media available and online study resources.

Transport Located outside the M25, there's easy access to central London by train as well.

⁶⁶ STUDENT VIEW ⁹⁹

"Reading has the best of both worlds: a campus-based community which is minutes away from a buzzing town centre!"

UNIVERSITY PROFILES

Reading 341

Robert Gordon University

Schoolhill
Aberdeen AB10 1FR

t 01224 262000
e admissions@rgu.ac.uk
↗ www.rgu.ac.uk

》 further links

ACCOMMODATION accommodation@rgu.ac.uk
STUDENTS' UNION www.rguunion.co.uk

1510   93.5   38.2   18.3   97.8

● Aberdeen

RGU is a modern university of more than 13,000 students. The city-centre campus at Schoolhill is the hub of student life; a second campus lies three miles away at Garthdee. The emphasis at RGU is firmly on vocational and professional courses, and a wide range of placement options is on offer, both here and abroad. As a result, RGU has one of the best graduate recruitment records in the UK. Aberdeen is a smart and pleasant city with a cosmopolitan, wealthy feel, thanks to North Sea oil.

Fees Scottish and EU students from outside the UK pay no tuition fees. UK students' tuition fees will be £1,775 in 2008-09.

Bursaries Young students' bursaries for Scottish students under 25 from low-income families. Supplementary grants are also available for eligible students. A range of scholarships is available from some of the UK's largest companies, particularly for courses in engineering, computing and management. Sport scholarships are available, too.

Accommodation Guaranteed for non-local first-years. Rent from £62 to £81.50 a week.

Facilities RGU has invested over £10m in a sports facility.

Transport Transport between campuses is easy. Aberdeen is two-and-a-half hours' drive from Edinburgh or Glasgow, or take one of the regular trains. Seven hours by train from London.

❝ STUDENT VIEW 》
"It's a place where anything seems and is possible, and a place to learn, love and have fun."

Roehampton University

Erasmus House
Roehampton Lane
London SW15 5PU

t 020 8392 3232
e enquiries@roehampton.ac.uk
↗ www.roehampton.ac.uk

》 further links

ACCOMMODATION accommodation@roehampton.ac.uk
STUDENTS' UNION www.roehamptonstudent.com

2215   94.0   34.3   20.2   93.7

London

Roehampton is a campus university based in a scenic parkland location overlooking Richmond park. The campus is close to the chi-chi London districts of Richmond and Putney, and central London is easily accessible by train. Significant proportions of Roehampton's 8,000 students are mature or from an ethnic minority, and women outnumber men by three to one.

Fees £3,145 a year for all full-time undergraduate courses in 2008.

Bursaries £500 for full-time UK students in receipt of a full or partial maintenance grant. Other scholarships and awards available.

Accommodation Most first-years can live in university accommodation on or near campus. Costs range from £86 to £104 a week.

Facilities The library contains a cybercafe, there are innovative teaching facilities and sports resources are enjoying multimillion pound development work.

Transport Only 20 minutes to London by train. From there, the world's your oyster.

❝ STUDENT VIEW ❞

"Although Roehampton is on the doorstep of cosmopolitan London, it doesn't quite feel like it because of the tranquil setting. But more pace and excitement is just a bus ride away. We're all one site, so everyone mixes — and the vibe is so welcoming that you can't help but be yourself."

Rose Bruford College

Burnt Oak Lane
Sidcup
Kent DA15 9DF

t 020 8308 2600
e enquiries@bruford.ac.uk
↗ www.bruford.ac.uk

》 further links

ACCOMMODATION 020-8308 2638
STUDENTS' UNION www.student-union.org.uk/
Rose-Bruford-College-Student-Union.htm

195   88.9   23.1   15.8   95.3

London

Rose Bruford is a drama school based in attractive grounds near Sidcup, Kent, on the outskirts of south-east London. It offers a range of degree courses in theatre and performance, validated by the University of Manchester. Facilities include two theatres – the 330-seat Rose and the Barn theatre – as well as studios for rehearsals, design, lectures, teaching and recording, plus lighting labs and workshops.

Fees £3,070 for full-time undergraduate courses.

Bursaries Eligible students can apply for a bursary of around £300. Other awards are available.

Accommodation There are limited places available for first-years in university-owned accommodation at a price of around £85 a week.

Facilities There's an extensive library, including impressive specialist collections. Unsurprisingly, facilities for performance are good.

Transport 25 minutes into London.

Royal Academy of Music

Marylebone Road
London NW1 5HT

t 020 7873 7373
e registry@ram.ac.uk
↗ www.ram.ac.uk

》 further links

ACCOMMODATION www.lon.ac.uk/halls
STUDENTS' UNION www.ram.ac.uk/whoswho/Students+Union

| 45 | 47.7 | 16.7 | 16.3 | 97.1 |

Founded in 1822, the Royal Academy is one of the oldest and most prestigious conservatoires (schools of music) in the UK. It is based in upmarket Marylebone, central London, and musicians study for University of London degrees in varying programmes of study including instrumental performance, composition, jazz, musical theatre and opera. A huge range of orchestras and ensembles give public performances in spaces such as the 400-seat Dukes Hall. The student community is international, with more than 50 countries represented.

Fees £3,145 for full-time undergraduate programmes in 2008.

Bursaries Means-tested bursaries are available, as well as other awards and scholarships.

Accommodation The academy cannot provide accommodation, but students can apply for a place in one of the University of London's halls.

Facilities Truly impressive facilities for performance and rehearsal.

Transport The academy is in the heart of London, providing easy access to all parts of the city and beyond.

⟨⟨ STUDENT VIEW 》》

"You learn so much so quickly here. The one-to-one lessons are incredibly valuable but you also have time to figure out how you want to develop yourself. There are so many opportunities to perform and make music and the other people you meet are amazing."

Royal Agricultural College

Stroud Road
Cirencester GL7 6JS

t 01285 652531
e admissions@rac.ac.uk
↗ www.rac.ac.uk

>> **further links**

ACCOMMODATION lettings@rac.ac.uk

165   42.8   37.3   19.8   91.5

Cirencester

The Royal Agricultural College is a single-campus university college in Cirencester, Gloucestershire, which offers BSc honours degrees in agriculture, business, equine management and land management. Situated in an Oxbridge-style quadrangle in attractive parkland, the college is a charming place to live and study.

Fees £3,145 for full-time undergraduate courses in 2008.

Bursaries Students are entitled to a means-tested bursary of up to £1,500.

Accommodation The college has study bedrooms for up to 300 students. Costs vary. There is a lettings service to help students find private-sector accommodation in Cirencester.

Facilities Facilities include three working commercial farms with a 250-cow dairy herd, a 1,650-ewe breeding flock, and 250 hectares of crops including organic produce.

Transport From Cirencester there's easy public transport.

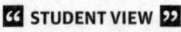 **STUDENT VIEW** >>

"I've met some great friends here and there's an excellent feeling on campus. The course is varied enough to keep anyone interested and the resources are good too."

Royal College of Music

Prince Consort Road
London SW7 2BS

t 020 7859 3643
e info@rcm.ac.uk
↗ www.rcm.ac.uk

》 further links

ACCOMMODATION collegehall@rcm.ac.uk
STUDENTS' UNION No SU web address

65   1.9   98.1

London

London's Royal College of Music is one of the top conservatoires in the country, attracting more than 600 students from 49 countries. The undergraduate BMus lasts for four years; tuition covers up to 90 minutes a week of principal study, plus extra options and ensemble activities. There is also a BSc in physics with studies in musical performance, taught at both RCM and Imperial. Facilities are top-notch and the RCM is aware that it has a duty to prepare students for viable careers in a difficult industry.

Fees £3,145 for full-time undergraduate courses in 2008.

Bursaries £1,000 a year for students receiving a maintenance grant of between £2,410 and £2,835.

Accommodation The college has a hall of residence, College Hall, near Ravenscourt Park in west London. It sleeps about 170 students, and includes practice rooms. Fees are around £65 to £115 per week including bills.

Facilities Facilities include the 400-seat Britten Theatre and the RCM's digital studios.

Transport Very easy: you're in the middle of London.

❝ STUDENT VIEW ❞
"It's full of like-minded people who want to have a great time as well as making great music."

Royal Holloway, University of London

Egham
Surrey TW20 0EX

t 01784 434455
e admissions@rhul.ac.uk
↗ www.rhul.ac.uk

》 further links

ACCOMMODATION accommodation@rhul.ac.uk
STUDENTS' UNION www.surhul.co.uk

| 1320 | 74.7 | 22.2 | 11.8 | 96.3 |

Though part of the University of London and within easy reach of the capital, Royal Holloway is actually based in Egham, Surrey, giving a sense of space and calm. The campus is 55 hectares of parkland within walking distance of Windsor Great Park. Teaching and research are both of the highest order and graduates enjoy a good graduate employment rate.

Fees £3,145 a year for all full-time undergraduate courses in 2008-09.

Bursaries £750-a-year bursaries for all students who qualify for partial or full grants. Other awards for excellence are also available.

Accommodation Prioritised for eligible first-years. Prices range from around £65 to £125 a week, with a choice of self-catering or catered.

Facilities Victorian Boilerhouse Theatre and the state-of-the-art lecture hall add to the architectural merit of the campus.

Transport Well serviced by road and rail, not least because London is less than 20 miles away.

❝ STUDENT VIEW ❞

"If you want to get a meaningful degree, live in a safe area with good quality social life, and nice facilities, then give Royal Holloway some serious consideration. The campus environment is kept very green which makes it a good place to relax in too."

Royal Northern College of Music

124 Oxford Road
Manchester M13 9RD

t 0161 907 5200
e info@rncm.ac.uk
↗ www.rncm.ac.uk

》 further links

ACCOMMODATION 0161 907 5219
STUDENTS' UNION http://www.rncmsu.co.uk

110   7.1   98.7

Manchester

The Royal Northern College of Music is based in a single building in the south of Manchester. Students take the four-year BMus in order to develop their performance or composition skills to professional standards — but the course also includes "supporting professional studies", such as the music business or teaching, plus "academic studies", which relate theoretical studies to practice. There is a huge range of ensembles, plus programmes in opera, chamber music and early music.

Fees £3,145 for full-time undergraduate courses in 2008-09.

Bursaries Up to £1,050, means tested. Scholarships are also available.

Accommodation The college has a hall of residence two minutes' walk away with places for 316 students. Costs are £87.25 per week.

Facilities The 616-capacity Bruntwood Theatre is one of the largest performance spaces in Manchester.

Transport Well serviced by road and rail. Oxford Road station is eight minutes' walk and London is two-and-a-half hours by train. Manchester airport is 15 minutes away.

《 STUDENT VIEW 》

"Whatever direction you want to take as a musician, you can find a platform to express and develop your interests. There are always students willing to collaborate. I've learned so much through working with my peers, tutors and staff of the college at many different levels, from performing to promoting and everything in-between."

Royal Scottish Academy of Music and Drama

100 Renfrew Street
Glasgow G2 3DB

t 0141 332 4101
e musicadmissions@rsamd.ac.uk
dramaadmissions@rsamd.ac.uk
⌘ www.rsamd.ac.uk

》 further links

ACCOMMODATION www.libertyliving.co.uk
STUDENTS' UNION www.rsamd-su.co.uk

165   89.2   10.1   94.1

Glasgow

RSAMD in Glasgow now attracts students from more than 20 countries. Music courses include the four-year BMus, plus a BEd for prospective music teachers and a BA in Scottish music. Drama courses include acting, digital film and technical arts; there is also a four-year BA in contemporary theatre.

Fees Undergraduate full-time fees will be £1,775 for new entrants, though Scottish students have this paid for them.

Bursaries Scholarships and bursaries are available.

Accommodation All first-year students can be accommodated by LibertyLiving, a private student halls provider. Rates are between £95 and £150 a week.

Facilities Facilities and venues include the Sir Alexander Gibson Opera School and the 344-seat New Athenaeum Theatre, plus a studio theatre and concert hall.

Transport Easily accessible from major roads. The airport is handy, as are the stations.

❝ STUDENT VIEW ❞

"Studying here has really allowed my own skills as a performer to develop: the support, encouragement and inspiration from teachers and other students is great. With so many creative people all studying and living together, there's always something going on!"

Royal Veterinary College

Royal College Street
London NW1 0TU

t 020 7468 5149
e registry@rvc.ac.uk
↗ www.rvc.ac.uk

Hawkshead Campus Hawkshead Lane, North Mymms, Hatfield, Hertfordshire AL9 7TA

》 further links

ACCOMMODATION www.lon.ac.uk/halls
STUDENTS' UNION No web address currently

310   76.3   24.9   1.8   99.3

Part of the University of London, and founded in 1791, the RVC was the UK's first veterinary school. It remains the largest and is based at two campuses: Camden, north London, and Hawkshead in Hertfordshire. Undergraduates can choose from the BVetMed, a five-year programme leading to qualification as a vet; a BSc in bioveterinary sciences for students looking for a career in the biotechnological, agricultural and pharmaceutical industries as well as organisations such as the Institute of Animal Health; and a foundation degree or BSc in veterinary nursing. Students may also take a "gateway" course, which leads on to the first year of the veterinary medicine degree.

Fees Tuition fees for full-time undergraduates are £3,145 for 2008-09.

Bursaries In 2008-09 the college will provide bursaries for undergraduates who qualify for a maintenance grant, up to £1750. It is also introducing merit scholarships to the value of £3,000 for every year of the course.

Accommodation RVC can provide places in halls for 95 per cent of first-year undergraduates, either in self-catering facilities or catered intercollegiate halls. Charges in 2008-09 ranged from £110 to £117.60 a week, but self-catering halls have a 50-week minimum let.

Facilities Research and treatment facilities are used by the profession, meaning students have access to top-class resources.

Transport Located in and around London, providing easy access to and from all campuses and to other parts of the city and beyond.

❝ STUDENT VIEW 》

"The course is demanding and the standards are high – but you know you're getting a good education. The college has great resources and the central location is a big bonus. There's always a buzz in the air."

Royal Welsh College of Music & Drama

Castle Grounds
Cathays Park
Cardiff CF10 3ER

t 029 2034 2854
e music.admissions@rwcmd.ac.uk
     drama.admissions@rwcmd.ac.uk
↗ www.rwcmd.ac.uk

》 further links

ACCOMMODATION studentservices@rwcmd.ac.uk
STUDENTS' UNION www.rwcmd.ac.uk/international
                _students/student_life.asp

Cardiff

This highly respected music and drama school is based in Cardiff, a thriving centre for the creative industries. Its campus is in the city centre, in the grounds of Cardiff Castle. The college has 640 students. It offers four undergraduate degrees, a three-year BA in acting, theatre design or stage management, plus the four-year BMus. The events calendar includes more than 300 public performances annually.

Fees Undergraduate fees for 2008–09 will be £3,145.

Bursaries Competitive entry scholarships are available for up to the full amount of the tuition fee. The National Bursary Scheme in Wales means students in receipt of a full maintenance grant get another £310.

Accommodation New students are guaranteed a room in halls and cost £79.95 a week for a 42-week contract including bills. Private-sector rents are around £220 a month, and a Find-A-Friend service helps you find fellow students to share with.

Facilities Facilities include the Anthony Hopkins Centre, two recital galleries, studio theatres, a recording studio, courtyard performance space, Bute Theatre, workshops and 50 music practice rooms.

Transport Cardiff airport is nearby, there is a coach service to London and frequent trains.

❝ STUDENT VIEW ❞
"Be prepared: the course is tough. But it's a great start for a career in the industry. The social life on campus is very active and Cardiff is a great place to go out."

University of St Andrews

St Andrews
Fife KY16 9AJ
Scotland

t 01334 476161
e student.recruitment@st-andrews.ac.uk
↗ www.st-andrews.ac.uk

》 further links

ACCOMMODATION studacc@st-and.ac.uk
STUDENTS' UNION www.yourunion.net

1155   60.9   15.2   5.0   94.8

St Andrews is a prestigious academic centre renowned for the quality of its teaching and research and has a reputation for being a bit posh. Prince William did study here, after all, there's a high independent-school intake and a raft of arcane traditions. But St Andrews does have an active commitment to widening access. It's certainly popular with applicants and has one of the lowest drop-out rates in the UK. The location is special – a small, historical town tucked up on the coast of north-east Scotland.

Fees Scottish and EU students from outside the UK pay no tuition fees. For other UK students, tuition s of £1,735 (£2,760 for medicine).

Bursaries Subject-based scholarships are available. Scholarships awarded on the basis of financial need for UK and EU students. Other bursaries and awards available.

Accommodation Guaranteed for eligible first-years. Prices range from around £54 to £162.

Facilities The university spends about £1.4m on books and journals each year. Sports facilities extend over 25 hectares.

Transport St Andrews is a walking town: you can get from one end to the other in under an hour. The nearest train station is Leuchars, which is on the main train line from London via Edinburgh. The nearest city is Dundee, approximately 30 minutes by bus or car. Edinburgh is 50 miles south and can be reached by bus, train or car. There is a small airport at Dundee and an international airport at Edinburgh.

❝ STUDENT VIEW ❞

"A small town means you have to make your own fun. You can walk across town in 25 minutes, taking a break for ice cream halfway, so the onus is on you to be inventive in finding means of procrastination or to join one of the many societies that make things happen in town."

St George's, University of London

Cranmer Terrace
London SW17 0RE

t 020 8672 9944
e See individual courses on the website
for contact details
↗ www.sgul.ac.uk

》 further links

ACCOMMODATION www.sgul.ac.uk/halls
STUDENTS' UNION www.student.sgul.ac.uk

555   77.1   25.0   4.1   99.0

London

St George's is one of the UK's best-known medical schools, and shares a site with
St George's Hospital in Tooting, south London. As well as the five-year course in
medicine, St George's offers degrees in health sciences (diagnostic or therapeutic
radiography and physiotherapy), biomedical informatics, biomedical sciences,
nursing, midwifery, social work, and a four- or five-year MPharm in pharmacy.

Fees £3,145 for full-time undergraduate courses in 2008.

Bursaries Between £1,230 and £155 for students entitled to a full or partial maintenance grant,
on a sliding scale.

Accommodation Rooms in halls cost from around £65 to £95 a week. For the past few years it
has been able to accommodate all students who wanted a room.

Facilities Specialist library resources and overnight computer access. There's a huge range of
clinical study material to work with, courtesy of St George's.

Transport It's in London, near Tooting Broadway underground station, so good for transport.

❝ STUDENT VIEW ❞

*"The course is great and there is always help there when you need it. You can immerse yourself in the
theory and you're learning the hands-on skills you'll need in the job too. The student community is very
close and friendly."*

St Mary's University College, Belfast

191 Falls Road
Belfast BT12 6FE

t 02890 268320
↗ www.stmarys-belfast.ac.uk

》 further links

ACCOMMODATION 02890 327678
STUDENTS' UNION www.smsu.co.uk

250   100.0   43.9   4.9   95.0

St Mary's is a college of Queen's University Belfast that mostly provides teacher training in the Catholic tradition. It currently offers undergraduate degrees in primary or secondary education (including specific subject studies), and a three-year BA in liberal arts, which includes modules in human development studies, Ireland in Europe, and options from a range of humanities subjects including Gaeilge (Gaelic) and religious studies.

Fees £3,145 for full-time undergraduate courses.

Bursaries Students in receipt of a full grant will receive a bursary of £1,230, while those getting a partial grant will receive a bursary of £515.

Accommodation Accommodation is available either in the private sector or in halls at Stranmillis University College or Queen's University Belfast itself.

Facilities There's a modern library and computing facilites; students are also entitled to use computing resources at Queen's University Belfast.

Transport Frequent buses to the bus and rail centre two miles away. Central station is 15 minutes by bus. Belfast's airports are easily accessible.

⁴⁴ STUDENT VIEW ⁷⁷

"You get to meet lots of different people in a friendly community. My course has been challenging and interesting and now is a great time to live in Belfast. I love it!"

St Mary's University College Twickenham

Waldegrave Road
Strawberry Hill
Twickenham TW1 4SX

t 020 8240 4000
e admit@smuc.ac.uk
↗ www.smuc.ac.uk

》》 further links

ACCOMMODATION   accommodation@smuc.ac.uk
STUDENTS' UNION   www.smuc.ac.uk/Life-and-support
/Lifestyle/SU.htm

990   94.5   37.6   12.8   96.8

London

St Mary's University College was founded in 1850 as a Catholic teacher-training college, and about a third of its students still take teaching courses, including PGCEs. Other courses include coaching science, drama, film and TV, health and exercise, various sports degrees, history and management studies. Its 2,500 undergraduates gave it good ratings in recent national student surveys. St Mary's was granted its own degree-awarding powers in 2006 and is making plans to slightly increase its size to gain university status.

Fees   £3,145 for full-time undergraduate courses in 2008.

Bursaries   All students are eligible for £310, and up to £700, means tested.

Accommodation   First-years are generally guaranteed accommodation. Prices vary.

Facilities   Good sports facilities — it is the Institute of Sports' leading centre in London. The college has also been identified as a training base for the 2012 Olympics.

Transport   Trains to Waterloo Station from Strawberry Hill every 35 minutes. Or take the train to Richmond underground station from where you can travel in on the district line. The M3 and M4 are close by.

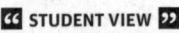 **STUDENT VIEW 》》**

"The course is well structured and the facilities are good.
There's always a chance to chat to other students and teachers too."

University of Salford

Salford
Greater Manchester M5 4WT

t 0161 295 5000
e course-enquiries@salford.ac.uk
↗ www.salford.ac.uk

>> **further links**

ACCOMMODATION www.accommodation.salford.ac.uk
STUDENTS' UNION www.salfordstudents.com

3365   96.7   34.3   25.4   91.2

The university has an attractive waterside location in vastly regenerated Salford.
It's about a mile-and-a-half from Manchester city centre. Just under 20,000 students
study here, with many international students among them. Courses are created
with future careers in mind, and there are some interesting options to choose from.

Fees £3,145 for full-time undergraduate students in 2008.

Bursaries £310 for students in receipt of a full maintenance grant. Further bursaries for
excellence, in particular subjects and for local students are also available, among others.

Accommodation Cost of accommodation per week is £53.27 to £74.69, among the lowest in the
country. University accommodation is guaranteed for all students provided they have accepted an
unconditional offer of admission to the university and have submitted an online application form
by the deadline.

Facilities The leisure centre is open seven days a week. There are five libraries and good access
to computers.

Transport It has excellent transport links, with Salford Crescent railway station on campus and a
regular bus service. It is only a couple of minutes' drive from the motorway network and less than
20 minutes' drive from Manchester international airport. The university provides a free bus
service between the campus buildings and the student accommodation.

‹‹ STUDENT VIEW ››

*"Salford has all the best bits of the other Manchester unis, culture to rival Oxford, nightlife to rival Sheffield,
history to rival York, and then adds a little something extra. I think it's called being in Salford!"*

School of Oriental and African Studies (Soas)

Thornhaugh Street
Russell Square
London WC1H 0XG

t 020 7637 2388
e study@soas.ac.uk
↗ www.soas.ac.uk

》 further links

ACCOMMODATION www.sshl.org.uk
STUDENTS' UNION www.soasunion.org

540   70.1   20.9   15.6   94.1

London

Soas is part of the University of London and enjoys a central location in student-centric Bloomsbury, with a second campus a short distance away near King's Cross. It's the UK's only higher education institution to focus on the languages, cultures and societies of Africa, Asia and the Middle East, with a worldwide reputation for its teaching and research. There are around 4,000 students (about half of them are postgraduates) representing 100 countries, making for a close-knit, cosmopolitan and fascinating student population, with great student-to-teacher ratios.

Fees £3145 for full time undergraduate courses in 2008.

Bursaries £720 for students who receive the maximum maintenance grant. £410 for students who receive a partial maintenance grant.

Accommodation First-years are accommodated wherever possible and Soas has access to a range of halls of residence — both its own and intercollegiate University of London halls. Costs vary, but anticipate around £100 a week.

Facilities The library is recognised as a collection of national importance and IT provision is very good.

Transport It's very central, near Euston, St Pancras and King's Cross.

〈〈 STUDENT VIEW 〉〉

"Most begin at Soas with a keen interest in the non-Western world. Everyone leaves with a plethora of obscure knowledge, a yearning for more, and a desire to make a positive mark on the world. Soas attracts a wide assortment of personalities who converge to discover and take pleasure in a fusion of world food, music, religion, culture, and ideas and immerse themselves in the uniqueness of the Soas bubble."

School of Pharmacy

29-39 Brunswick Square
London WC1N 1AX

t 020 7753 5800
e registry@pharmacy.ac.uk
↗ www.pharmacy.ac.uk

》 further links

ACCOMMODATION www.lon.ac.uk/halls
STUDENTS' UNION www.pharmacy.ac.uk/395.html

160   82.8   33.0   4.9   100.0

Part of the University of London, this specialist's only undergraduate degree is the Master of Pharmacy, or MPharm, which entitles graduates, after a further year of pre-registration training, to sit Royal Pharmaceutical Society exams and register as a pharmacist. Students can choose specialist options or undertake a research project, and there is also a chance to study abroad in the third year. The college is based in Bloomsbury, in the heart of London.

Fees £3,145 for full-time undergraduate courses in 2008.

Bursaries Students receiving the full maintenance grant will be eligible for at least £500, and then on a sliding scale. Students will be eligible for the same amount again if they achieve certain high grades at A-level.

Accommodation Students from outside London can apply to live in intercollegiate halls. Most first-years are allocated a place.

Facilities You can join two student unions: the school's own and the University of London Union, a 10-minute walk away. ULU has great sports and recreational facilities. Teaching facilities are state of the art.

Transport Located in the heart of London.

Scottish Agricultural College

Edinburgh Campus
King's Buildings, West Mains Road
Edinburgh EH9 3JG

t 0800 269453
e recruitment@sac.ac.uk
↗ www.sac.ac.uk

Aberdeen Campus Craibstone Estate, Aberdeen AB21 9YA
Ayr Campus Auchincruive, Ayr KA6 5HW

>> **further links**

ACCOMMODATION Edinburgh, 0131 535 4041/49, 0131 535 4391
Aberdeen 01224 711012; Ayr 01292 525203
STUDENTS' UNION No SU web address

SAC offers courses designed to support the land-based industries and rural economy. Courses range from agriculture to business studies, environment, conservation, garden design and tourism. SAC has three campuses across Scotland – in Edinburgh, Aberdeen, and Ayr.

Fees Scottish students pay no fees. £1,735 for students from elsewhere in the UK in 2007.

Bursaries Scottish students benefit from a range of support from the Scottish executive, but SAC itself also has a limited "centenary bursary" of up to £2,000.

Accommodation In Edinburgh, some first-year students can be accommodated in University of Edinburgh halls (average price is around £90 per week). In Aberdeen and Ayr there are self-catering halls of residence, and most first-years can be accommodated. Costs are £80 a week in Aberdeen and £54 in Ayr.

Facilities SAC has farms distributed around Scotland, with organic, livestock, arable and dairy farming represented. Science courses at SAC are supported by modern, well-equipped teaching laboratories and each campus has its own library.

Transport Good. Even the airport is pretty close.

66 STUDENT VIEW 99

"I wanted a course that would prepare me for the career I wanted, and that's what I've found. It's exceeded my expectations. There's a friendly atmosphere and the campus is really lovely."

University of Sheffield

Western Bank
Sheffield S10 2TN

t 0114 222 1255
e ug.admissions@sheffield.ac.uk
↗ www.sheffield.ac.uk

》 further links

ACCOMMODATION studentoffice@sheffield.ac.uk
STUDENTS' UNION www.shef.ac.uk/union

| 4475 | 83.8 | 21.3 | 6.8 | 94.3 | Sheffield |

Sheffield is always a popular choice, and the university has almost 24,000 students. The student media are especially well thought of. University buildings are clustered close together about a mile to the west of the city centre. The clubbing here is particularly good. Sheffield has a strong academic reputation and provides good career prospects.

Fees £3,145 a year for all full-time undergraduate courses in 2008.

Bursaries There are three types of bursary available: income, prior achievement and outreach. You may qualify for one or all three. First, income-based: £680 a year for those from a household with income below £16,785, £420 a year for those from a household with income between £16,785 and £34,615. Second, prior achievement: up to £1,625 dependent on A-grades at A-level, subject of study and household income. Those with a household income of less than £16,785 who achieve three A grades at A-level get the full £1,625 regardless of subject of study. Third, the outreach bursary scheme awards up to £840 to eligible students.

Accommodation Guaranteed for eligible, non-local first-years. Catered accommodation from £98 to £130 a week, self-catering from £70 to £110 a week.

Facilities The students' union is award-winning and has great facilities and events.

Transport The central position makes it good for getting around the country and there's a decent local public transport system.

❝ STUDENT VIEW ❞

"It's the UK's greenest city so it's got plenty of parks and open spaces. In general, the teaching staff are extremely helpful and committed to their subject. Definitely consider studying at Sheffield!"

Sheffield Hallam University

City Campus
Howard Street
Sheffield S1 1WB

t 0114 225 5555
e enquiries@shu.ac.uk
↗ www.shu.ac.uk

》 **further links**

ACCOMMODATION accommodation@shu.ac.uk
STUDENTS' UNION www.hallamunion.shu.ac.uk

| 5240 | 95.5 | 32.6 | 12.9 | 91.5 |

With 30,000 students, Sheffield Hallam is one of the largest universities in the country. It's based on two campuses, one in the bustling city centre and the other in the leafy suburbs. The university takes its links with business seriously, and has England's largest number of students on courses with work placements. Sheffield has great facilities and good transport links. It claims to be the greenest city in England, and is within easy reach of Leeds, Manchester and the Peak District.

Fees £3,145 for full-time undergraduate courses in 2008.

Bursaries £700 for eligible students in receipt of at least £1,000 in maintenance support. An access bursary of £300 is also available for students from certain schools.

Accommodation Guaranteed for first-years in either university-owned, partnership or privately owned accommodation. Prices are reasonable.

Facilities Good learning and teaching facilities, a lively students' union, plentiful sports provision and one of the UK's leading universities in e-learning.

Transport Easy to hop on a train to London, Leeds or Manchester. Good public transport.

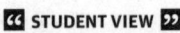 **STUDENT VIEW** 》
"You are not too far from bigger cities like Leeds and Manchester and not too far away from the Peaks if you want to escape to the countryside. It's a great place to go out, meet people, and socialise."

University of Southampton

Highfield Campus
University Road
Southampton SO17 1BJ

t 023 8059 5000
e prospenq@soton.ac.uk
↗ www.soton.ac.uk

Bodrewood Campus Biomedical Sciences Building, Bassett Crescent East, Southampton SO16 7PX

Southampton General Hospital Tremona Road, Southampton SO16 6YD

National Oceanography Centre Waterfront Campus, European Way, Southampton SO14 3ZH

Winchester School of Art Park Avenue, Winchester SO23 8DL

》 further links

accommodation@soton.ac.uk
STUDENTS' UNION www.susu.org

3525   82.7   20.0   8.5   93.7

Southampton

Founded in 1952, Southampton is an innovative university with a diverse student population. Its main Highfield campus is located two miles from the centre, with other sites spread across Southampton and Winchester. The active students' union recently launched a TV station to accompany its award-winning radio station. The National Oceanography Centre is here, and the university performs well academically on all fronts.

Fees £3,145 for all full-time undergraduate courses in 2008.

Bursaries £1,000 a year for UK undergraduate students from families earning less than £25,000; £500 a year for students from families earning between £25,001 and £32,000. A wide range of other bursaries are also available. Many subject-specific scholarships.

Accommodation Guaranteed for eligible first-years. Part-catered halls or flats: £101.85 to £145.60 a week.

Facilities Highfield Campus hosts three internationally celebrated arts venues, there are seven libraries and around 1,700 Windows PCs in dedicated rooms in all halls and on all campuses.

Transport Good train and motorway links.

❝ STUDENT VIEW ❞

"Southampton has a strong and increasing academic credibility, it's a great place with great people and a lot to do. Anyone can come to Southampton, get involved, and come out the other side a better person for it."

Southampton Solent University

East Park Terrace
Southampton SO14 0YN

t 0845 6767000
e enquiries@solent.ac.uk
↗ www.solent.ac.uk

》 further links

ACCOMMODATION accommodation@solent.ac.uk
STUDENTS' UNION www.solentsu.co.uk

| 2680 | 96.0 | 35.5 | 17.0 | 93.5 |

Southampton

Southampton Solent is one of the UK's newest universities, based in a lively city on the south coast. It is a modern university, with more than 17,000 students on work-related courses. It's close to the city centre and the waterfront. Unsurprisingly, maritime studies is a particular strength here, including courses in the design of yachts and small craft. Graduate employment rates are a particular source of pride.

Fees £3,145 for full-time undergraduate courses.

Bursaries £1,050 for students with a household income of less than £18,360, then on a descending sliding scale. Other awards are also available.

Accommodation Southampton Solent expects to be able to provide accommodation for all first-years who request it. Prices from £84.50 to £99.95 a week.

Facilities The university has a large sports centre and its own newly opened watersports centre at Warsash, on the river Hamble. An innovative "laptops for loan" service enables students to borrow laptops with the specific software packages they need for their course, from word processing to design software.

Transport The city has excellent transport links by road, rail and air, thanks to the nearby Southampton international airport.

❝ STUDENT VIEW ❞
"The best place to be for an all-round university experience. Its location, the nightlife, and the sports are amazing. It's everything you want from your university."

Staffordshire University

College Road
Stoke-on-Trent
Staffordshire ST4 2DE

t 01782 294000
e admissions@staffs.ac.uk
↗ www.staffs.ac.uk

Leek Road Campus Stoke-on-Trent ST4 2DF
Stafford Campus Beaconside, Stafford ST18 0AD
Lichfield Campus The Friary, Lichfield, Staffordshire WS13 6QG

》 further links

ACCOMMODATION www.staffs.ac.uk/study_here/student_services
/accommodation/index.jsp
STUDENTS' UNION www.staffsunion.com

2575   97.7   36.6   19.2   90.7

The university is located on two main campuses, in Stoke and Stafford, with a satellite campus in Lichfield. The Stoke campus lies close to the centre of Stoke-on-Trent, with easy access to the railway station and amenities. The Stafford campus is a mile-and-a-half from Stafford town centre — a lively and picturesque market town. The business-orientated Lichfield campus lies 15 miles from Stafford and is set near to the beautiful cathedral city. The university boasts a lively students' union and the cost of living in the area is relatively low. In total, there are around 15,500 students.

Fees Currently £3,000 a year for all full-time undergraduate courses.

Bursaries If your family income is £20,817 or less, you will be eligible for a £1,000 bursary a year; between £20,818 and £25,521, you will be eligible for £850 a year; between £25,522 and £30,810 you will be eligible to receive £500 a year.

Accommodation University-managed accommodation costs around £80 a week for ensuite rooms and around £55 a week for standard rooms.

Facilities Facilities include a professionally equipped media centre, music, film, TV and radio studios, a crime-scene house, nature reserve, drama studio and mock courtroom.

Transport Stoke station is a minute away and has pretty good links in all directions.

❝ STUDENT VIEW ❞

"Staffs prepares you for the real world and really supports everyone. It's given me some great life experiences — I've made loads of mates, got involved in lots of activities, learned the value of budgeting and managing my time and I am generally having a great time."

University of Stirling

Stirling FK9 4LA

t 01786 473171
e admissions@stir.ac.uk
↗ www.stir.ac.uk

》 further links

ACCOMMODATION www.studaccom.stir.ac.uk
STUDENTS' UNION www.susaonline.org.uk

| 1345 | 91.7 | 26.2 | 7.6 | 95.9 |

Stirling's campus is set in 120 hectares at the foot of the Ochil Hills. It boasts its own loch. Stirling, three miles away, is also pretty, with a castle and old town. There are excellent facilities for sport and a recently refurbished arts centre on campus. There are around 6,000 students. Many are local, but there's also a good representation of international students. Stirling is proud of the flexibility of its degrees: with no faculty boundaries, students can choose from a very wide variety of subject combinations.

Fees Scottish and EU students from outside the UK pay no tuition fees. For other UK students, annual tuition fee of £1,735.

Bursaries Young students' bursaries for Scottish students under 25 from lower-income groups. Other grants also available, plus a range of scholarships.

Accommodation All first-years are guaranteed accommodation should they want it. Weekly prices from £59.45 to £88.

Facilities There are 24-hour computer labs, the MacRobert arts centre with theatre and cinema, extensive sports facilities and a publicly accessible art collection.

Transport Stirling is well connected to the UK road and rail networks and is only 45 minutes from both Edinburgh and Glasgow.

❝ STUDENT VIEW ❞

"Stirling combines excellent history, beautiful scenery, a modern outlook, and a variety of courses. And there's a lovely loch!"

Stranmillis

Belfast BT9 5DY

t 028 9038 1271
↗ www.stran.ac.uk

》 further links

ACCOMMODATION www.stran.ac.uk/informationfor/undergraduatestudents
/studentservices/accommodationcatering

STUDENTS' UNION www.stran.ac.uk/informationfor/undergraduatestudents
/studentservices/studentsunion

| 275 | 100.0 | 32.9 | 4.1 | 90.5 |

Stranmillis is a college of Queen's University Belfast, offering three undergraduate degrees: a BEd in either primary or post-primary education, a BA in early childhood studies and a BSc in health and leisure studies. Its campus is based in a conservation area one mile south of the city centre. The college is proud of being an inter-faith institution.

Fees £3,145 for full-time undergraduate students.

Bursaries Up to £1,025, means tested.

Accommodation The college can provide rooms for 400 students. Rents are £80 a week.

Facilities There's a well-stocked library that will loan laptops to students.

Transport An hour by air from London. Good links with Northern Ireland and the Republic of Ireland.

❝ STUDENT VIEW ❞

"I always knew I wanted to do this type of degree and the course covers all the areas that you need for your future career. The lecturers are very supportive and it's great being able to discuss things with them and the other students."

University of Strathclyde

John Anderson Campus
16 Richmond Street
Glasgow G1 1XQ

t 0141 552 4400
e scls@mis.strath.ac.uk
↗ www.strath.ac.uk

Jordanhill Campus 76 Southbrae Drive, Glasgow G1 1XQ

》 further links

ACCOMMODATION student.accommodation@strath.ac.uk
STUDENTS' UNION www.strathstudents.com

3020   92.5   28.9   16.3   95.3

Glasgow

Strathclyde tailors degrees and teaching towards the requirements of future employers. It also acknowledges that students come to university to do more than just learn, and encourages them to get involved in student activities or check out what Glasgow has to offer. There are over 20,000 students, split between the central John Anderson campus (where many students also live) and another to the west.

Fees Scottish and EU students from outside UK pay no tuition fees. For other UK students, annual tuition fee of £1,775.

Bursaries There are a range of scholarships on offer.

Accommodation Guaranteed for first-years. Prices £60 to £90 a week.

Facilities Some of the best student libraries in Scotland, with specialist collections for the subjects taught here.

Transport Two railway stations and an airport, plus good public transport.

《 STUDENT VIEW 》

"Glasgow is great — there are about two pubs and a club for every person! With three universities, numerous free external libraries, and bookshops you will never be short of a book. A Strathclyde degree is worth more salt than one from elsewhere, it's in the middle of town, and it's on the bus route!"

University of Sunderland

City Campus, Edinburgh Building
Chester Road
Sunderland SR1 3SD

t 0191 515 2000
e student-helpline@sunderland.ac.uk
↗ www.sunderland.ac.uk

Sir Tom Cowie Campus at St Peter's St Peter's Way, Sunderland SR6 0DD

》 further links

ACCOMMODATION residentialservices@sunderland.ac.uk
STUDENTS' UNION www.sunderlandsu.co.uk

2240   97.4   41.7   19.0   91.3

The university has a total student population of more than 14,000, based at two main sites. Sunderland is a modern city, close to Newcastle and within easy reach of some stunning coastal scenery. The city has been the focus of regeneration and investment and is continuing to grow and develop. Courses focus on vocational development.

Fees £3,145 a year for all full-time undergraduate courses.

Bursaries £965 over three years, available to all, subject to progress. £525 per year to those with a household income under £39,305. Other financial support available.

Accommodation Guaranteed for eligible first-years.

Facilities Libraries have good IT facilities, including a large number of PCs, scanners, networked printing facilities and wireless access to the internet. You can also borrow laptops.

Transport There are good train links around the north-east. Road and rail transport to the rest of the UK is OK.

⟨⟨ STUDENT VIEW ⟩⟩

"It's the place where you find yourself, make some of your best friends, enjoy a great standard of education, have some great laughs, and maybe some cries — overall, it's life-changing."

University of Surrey

Guildford
Surrey U2 7XH

t 01483 300800
e ug-enquiries@surrey.ac.uk
↗ www.surrey.ac.uk

》 further links

ACCOMMODATION www.surrey.ac.uk/accommodation
STUDENTS' UNION www.ussu.co.uk

1505	88.6	22.5	10.5	96.6

The main campus is on Stag Hill in Guildford, adjacent to the cathedral. It's charming parkland with its own lake. The new Manor Park campus, just under a mile away, has been undergoing recent development. Guildford has easy links to London. 80 per cent of the 12,000-strong student population study on courses that include a work-based professional training year. The university is famous for its consistently outstanding employment record.

Fees £3,145 for full-time undergraduate courses in 2008.

Bursaries Up to £2,000 depending on family income. A further range of scholarships is available.

Accommodation All first-years are guaranteed university accommodation if they apply by the deadline.

Facilities Great resources for sport and physical activity. There's a dedicated art gallery on campus and good study facilities.

Transport London is half an hour away by train.

❝ STUDENT VIEW ❞

"The cobbled streets of Guildford are just ten minutes' walk from the university campus, where there's a huge landscaped lake, a fountain, and a variety of sculptures, not to mention the lost ducks that can be found across the campus. The reputation Surrey has for graduate employment certainly makes me feel confident about the future."

University of Sussex

Sussex House
Brighton BN1 9RH

t 01273 606755
e information@sussex.ac.uk
⚲ www.sussex.ac.uk

2155   84.8   20.0   11.7   93.1

Brighton

The university is situated entirely within an area of oustanding natural beauty – the South Downs. It is also only four miles from lovely Brighton. As well as good amenities on campus, there is a large and active students' union. Sussex has a good academic reputation – the English department is particularly strong – and a history of innovative approaches to teaching.

Fees £3,145 for full-time undergraduate courses in 2008.

Bursaries £1,000 a year for all students with a family income of £25,000 or less. More support is also available.

Accommodation Guaranteed for eligible first-years. Expect to pay between £80 and £110 a week.

Facilities IT facilities have 24-hour access in many cases and the library is open weekends and evenings. There's an extensive sports programme.

Transport London is under an hour by train. Gatwick is half that.

 STUDENT VIEW 》

*"Sussex is a beautiful campus, the people are bizarre in a brilliant way,
and you couldn't look for a better city than Brighton."*

Swansea University

Singleton Park
Swansea SA2 8PP

t 01792 205678
e admissions@swansea.ac.uk
↗ www.swansea.ac.uk

》 further links

ACCOMMODATION accommodation@swansea.ac.uk
STUDENTS' UNION www.swansea-union.co.uk

2710   92.4   26.8   11.0   93.9

Swansea

A hot contender for any "best campus" award going, Swansea sits in parkland overlooking the Swansea Bay, on the edge of the stunning Gower peninsula. Surfers, walkers and climbers adore it here. It's a short trip into the centre of Swansea, Wales's second city. The university is a consistently popular choice. The student population numbers about 12,000 undergraduates, and Swansea has a solid academic reputation and a good employment rate.

Fees £3,145 for full-time undergraduate courses in 2008. Students who normally live in Wales (and EU students) will be entitled to a "fee grant" from the Welsh Assembly government.

Bursaries and scholarships The university offers a number of scholarships, bursaries and prizes.

Accommodation 98 per cent of first-years normally in university accommodation. Prices £63 to £94 a week.

Facilities Among the best rates of computing provision in the country; students can also borrow laptops. The library is open until 2am during term time. The £20m sports village, home to the 50m Wales National Pool, is adjacent to campus.

Transport The university's major sites are easily accessible. Cardiff is an hour away and is well served by road and rail links.

❝ STUDENT VIEW ❞

"Swansea is a beautiful place to be, with the university overlooking Swansea Bay and the Gower within easy reach. The on-campus facilities are also of a high standard. The nightlife is fantastic, and it's close to some of the best beaches in Britain."

Swansea Metropolitan University

Mount Pleasant Swansea SA1 6ED	**t** 01792 481000 **e** enquiry@smu.ac.uk ↗ www.smu.ac.uk

》 further links

ACCOMMODATION accommodation@smu.ac.uk
STUDENTS' UNION www.metsu.org

850   97.8   37.9   24.1   94.3

SMU is based on several campuses in and around Swansea, with easy access to the Gower peninsula. It offers courses in three main areas – arts and design; applied design and engineering; and a third faculty broadly called "humanities", but also encompassing accounting, business and tourism. It focuses on vocational education and its employment rates are good.

Fees £3,145 for full-time undergraduate courses in 2008, though Welsh students are entitled to a "fee grant" from the Welsh Assembly government.

Bursaries Means-tested and around £300. Other awards are available.

Accommodation There's a range to choose from and fees range from £49 to £65 a week.

Facilities There are three libraries, each with their own computing facilities attached.

Transport Swansea enjoys excellent road and rail links with all parts of Britain.

❝ STUDENT VIEW ❞

Swansea is a beautiful place to spend three years – especially if you spend it at this university! I loved my course and found it really inspiring. Lecturers treat you as an individual. Students come from all over the place but we all get on really well. Coming here was one of the best decisions I ever made!"

University of Teesside

Middlesbrough
Tees Valley TS1 3BA

t 01642 218121
e registry@tees.ac.uk
↗ www.tees.ac.uk

》 further links

ACCOMMODATION accommodation@tees.ac.uk
STUDENTS' UNION www.utu.org.uk

2275   98.5   45.6   14.2   88.1

Middlesbrough

Teesside's campus is close to the centre of Middlesbrough, a town undergoing a transformation. Alongside a wide range of bars, cafes and clubs is a stunning new art gallery, Middlesbrough Institute of Modern Art. You're a short hop up to Newcastle for shopping or you can head out into the lovely scenery. Student numbers now exceed 22,400, with widening participation a priority: 98.5 per cent of young full-time degree entrants attended state schools or colleges.

Fees £3,145 a year for all full-time undergraduate courses in 2008.

Bursaries £1,025 per year for those from families earning £25,000 or less. Other support, including excellence scholarships and subject specific scholarships of up to £1,000 also available. Elite athlete bursary scheme of up to £2,000.

Accommodation Priority is given to first-year students although the university says they are normally able to offer accommodation to all students who apply for it. Rents in the range of £40 to £70 a week.

Facilities An award-winning student union, and some brand new learning resources on campus, thanks to a programme of recent investment. Among unique facilities is the crime scene laboratory for all you budding CSI officers.

Transport City centre campus, with direct rail links to York or Newcastle (both an hour away), Leeds and Manchester. The airport is 20 minutes away with direct flights to London.

⟨⟨ STUDENT VIEW ⟩⟩

"Most of your lectures will be in new buildings with top-class facilities, everything is within walking distance, and it's a cheap place to live. You'll also meet plenty of people and have loads of fun."

Thames Valley University

Thames Valley University

t 0800 036 8888
e learning.advice@tvu.ac.uk
↗ www.tvu.ac.uk

Ealing Campus St Mary's Road, Ealing, W5 5RF
Slough Campus Wellington Street, Slough, Berkshire SL1 1YG
Brentford Campus Paragon House, Boston Manor Road, Brentford, Middlesex TW8 9GA
Reading Campus Kings Road, Reading, Berkshire RG1 4HJ

》 further links

ACCOMMODATION uas@tvu.ac.uk
STUDENTS' UNION www.tvusu.co.uk

1990 96.2 36.7 22.0 94.6

TVU is based on four campuses — Brentford, Ealing, Reading and Slough. It's not too far to go to get to the wild and crazy heart of London. There is a large, mixed student body, with lots of mature, part-time and ethnic minority students. Most are local and often commute from home

Fees £3,145 for full-time undergraduate courses in 2008–09.

Bursaries Students with a household income below £25,000 are eligible for £1,030. Students with a household income between £25,000 and £40,000 eligible for a bursary of £515. Other support — including a £5,000 excellence award — is available.

Accommodation There are residences at Ealing (accessible to Brentford and Slough) and Reading. Expect to pay around £100 a week.

Facilities Learning resource centres at each site are well stocked and updated regularly. They have long opening hours; some with 24-hour access.

Transport There are shuttle buses between campuses, all of which (especially Ealing) are within easy striking distance of London.

❝ STUDENT VIEW ❞

"Ealing is a great place to live, especially during the summer. There are a lot of trees and greenery while at the same time it has quite a few restaurants and shops. There is a lot of up-to-date equipment and the bar is where all the magic happens!"

Trinity College Carmarthen

Carmarthen SA31 3EP

t 01267 676767
e registry@trinity-cm.ac.uk
↗ www.trinity-cm.ac.uk

》 further links

ACCOMMODATION d.doyle@trinity-cm.ac.uk
STUDENTS' UNION www.trinitysu.co.uk

440   99.4   46.9   15.0   95.8

Carmarthen

Trinity College Carmarthen (Coleg y Drindod Caerfyrddin) is a church college within the University of Wales. It offers arts and humanities degrees in a range of subjects from acting to film studies to Christianity and community studies. Students are based on a picturesque single campus in south Wales, with easy access to lovely countryside and the busy market town of Carmarthen.

Fees Latest available figures — which are for 2007, not 2008 — were £3,070 a year. That's likely to have risen.

Bursaries Means-tested bursary of around £300 for students from low-income homes. Also, a range of support for specific purposes, like accommodation or childcare, or for other eligible candidates, with varying criteria.

Accommodation The vast majority of first years can live on campus, in single study bedrooms. Rent is around £90 a week.

Facilities There's a sports hall (featuring a climbing wall) and fitness suite. The students' union is active and arts facilities in particular are very good, including a fully equipped theatre.

Transport Close to the town centre and to the station for major rail links. Good access to the main road network.

❝ STUDENT VIEW ❞

"The college is friendly and welcoming. There is a family feel about it.
I'm gaining confidence by being on the course and the lecturers are always willing to help."

Trinity Laban

King Charles Court
Old Royal Naval College
Greenwich, London SE10 9JF

t 020 8305 4300
e info@trinitylaban.ac.uk
↗ www.trinitylaban.ac.uk

》 further links

ACCOMMODATION www.opalstudents.com
STUDENTS' UNION Internal access only

130   75.0   18.6   98.0

London

Trinity Laban is a conservatoire for music and dance, formed in 2005 from the merger of Trinity College of Music and the Laban school of dance. It is based in Greenwich – a nice corner of south-east London. There's a range of specialised programmes available, including degrees in dance theatre, performance and Indian music.

Fees Latest figures for 2008 were £3,145.

Bursaries There is a means-tested bursary and a range of other support, including scholarships for excellence.

Accommodation The nearby privately owned McMillan Student Village can house most new students. Prices start at around £144 a week.

Facilities As you might expect, there are superb resources for practice and performance.

Transport It's in London, so ready access to the underground, national rail and bus services.

◄◄ STUDENT VIEW ►►
"The college is full of inspiring teachers and the students continue to generate a huge range of exciting and innovative music and dance."

UHI Millennium Institute

Executive Office
Ness Walk IV3 5SQ

t 0845 272 3600
e info@uhi.ac.uk
↗ www.uhi.ac.uk

》 further links

ACCOMMODATION uhi.ac.uk/accommodation
STUDENTS' UNION www.uhisa.org.uk

225   100.0   52.0   35.3

UHI Millennium Institute (UHI) is the only higher education institution in the Highlands and Islands of Scotland – covering 15 sites as far away from each other as Shetland, Lewis, Argyll and Perth. As well as more general vocational courses, the institute offers degrees in areas reflecting local industries and culture – such as aircraft engineering, Gaelic music, marine science, sustainable forestry and golf management. Many courses are offered on one site only.

Fees £1,775 for new students in 2008. Scottish students have their fees paid for them.

Bursaries There is a young person's bursary for eligible Scottish students, and further financial support available.

Accommodation There is a wide variety of accommodation available at the 15 sites. Some have halls and others will assist you in finding private accommodation. Prices vary.

Facilities Obviously vary according to where you study. UHI is good at off-campus delivery.

Transport Depends on where you are but plan seven hours for the train to London; less by air. All campuses are easily accessible by bus.

❝ STUDENT VIEW 》

"I did my science degree in rural development entirely online, with some video conferencing and audio classes, although the tutors were always on hand to help me. This study method enabled me to be independent and I had a part-time job so I was learning and earning at the same time."

UHI colleges

Aygrll College UHI
West Bay, Dunoon, Argyll PA23 7HP   **t** 0845 230 9969

Highland Theological College UHI
High Street, Dingwall, Ross-shire IV15 9HA   **t** 01349 780000

Inverness College UHI
3 Longman Road, Longman South, Inverness IV1 1SA   **t** 01463 273000

Lews Castle College UHI
Stornoway, Isle of Lewis HS2 0XR   **t** 01851 770000

Lochaber College UHI
Colaisde Lochaber OGE, An Aird, Fort William, Inverness-shire PH33 6AN   **t** 01397 874000

Moray College UHI
Moray Street, Elgin, Morayshire IV30 1JJ   **t** 01343 576000

NAFC Marine Centre UHI
Port Arthur, Scalloway, Shetland ZE1 0UN   **t** 01595 772000

Ness Foundation
Ness House, Dochfour Business Centre, Inverness IV3 8GY   **t** 01463 220 407

North Highland College
Ormlie Road, Thurso, Caithness KW14 7EE   **t** 01847 889000

Orkney College UHI
Kirkwall, Orkney KW15 1LX   **t** 01856 569000

Perth College UHI
Crieff Road, Perth PH1 2NX   **t** 0845 270 1177

Sabhal Mòr Ostaig UHI
An Teanga, Slèite, Isle of Skye IV44 8RQ   **t** 01471 888000

Scottish Association for Marine Science UHI
Dunstaffnage Marine Laboratory, Oban, Argyll PA37 1QA   **t** 01631 559000

Sustainable Development Research Centre
The Enterprise Park, Forres, Moray IV36 2AB   **t** 01309 678111

Shetland College UHI
Gremista, Lerwick, Shetland ZE1 0PX   **t** 01595 771000

University of Ulster

York Street
Belfast
Co. Antrim BT15 1ED

t 08700 400 700
e registryjn@ulster.ac.uk
↗ www.ulster.ac.uk

Jordanstown Campus Shore Road, Newtownabbey, Co. Antrim BT37 0QB
Coleraine Campus Cromore Road, Co. Londonderry BT52 1SA
Magee Campus Northland Road, Londonderry BT48 7JL

>> **further links**

ACCOMMODATION ulster.ac.uk/-accommodation
STUDENTS' UNION www.uusu.org

4995   99.9   46.8   22.5   94.4

Belfast

The 23,000 students, many of whom are from Northern Ireland, are spread over four campuses in Belfast, Coleraine, Jordanstown and Magee (in Derry). A fifth, Campus One, is an online e-learning service.

Fees £3,145 for full-time undergraduate courses in 2008–09.

Bursaries £1,040 per year where household income below £18,360. £620 per year where household income is between £18,361 and £21,000. £310 per year where household income is between £21,101 and £39,305. Other support also available.

Accommodation Guaranteed for eligible first-years. Weekly prices range from around £45 to £90.

Facilities There is an impressive sports centre at Jordanstown, arts venues at Coleraine and good learning resources.

Transport There are road and rail connections between the campuses plus airports and ports.

❝ STUDENT VIEW ❞

"The scenic views from the campuses are outstanding and there are lots of local services both on and off campus. The university has really established itself with a large number of facilities and the teaching staff are friendly and approachable. University is the best days of your life. Enjoy the craic, the thrill, and the excitement!"

University College Birmingham

Summer Row
Birmingham B3 1JB

t 0121 604 1000
e marketing@ucb.ac.uk
↗ www.ucb.ac.uk

》 further links

ACCOMMODATION accommodation@ucb.ac.uk
STUDENTS' UNION www.bcftcs.ac.uk/asp/STU-studentGuild.asp

| 540 | 93.8 | 45.4 | 16.9 | 93.2 |

UCB (formally known as the Birmingham School of Food, Tourism and Creative Studies) offers a range of undergraduate courses, mainly centred around the hospitality industries. There are around 6,500 students in total on a range of short courses and engaged in full- and part-time studies. The specialist nature of the college means that students have access to tailored facilities. There are also close links to employers. Birmingham is a fun place to study with all the attractions of a big city on your doorstep.

Fees £3,145 for full-time undergraduate students in 2008–09.

Bursaries Students from households with an income of less than £25,000 a year will receive a bursary of £1,050; students from households with an income of between £25,001 and £42,500 will receive a bursary of £630. Students from households with an income of between £42,501 and £60,000 will receive a bursary of £315 per annum.

Accommodation More than 1,000 students can be accommodated in halls. Rent is between £67 and £137 a week.

Facilities There are restaurants and a spa that are used both as learning resources and as commercial centres: the public is actively encouraged to make use of them and, of course, so can students.

Transport A convenient location within easy reach of the city centre. Birmingham itself is well served by road, rail and air.

❝ STUDENT VIEW 》

"The student body is really international, which is great. I have made friends with people I never would have met if I hadn't come here. It quickly feels like home."

University College London

Gower Street
London   WC1E 6BT

t   020 7679 2000
e   Enquiries via the website
↗   www.ucl.ac.uk

>> **further links**

ACCOMMODATION   ucl.ac.uk/-accommodation
STUDENTS' UNION   www.uclu.org

2405   62.4   17.5   5.7   96.2

London

UCL is big and is consistently ranked among the best universities in the world, with an emphasis on innovative teaching and research excellence (it got its 20th Nobel prize in 2007). Its Bloomsbury base is convenient for central London and is famous for its literary and educational heritage.

Fees   £3,145 a year for full-time undergraduate courses in 2008–09.

Bursaries   Up to £2,700 a year, depending on household income.

Accommodation   Guaranteed for eligible first-years. Weekly prices range from £97 to £139 for catered accommodation and from £66 to £133 for self-catering.

Facilities   Excellent library facilites on-campus theatre, a fitness centre and a great students' union.

Transport   Easy access to the London transport network and a couple of mainline stations; and the Eurostar terminal is only up the road.

&& STUDENT VIEW >>
"UCL is an academic juggernaut and you could pile every adjective on to London and it still wouldn't really do it justice. You have every resource on your doorstep and UCL boasts academic heavyweights in every field."

University of Wales Institute, Cardiff

Western Avenue
Cardiff CF5 2YB

t 029 2041 6070
e uwicinfo@uwic.ac.uk
↗ www.uwic.ac.uk

》 further links

ACCOMMODATION accomm@uwic.ac.uk
STUDENTS' UNION www.uwicsu.co.uk

1915　　93.8　　25.7　　14.4　　92.3

Cardiff

UWIC is one of the leading new universities in Wales. It's also a top sporting university with first-class facilities and is to invest £46m in redeveloping and updating the campus facilities. The university is split between four campuses. There's some lovely countryside within easy reach and good transport links to the rest of the UK.

Fees £3,145 a year for all full-time undergraduate courses. Welsh students are eligible for a fee grant from the Welsh assembly government of £1,890.

Bursaries £750 for students with a household income of less than £17,920, £500 for students with a household income of £17,921 to £27,135 and £300 for students with a household income of between £27,136 and £38,325. Other support is also available.

Accommodation Not guaranteed, but UWIC will help with finding suitable private accommodation. Rooms cost between £70 and £101 a week.

Facilities Learning materials are available on all campuses, as well as computing facilities. Resources for sport and especially good.

Transport There's a university shuttle bus between campuses, the city centre and popular student housing areas. Cardiff is good for road and rail: London is two hours by train.

❝ STUDENT VIEW ❞

"A top-class new university that has amazing facilities for any individual, whatever their subject, and that is based in an area with a fantastic and buzzing atmosphere. Cardiff really is the place to be!"

University of Warwick

Coventry CV4 7AL

t 02476 523523
e student.recruitment@warwick.ac.uk
↗ www.warwick.ac.uk

》 further links

ACCOMMODATION accommodation@warwick.ac.uk
STUDENTS' UNION www.warwicksu.com

| 2585 | 76.0 | 18.7 | 3.3 | 93.9 |

● Coventry

Warwick actually lies about three miles outside the centre of Coventry and on the border of Warwickshire. Warwick does have its own castle, though. Coventry has all the other mod cons you require, though the1960s main campus is well equipped. Consistently rated among the best universities in the country, Warwick is something of a leader in the academic field.

Fees £3,145 for full-time undergraduate courses in 2008–09

Bursaries £1,800 to all students with a family income of £36,000 or less. Further support also available.

Accommodation Guaranteed for all first-years. There are around 6,000 on-campus rooms, and a stock of off-campus rooms. Self-catering halls range from approximately £70 to £115 a week.

Facilities There's an impressive art collection on show at the arts centre, good sports facilities and a large library.

Transport Close to the M1/M6 intersection and half an hour to Birmingham by train; an hour and a quarter to London.

❝ STUDENT VIEW ❞
*"It's a place where it's very easy to feel at home, with a very strong identity.
It's easy to settle into in the first year and it has a strong 'work hard, play hard' ethic."*

University of the West of England, Bristol (UWE Bristol)

Frenchay Campus
Coldharbour Lane
Bristol BS16 1QY

t 0117 32 83333
e admissions@uwe.ac.uk
↗ www.uwe.ac.uk

Bower Ashton Campus Kennel Lodge Road, Bower Ashton, Bristol BS3 2JT

St Matthias Campus Oldbury Court Road, Fishponds, Bristol BS16 2JP

Glenside Campus Blackberry Hill, Stapleton, Bristol BS16 1DD

Hartpury College Hartpury House, Hartpury, Gloucester GL19 3BE

Bath Education Centre First floor, Education Centre, Royal United Hospital, Combe Park, Bath BA1 3NG

Gloucester Education Centre Hartpury House, Hartpury, Gloucester GL19 3BE

Swindon Education Centre Great Western Hospital, Marlborough Road, Swindon SN3 6BB

》 further links

ACCOMMODATION accommodation@uwe.ac.uk
STUDENTS' UNION www.uwesu.org/ez/

5340   88.3   28.6   18.6   93.6

Bristol UWE has a student population of almost 30,000 and an impressive graduate employment record. Bristol UWE has four campuses across the city, which is the largest in the south-west, with an impressive music scene and cultural life.

Fees £3,145 for all full-time undergraduate courses in 2008–09.

Bursaries £1,250 annually for students receiving a full grant. £750 for those with household income of between £18,361 and £27,000. £1,250 for UK undergraduates who have completed a recognised access course.

Accommodation Guaranteed for eligible first-years (there's a brand new student village on the Frenchay campus). Self-catering accommodation costs from £50 to £108 a week.

Facilities 24/7 access to computing facilities and a brand new sports centre.

Transport A university run bus service links the campuses to the city centre. On major rail routes, close to the M4 and M5 and not far from Bristol airport.

❝ STUDENT VIEW ❞

"I have loved my time at UWE and the social side and atmosphere are brilliant. There are great opportunities to get involved for those wanting more than an average degree. One of the main advantages is that it is based in Bristol; I knew that this was a place I wanted to spend the next three years of my life."

University of the West of Scotland

Paisley PA1 2BE

t 0141 848 3000
e info@uws.ac.uk
↗ www.uws.ac.uk

Ayr Campus Beech Grove, Ayr KA8 0SR
Dumfries Campus Maxwell House, Dumfries DG1 4UQ
Hamilton Campus Almada Street, Hamilton ML3 0JB

》 further links

ACCOMMODATION accommodation@uws.ac.uk
STUDENTS' UNION www.upsa.org.uk

1950   98.0   41.3   23.5   91.3

The University of the West of Scotland (formerly University of Paisley) is based on four campuses in the south and south-west of Scotland. The main campus is in Paisley, six miles from Glasgow; a second is in Ayr, a third outside Dumfries and the fourth in Lanarkshire. The university is one of Scotland's most vocational higher education institutions and students can take the option of a year's paid work placement as part of many degrees.

Fees Students resident in Scotland or in non-UK EU countries may be eligible for free tuition. For other UK students, annual tuition fee of not less than £1,735.

Bursaries Young students' bursaries for Scottish students under 25 from low-income families. Other grants available, plus university prizes and awards for achievement.

Accommodation Students from outside a 25-mile radius are given priority. University self-catering accommodation costs around £52 to £61 a week.

Facilities The £6.8m library on the Paisley campus has room for 1,000 studious students. Extensive sports facilities take care of the less studious.

Transport By train, the main campus is 10 minutes from Glasgow. One hour from Edinburgh.

❝ STUDENT VIEW 》

"It's very student friendly. As it is so close to Glasgow city centre there are many places to go to have fun — and studying is made easy with such an environment."

University of Westminster

309 Regent Street
London 1B 2UW

t 020 7911 5000
e course-enquiries@westminster.ac.uk
↗ www.westminster.ac.uk

》 further links

ACCOMMODATION unilethousing@westminster.ac.uk
STUDENTS' UNION www.uwsu.com

3730 94.7 42.0 17.2 88.2

Three of its campuses are bang in the middle of town; Harrow is slightly further flung, though still on the tube. In London, everything you could want is within easy reach. Westminster has a longstanding commitment to equal opportunities; lots of courses can be studied part-time and the student body is fantastically diverse. It puts careers at the centre of its mission.

Fees £3,145 a year for all full-time undergraduate courses in 2008–09.

Bursaries Bursaries at £310 a year for those receiving a grant. The university's scholarship programme is the largest of its kind in the UK, with £4.3 million being awarded annually to over 500 students

Accommodation There are around 1,400 beds available to students across six halls in Harrow, Hoxton, Highgate, Victoria, Marylebone and Lambeth. Priority is given to those living more than 25 miles from campus. Halls cost around £85.40 to £138 a week.

Facilities Recently revamped gym facilities and there's a 20-hectare sports ground by the river in Chiswick. Libraries on all sites, with 24-hour access in Harrow and Marylebone. The student union boasts a £1m venue and there's an award-winning student radio station. There's also an underground exhibition space at Marylebone campus.

Transport Three of the four campuses are in central London with excellent links. The fourth, in Harrow, is a 20-minute tube ride away, or there's a 24-hour bus service.

◀◀ STUDENT VIEW ▶▶

"There's a great community on campus and lots of things to do throughout the week.
Central London always has stuff to offer if the university nights don't provide enough.
I'm proud of our campuses, locations, and what we have to offer."

University of Winchester

West Hill
Winchester SO22 4NR

t 01962 841515
e course.enquiries@winchester.ac.uk
↗ www.winchester.ac.uk

Chute House Campus Church Street, Basingstoke RG21 7 QT

》 further links

ACCOMMODATION housing@winchester.ac.uk
STUDENTS' UNION www.winchesterstudents.co.uk

| 1230 | 96.0 | 31.7 | 12.0 | 93.3 |

Winchester

Winchester is a fairly small university, with around 3,000 full-time students and a similar number on part-time courses, which makes for a friendly, informal environment. Its long history as a teacher-training college means that education is still a focus, but there's a wide range of other degrees on offer, too. Winchester is a lovely cathedral city. There's another campus in Basingstoke.

Fees £3,145 for full-time undergraduate courses in 2008–09.

Bursaries All students who are entitled to a full maintenance grant are also entitled to £820 annually. Students whose household income is £25,000–£39,305 are entitled to an annual bursary of £410. Other scholarships and awards available.

Accommodation On-campus accommodation guaranteed to all first-year full-time undergraduates who hold Winchester as their firm choice and apply before the deadline. Costs range from £79 to £102 a week.

Facilities The new £10m University Centre includes a 1,200-capacity venue space. 2008 will see the completion of an Olympic-standard athletics track and an all-weather hockey and general sports pitch.

Transport A 10-minute walk to the city centre and the train station. Winchester is one hour away from London and 20 minutes from Southampton. Bus services are good.

❝ STUDENT VIEW ❞
"There is something about being a student here that you can't quite put your finger on.
Whether it's due to the sense of family or the feel of the city itself, it's both a great place to live and study."

University of Wolverhampton

Wulfruna Street
Wolverhampton WV1 1SB

t 01902 322222
e enquiries@wlv.ac.uk
↗ www.wlv.ac.uk

Compton Park Campus Compton Road West, Compton, Wolverhampton WV3 9DX
Telford Campus Shifnal Road, Priorslee, Telford TF2 9NT
Walsall Campus Gorway Road, Walsall WS1 3BD

》 further links

ACCOMMODATION residences@wlv.ac.uk
STUDENTS' UNION www.wlv.ac.uk

3540   99.0   50.0   21.1   88.9

Wolverhampton has around 24,000 students, including a growing number from Europe and overseas, and £120m of new buildings. The university stresses innovation and enterprise, encouraging student "start-up" companies. It has a successful focus on employability, with excellent business links, collaborative working and opportunities for students to gain experience. Wolverhampton is a bustling city and its four campuses are easily accessible.

Fees £3,145 for full-time undergraduate courses in 2008-09.

Bursaries £500 a year for students with family income of £25,000 or less, or £300 a year for students with family income is £25,000 to £35,000. In addition, there is a £1,000 grant for eligible first-year undergraduate students from the West Midlands region.

Accommodation Almost 2,000 places available. Prices range from £58 to £85 a week.

Facilities Each campus has a learning centre. There is a strong focus on IT and audio-visual facilities. Walsall campus's sports centre plays host to many large regional, national and international sports events and is one of the few national judo centres of excellence, being used as the training facility for 2012 Olympic contenders. The Arena Theatre, based on the city campus, is one of the busiest and most successful theatres in the Midlands.

Transport All campuses are linked by a free shuttle bus. Wolverhampton has excellent transport links and Birmingham is just a short train or tram ride away.

❝ STUDENT VIEW 》

"The university is constantly trying to improve itself. It's investing in all its campuses and the learning centres are bursting with books and journals."

University of Worcester

Henwick Grove
Worcester WR2 6AJ

t 01905 855000
e study@worc.ac.uk
↗ www.worcester.ac.uk

》 further links

ACCOMMODATION accommodation@worc.ac.uk
STUDENTS' UNION www.worcsu.com

1050   96.8   34.9   18.6   93.2

● Worcester

Hayfever sufferers might be interested to learn that all of the UK's national pollen forecasts are now supplied by the university's pollen and aerobiology research unit. It is investing £60m in a unique library and history centre, which will be the first joint university and public library in the UK. There are currently 8,000 students and the majority come from the local area, but applications from further afield are increasing. Worcester itself is a charming city.

Fees £3,145 a year for all full-time undergraduate courses in 2008–09.

Bursaries £500 for every new student, rising to £625 for students in receipt of a partial grant and £750 for those on full maintenance grant. 40 scholarships of £1,000 available after the first year of study to reward outstanding achievement. Other awards and support also available.

Accommodation Eligible first-years with the university as their firm choice will normally be given accommodation. Prices are from £60 to £95 a week.

Facilities The Peirson Library has over 150,000 books and 600 journal print titles, and 150 computers are available. Computers are also available in 24-hour open access rooms across the campus. Excellent sports facilities, too.

Transport The campus is a 15-minute walk from the city centre. A frequent bus service also links the two. Worcester has good rail and motorway links (M5) which put Birmingham within 45 minutes and London just over two hours from the city centre.

◀◀ STUDENT VIEW ▶▶

"Worcester is a great place — it offers loads to do, with a great city backdrop.
There is an overriding sense of community, making it a really friendly place to live and study."

Writtle College

Chelmsford
Essex CM1 3RR

t 01245 424200
e info@writtle.ac.uk
↗ www.writtle.ac.uk

>> **further links**
ACCOMMODATION student.services@writtle.ac.uk
STUDENTS' UNION www.writtlesu.com

| 210 | 94.9 | 27.7 | 15.3 | 92.6 |

Writtle College is an agricultural college based two miles from Chelmsford in Essex. It is now a partner college of the University of Essex and offers courses in a full range of land-based subjects. The main campus is surrounded by its own estate, farm and gardens — the college says this serves as a "green laboratory" for students.

Fees Most recent available figures — for 2007 — had students paying £2,765.

Bursaries Eligible students are entitled to a means-tested bursary, starting at around £300; you get more in your second and third years.

Accommodation Most first-years live in halls, at a cost of between £89 and £111 a week.

Facilities The active students' union keeps things lively on campus and a range of sporting facilities are available.

Transport Situated two miles from the town centre of Chelmsford and just a few minutes' walk from the main bus route through Writtle village. There are buses from Chelmsford station to the campus.

<< STUDENT VIEW >>

"I wasn't looking for a big university in a big city. I was looking for a college that took pride in having a more personal approach, was multicultural, and had a good supportive faculty. I found all of these qualities in the hidden gem that is Writtle College."

University of York

Heslington
York YO10 5DD

t 01904 430000
e admissions@york.ac.uk
↗ www.york.ac.uk

King's Manor University of York, Exhibition Square, York YO1 7EP

》 further links

ACCOMMODATION accommodation@york.ac.uk
STUDENTS' UNION www.yusu.org

| 2050 | 77.9 | 17.1 | 4.8 | 93.5 |

York enjoys a collegiate system similar to Oxbridge, though the divisions don't seem to be as rigid as at those universities. Most students are based on the landscaped campus on the outskirts of the city. The campus is undergoing a process of expansion and improvement to its buildings. York is an interesting city, with a history stretching back to Roman times and the evidence of it all around you.

Fees £3,145 for full-time undergraduate degrees in 2008–09.

Bursaries For students with a household income of up to £25,000 a bursary of £1,400. For students with a household income of between £25,001 and £35,000 a bursary of £700, and for students with a household income of between £35,001 and £40,000 a bursary of £350.

Accommodation Guaranteed for first-years. University residences cost between £73 and £87 a week.

Facilities Libraries, computer rooms, restaurants, bars, shops, a fully equipped sports centre, tennis and squash courts, health centre, theatres and concert halls are all within easy walking distance.

Transport The campus itself is compact and generally traffic-free. York city centre is 20 minutes' stroll away, or less than 10 minutes by bus — a fast, direct service runs every 10 minutes. Much of the city is pedestrianised and there are plentiful cycle routes. A fast all-night train puts Leeds and Manchester within easy reach.

❝ STUDENT VIEW ❞

"The university, the surrounding area, and the city are fantastic places to live. The pleasant aura that surrounds the university enables students to study as they wish to. York attracts some of the best and most exciting staff around. And literally every student is involved in campus life in some way."

York St John University

Lord Mayor's Walk
York YO31 7EX

t 01904 624624
e admissions@yorksj.ac.uk
↗ www.yorksj.ac.uk

》 further links

ACCOMMODATION accommodation@yorksj.ac.uk
STUDENTS' UNION www.ysjsu.com

1315   94.3   31.4   13.1   93.0

St John's descends from two Victorian Anglican teacher-training colleges. Over the years, it has had various incarnations and it won full university status in 2006. There are around 6,000 students and almost half of them are over 21. There's also a male to female ratio of 30:70. The campus is located almost literally a stone's throw from York Minster, the medieval cathedral.

Fees   £3,145 for all full-time undergraduate degrees in 2008–09.

Bursaries   If your household income is less than £18,360 you will receive a bursary of £1,570. Between £18,361 and £20,970, you'll receive £1,050. Between £20,971 and £25,000 you will receive £525.

Accommodation   Nearly all first-years who want to can live in student accommodation. A range of types at different prices is available, and 2008 sees the opening of £10m worth of new accommodation.

Facilities   Recent investment has seen new facilities for study and teaching being built on campus. There is good sports provision — including a climbing wall, an internet cafe and impressive lecture theatres.

Transport   St John's is just a few minutes' walk from the city centre. The city is on the main east-coast rail line — handy for London and Edinburgh. Leeds and Manchester are easy to get to.

❝ STUDENT VIEW ❞

"The teaching staff are extremely helpful and encourage me to explore and develop new ideas in my course. Studying at York St John was a brilliant experience from beginning to end."

Acknowledgments

Thanks to

The universities who responded to requests for information and also to
Matt Hiely-Rayner, Julie Whittaker and Lorna Lines of Campus Pi at Brunel University,
Jon Bentham, Helen Brooks, Lisa Darnell, Liz Ford, Amelia Hodsdon, Poppy Hughes,
Donald Macleod, Lucy Mangan, Jessica Moore, Bryony Newhouse, James Wignall
and Alice Woolley.

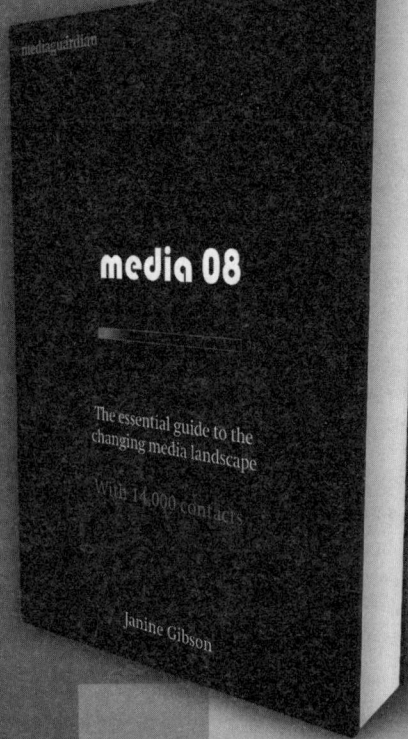